Interactive System DESIGN

Interactive System DESIGN

William M. Newman
Michael G. Lamming
Rank Xerox Research Centre, Cambridge

ADDISON-WESLEY

Harlow, England • Reading, Massachusetts • Menlo Park, California • New York
Don Mills, Ontario • Amsterdam • Bonn • Sydney • Singapore
Tokyo • Madrid • San Juan • Milan • Mexico City • Seoul • Taipei

Cover designed by Designers & Partners of Oxford
incorporating design drawings for a memory aid by M. Flynn and M. G. Lamming
and printed by The Riverside Printing Co. (Reading) Ltd.
Typeset by VAP Group Ltd, Kidlington.
Text designed by Sally Grover.
Line diagrams drawn by the authors and PanTek Arts.
Printed in Great Britain at the University Press, Cambridge.

First printed 1995. Reprinted 1996.

ISBN 0-201-63162-8

British Library Cataloguing in Publication Data
A catalogue record for this book is available from the British Library.

Library of Congress Cataloging in Publication Data
Newman, William M., date–
    Interactive system design / William M. Newman, Michael G. Lamming.
      p.   cm.
    Includes index.
    ISBN 0-201-63162-8
    1. Human–computer interaction.   2. System design.   I. Lamming,
Michael G.   II. Title.
QA76.9.H85N48   1995
004.2'1'019—dc20
                                      95–3377
                                        CIP

*To Anikó
and Phyllis*

FOREWORD

Ever since people first started building computers they have been designing mechanisms for interacting with them. But it is a surprisingly recent
development that human–computer interaction (HCI) has become a focus
of interest in its own right, rather than a peripheral add-on to the 'real'
business of computational science and design. Not so long ago, concern
with what was called 'human factors' was limited to some thoughtful programmers and a few psychologists who happened to study how people
used complex devices. With the advent of the personal computer, a trend
that had been building for many years came to centre stage, bringing
interactions into the spotlight. Processing power and programming convenience were no longer the central arenas of competition in the software
industry. The look and feel of a product became its dominating characteristic, and fortunes were made and lost because designers understood (or
failed to understand) how their software would be encountered by users
in their own context, not a context of data processing and computation.

The HCI world came into its own with the graphical user interface
(GUI), showing that it could be relevant to the design of successful productivity software. Today the market is shifting yet again. Computers are
proceeding through the phase where software emphasis has been on productivity and business, into a consumer phase in which purchase and use
choices are driven by feelings of engagement and appeal. The focus continues to shift away from the computer towards the human side of the
equation. The emphasis is on design, with all of the human aspects it
brings into focus.

The shift from a machine-centred to a human-centred perspective creates difficulties for teaching HCI as a part of computer science. The style
of teaching that has worked well for more traditional areas of computing
doesn't translate easily to the more open-ended problems of designing for
people. Rather than being able to offer carefully staged incremental exercises that have correct answers, we are faced with the difficulties of developing a professional sense of design, in which problem formulation is as
important as problem solving, in which aesthetics plays a role along with
function, and in which there is rarely a correct solution.

It is tempting to continue teaching what is most easily conveyed, carefully explaining the detailed principles of windows and menus, the mechanisms of selection and command execution, and the world of GUI
widgets. But this would be shortsighted. Though it is always necessary for
the designers of software and its interactions to have a mastery of current

mechanisms and techniques, it is never sufficient. The majority of today's students will not be working in a world bounded by current familiar examples. They will design interactions that move beyond the desktop and even beyond the extended desktops of PDAs and wall-sized whiteboards. The human–computer interface of the future will not be perceived as the interface to a computer, but as a pervasive part of the environment we all inhabit.

Our challenge, then, is to find ways to convey to today's students of software design the underlying concepts and competencies that will not be bound either to the current GUI or to the specific details of its successors. Newman and Lamming offer a significant new step in that direction. This book embodies some critical principles of learning that have all too often been overlooked in our computing curricula:

(1)   Learning happens most effectively in the process of encountering real situations.

(2)   Real situations demand the integration of multiple disciplines and skills.

(3)   Generalization of learning happens through the interplay of theory and practice.

The first of these is at the heart of teaching in traditional design-oriented disciplines, which emphasize the study of classical examples and engagement in projects. Budding architects are introduced to the great genres of the past: the Greek temple, the Gothic cathedral, the modern and post-modern skyscraper. They learn what is important (and what is possible) by understanding how each of these very different traditions has dealt with the same fundamental problems in its own way. For, after all, people and their needs are very much the same from millennium to millennium. The same is true in HCI – we need to ground the discussion in experience of systems that have been built and tested and in the methods that have been found to work well in practice. Newman and Lamming have based their book on a rich array of real-world examples and methods from which the student can learn the emerging traditions of our young field.

The second point is almost a defining element of the discipline: HCI does not lie within the traditional boundaries of computer science or human factors. It also touches on many of the disciplines that have dealt systematically with human activity, including philosophy, psychology, anthropology and the social sciences. We need not turn computer students into amateur professionals in all these areas, but it is critical to provide a basic familiarity with the key insights and methods that each discipline has to offer for software interaction design. The premium is on integration, and only by introducing each of the components can we foster the judgement that is needed in making design decisions. This book draws on a wide range of disciplines, and goes into depth in those areas where the authors see a need for the software designer to know how the methods can really be applied in practice.

Finally there is the interplay between practice and theory – practice showing where the hard problems lie, and theory giving tools to solve those problems.

Deep learning takes place in the interplay between the engagement of experience and the articulation of a structured analysis. The student encounters a real problem, a real setting, which offers possibilities that are not yet formulated into requirements and specifications. In the process of struggling to define the problem and its possible answers, the student makes use of the tradition that has developed for finding appropriate distinctions and laying out the essence of the problem. This provides a foundation on which rigorous analyses and methods can be brought to bear. Newman and Lamming offer formal methods of analysis that the student can use effectively, to complement the less structured and more experiential aspects of design.

Of course, no book alone can achieve these educational goals. The kind of knowledge we want our students to achieve is not 'book knowledge'. The teaching methods and activities of our departments will have to shift to a design-oriented approach, and this will take a continuing evolution of our educational structure. I am glad that this book is available to serve as a resource in that evolution, helping to make it possible to bring our theory into practice.

Terry Winograd
Stanford University, January 1995

PREFACE

Interacting with computer technology has become an essential part of everyday life. Computer-based interactive systems provide support to an ever widening range of human activities, some as simple as checking one's bank balance, others as complex as flying a passenger aircraft. It is becoming increasingly important that these systems should be usable, reliable and cost-effective, and this means ensuring that they are well designed.

We have written this book for those involved in the design of interactive computer systems and for those who are learning to become designers. In it we present a range of methods essential to solving the problems encountered in designing systems that are interactive by nature. Principal topics covered include problem definition, user study methods, systems analysis and design, requirements definition, prototyping, and a range of methods for designing and evaluating user interfaces.

A major objective of ours has been to provide readers with a framework that can link together all aspects of designing computer-based systems for human use. In other words, we are offering a means of integrating methods specific to interactive systems (such as user interface design) with methods of a more general nature such as systems analysis and requirements definition – methods normally treated as a part of software engineering. We do this to make sure that the sets of methods are not treated each in isolation, but are collectively given the attention they deserve.

We are trying here to address a serious problem facing the computer industry and the institutions that train the industry's future designers. Basically, system design methods have changed much less rapidly in the last two decades than the systems themselves and the ways these systems are used. It is still common for software to be designed with little or no attention to the human activity it supports. There is an overall tendency to treat interactive system design as a 'special case' of software design. These practices are inappropriate in an era when interactive systems have become so widespread, and when virtually every software system built has an interactive user interface of some kind. It would be better, we think, if interactive systems were treated as the norm, and so we offer here a way of treating them as such.

Challenges

There are many challenges in writing a book of this kind. We will highlight three in particular, concerning the designer's need for *self-sufficiency*, *underlying concepts* and *access to real-world data*.

We want our readers to gain familiarity with a full range of methods, so that they can tackle entire problems in interactive system design on their own if necessary. Unless they can achieve this degree of self-sufficiency they will rely on the help of experts to deal with interactive aspects of system design. This is risky, because experts are not always around to help when interactive systems are designed. Furthermore, when experts are brought into the team the designer is always better off knowing something of their area of expertise. This is why we include topics that some might consider specialized, such as Chapter 8's usability analysis methods and Chapter 10's statistical techniques for checking the validity of evaluations.

We are also concerned to make sure that the reader has an adequate foundation of underlying concepts to carry out design. The challenge here has been to extend the theoretical base of system design. The largely mathematical body of theory supporting computer science is simply inadequate to deal with interactive situations. The solution to this problem is usually to draw on psychological theories, but these are of limited use in collaborative situations where people interact with other people as well as with computer systems. We have therefore taken a multidisciplinary approach, offering a model of human performance based primarily on cognitive theory, but supplemented with concepts drawn from recent sociological and anthropological research.

Our third concern is to place system design in a context of real-world human activity. Success in design involves understanding the context into which the designed artefact will be introduced – the 'outer environment' of design identified by Herbert Simon (1981). By tradition, the context for which software is designed is simply another software system. An operating system, for example, is designed to be 'used' by application programs. When interactive systems are designed, however, the context of use is the human activity that the system will support, and this is much more difficult to understand. Indeed it is hard to find well-documented examples of real-life activity. We have nevertheless managed to collect together a number of examples, covering a broad spectrum from air traffic control to police work and collecting payment on unpaid bills. We use these examples to help the reader gain a broader and deeper understanding of the kinds of activities that interactive systems can support.

Our whole approach is thus centred around the need to design systems that support human activity. This is not greatly different from the 'user centred' approach advocated by other writers. The point we emphasize is the need to understand and support the tasks and processes that users perform; this is the way to ensure understanding and support of the users themselves.

Readership

The book's overall purpose is to assist readers in becoming effective system designers. It should be of value, therefore, to practitioners and students alike. As regards practitioners, our primary readership includes designers themselves, software engineers, system analysts, researchers and human factors engineers. We would expect parts of the book to appeal to a wider set of practitioners, however, including product managers, technical writers, marketeers, and indeed anyone closely associated with the development of interactive systems. The first seven chapters are oriented particularly towards this wider readership.

In the teaching context the book can serve a number of functions. Taken as a whole, it can serve as a text for courses on user interface design and human–computer interaction (HCI), for it covers all of the major topics generally included in such courses. The full set of topics, shown below in Figure 0.1, will typically be spread over an entire semester.

The first six or seven chapters can be used more widely, as shown in the darker shaded areas of the diagram. They can be used, for example, to introduce a course on software engineering, or (with Chapters 8 and 9) to teach a short course on interactive system design to non-majors. None of the material in the book is of a highly technical nature. The later chapters go into design methods in greater detail, however, and are likely to appeal more to students who are majoring in computer science or information science.

Structure

The book is divided into four parts. It starts with a set of four chapters on foundational topics. These are followed by three chapters on system design and three more on evaluation. By this route the book covers the basic framework of design before turning to user interface design, which is covered in the final five chapters.

Each part of the book is organized around a set of methods and concepts. We think it best to recommend methods only if they have worked well in practice. Therefore we include methods that we personally have found useful in our design work. For the most part these methods have been developed elsewhere and have been thoroughly tried and tested by teachers and practitioners. Some of the concepts and representations are our own, however, because we could find nothing else capable of doing the job.

In Part I, for example, we begin with an introductory chapter and then focus on **Problem definition**, the topic of Chapter 2. We emphasize here the need to identify the design problem, and to distinguish this from the *situation of concern* that gives rise to designing the system. We introduce a number of key concepts, including usability factors and representations of human activities, and we suggest the use of a single-sentence problem statement to bring together the components of the design problem.

Also in Part I, Chapter 3 (**the Human Virtual Machine**) introduces a number of important theoretical concepts. Our primary purpose here is to

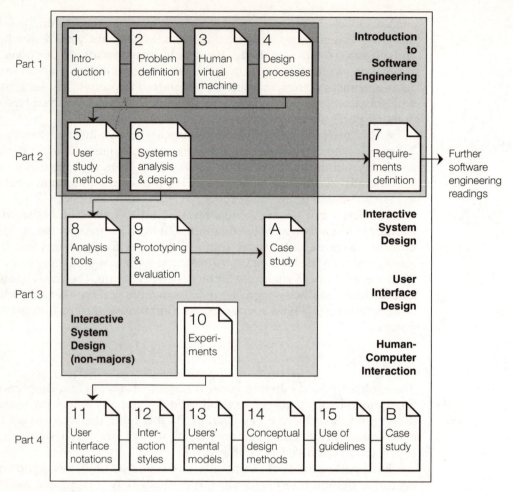

Figure 0.1   The chapters of the book and the courses in which they may be used.

offer a model of the workings of the 'machine' that performs human activities. Many aspects of human behaviour can be explained by the psychological theory of human information processing, but in order to cover behaviour in social settings this theory needs to be supplemented with findings drawn from anthropological and sociological research.

The remaining chapter in Part I, Chapter 4, provides an explanation of how the methods in the book link together and how the various design representations form the essential links.

Part II is concerned with system design, and in its initial Chapter 5 we therefore explain how to gather data about human activity in preparation for design. This leads into the important material of Chapter 6, **systems analysis and design**, which explains how observations of human activity are transformed into outline designs. It explains the nature of the analysis that takes place here, a topic that has rarely received much attention. This chapter is essential reading for anyone wanting to understand how analysis contributes to system design, and how interactive system design relates to software engineering. In the following Chapter 7 we cover requirements definition, and forge the link with software engineering more strongly. We explain the need to define, in a set of requirements, a *usable functional form*; we also explain why this can sometimes lead to writing voluminous sets of requirements.

Part III complements Part II; it explains how, in the course of design, interactive systems are evaluated in terms of their usability. Methods for checking usability are presented under two headings. Chapter 8 covers methods for evaluation 'on paper', before the design has been implemented. These methods are important because they can be applied early in the design and can sometimes save a great deal of unnecessary prototyping effort.

Chapter 9, **prototyping and evaluation**, plays a central role in Part III. It covers a number of methods for evaluating working prototypes, all of them following a general six-step evaluative process. This chapter introduces the concept of documenting the evaluation in terms of the performance requirements that the system is to meet, and it suggests a 'pro forma' notation for doing this. Chapters 8 and 9 may be considered for inclusion in a course organized around Parts I and II of the book. In Chapter 10 we explain how the results of prototype evaluation are checked for statistical significance, and offer a few simple methods.

In Part IV we cover user interface design. At the outset, Chapter 11 offers a number of different notations for describing user interfaces, and Chapter 12 explains the role of interaction styles and illustrates several different styles by means of a worked example. We place particular emphasis on **conceptual design**, by which an appropriate mental model is chosen for adoption by the user. We devote two chapters, 13 and 14, to this topic, presenting a range of design methods in Chapter 14. Chapter 15 covers the use of guidelines, explaining how to make use of sources of design knowledge and how to apply guidelines to answering questions of detailed design.

A number of case studies are included in the book. Some are used as linking material between the chapters; others illustrate methods, e.g., of evaluation and of choice of interaction style. Two detailed case studies are included at the ends of Parts III and IV respectively. The first describes a major exercise in analysing and evaluating the usability of a telephone operator's workstation, while the second covers a programme of research leading to the development of a portable memory aid.

Supplements

An Instructor's Manual is available for adopters of the text. It includes notes on how to design a course based on the book, notes on teaching from each chapter and nearly 400 overheads organised by chapter. To receive a copy, contact your local Addison Wesley Longman Sales Representative.

Further information about the book is available at:

http://www.aw.com/cseng/authors/newman/intsysdes/intsysdes.html

Please note that this material is constantly being updated.

Acknowledgements

We have been fortunate to receive a great deal of support and assistance during the four-year gestation period of this book. Our colleagues at the Rank Xerox Research Centre, Cambridge, have been a constant source of insight and learning, and the management of the Research Centre have remained patient and supportive despite our repeated inability to complete the writing task within the time allotted. We are particularly indebted to Bob Anderson, Manager of RXRC Cambridge, without whose support the book could not have been written. We are also most grateful to Richard Harper, who helped us to fashion the book's coverage of sociological aspects of system design.

The book benefited greatly from the reviews conducted along the way, and we would like to thank those who reviewed the book in its various stages of development: Bob Anderson, John Bates, Dik Bentley, Marge Eldridge, Stu Card, George Coulouris, Jean Dollimore, Paul Dourish, Jonathan Grudin, Richard Harper, Bill Hefley, Brian Inwood, Allan MacLean, Gary Perlman, Richard Rubinstein, Abigail Sellen and Ian Sommerville. We would like to thank Mike Flynn and Maureen Stone for their help in providing illustrations. We are most grateful to Mike Atwood, Wayne Gray and Bonnie John for their assistance with Case Study A. We were also greatly helped by the feedback we received from the students we taught from early versions of the book, at Cambridge University, Queen Mary Westfield College, the Joint Research Centre, Ispra, and ACM SIGCHI '92.

Many people assisted us with the mammoth task of getting the manuscript into its final form. We are especially grateful to Christine King at the Rank Xerox Research Centre, and to the Centre's administrative staff. We would also like to thank Simon Plumtree for his constant advice, and all other staff of Addison-Wesley who helped shepherd the book through editing and production. Finally, we express our deep gratitude to our families, whose tolerance, forebearance and support has meant so much to us while this book was taking shape.

William Newman
Mik Lamming

Cambridge, 1995

ACKNOWLEDGEMENTS

The publisher wishes to thank the following for their permission to reproduce photographs, figures and quotations:

Chapter 1
Figure 1.1(a): Cinematrix Inc., Novato CA. Figures 1.1(b) and 1.1(c): Rank Xerox Ltd.

Chapter 2
Figure 2.7: Rank Xerox Ltd. Figure 2.10: from Stifelman L. J., Arons B., Schmandt C. and Hulteen E. A. 'VoiceNotes: A Speech Interface for a Hand-Held Voice Notetaker.' (1993) *Proceedings of InterCHI '93 Human Factors in Computing Systems* (April 24–29, Amsterdam, Netherlands) ACM/SIGCHI, NY.

Chapter 3
Figure 3.1: from Greatbatch D., Luff P., Heath C. and Campion P. (1993) 'Interpersonal Communication and Human–Computer Interaction: An Examination of the Use of Computers in Medical Consultations.' *Intnl. J. of Interacting with Computers*, Vol. 5, pp. 193–216. By permission of the publishers, Butterworth Heinemann Ltd. ©. Figure 3.2: based on Landauer T. K. and Nachbar D. W. (1985). 'Selection from alphabetic and numeric menu trees using a touch-screen: Breadth, depth and width.' *Proceedings of CHI '85 Human Factors in Computing Systems* (San Francisco CA, April 14–18) ACM/SIGCHI, NY. Figure 3.3: from Barnard P. (1991) 'Bridging between Basic Theories and the Artifacts of Human-Computer Interaction.' In Carroll J.M., ed. *Designing Interaction: Psychology at the Human–Computer Interface*. Cambridge: Cambridge Univ. Press. Figure 3.4: from Card S. K., Moran T. P. and Newell A. (1983) *The Psychology of Human Computer Interaction*. Hillsdale NJ: Lawrence Erlbaum Associates. Pages 53 and 54: quoted from Goodwin M. H. (1991) 'Assembling a Response: Setting and Collaboratively Constructed Work Talk' by permission of the author. Figure 3.7: from Norman D. A. (1986) 'Cognitive Engineering.' In *User Centered System Design* (Norman D. A. and Draper S. W., eds.), pp. 31–65. Hillsdale NJ: Lawrence Erlbaum Associates. Figure 3.8: based on Norman D. A. (1986) 'Cognitive Engineering.' In *User Centered System Design* (Norman D. A. and Draper S. W., eds.), pp. 31–65. Hillsdale NJ: Lawrence Erlbaum Associates. Page 61: quoted from Lewis C. H., Polson P. G., Rieman J., Wharton C. and Wilde N. *Cognitive Walkthroughs: A*

Method for Theory-Based Evaluation of User Interfaces. CHI '92 Tutorial Notes, copyright Clayton L. Lewis and Peter G. Polson, by permission of the authors.

Chapter 4
Figure 4.4(b): from Goodwin C. and Goodwin M. H. (in press) 'Seeing as Situated Activity: Formulating Planes.' In Middleton, D., and Engestrom, Y. *Cognition and Communication at Work.* Copyright Cambridge Univ. Press, reprinted with the permission of Cambridge University Press. Figure 4.4(c): from Card S. K., Moran T. P. and Newell A. (1983) *The Psychology of Human Computer Interaction.* Hillsdale NJ: Lawrence Erlbaum Associates. Figure 4.4(d): Kenneth E. Kendall/Julie E. Kendall, *Systems Analysis and Design*, 2/e © 1992, p. 144. Reprinted by permission of Prentice-Hall, Englewood Cliffs NJ.

Chapter 5
Figure 5.3: from Bingham J. and Davies G. (1992) *Systems Analysis.* Reprinted with the permission of Macmillan Press. Figure 5.4: from Suchman L. and Wynn E. H. (1984) 'Procedures and problems in the office.' *Office: Technology and People.* vol. 1, p. 133, 1984. Reprinted by permission of Elsevier Science B.V. Figure 5.5: from Heath C., Jirotka M., Luff P. and Hindmarsh J. (1993). 'Unpacking Collaboration: The Interactional Organisation of Trading in a City Dealing Room.' *Proc. Third European Conf. on Computer-Supported Cooperative Work – ECSCW '93.* Reprinted by permission of Kluwer Academic Publishers. Figure 5.7: Rank Xerox Ltd. Figure 5.8: from Preece J., Rogers Y., Sharp H., Benyon D., Holland S. and Carey T. (1994) *Human Computer Interaction.* Wokingham: Addison-Wesley. Copyright © 1994 The Open University.

Chapter 6
Figure 6.5: From *Programmers at Work.* Copyright © 1986 Microsoft Press. Reprinted with permission of Microsoft Press. All rights reserved. Figure 6.11: quoted from Lewis C. H., Polson P. G., Rieman J., Wharton C. and Wilde N. *Cognitive Walkthroughs: A Method for Theory-Based Evaluation of User Interfaces.* CHI '92 Tutorial Notes, copyright Clayton L. Lewis and Peter G. Polson, by permission of the authors. Figure 6.15: from Hopkin V.D. (1988) 'Air Traffic Control.' In *Human Factors in Aviation* (Wiener E. L. and Nagel D. C., eds), pp. 639–663. San Diego CA: Academic Press.

Chapter 7
Figure 7.3(a): from *Programmers at Work.* Copyright © 1986 Microsoft Press. Reprinted with permission of Microsoft Press. All rights reserved. Figure 7.3(c): Copyright © North West Regional Health Authority.

Chapter 8

Table 8.1 and Figure 8.5: from Card S. K., Moran T. P. and Newell A. (1983) *The Psychology of Human Computer Interaction*. Hillsdale NJ: Lawrence Erlbaum Associates. Table 8.3: from Nielsen J. and Molich R. (1990). 'Heuristic evaluation of user interfaces.' *Proceedings of CHI '90 Human Factors in Computing Systems* (April 1–5, Seattle, WA) ACM/SIGCHI, NY.

Chapter 9

Figures 9.6, 9.7, 9.8, 9.9 and 9.10: HyperCard II.1 © 1987–1990 Apple Computer Inc. All Rights Reserved. Used with permission. Figure 9.12: from Bly S. and Minneman S. (1990) 'Commune: A Shared Drawing Surface.' *Proc. COIS '90, Conference on Office Information Systems* (Cambridge MA, April 25–27, 1990) pp. 184–192, by permission of ACM. Page 207: excerpted with permission from 'An Interview with Wayne Rosing, Bruce Daniels and Larry Tesler.' *BYTE Magazine*, February 1983 © by McGraw-Hill Inc., New York NY. All rights reserved. Figure 9.13: from Pedersen E. R., McCall K., Moran T. P. and Halasz F. G. (1993) 'Tivoli: An Electronic Whiteboard for Informal Workgroup Meetings.' *Proceedings of InterCHI '93 Human Factors in Computing Systems* (April 24–29, Amsterdam, Netherlands) ACM/SIGCHI, NY.

Chapter 10

Figures 10.13 and 10.14: from Ballas J. A., Heitmeyer C. L. and Pérez M. A. (1992) 'Evaluating Two Aspects of Direct Manipulation in Advanced Cockpits.' *Proceedings of CHI '92 Human Factors in Computing Systems* (May 3–7, Monterey, CA) ACM/SIGCHI, NY.

Case Study A

Figure A.8: from Gray W. D., John B. E. and Atwood M. E. (1993). 'Project Ernestine: Validating a GOMS Analysis for Predicting and Explaining Real-World Task Performance.' *Human Computer Interaction* Vol. 8, pp 237–309. Hillsdale NJ: Lawrence Erlbaum Associates.

Chapter 11

Figure 11.5(a): James Martin, *Design of Man–Computer Dialogues*, © 1973, p. 101. Adapted by permission of Prentice-Hall, Englewood Cliffs NJ. Figure 11.7: from Goodwin C. and Goodwin M. H. (in press) 'Seeing as Situated Activity: Formulating Planes.' In Middleton, D., and Engestrom, Y. Cognition and Communication at Work. Copyright Cambridge Univ. Press; reprinted with the permission of Cambridge University Press. Figure 11.8, dialog box on page 284, icon in Figure 11.9: Systems software © Apple Computer Inc. 1983–1992; All Rights Reserved. Used with permission.

Chapter 12

Figure 12.2: from *Apple Human Interface Guidelines: The Apple Desktop Interface* (page 21), © 1987 by Apple Computer, Inc. Reprinted by permission of Addison-Wesley Publishing Company, Inc. Figure 12.6: from NCSA Mosaic™ from the Software Development Group at the National Center for Supercomputing Applications. Figure 12.15: Ben Shneiderman, *Designing the User Interface, Second Edition* (p. 121), © 1992 by Addison-Wesley Publishing Company Inc. Reprinted by permission of the publisher.

Chapter 13

Figure 13.7: Copyright © 1933, 1961 James Thurber. From *My Life and Hard Times*, published by HarperCollins. Figure 13.9 desktop: Systems software © Apple Computer Inc. 1983–1992. All Rights Reserved. Used with permission. Microsoft Word icons reprinted with permission from Microsoft Corporation. MacPaint icon: MacPaint software is © 1989 Claris Corporation. All Rights Reserved. Figure 13.10: from Young R. M. (1983) 'Surrogates and Mappings: Two kinds of conceptual models of interactive devices.' In *Mental Models* (Gentner D. and Stevens A. L., eds.), pp. 35–52. Hillsdale NJ: Lawrence Erlbaum Associates. Figure 13.11: Copyright Thomson Training and Simulation. Figures 13.12 and 13.13. Microsoft Word icons reprinted with permission from Microsoft Corporation. Figure 13.14: from Moray N. (1992) 'Mental Models of Complex Dynamic Systems.' *Mental Models and Everyday Activities*, Proceedings of 2nd Interdisciplinary Workshop on Mental Models, © 1992 Neville Moray. Figure 13.15: from Lee J.D. (1992) *Trust, Self Confidence, and Operators' Adaptation to Automation*, Ph.D. Thesis, Univ. of Illinois, © 1992 John D. Lee.

Chapter 14

Page 353, quotes: from Norman D. A. (1986) 'Cognitive Engineering.' In *User Centered System Design* (Norman D. A. and Draper S. W., eds.), p. 47. Hillsdale NJ: Lawrence Erlbaum Associates. Figure 14.5(a) desktop: Systems software © Apple Computer Inc. 1983–1992. All Rights Reserved. Used with permission. Microsoft Word icons reprinted with permission from Microsoft Corporation. Figure 14.5(b): by permission of the Syndics of Cambridge University Library. Figure 14.5(c): from Rasmussen J. and Goodstein L. P. (1988) 'Information Technology and Work.' In *Handbook of Human–Computer Interaction*. (Helander M., ed.), pp. 175–201. Reprinted with permission from Elsevier Science B. V. Figure 14.6: Systems software © Apple Computer Inc. 1983–1992. All Rights Reserved. Used with permission. Figures 14.9, 14.10 and 14.11: MacDraw software is © 1989–1992 Claris Corporation. All Rights Reserved. Page 370: guidelines from Mayhew D. J. (1992) *Principles and Guidelines in Software User Interface Design*. Englewood Cliffs NJ: Prentice-Hall, reprinted with permission of the publishers. Page 370: guidelines from *Apple Human Interface Guidelines: The Apple Desktop Interface* (page 3), © 1987 by Apple Computer, Inc. Reprinted by permission of Addison-Wesley Publishing Company, Inc.

Chapter 15
Figure 15.1(a) and guideline on page 396: Ben Shneiderman, *Designing the User Interface, Second Edition* (p. 72), © 1992 by Addison-Wesley Publishing Company Inc. Reprinted by permission of the publisher. Figure 15.1(c): from Mayhew D. J. (1992) *Principles and Guidelines in Software User Interface Design*. Englewood Cliffs NJ: Prentice-Hall, reprinted with permission of the publisher. Figure 15.1(e) and (f): from *Apple Human Interface Guidelines: The Apple Desktop Interface* (page 43), © 1987 by Apple Computer, Inc. Reprinted by permission of Addison-Wesley Publishing Company, Inc. Figure15.3(a). Microsoft Windows screen shots reprinted with permission from Microsoft Corporation. Figure 15.3(b): Systems software © Apple Computer Inc. 1983–1992. All Rights Reserved. Used with permission. Figure 15.5: Copyright owned by Sun Microsystems, Inc. Used herein by permission. All other rights reserved. Page 377: guideline from *The Windows Interface, An Application Design Guide*. Copyright © 1987, 1992 Microsoft Corporation. Reprinted with permission of Microsoft Press. All rights reserved. Page 377: guideline from Mayhew D. J. (1992) *Principles and Guidelines in Software User Interface Design*. Englewood Cliffs NJ: Prentice-Hall, reprinted with permission of the publisher. Pages 378, 380, guidelines: Copyright owned by Sun Microsystems, Inc. Used herein by permission. All other rights reserved. Page 379, guideline from Mayhew D. J. (1992) *Principles and Guidelines in Software User Interface Design*. Englewood Cliffs NJ: Prentice-Hall, reprinted with permission of the publisher. Table 15.1: Ben Shneiderman, *Designing the User Interface, Second Edition* (pp. 72–73), © 1992 by Addison-Wesley Publishing Company Inc, reprinted by permission of the publisher; and from Nielsen J. and Molich R. (1990). 'Heuristic evaluation of user interfaces.' *Proceedings of CHI '90 Human Factors in Computing Systems* (April 1–5, Seattle, WA) ACM/SIGCHI, NY. Pages 398-399: guidelines from Mayhew D. J. (1992) *Principles and Guidelines in Software User Interface Design*. Englewood Cliffs NJ: Prentice-Hall, reprinted with permission of the publisher. Page 405, guidelines: Copyright owned by Sun Microsystems, Inc. Used herein by permission. All other rights reserved. Pages 405–406, guidelines; page 407, Figure 15.22; and pages 408–409, guidelines; all from *The Windows Interface, An Application Design Guide*. Copyright © 1987, 1992 Microsoft Corporation. Reprinted with permission of Microsoft Press. All rights reserved. Figure 15.21: from NCSA Mosaic™ from the Software Development Group at the National Center for Supercomputing Applications. Figure 15.23. Microsoft Windows screen shots reprinted with permission from Microsoft Corporation. Plate 8: from Stone M. C., Cowan W. M. and Beatty J. C. (1988) 'Color gamut mapping and the printing of

digital color images.' *ACM Trans. on Graphics*, Vol. 7 no. 4 (October 1988). pp. 249–292. Plate 9: from Lamming M.G. and Rhodes W. R. (1990) 'A Simple Method for Improved Color Printing of Monitor Images.' *ACM Trans. on Graphics*, Vol. 9 no. 2 (October 1990). pp. 346–375.

Case Study B
Figures B.2 and B.3, Table B.1: Rank Xerox Ltd. Figure B.5: from Newman W. M., Eldridge M. A. and Lamming M. G. (1991) 'Pepys: Generating Autobiographies by Automatic Tracking.' *Proc. Second European Conf. on Computer-Supported Cooperative Work – ECSCW '91*. Reprinted by permission of Kluwer Academic Publishers. Figures B.6, B.8, B.9, B.11, B.12, icon and screen designs on pages 434–439: Rank Xerox Ltd.

CONTENTS

Foreword   vii

Preface   xi

PART I   The framework

CHAPTER 1   Introduction   3

1.1   **Interactive systems**   3

1.2   **Success in interactive system design**   4
1.2.1   What are interactive systems?   6
1.2.2   Why do we design them?   6
1.2.3   How do we know if we have succeeded?   7
1.2.4   What happens if we fail?   8
1.2.5   How do we maintain a track record of success?   9
1.2.6   Creativity in engineering design   10

1.3   **The nature of the methods we use**   10
1.3.1   Analysis and synthesis   11
1.3.2   The supporting activities   11

1.4   **In conclusion**   12

Further reading   13

CHAPTER 2   Defining the problem   15

2.1   **Introduction**   15

2.2   **The problem statement**   16
2.2.1   The one-sentence problem statement   17
2.2.2   Whose problem are we solving?   17

2.3   **The situation of concern and the course of action**   18
2.3.1   Human activity as the causal link   19

2.4   **The activity to be supported**   20
2.4.1   Tasks: Units of goal-directed activity   20
2.4.2   Designing a tool to support the task   22

2.4.3   Processes: Linking tasks to achieve longer-term goals   23
2.4.4   Formation of processes: The effect of multiple dependencies 24
2.4.5   How we discover processes   26
2.4.6   Designing systems to support processes   27

2.5   **The user**   **29**
2.5.1   Addressing the general needs of the human user   29
2.5.2   Addressing specific user needs   29

2.6   **Usability**   **30**
2.6.1   Usability factors   30
2.6.2   Our choice of usability targets   31
2.6.3   Improving levels of performance   32

2.7   **The form of the solution**   **32**
2.7.1   Describing the form of solution   32
2.7.2   What we define in the problem statement, and why   33
2.7.3   Exploiting in-house expertise or technology   34
2.7.4   Innovative forms of solution   36

2.8   **Conclusion: What follows after problem definition?**   **37**

        Exercises   38

        Further reading   39

CHAPTER 3   **The Human Virtual Machine**   **41**
3.1   **Introduction**   **41**

3.2   **Types of theory useful in system design**   **42**
3.2.1   Explanatory theories   42
3.2.2   Empirical laws   44
3.2.3   Dynamic models   44
3.2.4   The Human Virtual Machine   46

3.3   **Psychological models of human information processing**   **48**
3.3.1   Information processing subsystems   48
3.3.2   Cycle times and task performance   50

3.4   **Sociological and anthropological theories of human behaviour** **53**
3.4.1   Cognitive versus social perspectives   53
3.4.2   Factors that distinguish the social perspective   54
3.4.3   Examples of theories of social behaviour   55

3.5   **Theories of the organization of human activity**   **57**
3.5.1   Problem-solving models   58
3.5.2   Norman's model of task performance   59
3.5.3   A theory of exploratory learning   61

3.6   **Sociological theory of group organization**   **62**
   3.6.1   Modelling users' reasoning about choice of tools   65

3.7   **Conclusion**   **67**

Exercises   67

Further reading   68

CHAPTER 4   **Design processes and representations**   **69**
   4.1   **Introduction**   **69**

4.2   **Understanding design**   **70**
   4.2.1   The multiple processes of interactive system design   70
   4.2.2   Design representations   71

4.3   **Studying the user**   **72**

4.4   **Modelling the user's activity**   **75**

4.5   **Developing the specification**   **78**
   4.5.1   The problem statement as a specification   78
   4.5.2   The requirements document   79
   4.5.3   Subdivision of the design   80
   4.5.4   Designing the user interface   80

4.6   **Analysing the design**   **83**
   4.6.1   Analysis of the organization of activities   83
   4.6.2   Analysing performance levels   84

4.7   **Empirical evaluation**   **85**

4.8   **In summary: The processes of design**   **86**

Exercises   87

Further reading   87

PART II   **System design**

CHAPTER 5   **User study methods**   **91**
   5.1   **Introduction**   **91**
   5.1.1   When do we conduct user studies?   92
   5.1.2   How do we ensure quality?   93
   5.1.3   Data collection methods   93

5.2   **Interviews**   **94**
   5.2.1   The basic method   94

5.2.2	Effective interviews	96
5.2.3	Recording the interview	99

5.3 Observation — **99**
5.3.1	Video recording	99
5.3.2	Concurrent verbal accounts	100
5.3.3	Passive observation	100
5.3.4	Ethnographic field study	101
5.3.5	Action research	103

5.4 Questionnaires — **103**
| 5.4.1 | Questionnaire design issues | 103 |
| 5.4.2 | Questionnaires by electronic mail | 105 |

5.5 Conclusion — **107**

Exercises — 107

Further reading — 108

CHAPTER 6   Systems analysis and design   109

6.1 Introduction — **109**
| 6.1.1 | The processes of systems analysis and design | 110 |
| 6.1.2 | The place of prototyping and evaluation | 111 |

6.2 Approaches to modelling the user's activities — **114**
6.2.1	Task-oriented modelling and analysis	114
6.2.2	Process-oriented methods	114
6.2.3	Activity models, normative and descriptive	114
6.2.4	How we use models of activities	115

6.3 Methods based on task models — **117**
| 6.3.1 | Hierarchic task models | 117 |
| 6.3.2 | Analysing the task model | 119 |

6.4 Task analysis and design: An example — **120**
6.4.1	First attempt: Studying the activity	120
6.4.2	Modelling the activity	120
6.4.3	Synthesizing an initial solution	120
6.4.4	Specifying the initial solution	122
6.4.5	Analysing the initial solution	123

6.5 Systems analysis methods — **124**
| 6.5.1 | The need for systems analysis | 124 |
| 6.5.2 | Viewpoints | 124 |

6.6 Software systems analysis — **125**
| 6.6.1 | Data modelling | 125 |

6.6.2   Data-flow diagrams   126
6.6.3   Analysis   126
6.6.4   Analysis of the Commission study   128
6.6.5   Allocating functions from the system model   129

6.7   User-participative methods   **131**
6.7.1   The method in outline   131
6.7.2   Participative design at the Commission   133
6.7.3   User-participative methods: Pros and cons   136

6.8   Summary   **137**

Exercises   138

Further reading   139

CHAPTER 7   Requirements definition   141
7.1   Introduction   **141**

7.2   How requirements serve design   **142**
7.2.1   Support for validation   143
7.2.2   Support for verification   143

7.3   Defining requirements   **144**
7.3.1   Who reads requirements documents?   144

7.4   Defining requirements for interactive systems   **147**
7.4.1   Continuing the Commission example   147
7.4.2   Defining the functional form   149
7.4.3   Identifying the users   149
7.4.4   Setting performance requirements   151
7.4.5   Requirements for other layers of technology   154

7.5   Validating requirements   **156**
7.5.1   Analytical methods of validation   156
7.5.2   Building and testing prototypes   157
7.5.3   On documenting the prototype's design   157

7.6   Requirements and innovation   **158**

7.7   Verification against performance requirements   **159**

7.8   Conclusion   **160**

Exercises   160

Further reading   161

PART III   System evaluation

CHAPTER 8   Usability analysis and inspection   165
  8.1   **Introduction**   165

  8.2   **Answering usability questions**   166
    8.2.1   Two approaches to measuring usability   166

  8.3   **Analysis as a two-stage process**   167
    8.3.1   Determining the sequence by walkthrough   168
    8.3.2   Determining the sequence empirically   168
    8.3.3   Folding in the usability analysis   169
    8.3.4   Methods of analysis   169

  8.4   **Analysis techniques based on the GOMS model**   169
    8.4.1   The GOMS model   170
    8.4.2   Keystroke-Level Analysis   171

  8.5   **Analysis by Cognitive Walkthrough**   176
    8.5.1   The underlying model of exploratory learning   177
    8.5.2   Cognitive Walkthrough: An example   178

  8.6   **Heuristic Evaluation**   182
    8.6.1   The method of evaluation   183

  8.7   **Conclusion**   186

  Exercises   186

  Further reading   187

CHAPTER 9   Prototyping and evaluation   189
  9.1   **Introduction**   189

  9.2   **Evaluation in support of design: The formative approach** 190
    9.2.1   Evaluating against requirements   190
    9.2.2   The summative approach, and its drawbacks   191
    9.2.3   Methods of formative evaluation   192
    9.2.4   Choosing between the methods   193

  9.3   **Conducting the investigation**   194
    9.3.1   The basic stages of evaluation   194
    9.3.2   Experimental design and analysis   195
    9.3.3   Documenting the planned investigation and its result   196
    9.3.4   Documenting with the aid of pro formas   197

  9.4   **Prototyping**   198
    9.4.1   Prototyping in interactive system design   199

9.4.2 Prototyping tools   200
9.4.3 An overview of HyperCard   200
9.4.4 HyperCard programming: The HyperTalk language   202

9.5 **Learning while prototyping**   **203**

9.6 **Informal testing of prototypes**   **204**
9.6.1 Goals of informal testing   204
9.6.2 Conducting the investigation   205

9.7 **Iterative field tests**   **208**
9.7.1 Participative evaluation   208
9.7.2 Stages in field testing   209

9.8 **Case study: Evaluating a meeting support tool**   **210**
9.8.1 Setting up the experiment   210
9.8.2 The pro forma plan   211
9.8.3 Results   212

9.9 **Conclusion**   **212**

Exercises   213

Further reading   214

CHAPTER 10   Experiments in support of design   215
10.1 **Introduction**   **215**

10.2 **The purpose of controlled experiments**   **216**
10.2.1 Evaluation when usage is predictable   216

10.3 **Populations and samples**   **218**
10.3.1 Populations   218
10.3.2 Samples and sample means   219
10.3.3 Confidence levels   219

10.4 **The design of two-sample experiments**   **220**
10.4.1 Measurements in the context of task performance   221
10.4.2 The variables in the experiment   222
10.4.3 Nuisance variables   223
10.4.4 The stages of the experiment   223

10.5 **Establishing confidence levels**   **224**
10.5.1 Normal distributions   225
10.5.2 Population variance and standard deviation   227
10.5.3 The null hypothesis   229
10.5.4 Some simple methods of statistical analysis   230

10.6   **Basic calculations of variance and standard deviation**   **231**
10.6.1   Sums of squares of differences from the mean   231
10.6.2   Degrees of freedom   232
10.6.3   Variance and standard deviation of a sample   233

10.7   **Comparisons of two samples: The *t* test**   **233**

10.8   **Using *t* values to derive confidence intervals**   **236**

10.9   **Chi-square analysis of categorical data**   **239**

10.10   **Illustrations of the methods: Testing the ticket machine**   **240**
10.10.1   The question of speed of operation   241
10.10.2   The question of preferred journey type   242

10.11   **Case study: Evaluating a cockpit display**   **243**
10.11.1   The design problem: Reducing automation deficit   243
10.11.2   The experiment   244

10.12   **Conclusion**   **246**

Exercises   247

Further reading   248

CASE   Evaluation and analysis of a telephone
STUDY A   operator's workstation   249

PART IV   User interface design

CHAPTER 11   User interface notations   271
11.1   **Introduction**   **271**

11.2   **The use of representations in design**   **272**
11.2.1   The roles of representations   272
11.2.2   Representational strategies   274
11.2.3   Strategies for describing the user interface   276

11.3   **User actions: Defining input syntax**   **276**

11.4   **Appearance: Describing system output**   **278**

11.5   **Describing interactive objects**   **279**

11.6   **Describing methods of operation**   **284**
11.6.1   An example: Extracting methods from
         Object State Transition Charts   285
11.6.2   Describing action sequences with the UAN   285

11.7	**Describing by prototyping**	**287**
11.8	**Conclusion**	**290**
	Exercises	290
	Further reading	291

CHAPTER 12	Interaction styles	**293**
12.1	**Introduction**	**293**
	12.1.1 What are interaction styles?	294
12.2	**Three categories of style**	**294**
	12.2.1 Key-modal interaction styles	295
	12.2.2 Direct-manipulation styles	296
	12.2.3 Linguistic styles	297
12.3	**A survey of interaction styles**	**299**
	12.3.1 The example: Purchasing from a hardware catalogue	299
12.4	**Menu-based interaction**	**300**
	12.4.1 Principles of menu-based interaction	301
	12.4.2 Variants of menus	301
	12.4.3 Hypertext embedded menus and the World Wide Web	301
	12.4.4 Properties of menu-based interaction	303
12.5	**Question and answer**	**305**
	12.5.1 Properties of question and answer	306
12.6	**Function-key interfaces**	**307**
	12.6.1 Principles of function-key interfaces	307
12.7	**Voice-based interaction**	**309**
12.8	**Graphical direct manipulation**	**311**
	12.8.1 Properties of graphical direct-manipulation interfaces	312
12.9	**Forms fill-in**	**313**
	12.9.1 Properties of forms fill-in	315
12.10	**Command-line interaction**	**315**
	12.10.1 Properties of command-language interaction	316
12.11	**Text-based natural language**	**317**
12.12	**Choice of interaction style**	**319**
	12.12.1 Narrowing down the choice	319
	12.12.2 Style-specific design knowledge	320
	12.12.3 Combining styles and maintaining consistency	320

| | | Exercises | 321 |
| | | Further reading | 322 |

CHAPTER 13		**Conceptual design: The user's mental model**	**323**
	13.1	**Introduction**	**323**
	13.2	**Understanding software systems**	**324**
	13.2.1	Programmers' misunderstandings	324
	13.2.2	Users' problems with conceptual mismatch	325
	13.2.3	The problem of learning on the job	325
	13.3	**The user's mental model**	**326**
	13.3.1	Runnable mental models	326
	13.3.2	Running a mental model: A simple example	329
	13.3.3	How the system image helps form mental models	331
	13.4	**The form of the mental model**	**331**
	13.4.1	Recurring forms of mental model	333
	13.4.2	State transition models	333
	13.4.3	Object-action models	333
	13.4.4	Mapping models	335
	13.4.5	Analogical models	336
	13.5	**Mental models of complex systems**	**338**
	13.5.1	Lattices of causal relationships	338
	13.5.2	Mixed forms of mental model	342
	13.5.3	Running different forms of mental model	342
	13.6	**The interaction cycle and the user's understanding**	**343**
	13.6.1.	In conclusion: How we tackle conceptual design problems	345
		Exercises	346
		Further reading	346

CHAPTER 14		**Conceptual design: Methods**	**347**
	14.1	**Introduction**	**347**
	14.2	**The intended mental model**	**348**
	14.2.1	How the choice of mental model influences design	348
	14.2.2	Retrofitting the mental model	349
	14.2.3	The intended mental model and the style of interaction	349
	14.2.4	In summary	350
	14.3	**Hiding the system model**	**350**
	14.3.1	In summary	353

14.4   Designing the system image   **353**
    14.4.1   The user interface as the presenter of the system image   353
    14.4.2   Maintaining the currency of the system image   355
    14.4.3   Maintaining system-image consistency   356
    14.4.4   Progressive reinforcement of the system image   357
    14.4.5   In summary   357

14.5   Walkthrough analysis   **358**
    14.5.1   Cognitive Walkthroughs: The technique in outline   358
    14.5.2   Extending the walkthrough technique   358
    14.5.3   In summary   368

14.6   Conceptual design heuristics   **369**
    14.6.1   A sample of conceptual design heuristics   369
    14.6.2   In summary   371

    Exercises   372

    Further reading   372

CHAPTER 15   Designing to guidelines   373
15.1   Introduction   **373**

15.2   Guidelines: What are they, and why do we need them?   **374**
    15.2.1   Why do we need guidelines?   374

15.3   How we use guidelines   **375**
    15.3.1   The roles of guidelines   376
    15.3.2   Limitations of guidelines   379
    15.3.3   Contexts of guideline use   382

15.4   General design principles   **383**
    15.4.1   General principles   384

15.5   An example: The design of the Economic Update system   **386**
    15.5.1   The Economic Update problem   386
    15.5.2   Applying general principles   387
    15.5.3   Applying other categories of guideline   388

15.6   Guidelines for the design of effective displays   **388**
    15.6.1   Screen design guidelines   388
    15.6.2   Graphic design guidelines   389
    15.6.3   Applying screen design guidelines to the
             Economic Update application   389

15.7   Guidelines for the use of colour   **392**
    15.7.1   Colour terminology   392
    15.7.2   Choice of colours   392

15.7.3   Colour vision limitations   393
15.7.4   Colour vision impairment   393
15.7.5   Accuracy in colour rendering   394

15.8   Guidelines in support of interaction styles   **395**
15.8.1   The contribution of research   395
15.8.2   A voice-based Economic Update interface   398

15.9   The use of style guides   **400**
15.9.1   Style guidelines for the World Wide Web   401
15.9.2   Style guides for windowing environments   402
15.9.3   Designing the components of windowed applications   405
15.9.4   Designing drop-down menus for a windowed Economic
         Updates system   406

15.10   Conclusion   **409**

Exercises   410

Further reading   410

CASE
STUDY B   Designing a human memory aid   411

Design problems   441

Bibliography   445

Index   457

PART I

The framework

1 Introduction

2 Defining the problem

3 The Human Virtual Machine

4 Design processes and
   representations

CHAPTER 1

Introduction

Chapter objectives:

This chapter introduces the topic of interactive system design. Its aims are:

- To explain what interactive systems are
- To explain what it means to design a successful interactive system
- To emphasize the need for sound engineering methods of design
- To indicate the range of methods needed in interactive system design, and the contributions they make.

1.1 Interactive systems

In today's world, interacting with computer-based devices and systems is commonplace. Even home TV sets and wristwatches contain large amounts of software. Interacting with computers, once just a privilege of the professional and clerical workforce, is now something that everybody does. The designers and builders of interactive systems have been propelled into positions of real influence in society. It is imperative they do their job well.

This book is about doing interactive system design and doing it well.

1.2 Success in interactive system design

What does it mean to do a good job of designing an interactive system? This question has a long answer and a shorter one. The long answer unfolds, piece by piece, in the course of this book. It reveals a wide range of methods for solving design problems, and a supporting framework of processes and representations.

Even this cannot be a full answer, however. Even in a book ten times as long it would be hard to provide readers with a complete set of design methods; for the field of interactive computing has now expanded to the point where no one person can know all about it. And it is still expanding, faster than ever. It has become a focal point for technological innovation on a massive scale. Every year, new ideas for interacting with computers are made public. A few are illustrated in Figure 1.1.

The shorter answer to the question breaks down into answers to several subsidiary questions:

• What are interactive systems?

• Why do we design them?

(a)

Figure 1.1 Novel uses of interactive technology: (a) audience participation with the aid of the Cinematrix system, which can sense bi-coloured wands held up by participants (courtesy Cinematrix Inc.); (b) the DigitalDesk, which allows the user to interact with paper documents and with electronic documents projected from overhead (Wellner, 1991, courtesy Rank Xerox Ltd); (c) a hand-held memory aid, capable of assisting the user in retrieving details of past events (Lamming and Flynn, 1994, courtesy Rank Xerox Ltd).

- How do we know if we have succeeded?
- What happens if we fail?
- How do we maintain a track record of success in design?
- How can we also retain our creativity?

(b)

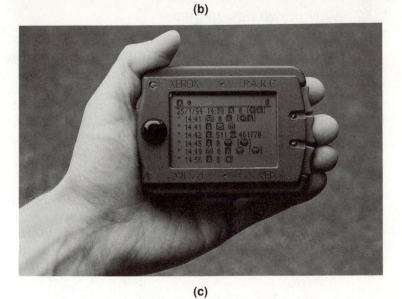

(c)

Figure 1.1   *Continued*

By addressing each question briefly, we will begin to see what interactive system design is about. We will see that it relies on the use of a wide range of design methods, each of which makes an essential contribution to the progress of design.

1.2.1   What are interactive systems?

As its name indicates, an interactive system supports communication in both directions, from user to computer and back. It does this in a way that enables it to follow the pace and direction of the user's activity. The user takes actions such as pressing buttons, pointing with a 'mouse' or typing in text. The system reacts accordingly, perhaps by displaying information, perhaps by activating machinery or performing some other useful service, perhaps just by waiting for the user's next action. All of this takes place via the system's **user interface**, the part of the system that provides access to the computer's internal resources.

The most crucial property of any interactive system is *its support for human activity*. This is what makes it worth having. It may enable us to do things faster, with fewer errors, with less prior learning, with greater resultant quality, or perhaps just with greater fun and satisfaction. These are some of the benefits that justify the money spent on it. But if instead it interferes with our activities it becomes a source of trouble. We must spend more time doing the same amount of work or clearing up problems that the system has caused, and sooner or later we must discard the system or replace it with a better design.

1.2.2   Why do we design them?

The need to replace an obsolete or inadequate system is a common reason for embarking on a design exercise. But we get drawn into design activities for many other reasons besides. We may identify a human problem that needs solving, such as a disadvantaged group of people. We may see an opportunity for commercial profit. We may be students, tackling design problems in order to learn how to design. Or we may simply be designers by profession, serving on teams whose task is to produce a new artefact; it is our job to produce a satisfactory solution to the design problem.

Whatever the circumstances that draw us into interactive system design, there is always a context for which the system is targeted. Checkland has called this context the **situation of concern** (Checkland and Scholes, 1990). There is something unsatisfactory about this situation, and we need to find a means of resolving it. We need to reduce the plight of disadvantaged people, or perhaps we just need to plug a gap in the company's product line. We see a way of doing this by means of a new interactive system, such as a computerized water-purifier or an electronic game, and therefore we set about designing it.

Of course, there are often several different ways of resolving a situation of concern. A water pipeline might do the job better than an interactive purifier, and a game licensed from another supplier might generate more profit than a new design. We shouldn't adopt the system-design route blindly, ignoring these alternatives.

Ultimately we design interactive systems because we see activities that they can support, and we can tell that this will lead to resolution of the situation of concern. We can see that this is the most cost-effective way of getting there. The support of people's activities provides the missing link between an unsatisfactory situation and its resolution. It engages us in interactive system design.

1.2.3   How do we know if we have succeeded?

As designers, we want to know if we have done a satisfactory job. This is not just a matter of feeling good or justifying our designer's pay. If we do not know how well we have done, we cannot tell whether we are making progress from one job to the next – we are designing 'blind', unable to see whether one method works and another doesn't.

The true measure of design success is, of course, the resolution of the situation of concern. But there are several reasons why we might like to use other measures. For one, we won't find out right away whether our design has resolved the situation. We will have to wait, perhaps several years, perhaps indefinitely. For another, the situation may take an unexpected turn for reasons that have nothing to do with our design. Political or economic factors, not design quality, may determine the outcome.

We need an interim, localized measure of design success. We find it in measuring how well our system supports people in their activities. If these activities are worth doing they are worth doing well, and if our system enables people to perform them better, to a degree that justifies the cost of the system, we can consider the design a success.

For this reason, interactive system design is concerned with ways of measuring how well people perform activities with the aid of systems. There is no single way of measuring this; indeed the factors that contribute to a well-performed activity are numerous. They include, at a very minimum, the speed with which the activity is performed with the aid of the system, the ease with which people can learn to use it, and the number of errors that occur. Our collective term for them is **usability factors**. A short list of them is shown in Figure 1.2.

System design is not concerned only with achieving usability. Systems need to be robust, easy to maintain, easy to upgrade, secure against intruding 'hackers', socially acceptable. At the same time, they need to meet cost targets. Only if they measure up in these respects too can they be considered truly well engineered. We need to keep these factors in mind too as we design interactive systems. But methods for

- The **speed of performance** of the activity, which affects **how many people** are needed to perform it
- The **incidence of errors** while performing the activity
- The users' ability to **recover from errors** that occur
- The magnitude of the users' task in **learning to use the system**
- The users' **retention of learned skills**
- The users' ability to **customize** the system to suit their way of working or the situation of use
- The ease with which people can **reorganize activities** supported by the system – their own activities and other people's
- Users' **satisfaction** with the system.

Figure 1.2   A short list of usability factors, indicators of how well a system supports the performance of activities by users.

achieving all of these properties in systems lie outside the scope of this book. This book is about the special methods needed when interactive systems are designed.

1.2.4   What happens if we fail?

There is always an element of risk in design. We set our sights on producing a design that will have the desired effect; by diligent design we hit the target most of the time, but occasionally we miss. What happens then?

Failures in interactive system design often go unnoticed. An interactive system may have serious design flaws that undermine its usability, but its users will still manage to steer around these flaws and get their work done (Zuboff, 1988). They will often gain satisfaction from their ability to devise work-arounds for system problems; if they cannot make the system work, on the other hand, they are quite likely to attribute this to their own stupidity (Norman, 1988). To the outside world, the only evidence of design failure is the frequency with which systems are said to be 'giving trouble today' or are 'out of action at the present moment', phrases commonly used to hide that fact that usability problems have struck again.

Although design failures can remain hidden from the public eye, this is not always the case. Eventually a design problem will cause a failure that even the best work-arounds cannot hide. A frequent source of these failures is lack of attention to preventing user errors.

A widely used text editor uses the character '.' to select the line of text that is currently being edited, and ',' to select the entire document. These are on two adjacent keys of the keyboard, so it is highly likely that the wrong key will sometimes be pressed. The results can be unfortunate – we can easily destroy the entire file of text when we mean to delete one line.

If we are trying to correct the text *A heavy poll is expected* to read *A heavy turnout is expected* by substituting the text *turnout* for *poll*, and we type a comma instead of a period, we will change *poll* to *turnout* throughout the document. An instance of such a mistake was reported in the British press: all of the election documents for a candidate named Pollack were printed with the name Turnoutack instead. A 'computer failure' was blamed (Neumann, 1991).

The results of failures in interactive system design are rarely amusing for those directly affected. An ambulance dispatch system, introduced in London in 1992, caused long delays in ambulances reaching the scenes of emergencies, and had to be taken out of service within days of its introduction. There were many flaws in its design, some of them in the user interface. The inquiry report mentions, among possible contributing factors, the failure of ambulance crews to press the correct status button on their mobile control panels, or pressing them in the wrong order. In another passage it describes a problem with the display of messages to control-room staff:

> The number of exception messages increased rapidly to such an extent that staff were unable to clear the queue. As the exception message queue grew the system slowed. The situation was made worse as unrectified exception messages generated more exception messages. With the increasing number of 'awaiting attention' and exception messages it became increasingly easy to fail to attend to messages that had scrolled off the top of the screen (London Ambulance Service, 1993).

An especially tragic case occurred in 1988 when the USS *Vincennes* shot down an Iran Air A300 Airbus, with 290 people aboard. The Aegis weapons system aboard *Vincennes* had sophisticated software for identifying and tracking potentially threatening targets, but was unable to provide the crew with up-to-date altitude information on its large-screen display. Instead, altitude had to be read from other consoles, and in the confusion of the situation an incorrect reading was taken. The Airbus, which had levelled off at 12 500 feet, was taken to be an F-14 fighter descending towards the *Vincennes* from 9000 feet. Ironically, an escort ship to the *Vincennes*, using older equipment, was able to read the plane's altitude quite correctly as 12 500 feet, but could not intervene in time (Lee L., 1992).

1.2.5   How do we maintain a track record of success?

We would like to know that every design we undertake has a good chance of success, and that failures of the kind just described will not occur. The best way to guarantee this is to go about the design in an organized way, making systematic use of the practices and methods that successful designers have used in the past.

We can benefit from taking a broad look at how design is done. We need not limit ourselves to interactive system designers. We can learn, for example, from the methods of architects, industrial designers, electronic circuit designers, bridge builders and many others.

In particular, we can benefit from looking at how *engineering design* is done. Engineers have a professional concern with organizing the design and construction of artefacts that affect our surroundings (see Rogers, 1983). In many branches of engineering, designers regularly achieve the kind of track record of success that we strive for in the computer field. They build skyscrapers that survive earthquakes, ships that stay afloat, phone systems that can connect you to anywhere, anytime. If we want to be just as successful, we must learn how to work as engineers.

1.2.6   Creativity in engineering design

But can we retain our creativity as system designers if we operate as engineers? Won't our ability to innovate be affected? The answer is that engineering, too, is about creativity and innovation. It is about making it easier to do some of the laborious aspects of design, such as analysing performance, testing for safety or ease of use, integrating together component parts, tracking down obscure pieces of design knowledge. When these aspects of design are made easier it becomes easier to be creative, because there is less effort involved in turning novel ideas into reliable products, and less danger of spending time exploring dead ends.

When engineers innovate, however, they need a broader range of tools and methods than when they follow well-trodden paths. They need methods for studying unfamiliar application domains and for making sense of what they have observed there. They need ways of describing novel solutions to design problems. They need to know how to test new designs, even when it is not clear how they will be used. Sometimes they need to become researchers in order to fill a gap in the available engineering knowledge. In addition, they need to know when to use one method rather than another, because each has its strengths and weaknesses.

If we have such a set of methods at our disposal, we can approach the design of interactive systems in an organized way, whether or not we are adopting an innovative approach. We can maintain a more consistent level of quality in our designs, and see progress as we move from one design project to the next.

1.3   The nature of the methods we use

There is no single 'methodology', or sequence of steps, that leads to a successful outcome in interactive system design. Such is the breadth of applications for interactive technology, we cannot assume that the method we applied successfully to one design problem will apply to another. Instead we need to gain an understanding of the problem, and then address it with the available methods, applying them where they are needed.

1.3.1 Analysis and synthesis

One thing we always experience during design is a need to shift constantly between two kinds of design activity, *analysis* and *synthesis*. During analysis we test the design to determine whether it is meeting our targets for usability and software quality. During synthesis we shape the design, drawing on fresh ideas and on solutions to similar problems that have worked well in the past. We try to devise an effective user interface through which the user can access the system's functionality.

Analysis is a key component of the process, for it enables us to understand how the system is likely to affect the user's activity. Will things get done faster and with fewer errors? Or will things be much as before? To answer these questions we try to gain a clear picture of how the user's activity will be performed; we build a *model* of the performed activity, from which we can take performance measurements and make assessments of usability. These measurements and assessments in turn feed into the enhancement of the design. The two-stage process, shown in Figure 1.3, is repeated many times over during the course of design.

1.3.2 The supporting activities

A variety of design activities support this two-stage process. Some are concerned with user studies, some with evaluation, some with user interface design. They mostly cluster around one or other of the two main steps in the cycle, in support of analysis or synthesis. There is no clear dividing line, however; some activities spread across the whole cycle.

In Figure 1.4 this supporting role of design methods is shown overlaid on the basic diagram of Figure 1.3. Only those methods concerned specifically with the interactive properties of the system are shown here. The methods are labelled with names that correspond to the topics covered in this book.

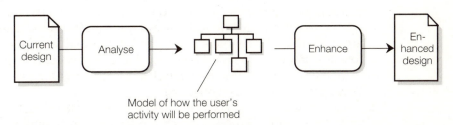

Figure 1.3 The basic iterative step of interactive system design, in which the current design is analysed in order to build a model of how the user is expected to perform their activity with the system's support. This enables assessments to be made of the design's usability, which feed into the enhancement of the design. Then the process repeats.

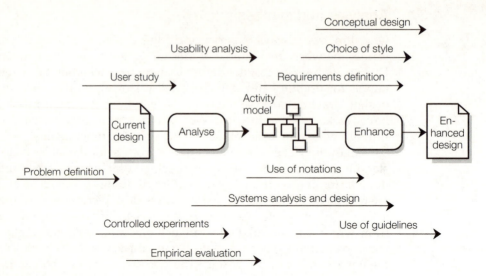

Figure 1.4   The design activities that contribute to the basic iterative cycle.

Figure 1.4 conveys the way in which this collection of methods supports interactive system design. Each of the methods is available for use
throughout the design process, although some of them tend to get used
early and others later on. Depending on the nature of the design problem,
each one plays a greater or lesser role. Every iteration in the design will
involve the use of one or more techniques for analysis, and one or more
for enhancing the design further. As we gain familiarity with the methods
we become more adept at choosing when to apply them; this makes us
more effective as designers.

1.4   In conclusion

These, then, are some of the issues raised by the need to do a good job of
designing interactive systems, and by the availability of a range of methods for use in design. We shall be discussing the methods, and how they
are applied, in the chapters that lie ahead. We shall also be referring back
to many of the issues raised here – the focus of design on situations of concern, the concept of usability, the risks of design failure, and the need to
apply sound engineering practices.

Most of all, we will be concerned with understanding how to support
people's activities. This is the central purpose of designing interactive systems. It is also a factor that makes their design challenging and endlessly
absorbing, for people's activities are highly complex and infinitely varied.
As technologies advance, new opportunities are created to provide them
with better support than before. We are assured of an unending supply of
design problems to exercise our design skills.

Further reading

Rogers G. F. C. (1983). *The Nature of Engineering: a Philosophy of Technology*. Macmillan

A short but insightful account of engineering practice and its approach to innovative design.

Lee L. (1992). *The Day the Phones Stopped*. New York: Donald I. Fine Inc.

An absorbing account of some of the ways in which computer failures, including interactive system design failures, affect our lives.

London Ambulance Service (1993). *Report on the Inquiry into the London Ambulance Service*. Available from: Communications Directorate, South West Thames Regional Health Authority, 40 Eastbourne Terrace, London W2 3QR

A cautionary tale for interactive system designers. The report was issued after an inquiry into a dispatch system that failed almost immediately after its introduction. It includes a detailed account of the course of the system's development and the problems encountered along the way.

CHAPTER 2

Defining the problem

Chapter objectives:

Interactive system design is concerned with solving problems, and before we proceed any distance into design we need to know what the problem is. This chapter explains:

- The nature of the design problems we are likely to encounter
- The range of tasks and processes that interactive systems can support
- The importance of usability in measuring how well a system supports the user's activity
- How we focus on a particular form of solution
- How to write a one-sentence problem statement.

2.1 Introduction

Designing an interactive system leads us into many challenging areas of work. There is a need – as later chapters in this book will explain – to perform studies and analyses, define requirements, design user interfaces, build prototypes and conduct evaluations, to name just a few activities. Each one plays a crucial part in the overall design of the system.

To make sure that all of this effort is well spent, we must state quite clearly what problem we are trying to solve. We must define the objectives of the design project. Then, with a clear problem statement to guide us, we can keep track of progress as we home in on a satisfactory solution. When we lack such a problem statement, our project can drift dangerously off-course, leaving us perhaps with a solution to the wrong problem or, worse still, with no solution at all.

This chapter provides an introduction to the task of preparing a problem statement – a definition of design objectives. The topic of 'defining the problem' brings us face to face with four fundamental issues in interactive system design:

- Identifying the **human activity** that the proposed interactive system will support;

- Identifying the people, or **users**, who will perform the activity;

- Setting the **levels of support** that the system will provide, otherwise known as the system's **usability**;

- Selecting the basic **form of solution** to the design problem.

Of course, by defining these four aspects of the problem we don't settle them once and for all. On the contrary, each issue evolves into a major area of design work. The human activity supported by the system becomes a focus of study and a target for change; so does the person performing it. Levels of support are defined with increasing precision so as to provide yardsticks for evaluation. And the form of solution, initially described in just a few words, gradually expands into a statement of requirements, which in turn leads to a specification of the design and, ultimately, to a working interactive system.

2.2 The problem statement

The problem statement defines the objectives of design. It may be as short as a single sentence, e.g., 'Design a cash-operated machine for quick, easy purchase of railway tickets by passengers.' A design problem such as this will usually arise out of a situation that needs changing; for example, queues of passengers at ticket counters are getting too long. We call this the **situation of concern**, and the purpose of the interactive system is to resolve it (Checkland and Scholes, 1990). In order to define the design problem we must identify a human activity or activities that the system can support (in this instance, ticket purchase by passengers). We will also want to specify what it means to achieve an adequate level of support; for example, ticket purchase must be rapid and easy. Finally, we must ensure that there is a means of providing an interactive solution to the design problem.

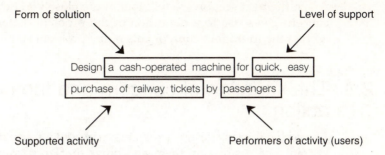

Figure 2.1 The one-sentence form of the problem statement, showing the four essential components defining the supported activity, the user, the level of support and the form of solution.

2.2.1 The one-sentence problem statement

Problem statements vary in length and detail. Sometimes they run to half a page or so, perhaps identifying each of the separate activities that the system must support. In this chapter we will use a concise, one-sentence form of statement that provides a place for each of the essential components. This form is shown in Figure 2.1.

2.2.2 Whose problem are we solving?

The design problems we tackle may arise out of situations that are themselves problems. Thus the problem of designing a ticket machine arises out of the problem of long queues at ticket counters. Another design problem we will discuss in this chapter is the provision of interactive workstations to support telephone assistance operators (the people who answer when we dial 0). This design problem arises out of the phone company's problem of rising operating costs. In each case there's a **causal link** between the overall situation of concern – long queues, rising operating costs – and the design problem we tackle.

A major purpose of problem definition is to transform the situation of concern into a design problem, that is, to find the causal link between one problem and the other. In this way we can focus on the kind of problem we designers are equipped to solve, a problem in interactive system design. It is this *design problem* that we attempt to solve. If we can identify the design problem correctly at the outset, then designing and building the system should enable someone to resolve the situation of concern. It is important to recognize that this 'someone' may not be a member of the design team. Often it is more appropriate to regard this person or organization as the *client* for the design – a point to which we will return at the end of this chapter.

In the next section we will look more closely at how the situation of concern gives rise to a definition of the problem. Later sections discuss each of the four main components of the problem statement.

2.3 The situation of concern and the course of action

As we have seen, design problems arise out of **situations of concern**. Within such a situation there are things that aren't quite right. Perhaps there is a problem that must be sorted out or things that people need, or perhaps there is an opportunity that will be lost unless it is seized without delay. Whatever the source of concern, it needs to be resolved; that is, something about the situation needs to be changed. This will involve an appropriate **course of action**, applied to particular components of the situation (Figure 2.2).

We have already seen an example of a situation of concern, in the form of long queues of railway passengers at ticket counters. The course of action adopted here is the provision of ticket machines. It applies to a particular component of the situation; that is, passengers' purchase of tickets.

The other example given of a situation of concern related to controlling operating costs in a phone company. Many factors contribute to these costs, including employee salaries, capital investment in switching and transmission equipment, interest on borrowing, employee travel expenses, and so forth. We could tackle the situation of concern in a wide variety of ways. For example, we could look for ways to reduce borrowing by selling off some of the company's assets. We could explore ways to cut the cost of employee travel. Neither of these is likely to involve the use of interactive systems. But if we were to look at the company's salary bill, and were to find that the cost of assistance operators' wages had been

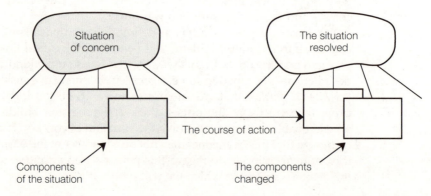

Figure 2.2   How a situation of concern is resolved, by applying a course of action to one or more components of the situation. Based on Checkland and Scholes, 1990.

rising sharply, we might consider the use of interactive technology to bring this cost down.

An important point is emerging here: problems in interactive system design arise when we see *ways to resolve a situation of concern through the use of interactive technology*. The design problem becomes one of changing particular components of the situation so that the desired overall change is achieved. There is a causal link between altering the component and altering the situation as a whole – changing one will lead to changing the other. Problem definition involves identifying this causal link.

2.3.1 Human activity as the causal link

As we saw in Chapter 1, interactive systems support human activity directly; they are able to provide this support as the activity is being carried out. Hence if we want to find a way to use interactive technology to resolve a situation of concern, we look for activities that the technology can support. These activities provide the causal link.

Figure 2.3 shows how interactive systems achieve the changes we seek. They replace or augment existing support systems, which themselves may or may not be interactive. In this way, an interactive system can improve the performance of certain human activities that are affecting the situation of concern. As a result, the situation itself improves.

In order to define the design problem, therefore, we must identify the activity or activities to support. There may be many activities affecting the

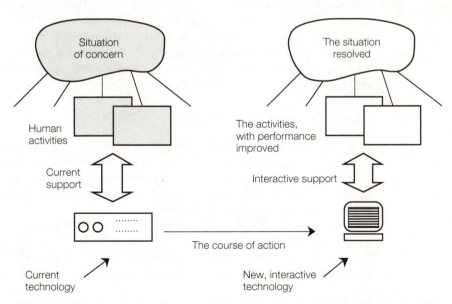

Figure 2.3   Changing the means of support produces the improvements in activities' performance that address the situation of concern.

situation of concern, and the choice may not be an easy one. Even in the simple case of railway ticket purchase there is a choice of at least four activities to support:

- Ticket purchase by passengers
- Ticket preparation by clerks
- Payment handling by clerks
- Record keeping by clerks.

Whatever the range of activities, we need to study each activity in turn, with a view to applying interactive technology so as to bring about the necessary overall changes.

2.4 The activity to be supported

We make a crucial step towards defining the problem when we select the activity or activities to be supported. Our aim here is to identify people's activities whose performance we can improve so as to resolve the situation of concern. There are two basic approaches: we may focus our attention on individual *tasks*, or look more broadly at linked sets of tasks representing *processes*.

In this section we will discuss tasks and processes, viewing them from two angles each. First, we will look at how we identify the activity in question – how we discover it amongst the complex, infinitely varying activities that we see people performing. Second, we will discuss what it means to support the activity. By treating these two aspects of tasks and processes we will be in a position to discuss, in the following sections, how we assess the level of support that the system needs to provide, and what we should say about the form of solution.

2.4.1 Tasks: Units of goal-directed activity

A **task** is a unit of human activity, carried out in order to achieve a specific goal. The performance of a task usually involves a sequence of steps, each step contributing in some way towards achieving the task's goal (Diaper, 1989b). The fact that tasks have separate goals helps us to distinguish between one task and the next.

An example of a task, illustrating how each step contributes towards achieving a common goal, is the purchase of a railway ticket. The following list shows a sequence of steps that a railway traveller might carry out; the steps in the ticket-purchase task are shown emphasized:

- Study list of train departures.
- Mentally note time and platform number of next train.

- **Stand in line at ticket counter.**

- **On reaching counter, state destination and journey type.**

- **Receive quote for price of ticket.**

- **Pay money.**

- **Receive ticket and change.**

- Walk over to drinks machine.

- Insert money.

- Press button for black coffee.

- Wait for cup to drop and contents to be poured.

- Remove cup from machine.

When we study people's activities we can often separate one task from another by looking for changes of goal. During a task's performance, each step will tend to contribute in some way towards achieving the task's goal. Steps that don't appear to contribute are likely to represent parts of other tasks.

In the above list, we can see that each of the emphasized steps contributes in some way to the goal of purchasing the ticket. The preceding two steps cannot be linked directly to the ticket-purchase goal, and we conclude that they belong to another task whose goal is to find the next train. Likewise the last five steps contribute to the goal of obtaining a cup of coffee.

We can describe tasks in terms of the goals they achieve and the steps they involve. One way to do this is to write a list of steps under the heading of the task goal, as shown in Figure 2.4(a); a second method is to use a graphical notation such as that of Figure 2.4(b). Both of these are examples of **hierarchic task description** that show each step as a contributor to a 'parent' goal.

It is important to realize that the sequences of steps we observe are only instances of the many different sequences that people may follow in performing tasks. During the task's performance, all sorts of situations can arise; for example, the previous user of the drinks machine may have left the machine with money in it, or the cup may tip over while it is being filled. These situations will affect the sequence of steps. Suchman has used the term *situated action* to draw attention to the way in which the surrounding circumstances affect the course of action (Suchman, 1987).

The circumstances at the outset of the task are particularly important, because there is often a choice of methods for performing the task (for example, using the drinks machine versus going to the snack bar). We need to understand what causes people to choose one method rather than another, because we are aiming to design a means of support that people will prefer to the means they already have.

1   Find time of next train

1.1   Study list of train departures

1.2   Mentally note time and platform number of next train

2   Purchase ticket

2.1   Stand in line at ticket counter

2.2   On reaching counter, state destination and journey type

2.3   Receive quote for price of ticket

2.4   Pay money

2.5   Receive ticket and change

3   Obtain cup of coffee

3.1   Walk over to drinks machine

3.2   Insert money

3.3   Press button for black coffee

3.4   Wait for cup to drop and contents to be poured

3.5   Remove cup from machine.

(a)

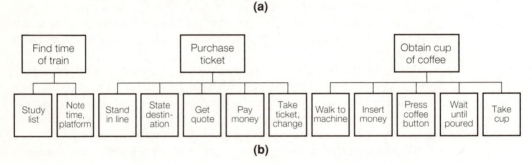

(b)

Figure 2.4   Hierarchic task descriptions, (a) using a text notation, (b) using a diagrammatic notation.

2.4.2   Designing a tool to support the task

Many of the individual tasks that people perform can be supported with the aid of interactive technology. We could probably think up an interactive solution to assist each of the tasks shown in Figures 2.4(a) and 2.4(b). However, every task we observe already has its existing means of 'support', even if this is as simple as a printed list of train departures. An interactive solution should be demonstrably better than available means of support, otherwise people won't use it.

Designing a means of support for an individual task is a matter of designing a *tool* for use in the task's performance. We are designing something that people can pick up or switch on, and then later put down or turn off, just like a hammer or a vacuum cleaner. The tool's design should reflect this. The person performing the task should be able to access the tool, turn it on and use it, all within the time-frame of the task's performance.

Since people are often free to choose which tools they use, there is no guarantee they will accept a new interactive tool when it is offered to them. Instead, the new tool will have to *compete* with the tools already available. If people perceive the new tool as inferior to those already available, they probably won't use it. But if the tool enables tasks to be performed better or faster, people who use it once will probably use it again – at least, until someone comes up with an even better design!

2.4.3   Processes: Linking tasks to achieve longer-term goals

In a great many of the situations of concern we encounter, we don't find individual tasks that need support. Rather, we find people performing tasks that are part of a linked series, distributed over time and possibly involving a number of other people. These linked tasks represent a **process**, sometimes called a *business process* in organizational settings. Like single tasks, entire processes can be supported by technology, and this is often an effective way of resolving situations of concern.

Processes are performed with a view to achieving goals, sometimes very similar to the goals of individual tasks. For example, when a mail-order company receives an order, it sets in motion a process whose goal – delivering the product in return for the customer's money – is basically the same as the goal of the clerk who sells a railway ticket. Unlike selling tickets, however, handling mail orders involves a number of separate tasks, carried out at different times and often by different people. If we ignore for the moment the tasks that arise in exceptional conditions (for example, cancellation of orders), we will find that the main tasks are:

Task 1:   Checking the customer's credit status

Task 2:   Checking the availability of the product

Task 3:   Accepting the order, provided it checks out

Task 4:   Shipping the product

Task 5:   Invoicing the customer

Task 6:   Filing paperwork in readiness for arrival of payment

Task 7:   Checking the amount on the filed invoice when payment is received, and marking the invoice paid

Task 8:   Issuing a receipt to the customer

Task 9:   Banking the payment

Task 10:   Filing paperwork for the completed transaction

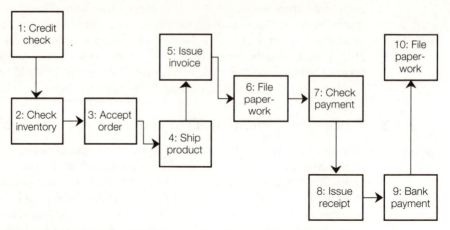

Figure 2.5   The mail-order process, shown as a simple sequence of tasks.

Once the final set of paperwork has been filed and the money banked, the mail-order process has achieved its goal and can be terminated. Figure 2.5 shows how the ten tasks might be performed in simple sequential order.

2.4.4   Formation of processes: The effect of multiple dependencies

Why do processes like this exist? Why is a whole series of tasks sometimes needed to achieve virtually the same result as a single task? If we want to apply interactive technology to the support of processes, we should understand how they are formed in the first place.

When we look at the individual tasks that make up a process, we will see that each one depends in some fashion on a crucial resource, sometimes known as the *task object* (Carey *et al.*, 1989). This dependency places constraints on the performance of the tasks – on when they can be performed, by whom, in what sequence. A familiar example is our dependence, when we telephone somebody, on that person's availability at the other end. Here the person is the crucial resource; if he or she isn't available we must leave a message or try again later, and thus we enter into the process of playing 'telephone tag'. The more an activity depends on resources in this way, the more difficult it is to perform as a simple task, and the more likely it is to break up into several linked tasks and thus transform into a process.

Tasks depend on resources of several different kinds. There are those lying within the domain of information systems and those that lie outside (Carey *et al.*, 1989). Those outside include inanimate objects such as machinery (Moray, 1992); they also include people (Suchman, 1987). It may be helpful, therefore, to distinguish between task resources of three main kinds:

- **Files, lists and databases** that provide permanent storage for the information involved in task performance;

- **People** with specific skills or responsibilities;

- **Other ongoing processes** including physical processes in the real world, functioning of machinery and plants, and so on.

Dependency on one such resource doesn't necessarily make a task into a process. Indeed it is common for individual tasks to have such a dependency, or *focus*. The three railway-station tasks of Figure 2.4 focus respectively on a list (of departures), a person (the ticket clerk) and a machine (dispensing drinks). Once this resource has been 'captured', the task can be carried out without interruption.

Processes are likely to form when the activity has *multiple dependencies* – when the focus of attention shifts from one resource to another. If the next resource isn't immediately available, the activity must suspend. The person performing the activity must either sit and do nothing, or leave the activity in suspense and return to it later when the resource is available.

How the mail-order process is formed

The mail-order activity shows a number of dependencies that might cause suspension, and these are what lead to the formation of a process. Here are the main dependencies:

Task 1:   Checking the customer's credit status depends on **access to the accounts-payable file** showing invoices not yet paid.

Task 2:   Checking the availability of the product depends on **access to the inventory** of goods in stock.

Task 4:   Shipping the product depends again on **access to the inventory** in order to update it.

Task 6:   Filing paperwork, to be checked when payment is received, depends on **access to the accounts-payable file**.

Task 7:   Checking the amount on the filed invoice, when payment is received, and marking the invoice paid, depends first on **the customer's response to the invoice**, and then on **access to the accounts-payable file**.

Task 10:   Filing paperwork for the completed transaction depends on **access to the completed-sales file**.

A common technique for reducing the delays caused by multiple dependencies is to have different people perform tasks in parallel. Thus Task 1 might be performed by a credit assistant and Task 2 by the stores clerk. But this would introduce another dependency:

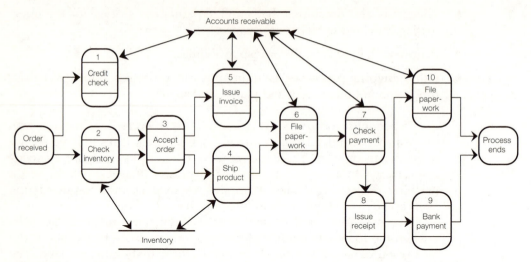

Figure 2.6   Process flow chart for mail-order, drawn using the notation of a *Data Flow Diagram*.

Task 3:   Accepting the order, provided it checks out, will depend on **receiving responses from the credit assistant and stores clerk**.

Ultimately the mail-order process may come to depend on three or four different people, and on three or more files or databases. A chart of the process is shown in Figure 2.6.

2.4.5   How we discover processes

If we study people in organizations and look at the tasks they perform, we will find that many of the tasks are parts of processes. We will see the various tell-tale features of process performance that arise from task dependencies:

- **Use of files and databases**, some of them shared between people;

- **Communication between people**, including indirect communication by means of forms, messages, voice-mail and other documents;

- **Synchronization** with real-world physical and mechanical processes;

- **Suspension** while waiting for information to become available, for people to respond, or for real-world processes to reach the appropriate state.

As an illustration, Figure 2.7 shows a sequence of tasks performed by a detective, as observed by a research team (Thornton and Harper, 1991). All of the tasks, except phoning home at 11:13 and taking lunch at 12:05, have the marks of tasks forming parts of processes. Some of the tasks are

10:35	Make telephone inquiries about a fraud case.
10:47	Visit the communications room to make sure a message has been passed on to a uniformed colleague.
10:54	Make a telephone inquiry about a rape case, trying to contact a doctor.
11:03	Answer telephone for colleague, take details to pass on.
11:05	Another officer asks the detective to accompany him in making an arrest; they discuss the case but decide not to proceed with the arrest.
11:13	More telephone enquiries regarding fraud case; phone home.
11:40	Answer phone to take details for another officer.
11:45	Another uniformed officer comes in to discuss a case.
11:50	Telephone inquiry regarding fraud case.
12:05	Lunch.

Figure 2.7   Observations of a detective's work over a 90-minute period, based on Thornton and Harper (1991). Times are in hours:minutes.

performed in support of other officers' work processes, such as the messages taken at 11:03 and 11:40. One particular process, the investigation of a fraud case, shows up several times.

Building a complete picture of a process involves lengthy investigations, possibly relying on observations as in this example, from which the connections between tasks are gradually pieced together. This is itself a kind of detective work. Methods for studying and modelling processes will be described in Chapter 5.

2.4.6   Designing systems to support processes

Much of the computer industry's business lies in developing systems to support work processes. The effectiveness of these systems lies not only in their provision of tools to perform tasks faster and better, but also in their support for the links between tasks and for the information resources that the tasks share. The tasks are supported in a systematic way, rather than piecemeal, by technology that truly represents a *system*.

When we set out to design a system to support a process, therefore, we look beyond merely improving the performance of tasks. One option we may have is to *automate* tasks, that is, replace them by software that performs the task automatically. This is an effective technique for saving labour costs, and thus for addressing situations of financial concern. Flight-deck automation has been very successful in this respect, automating many of the flight engineer's tasks and thus permitting the reduction of flight crews from three people to two.

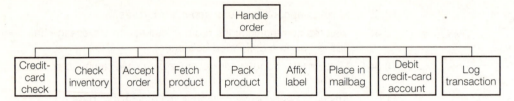

Figure 2.8   Reducing mail-order to a simple task.

A more general approach to process support is to reduce dependencies. This may not necessarily reduce the number of steps performed, but it may enable them to be linked more closely, and the whole process may be faster and more streamlined as a result.

It is feasible, for example, to support the mail-order process interactively so that it can be performed by just one person. If the customer provides a credit-card number, this can be checked online by the mail-order clerk, and so can the inventory, so that the order can be accepted on the spot. If the stock of products is kept close by, the same clerk can go and fetch the product, pack it in an envelope, affix a label printed by the system and put it in a mailbag. Meanwhile the system can debit the customer's credit-card account and log the transaction. The process has been reduced, in effect, to the single task shown in Figure 2.8.

Many of the interactive systems now in current use have succeeded in making processes simpler; some of them have even reduced processes to single tasks. Starting a car, for example, is simply a matter of turning a key, thanks to electronic ignition. In the days of vintage cars it was a true process, involving a series of steps such as retarding the ignition, adjusting the mixture, pumping fuel into the induction manifold, cranking the engine, and so on, with suitable pauses between steps (Wheatley and Morgan, 1964). Other examples of processes that have been simplified by interactive technology include:

- **word processing**, which enables the writer of a report to prepare a succession of drafts without the need to suspend while the report is retyped in the typing pool;

- **software development**, which once involved batch processing – submitting a program to the computer centre on punched cards to be run as part of the next batch – but which now permits a complete cycle of testing, debugging, source editing, recompiling, loading and running to be performed interactively as an uninterrupted sequence;

- **international telephone dialling**, which still occasionally involves the process of 'booking' a call via the operator, but which can increasingly be performed as a single task by the caller;

- **online airline and hotel reservation systems**, which enable us to book a flight or a vacation in minutes; these are tasks that once involved processes lasting days or weeks;

- **paging devices**, which allow telephone calls to be routed directly to the nearest phone, thus avoiding telephone tag.

2.5 The user

In conjunction with identifying the supported activity, we need to give thought to who will perform it. In other words, we need to identify the **user** of the proposed interactive system. By bringing the user into the design problem, we can focus properly on the user's needs, both general and specific.

2.5.1 Addressing the general needs of the human user

What does it mean to address the needs of the user? To a large extent, the answer lies in supporting the activity or activities users perform. We must not forget, however, that using an interactive system is a *human* activity. When we come to define how the system will be used, we need to make sure that this usage is consistent with the human user's physical and cognitive abilities, and with the social environment he or she inhabits. Otherwise we may make unreasonable demands on the user, and create a system that is intrinsically unusable.

A first step towards understanding how to address the user's needs is to take account of human performance and behaviour in general. This means looking at what is known about humans as physical, cognitive and social performers. Psychological research can tell us a great deal about the limits of human performance, and sociological and anthropological research can supplement this with observations about human behaviour in social settings. Out of this research have emerged *models* of human behaviour that can be useful in testing ideas for system designs. The next chapter is devoted to looking at general models of human behaviour, suitable for use in interactive system design.

2.5.2 Addressing specific user needs

Human beings also make specific demands and bring specific capabilities as potential users of new systems. They may have acquired particular skills and expertise, and the system's design should recognize this; it should use the terminology they know, and enable them to be creative and apply problem-solving or analytical skills. In a work environment, people have responsibilities, and need systems that help them to meet these responsibilities. A system that fails in this respect may not get used.

In some situations people will undergo training to use the systems, while in other cases they will receive no prior training and must be able to operate it in a 'walk-up-and-use' fashion.

The reason for identifying specific users at the time of problem definition is to ensure that adequate attention is paid to their particular skills, expertise, responsibilities, training, and working environment. We group these aspects of the user under the heading of 'user needs'. By pointing out, in the problem statement, that the system is to support 'purchase of tickets *by passengers*' or 'handling of collect calls *by telephone assistance operators*', we draw attention to the requirement to study and analyse user needs. In Chapters 5 and 6 we will look in detail at how this is done.

2.6   Usability

Designing an interactive tool or system is not just a matter of supporting a chosen activity. There is a need to achieve an improvement in the activity's performance, sufficient to resolve the situation of concern. Throughout design, therefore, we pay close attention to the system's likely influence on performance of tasks and processes. We start paying attention to this right at the outset, making sure that the problem statement makes due mention of targets for activity performance.

The central issue here is the system's **usability**. This is a collective term for all aspects of an activity's performance that can be affected by the use of technology (Whiteside *et al.*, 1988). The individual aspects are known as **usability factors**. Each one provides a measure of a particular aspect of the performance of activities when supported by the system.

2.6.1   Usability factors

What sorts of factors are we concerned with under the heading of usability? To answer this question, we need to consider which aspects of activity performance are affected by the introduction of systems. A list of the main usability factors will normally include the following:

- The **speed of performance** of the activity, which affects **how many people** are needed to perform it;

- The **incidence of errors** while performing the activity;

- Users' ability to **recover from errors** that occur;

- The magnitude of the users' task in **learning to use the system**;

- Users' **retention of learned skills**;

- Users' ability to **customize** the system to suit their way of working or the situation of use;

- The ease with which people can **reorganize activities** supported by the system – their own activities and other people's;

- Users' **satisfaction** with the system.

Most usability measures depend on the activity performed. This is especially true of factors such as speed of performance and ease of learning. The only effective way of specifying a system's speed of use is to define the activity to be performed and the speed of completing it. Likewise, setting targets for ease of learning makes a lot more sense if we specify what we want the user to learn to do. Learning to use a word processor, for example, varies in difficulty depending on whether you just want to type simple letters or you want to prepare complex, multi-column documents with illustrations.

2.6.2   Our choice of usability targets

In defining the design problem we will usually identify the principal usability factors we are concerned with. We will specify, for example, that purchase of railway tickets is to be faster than before, or that there will be fewer cases of people buying the wrong kind of ticket. We may set specific levels of performance to be achieved (for example, ticket purchase time) or we may leave these to be determined at a later stage in the design. The important question during problem definition is, what are the key factors? What aspects of activity performance are affecting the situation of concern?

In many cases, *speed of performance* is the key usability factor. There is a need to get the activity done faster or with fewer people. *Incidence of errors* is also likely to be of importance, because of the trade-offs with performance speed. Under pressure to increase speed, users may make more errors (Mayhew, 1992); and if they detect the errors they make, they will lose time in correcting them.

Ease of learning is sometimes a key factor because of the time and money involved in training. Consider the cost of training a thousand employees of an organization to use a new word processor. A two-day training course will cost 2000 days lost from work; that's ten working years!

In setting usability targets, it helps to consider whether we are supporting tasks or processes. Are we concerned, for example, with the time users devote to performing the activity, or the total elapsed time the activity takes? In the case of a simple task, such as buying a railway ticket, the two times are much the same. In the case of a process, such as mail order, the times are likely to be quite different, because several people may be involved and there will be lengthy periods of process suspension.

2.6.3 Improving levels of performance

We are usually concerned with *improving* the performance of activities, for this is how we hope to resolve the situation of concern. We cannot set targets for usability levels, therefore, unless we know what levels are already being achieved. Nor can we set targets unless we know what levels of improved performance are achievable.

There is a need to understand how tasks and processes are being performed at present, in order to assess the usability of the current support system. Of course, we may find ourselves trying to measure the 'usability' of low-tech or even non-tech systems, such as pen and paper or face-to-face conversation. This should not make any difference; we can measure speed of performance, errors, and so on, whether or not the activity is computer-supported.

There is also a need to set *realistic* targets for the levels of performance we can achieve with the new system. Defining the design problem is not just a matter of deciding how big an improvement is necessary in order to resolve the situation of concern. Suppose we cannot achieve it? Suppose, for example, we need to reduce training time to half a day, but the training course ends up taking a full day after all? These kinds of mistakes cause one situation of concern to be replaced with another.

Setting realistic targets is largely a matter of familiarity with the problem. When we tackle a new and unfamiliar problem, we may not know what levels of performance are easily achieved. It is all too easy to accept the challenge of meeting a target, and then find that it is impossible to meet. A lot depends on the form of solution we adopt. This brings us to the final topic in problem definition.

2.7 The form of the solution

By choosing interactive technology as a means of alleviating the situation of concern, we have already begun to focus on a form of solution. In effect, we have chosen the first four words of the problem statement to be, 'Design an interactive system . . .' or 'Design an interactive tool . . .'. Often the problem statement will say no more than this about the form of solution; after all, to say more would be to commence the design activity itself. There are circumstances, however, in which the problem statement needs to say more about the solution. We will look at some of the reasons in this final section.

2.7.1 Describing the form of solution

What would it mean, anyway, to say more about the form of solution? What sorts of details would we add? We have been talking throughout this chapter about the *support* that the interactive system will provide to people's activities. To define the form of solution means to specify how this support is to be made available.

Provision of interactive support involves numerous layers of technology and resources, including:

- **The user interface** with which the user interacts directly;

- **The application software** that supports the user interface;

- **The operating system** that provides standard services to both the user interface and its supporting software;

- **System resources** accessed via the user interface and supporting software: information storage, communication, printing, and so on;

- **The hardware** that supports all of these resources.

In the course of solving the design problem we will specify every layer of the design in sufficient detail for implementation to be carried out. We will probably pay most attention to the user interface, because this has a particularly direct impact on interactive support. We will need to pay attention also to the design of the interactive software. As regards the remaining layers, we are likely to look for existing solutions – existing operating systems, file systems, networks, workstations, and so on – so that we don't have to design these too.

2.7.2 What we define in the problem statement, and why

At the problem definition stage, it is necessary only to define the constraints that apply to the choice of solution. These constraints may arise for various reasons, including market pressures, opportunities to exploit available technology or expertise, and the need for compatibility with specific software or hardware. They may apply to any layer of the solution, leading us to specify, for example:

- an interactive tool that adheres to Apple Macintosh user interface standards;

- a system that makes use of proprietary speech-recognition software (an example we discuss further below);

- a system that runs in the Microsoft Windows NT operating system environment;

- a tool that can be run in the Windows NT, Apple Macintosh or X Windows environments;

- a system that can be linked to other applications currently in use within the user organization;

- a system for monitoring the status of a particular process plant;

- a system for linking together particular people at three specific sites;

- a system to run on a particular 'palmtop' computer with two megabytes of memory.

Constraints on the form of solution sometimes arise out of the situation of concern. Thus if the current version of a product is losing market share because of incompatibility with standard hardware or software, this may lead to setting up a project to develop a compatible version.

2.7.3   Exploiting in-house expertise or technology

A common reason for choosing a particular form of solution is to exploit intellectual property – to make use of technology that is 'owned' by the system developers, or to which they have preferential access rights. Intellectual property rights come about in various ways, e.g., through in-house research and development or through licensing agreements. When investments of this kind have been made, there may be a need to exploit them commercially. Again, this can become a cause for concern all of its own.

To take an example, let us look in more detail at the particular case of speech recognition mentioned in the above list of constraints. Suppose a consumer-products company has bought a licence to use some powerful software for storing and matching recorded voice records. A situation of concern is thus created – the company needs to find a way of exploiting its newly acquired technology. How should it go about defining the design problem? One approach might be to make a list of all of the human activities in which speech plays a key role, just as we listed all of the activities involved in railway ticket purchase; but this list would be tediously long, covering activities all the way from answering the telephone to negotiating a corporate takeover.

There is an opportunity here to take a more direct route towards defining the problem, as shown diagrammatically in Figure 2.9. The designed artefact needs to take advantage of the company's expertise in consumer products and access to speech-recognition software; this much can be taken for granted. The form of the solution can thus be narrowed to 'a consumer product incorporating speech-recognition software'. This in turn has the effect of narrowing the range of human activities worth considering. The eventual choice might be to support the recording and playback of voice notes, that is, to solve the following problem:

Design an interactive hand-held consumer product to support the quick and easy storage and retrieval of voice notes.

Figure 2.10 shows a device designed to solve this particular problem from Stifelman *et al.* (1993). It allows voice notes such as 'Call Tom' to be

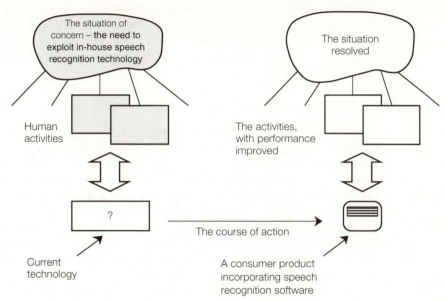

Figure 2.9 The first stage in defining the problem in a case where the nature of the solution is constrained.

Figure 2.10 Hand-held voice-note recorder, from Stifelman *et al.* (1993).

recorded, and includes the capability to organize notes into categories. For example, the user can speak into the device as follows: 'Calls . . . records . . . call Tom.' This will store the note in the 'Calls' category. Later, when he says 'Calls', the device will play back the notes in this category, including 'Call Tom'.

2.7.4   Innovative forms of solution

Novel forms of solution, like the device shown in Figure 2.10, are often discovered in the course of trying to fit technologies to activities. This is one way in which **innovation** can occur, that is, in which ideas can be transformed into artefacts and processes of practical use in society. It is common to take an innovative approach to the design of interactive systems, that is, to try a new form of solution rather than enhance one that is already in established use. In the computer business, with technology advancing rapidly and with hardware still falling in cost, existing forms of solution can become obsolete in a year or two. Designers often choose an innovative approach for this reason.

It is important to recognize that there is often a choice between trying something new and enhancing something that already exists. Innovation, although often the more attractive choice, often is also the most expensive, risky and time-consuming. The initial idea or invention doesn't become a working product overnight; it involves many stages of investigation, prototyping, testing, redesign, field trial, and so on, before it is safe to place in the hands of users. We may wish to take a position, when defining the design problem, on whether it should be solved by enhancing an existing form of solution or trying a new one. We will look briefly at the points in favour of each.

When it is enough to enhance an existing form of solution
Generally speaking, solving the problem with an existing form of solution is preferable to solving it by inventing a new one, if an existing solution can be found that will do the job. With an existing solution as a starting point, many of the design decisions are easier, the outcome is easier to predict, and thus the degree of risk is less. In an engineering sense, we are choosing to use the 'normal technology' that has been proven to work in the past, abandoning it in favour of new 'radical technology' only if we must (Kuhn, 1962; Constant, 1980).

An example of a situation that has favoured the enhancement of existing solutions is the support of telephone assistance operators, already mentioned several times in this chapter. It is common for these operators to use interactive workstations to control the switching of calls and to retrieve essential information, e.g., about billing rates (Gray *et al.*, 1992). Enhancements to workstation software are often required in order to achieve improvements in productivity and to extend the range of services supported. However, it is preferable to find a solution similar to the system currently in place, if at all possible. In this way, operators require less retraining, and use can be made of existing system components, such as billing-rate databases and digital switching systems.

If we were to tackle this situation, we would need to say little or nothing about the form of solution, because we could assume that it would be based on existing designs. We could simply state that the solution should take the form of an 'enhanced workstation':

> Design an enhanced workstation that enables a skilled operator to handle a full range of telephone-assistance calls, in an average of 2 seconds less time than at present.

Case Study A tells the story of how such a design problem was tackled.

When innovation is needed

Innovation in system design often becomes necessary when existing solution strategies begin to run out of steam. Every form of solution has its limits, and as it approaches these limits it demands more and more design effort to wring out each improvement in performance. Eventually the pay-off from enhancement is so little that it is better to invest the effort in trying something new.

An example of applying innovation to overcome inherent performance limits can be seen in the design of tollbooths for bridges and toll roads. How do we increase the flow of traffic through the tolls without installing more booths and toll collectors? One solution is to provide unmanned exact-change lanes with chutes to collect coins thrown by drivers. However, there is a limit to the speed at which drivers can deposit coins while passing through an exact-change lane, and this sets an upper limit to possible enhancements. Hence the introduction of the infrared pass card which enables drivers to pass through tolls at up to 100 kph.

When there is a need to take a radical approach to solving a design problem, we may decide to identify the approach in the problem statement:

> Design a tollbooth for road traffic based on smart cards and remote sensing techniques, to enable passage by drivers through the tollbooth at speeds of up to 100 kph.

2.8 Conclusion: What follows after problem definition?

In this chapter we have focused on the various aspects of drawing up a problem statement. We have seen how this starts with the identification of a situation of concern, and the discovery of a causal link connecting the situation to a human activity that can be enhanced by the use of interactive technology, thus addressing the situation of concern. We have seen

how the definition of the problem divides into specifying four components: the supported activity, the user, the level of support provided, and
the form of solution.

What follows next? Clearly, the next stage is to design the solution,
with a view to implementing and installing it. A design project therefore
gets under way, with the ultimate goal of seeing an interactive system
installed, and the situation of concern thus addressed. In this way the project serves those who must deal directly with the situation of concern;
they become the **client** for the system that will ultimately be delivered.

During design, each of the four parts of the problem statement needs
to be expanded and reformulated. The supported activity needs to be
defined and understood well enough to know how the interactive system
will support it. In conjunction with this, the levels of support will need to
be defined more precisely. This should help the client to see that the situation of concern will indeed be resolved.

The primary focus of the ensuing design work will be on the solution
itself – on the user interface and the underlying layers of supporting technology. The next step will normally be to specify the solution more fully,
so that it is possible to see just how it will address the situation of concern,
and at the same time to see that a solution is technically feasible. This step
represents only the first step towards completing the design of the system,
but it is an important one because it specifies the *requirements* that the
design must meet, making it clear to both client and designer that these
requirements are a valid restatement of the original problem. The topic of
requirements definition is taken up in Chapter 7.

Exercises

(1) What are the three kinds of resource on which tasks depend? Think of
examples of systems in which these dependencies can be seen.

(2) What distinguishes tasks from processes? What causes processes to form
in place of simple tasks? How can we reverse this, and turn processes
back into tasks?

(3) What are the four essential components of a problem statement?

(4) What is wrong with each of the following problem statements?

   (a) Find a way to help delivery drivers to reach their destinations without getting
   lost so often.

   (b) Design an interactive system for genealogical researchers.

   (c) Design a system to support concert pianists in giving recitals.

(5) Figure 5.7 shows the full day's transcript from which the excerpt in Figure
2.7 was taken. Find other examples of tasks and processes in Figure 5.7.

(6) Make a list of as many usability factors as you can. How many of these could you measure quantitatively?

(7) Write problem statements for the design of a mail-order system in the following situations of concern: (a) sales volume has grown to a point where one person can no longer handle orders; (b) sales volume has fallen, and the company can afford to employ only one person in its mail-order department.

(8) Think of three systems that don't work well for you (for example, fax machines, automated tellers) and write problem statements to define how the systems should be redesigned.

(9) Suppose you have identified a need to support the activity of rapid translation of unknown words while reading a foreign language document. How many possible forms of solution can you think of? How would you choose between them? What other aspects of the problem definition would contribute to making the choice?

(10) 'If the design problem can't be described in a single sentence, it isn't worth solving.' Discuss.

Further reading

Checkland P. and Scholes J. (1990). *Soft Systems Methodology in Action*. Chichester: John Wiley

Valuable for its explanation of how systems problems arise from situations of concern, and for its broad coverage of problem-solving strategies. Most of the material is not specific to computer-based solutions, but an appendix discusses IT system design.

Woodmansee G.H. (1984). 'The Visi On™ experience – from concept to marketplace'. In *Human Computer Interaction – Interact '84* (Shackel B., ed.), pp. 871–5. Amsterdam: North Holland

A rare example of an account of a design project that went wrong. Soon after this paper was written the Visi On product was abandoned, and this paper provides interesting glimpses of some of the contributing problems.

CHAPTER 3

The Human Virtual Machine

Chapter objectives:

The decisions we make during design are only as sound as the theories we base them on. What theories do we rely on in interactive system design? This chapter provides an answer by covering the following:

- The types of theory useful to interactive system designers
- The need for a model, or Human Virtual Machine, to help us understand and predict human behaviour
- Some simple examples of predictions we can make
- Useful theories of human social behaviour
- Models of how interaction takes place and how people learn to use systems through exploration.

3.1 Introduction

Designing an interactive system involves making predictions about the outcome. We draw up specifications for the system, predicting that there will be an improvement in the performance of the users' activities when the system is placed in their hands. We make these predictions, not just when the design is finished, but at every step along the way. The better we are at making these predictions, the easier our task will be and the better chance we have of achieving the outcome we want.

This chapter introduces some of the theories that help us to make predictions about the outcome of interactive system design. The theories in question have to do with the behaviour of people when using systems. They are useful in design for the simple reason that *predictions are themselves theories*. When we make a prediction, we are theorizing about what will ultimately happen. We might predict, for example, that a new design will be easier to learn than its predecessor. What we mean is, *in theory* it will be easier to learn. *In practice*, however, it may turn out harder to learn, showing our prediction to have been wrong. If we can lay our hands on better theories about people's usage of systems, we may be able to avoid making this kind of mistake.

Note that this chapter is specifically about theories of the human user, derived from psychological, sociological and anthropological research. It doesn't attempt to cover theories of the behaviour of computer programs. To build successful interactive software, we need both kinds of theories, because we make predictions about both kinds of behaviour – about the user's speed of task performance, for example, and the software's speed of execution. Theory of computation isn't covered here, however, because there are excellent computer-science texts on the subject; see, for example, Gordon (1988); Mattson (1993). The purpose of this chapter is to provide a complementary body of theory about the people who use interactive systems.

3.2   Types of theory useful in system design

Research into human behaviour has furnished us with a body of knowledge from which are derived the theories we use in design. As more research is done, the body of knowledge grows, and the theories become more numerous and more powerful. These theories fall into three basic categories: *explanatory theories*, *empirical laws* and *dynamic models*. In this section we will look briefly at each category of theory and the way it supports design. We will also discuss the concept of a *human virtual machine* as a general receptacle for all three kinds of theory.

3.2.1   Explanatory theories

The purpose of an **explanatory theory** is simply to explain observed human behaviour. We don't expect these kinds of theories to help us predict how system designs will turn out; their purpose is to explain things we see people doing, whether supported by interactive systems or not.

Although lacking predictive power, explanatory theories can provide very useful insights during design. When we come to evaluate a newly installed system, explanatory theories help us to understand why the system's impact is different from what we might have expected. They are also useful in the initial stages of studying users and analysing their needs.

For instance, in a study of doctors' use of desktop computers during consultation, Greatbatch *et al.* found that the conversation between doctor and patient was affected by the doctor's interaction with the computer, and that the patient was likely to speak only at certain points during the interaction (Greatbatch *et al.*, 1993). The patient was particularly likely to start speaking just after the doctor confirmed a command with the RETURN key (Figure 3.1).

[Transcript 1]

1	P:	The only thing other problem I do have u::hm
2		I sleep quite fitfully.
3	Dr:	Uh huh
4		(0.6)
5	P:	a:u::hm: With my previous doctor I did occasionally
6		go to him for: sleeping tablets.

[Transcript 2 – detail from Transcript 1 (lines 2–5)]

P: I sleep quite fitfully. ------ a:u::hm: With my...

                                        R   +++
                        * *   * *   *
                                        –
Dr: Uh huh

Key to symbols, Verbal elements:

[	Overlapping talk begins
]	Overlapping talk ends
(0.5)	Numbers in parentheses indicate silences, length given in seconds
(.)	A gap of less than 0.2 seconds
wo::rd	Colons indicate prolongation of the immediately preceding sound
( )	Transcriber was unable to hear what was said
(word)	Possible hearings
((text))	Transcriber's comments and descriptions

Visual elements:

-------	Party is gazing away from a co-participant
+	Significant changes in the screen image
*	Keystroke
*⁄–	Keystroke with greater force than normal
R	A RETURN or ENTER keystroke

Figure 3.1   Transcript of a conversation between a doctor and a patient, showing the patient resuming his conversation after the doctor has hit the return key; from Greatbatch *et al.* (1993).

To explain this pattern of conversation, Greatbatch *et al.* theorized that patients were treating the doctor's interaction like a second conversation, and saw the completion of the command as a chance to pick up the thread of their own conversation. If we were involved in redesigning the desktop system to provide better support to the consultation process, we might gain useful insights and ideas from this theory – it might help us to see how to assist the flow of conversation between doctor and patient, rather than hinder it.

3.2.2   Empirical laws

Empirical laws offer simple quantitative predictions of human performance. They come about through the discovery that human performance is repeatable under certain conditions. Typically the discovery will be made in a series of psychological experiments, and will show that a particular variable in human behaviour can be linked to some aspect of the action being performed. With the aid of empirical laws we can often make quick estimates of human performance, based on the type of action and the form of the user interface.

An example of an empirical law is Hick's Law (Hick, 1952). It states that the time T taken to choose between a number of alternative targets is a function of the number of targets n, and is related logarithmically:

$$T = k \log_2 (n + 1)$$

where k is a constant. Figure 3.2 depicts a graph of the times taken by users to select items from screen menus of different lengths, and shows that these times obey Hick's Law. Knowledge of this repeatable behaviour can be factored into the design of faster menu systems (Landauer and Nachbar, 1985). Later in this chapter we will discuss another empirical law, Fitts' Law, which enables predictions to be made of the time taken by the user to point to a target of a particular size.

3.2.3   Dynamic models

We will often want to make predictions of more complex human actions than simple selection of menu items or targets. We will want to understand how well the system supports an entire task involving a sequence of steps. In these cases, empirical laws cannot help because they apply only to isolated actions.

Instead, therefore, we use **dynamic models**, that is, models that predict how a whole sequence of actions will be performed. Some dynamic models are helpful in predicting the sequence of actions that the user will take; others can provide predictions of levels of performance if given the sequence of steps taken by the user.

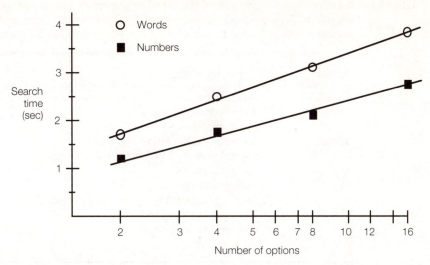

Figure 3.2   Selection time for menu items as a function of the number of options, showing adherence to Hick's Law (based on Landauer and Nachbar, 1985).

It is particularly common to use dynamic models to help predict the speed with which the user can perform an activity. We can do this if we know the sequence of actions that the user will follow; the model tells us how to calculate performance times from this sequence. In effect we 'run' the model over this sequence.

An example: A dynamic model of keyboard interaction speed

A simple dynamic model can be used to predict the speed of operation of keyboard-based user interfaces, in which all commands and data are entered as text. It enables us to determine how fast certain such commands will be, when typed by experienced users.

We can of course make a rough estimate of interaction speed by counting the number of keystrokes in each command, and dividing by the user's typing speed in keystrokes per second. To this value we would then add the time taken by the system to respond. Thus we would estimate the time to enter the 15-character command, NAME NEWMAN 55 <RETURN>, typed at two characters per second, to be 7.5 seconds. If the system then takes 2.5 seconds to respond, our prediction of the total time for the command will be 10 seconds.

But this dynamic model doesn't allow for the pauses that occur during the typing of such commands. In the course of developing their Keystroke-Level Model, described in Chapter 8, Card, Moran and Newell determined that even the most experienced users pause at certain places when entering text (Card *et al.*, 1983). They theorized that these pauses represented *mental preparation* by the user for the next stage in the task.

Table 3.1   A keystroke-level analysis of the speed of typing the command NAME NEWMAN 55 <RETURN>. Typing speed is assumed to be 0.5 sec per character, and the system's response time is 2.5 sec. Based on the Keystroke-Level Model (Card *et al.*, 1983).

Action	Cognitive operation	Predicted time (secs)
–	mental preparation (before command)	1.35
NAME	4 keyboard characters	2.00
	space character	0.50
NEWMAN	6 keyboard characters	3.00
–	mental preparation (before confirming)	1.35
	space character	0.50
55	2 keyboard characters	1.00
–	mental preparation (before confirming)	1.35
RETURN	1 keyboard character	0.50
-	response time	2.50
	Total	14.05

They measured the length of the pauses, establishing an average length of 1.35 seconds. They identified a number of places where pauses regularly occurred, such as before entering a command and before confirming an item of data. According to their model, the time taken by a two-characters-per-second typist to enter NAME NEWMAN 55 <RETURN> would be more than 14 seconds. This **keystroke-level analysis** is laid out in Table 3.1.

3.2.4   The Human Virtual Machine

These theories provide us with a variety of ways of explaining and predicting human performance. We can apply them to situations where interactive systems are in use and where they are not. Each theory allows us to explain or simulate some aspect of the performance of activities by people, such as speed of performance, ease of learning, errors, and so on. But how can we view the theories collectively? One way is to build a model of a 'human processor' based on the theories (Card *et al.*, 1983). We take a similar approach here, regarding the theories as components of a *human virtual machine*.

Step-by-step simulation of tasks and processes
The approach we take is rather like the approach taken by software designers in analysing and predicting the performance of computer programs. Software designers are also concerned about the speed of performance, and about the errors that occur as a result of 'bugs' in the program. Before building and testing the program, therefore, a software designer will often hand-check it by conducting a *walkthrough*, that is, a step-by-step simulation of what the machine would do. In the same way, we can

perform a simulation of what the human processor would do at each step in the performance of a task or process.

This approach is based on drawing an analogy between computers executing programs and people performing tasks, and we must guard against taking this analogy too far. In particular, we must not make the mistake of thinking that human activity is planned or programmed in the same sense as the steps performed by a computer (Suchman, 1987). Many of the things people do are in response to their immediate surroundings, as we will see later in this chapter. But where there is evidence of repeatable behaviour by people, we can often perform simple simulations of what these repeatable human processors might do.

Simplification by abstraction

We do not try to simulate the human processor in complete detail. For one thing, we don't have a complete and detailed understanding of how humans do things, so this approach would be bound to fail. But even if it worked, a full simulation would be impossibly time-consuming.

Again, therefore, we take a leaf out of the software designer's book, by not trying to represent the human processor in all its detail. Instead we look for simplifications and approximations that will enable us to gain most of the benefit of the full theory with a fraction of the effort. We arrive at an **abstraction**, or simplified model, of the human processor. In the software context we would use the term *virtual machine* for this abstraction, for we would be testing our programs against a 'machine' that is constructed partly from hardware and partly from the software that supports the programming language and operating environment.

In this chapter we will use the term **Human Virtual Machine** to describe the overall model that we use to explain and predict human behaviour. We treat theories about human behaviour as potential components of this Human Virtual Machine. Many of these same theories have been used before to construct overall models, an important example being the Model Human Processor constructed by Card, Moran and Newell, who drew primarily on theories in cognitive psychology (Card *et al.*, 1983). In this chapter we will be looking at possible extensions to the Model Human Processor, drawing on sociological and anthropological theories such as the explanatory theory of patients' interaction with doctors mentioned earlier.

Overlaps and gaps in the body of theory

We will notice one or two areas where theories of the cognitive and social domains overlap and provide mutual support. A simple instance of this can be seen in the example of doctor–patient interaction. The explanatory theory tells us that patients are likely to speak when the doctor finishes typing a command. But how does the patient know that the command is complete? Here keystroke-level analysis can help; it predicts that the doctor will pause for about a second between typing the command and typing the RETURN to confirm it. This characteristic combination of a pause followed by pressing RETURN is easy for a patient to recognize. The two bodies of theory combine to provide an improved explanation for the patient's behaviour.

We will also notice many aspects of human behaviour where the Human Virtual Machine lacks definition. In this respect it is very different from the virtual computing machine, which provides a complete model of the computer's behaviour at a particular level of abstraction. In the case of human behaviour, we simply don't know enough to construct a full model. The purpose of this chapter is to point out both the areas where we can make predictions and the very large areas where we cannot.

3.3   Psychological models of human information processing

From a psychological point of view, interacting with a computer is primarily a matter of processing information. There are other aspects to interaction, such as eye and hand movements, and we shall be concerned with these too. Primarily, we need to focus on understanding the processing of information that takes place between sensing external phenomena and causing external changes. Therefore we need to build a model of human information processing into our description of the Human Virtual Machine.

3.3.1   Information processing subsystems

Human information processing involves **multiple processors**; at least, all evidence points to this. Even without a psychological training, we can observe many instances of human multiprocessing. For example, we can see people talking while driving a car, which involves processing auditory information and responding with speech, meanwhile processing visual information from the view of the road ahead and issuing hand and foot movements to control the car. As we shall see, a multiprocessor model of information processing provides good explanations and predictions for human activity.

Each processor acts as a **subsystem** within the overall human information processing system. When a human task is performed, several subsystems are likely to be involved. The simple task of drawing a pencil line on a piece of paper involves the visual perceptual subsystem in sensing the position of the pencil, cognitive subsystems in determining whether corrective action is needed, and the motor subsystem in moving the hand. Many experiments have been conducted in which the speed and accuracy of performance of such tasks have been measured. These have helped

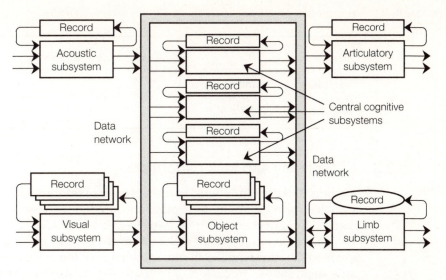

Figure 3.3   A simplified model of human information processing, from Barnard (1991). Each of the subsystems serves specific functions, e.g., processing auditory or visual information, and has a specialized memory holding a number of records. The subsystems communicate via a data network.

psychologists to deduce what subsystems must exist, how each is structured, how fast it operates and how much information it can store.

Thus we know that certain subsystems must be present for the perception of auditory and visual information, for vocal (or *articulatory*) communication, and for operating and sensing feedback from the motor system that operates the limbs. Subsystems are known to possess separate memories, and to process at different speeds. We know about the ways in which information is stored in the subsystems' memories; for example, the visual subsystem's records appear to store information about the shape of perceived objects, rather than raw images like computer frame stores.

The parts of the system we least understand are those with purely cognitive functions. We cannot be sure how many parts there are. Figure 3.3 shows a model of the human information processing system in which three separate central cognitive subsystems are identified (Barnard, 1991). In this chapter, however, we will treat these as part of a single cognitive subsystem.

There is also much uncertainty about the structure of the main human memory. However, a widely accepted theory is that human memory consists of a **working memory** with an effective capacity for about seven 'chunks' of information, and a **long-term memory** of virtually unlimited capacity. Our lack of knowledge about the cognitive subsystem is due to the difficulty of observing its operation: at best, we can observe what goes into and comes out of the adjoining subsystems.

Table 3.2   Information processing cycle times. From Card *et al.* (1983).

Subsystem	Average cycle time (msec)	Range (msec)
Perceptual (visual and auditory)	100	50–200
Cognitive	70	25–170
Motor	70	30–100

3.3.2   Cycle times and task performance

Despite all these limitations, models of human information processing are valuable for their ability to explain and predict the speed of task performance. A number of examples have been given in Card *et al.* (1983).

The reason that we can make use of the human information processing model in this way lies in our knowledge of the **cycle times** of the various subsystems' processors. These are summarized in Table 3.2. When tasks are performed that require the involvement of several processors in a serial fashion, performance times can be calculated by adding together the cycle times of the processors.

An example: Drawing a zig-zag line

A simple demonstration of this use of the model, quoted from Card *et al.* (1983), is the prediction of the rate of drawing an oscillating trace between two straight lines. Figure 3.4 shows a trace drawn at maximum speed for five seconds, using a pencil. The speed of drawing is basically limited by the motor subsystem, which can signal a reversal in direction once per cycle, or every 70 msec. Thus we would expect to find about 71 (= 5000/70) oscillations in a five-second trace.

The model also predicts how rapidly the ends of the pencil's travel are corrected. This involves the perceptual subsystem in following the trace, the cognitive subsystem in deciding that a correction is necessary, and the motor subsystem in making the correction. Each processor introduces a

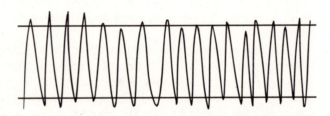

Figure 3.4   Drawing an oscillating trace as rapidly as possible between a pair of parallel straight lines; from Card *et al.* (1983).

cycle-time's delay. The total time for the sequence is therefore the sum of the cycle times, or $100 + 70 + 70 = 240$ msec. The maximum number of corrections possible during five seconds will therefore be about 20.

If you try drawing a zig-zag trace between two parallel lines you will probably achieve roughly the same figures. If you don't, this may indicate that your information-processing subsystems run faster or slower than usual!

Another example: Pointing at a target

Our model of human information processing is useful in predicting the speed of performance of a simple but very common task, namely pointing at a target on the screen. This is the task we perform when we select a key on a pocket calculator or when we move the mouse pointer to a screen icon. Our model can provide predictions of speed of pointing in terms of the target width W and the amplitude of movement (or distance) A.

The pointing task involves repeated use of several information processing subsystems. If our perceptual subsystem indicates that the mouse pointer is a certain distance away from the target, our cognitive subsystem initiates a motor action that moves it close to the target. There will

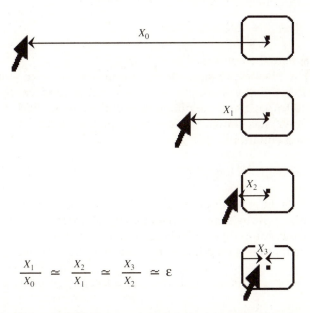

$$\frac{X_1}{X_0} \simeq \frac{X_2}{X_1} \simeq \frac{X_3}{X_2} \simeq \varepsilon$$

Figure 3.5   Successive iterations in the task of pointing to a target with a mouse. Three iterations are sufficient to bring the pointer within the target. The ratio of the error X_i to the perceived distance X_{i-1} is approximately the constant ε. Iteration terminates when the pointer is within the target. The value of ε is intentionally exaggerated here to illustrate the process.

be some error in positioning, however, so this process is repeated until the pointer is within the target. As Figure 3.5 indicates, the error can be assumed to be a constant proportion ε of the pointer's perceived distance X_i from the target.

Each iteration brings the pointer to ε times the previous perceived distance, where $\varepsilon < 1$. Thus after the first iteration the pointer is a distance εA away from the target (recall that A is the original distance). After two iterations the pointer is $\varepsilon^2 A$ away, and after n iterations the distance is $\varepsilon^n A$. Iteration continues until the pointer is perceived to lie within the target, that is, until the distance has reduced to half the target width W. Thus the number of iterations needed is given by the equation:

$$\varepsilon^n A \leq W/2$$

This gives the following expression for n, the number of iterations needed:

$$n = -\log_2(2A/W)/\log_2\varepsilon$$

Our information-processor model tells us that each iteration involves a cycle in turn from the perceptual, cognitive and motor subsystems, that is, $100 + 70 + 70 = 240$ msec, which we will call t. This gives a positioning time T_{pos} of nt, which we can express as:

$$T_{pos} = K\log_2(2A/W)$$

where the constant $K = -t/\log_2\varepsilon$

This expression for positioning time is known as *Fitts' Law* (Fitts, 1954). Experiments have shown that a good value for the constant K is 100 msec. Since the publication of the Law in 1954, research by MacKenzie (1992) has shown that better estimates result from using a slightly modified equation:

$$T_{pos} = K\log_2(A/W + 1)$$

Fitts' Law is simple to apply. If we wish to know how much of the user's time will be saved by using a target 0.5 cm wide instead of 0.2 cm, and if we assume that the average distance of travel A is 10 cm, Fitts' Law tells us that the two positioning times will be approximately:

$$T_{0.5} = 100\log_2(10/0.5 + 1) = 100\log_2 21 = 100 \times 4.39 \text{ sec} = 439 \text{ msec}$$

$$T_{0.2} = 100\log_2(10/0.2 + 1) = 100\log_2 51 = 100 \times 5.67 \text{ sec} = 567 \text{ msec}$$

Thus the choice of the larger target will save $567 - 439$ msec, or approximately 130 msec each time.

3.4 Sociological and anthropological theories of human behaviour

The environment in which interactive systems are used is a social setting; many social forces are at play, and some of them affect how systems are used. Lack of appreciation for social forces has been the downfall of many system designers, as far back as attempts in the 1940s to introduce coalmine automation (Trist and Bamforth, 1951). There is still a serious lack of useful theory about human social behaviour to support system design. Although more is understood now than in the 1940s, even more needs to be understood if we are to keep up with the expanding social impact of interactive systems.

This section looks at how the research of sociologists and anthropologists into routine human behaviour can augment our description of the Human Virtual Machine. It doesn't draw a sharp distinction between the two fields of research, although they have very different origins, anthropology starting from an interest in pre-literate cultures and sociology in urban cultures. Now the two fields have come close together in their approach to understanding how people use systems.

3.4.1 Cognitive versus social perspectives

What does it mean to take a social perspective onto the environment of use? How do the theories of sociologists and anthropologists differ from those we have just been discussing, based on cognitive science? To answer these questions, we'll start with an example, taken from Goodwin (1991).

Example

One situation that has been studied from both perspectives is the verbal interaction between aircraft pilots and controllers on the ground. In this example, the pilot of a scheduled flight (Atlantic flight 1091), which has just landed and has been assigned to Gate 7, is talking to the airport Flight Tracker (FT) who handles traffic from the runway to the gate:

> Pilot: Operations. Atlantic ten ninety-one's on the ground to gate seven.
> FT: Roger, ten ninety-one. Charlie...Alpha seven? Uh, shoo... Hold on one second, ten ninety-one...
>   That aircraft should be off the gate shortly. Stand by until seven clears, ten ninety-one.
> Pilot: Roger. Could you tell them we're gonna need ground power please.
> FT: That's affirm.

Psychologists have a strong interest in the cognitive processing that takes place in such an exchange, and in ways of modelling the processes with a view to understanding what problems might occur and how the exchange might be made more efficient. By studying a large number of examples of this gate-confirmation activity, they would be able to model its performance and possibly discover a different set of speech conventions that would enable faster or more reliable confirmation. A study of this kind, focusing on telephone assistance operators' conversation with callers, can be found in Gray *et al.* (1993).

Anthropologists, on the other hand, have an interest in the social behaviour that underlies this kind of work. They study the ways in which unusual situations are handled and look for explanations for unexpected behaviour, with a view to showing how mundane skills and common sense take care of situations that arise in social settings. Thus Marjorie Goodwin, the anthropologist who studied the Atlantic 1091 example, was interested in the momentary hesitation of the Flight Tracker. She found that a third person, the Ramp Planner, who was sitting with his back to the Flight Tracker, was instrumental in resolving an unexpected problem. Here we see the control-room conversation, including the remarks of the Ramp Planner (RP), shown in italics:

> Pilot: Operations. Atlantic ten ninety-one's on the ground to gate seven.
> FT: Roger, ten ninety-one. Charlie...Alpha seven? Uh, shoo... Hold on one second, ten ninety-one...
> *Alpha seven...*
> RP: *That plane should be pushin'.*
> FT: That aircraft should be off the gate shortly. Stand by until seven clears, ten ninety-one.
> Pilot: Roger. Could you tell them we're gonna need ground power please.
> FT: That's affirm.
> *Did you catch that, Ed?*
> RP: *Yeah.*

We can see how the Ramp Planner, realizing that the Flight Tracker is in difficulties, volunteers the essential information that *'That plane should be pushin''*. This enables the Flight Tracker to solve the problem, and turn the situation back into a routine one.

It is characteristic of these kinds of theories that they focus on the social context as a resource for problem solving, rather than on the cognitive capabilities of the individual. This particular study shows how the resources of the control room, and especially the co-workers 'listening in' to each others' activities, enable problems to be solved as a matter of course.

3.4.2   Factors that distinguish the social perspective

Research in anthropology and sociology identifies two major factors that characterize the social perspective on human behaviour:

- Recognition of the importance of the **social setting** – or the context in which the behaviour takes place. The social setting is responsible for major variations in behaviour (such as attending to one's own work or getting involved in someone else's) and cannot be ignored.

- Showing the **purpose** that underlies or motivates the things people do. Even a seemingly pointless action like the Flight Tracker's muttered 'Alpha seven...' can be seen to have the purpose of alerting other people in the room to the predicament of the speaker.

We will see evidence of these two factors in the following examples of sociological and anthropological theory.

3.4.3   Examples of theories of social behaviour

We will conclude this section with a couple of examples of theories drawn from studies of people in their social settings. They are both drawn from the results of detailed studies based on audio or video recordings. These studies have a different flavour from some of the more broad-brush sociological work we will be looking at later. They focus in on the fine-grained detail of the activity, and are able to compare similar activities in order to make generalizations. After looking at two examples, we will discuss how they might be applied to the design of an audio-video communication link.

As we shall see, this kind of research sometimes leads to the development of simple 'runnable' dynamic models. Thus the first example shows that we can predict roughly what telephone callers will say in response to the answer 'Hello', to within a small range of possible types of response. The second example shows that when two people are holding a conversation, changes in gaze direction by the listener have predictable effects. These are quite specialized models, but we can nevertheless incorporate them into our description of the Human Virtual Machine, so that we can predict more accurately what will happen when we apply technology in these kinds of situations.

Example 1: Opening sequences in telephone calls

We are all aware, probably without thinking about it, that we take turns during the opening of a phone call in a rather stylized way. For example, it is very rare for the person *making* the call to speak first. Usually the person *receiving* the call starts the ball rolling, saying 'Hello?' and possibly giving their name. A number of studies of these opening sequences have been conducted by Schegloff (1979); Figure 3.6 shows the nine basic forms of response to 'Hello' that he identified.

This model of phone-call openings is useful in the design of systems to automate one side of telephone calls. A simple example is the common answering machine; it complies with the model by taking the first turn in the opening sequence. The model helps explain why answering machines whose outgoing messages are silent tend to confuse the caller. The model is also useful in analysing more elaborate designs, such as telephone-operator workstations that issue a recorded initial turn (for example, 'Pacific Telephone, can I help you?'). One day, when speech-recognition technology improves to a point where it can recognize a wide

1	Greeting terms only:	Hello
2	Answerer's name queried:	Mister Smith?
3	Answerer's name stated:	Joe!
4	Questioning or noting answerer's state:	Hello. You're home
5	First topic or reason for call:	Hi, is Joey there?
6	Request to speak to another:	May I speak to Chris, please?
7	Self-identification:	Hi Fred. This is Peter
8	Identity questions:	Hello, who is this?
9	Jokes and joke versions of 1 to 8:	Goodbye!

Figure 3.6   Nine forms of response by a caller to the answerer's 'Hello' in initiating telephone conversations; based on Schegloff (1979).

range of words and phrases, we will probably start seeing systems that have been designed with the help of this model.

Example 2: How gaze direction punctuates conversation

Gaze direction is an important component of face-to-face conversation. We can build simple models of the effect of gaze, and can use these models to explain observations, such as difficulties in holding conversations with the partially sighted.

Contrary to popular opinion, it isn't necessary to maintain eye contact continuously in order to be an effective conversationalist. Studies by Goodwin have shown that people frequently turn their gaze away and back. However, there are certain patterns of gaze movement that can cause the speaker to pause or even restart the current sentence, as in these two examples from Goodwin (1981):

Barbara: Uh, my kids... [pause] ...had all those blankets.
Eileen: She — she's reaching the p — She's at the point I'm...

Goodwin showed that these behaviours were related to the direction of the hearer's gaze. The speaker (Barbara or Eileen) was in each case relying on the gaze of the hearer to indicate that the hearer was paying attention. By introducing a pause, Barbara was able to bring the hearer's gaze round to focus on her. In Eileen's case, she found that her hearer was looking elsewhere, and she had to restart her sentence twice before she secured the hearer's gaze.

Goodwin is offering a model of how the hearer's gaze direction affects speech. If the hearer's gaze is on the speaker before the speaker starts, the sentence should not be impaired. However, if the speaker is aware that the hearer is looking elsewhere, he or she may introduce a pause in order to attract the other's gaze. If the speaker discovers, during the sentence, that the hearer is looking elsewhere, he or she is likely to restart the sentence as a result.

How we might use the theories

These theories could be helpful in the design of systems supporting collaboration via audio and video. Two of the many questions that arise in the design of such systems are:

- What support is needed for the opening sequence when connections are set up?

- How important is the maintenance of eye contact?

The first question is an interesting one, because audio-video switches permit connections to be set up in a variety of sequences. The video connection can be made first, and the participants can open the audio connection when they have something to say. Conversely an audio connection via telephone can be extended to a full video connection if the need arises to see each other. A third possibility is that both two-way channels, audio and video, are opened simultaneously. Schegloff's study tells us that we should expect certain standard patterns of greeting to arise, and that the different sequences of connection may give rise to different opening greetings.

Suppose, for example, the video connection is made first. What kind of exchange is likely to occur when the audio connection is made? There won't be any need for the parties to identify themselves. But there may be some ambiguity about who should speak first.

Here the study by Goodwin can help us. It suggests that there may be benefits in providing an accurate simulation of eye contact. Few video-phone systems support changes in gaze accurately because this would involve placing the camera on the same axis as the centre of the video screen. The camera is usually mounted above the screen, which makes people appear to be looking down when they're actually looking straight at the other person's image on the screen. Inexperienced users of these systems may have difficulty in conducting conversations because their techniques for controlling the other person's flow do not work reliably.

Goodwin's study suggests that we may want to try to support a close simulation of eye contact, for this may enable the users to punctuate their conversations as if they were in the same room. They may have less trouble during opening sequences and turn-taking. Alternatively we might prefer to design the system to make simultaneous audio and video connections, since this is likely to lead to opening sequences more like the sequences of telephone users.

3.5 Theories of the organization of human activity

We need ways to support design through the analysis of widespread effects of new systems. The fine-grained theories we have discussed so far can help us, but only by analysing individual activities, one at a time. The impact of new systems is rarely limited to one or two activities; quite often there will be changes all over the organization, with benefits in one place being offset by problems in another. The introduction of a large-scale system will be justified in terms of its impact as a whole.

The problem here lies in predicting **changes in the way people organize their activities**. If we could predict exactly how people will organize their work, we could apply fine-grained analysis to each activity. We know perfectly well, however, that this is impossible. We know that the changing setting changes the way things are done, and we know of the aptitude of people for redesigning the way they do things. This problem ultimately prevents us from predicting the outcome of large-scale innovation.

Nevertheless we can apply theories of the organization of work to understanding the impact of systems. In some cases, where small-scale changes are intended, we can make predictions of their likely success. The theories available to us are of several kinds. Some are cognitively based, helping us to understand the performance of certain kinds of complex task, such as problem solving. Others have been developed from a social science perspective, focusing on the effects of systems on people's activities as a whole (Emery and Trist, 1960). We shall look at theories of both kinds.

3.5.1 Problem-solving models

There is a lot in common between theories relating to the organization of activities. They all propose models with a basically *functional* form, that is, in the form of a mechanism with several interconnected parts, each part serving a particular function. We find certain parts recurring in every such model: for example, we find parts that store *knowledge* about the domain of activity, parts that keep track of the *goal* of the current activity, and parts that make *choices* about the next action.

One of the reasons why our models tend to look rather alike is that they are mostly derived from the same source, the pioneering work of Newell and Simon on Human Problem Solving (Newell and Simon, 1972). They proposed a comprehensive Theory of Human Problem Solving that has inspired the work of many researchers over the intervening 20 years. Their theory encompasses ideas about human information processing, later incorporated in the Model Human Processor of Card, Moran and Newell; about the nature of the 'programs' that people follow in order to achieve goals; about the representation of knowledge about tasks, and about the ways people search for strategies to perform tasks.

Because the theories of Newell and Simon are so comprehensive they are difficult to apply to system design. They need to be approximated and narrowed down to make them applicable to specific problems – in other words, transformed into more of an engineering science. The next pages describe examples of simpler theories, some of them with a narrower focus, that can be applied more easily to system design.

3.5.2   Norman's model of task performance

The design of interactive systems involves detailed analysis and prediction of the performance of tasks. Don Norman (1986) has proposed a model of task performance that identifies seven stages of execution and evaluation of user actions. The model, shown in Figure 3.7, provides a framework for understanding how users' actions relate to their goals and to the systems they use.

The model depicts the stages of mental activity that may be involved in the user's achievement of a goal. These consist of,

- **Establishing the goal** to be achieved
- **Forming the intention** for action that will achieve the goal
- **Specifying the action sequence** corresponding to the intention
- **Executing the action**
- **Perceiving the system state**
- **Interpreting the state** as perceived
- **Evaluating the system state** with respect to the goal and intentions.

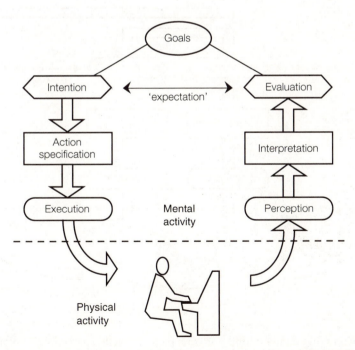

Figure 3.7   Norman's seven-stage model of interaction; from Norman (1986).

The model identifies two categories of mental activity concerned respectively with *execution* and *evaluation*. The execution stages lead from the goal to the performance of action, and the evaluation stages lead back from perceiving the resulting state of the system to its evaluation with respect to goals and intentions. It is only at the stage of system-state evaluation that the user can judge whether progress has been made towards achieving the goal, that is, how the results measure up to expectations.

During task performance the stages of action will not necessarily follow the sequence shown in Figure 3.7. Some stages may be left out, others may be repeated. If we are writing a memo, for example, and form the goal of 'fitting it onto one page', we may need to form a series of intentions, and evaluate the system state against each one, before this goal is reached. Thus we may try rewording a sentence so as to reduce its length, and then view the memo to see if it fits onto one page. Figure 3.8 shows the stages of action laid out according to Norman's model of interaction.

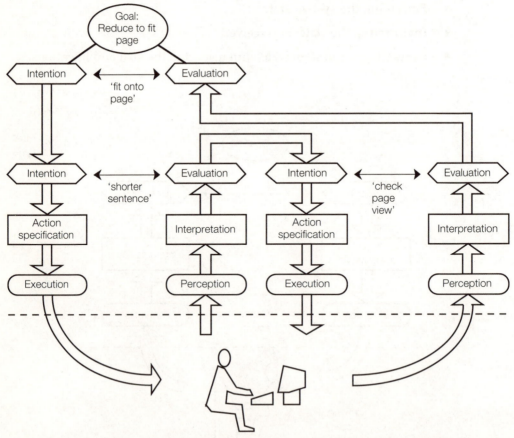

Figure 3.8   Modifying a memo to fit onto one page, modelled according to Norman's seven stages of interaction. Based on an example in Norman (1986).

This model has a number of practical uses in system design. Some of these will be explored in Chapters 13 and 14, when we discuss the user's conceptual model. Norman makes the point that there is a cognitive 'gulf' between the goal and the physical system used in achieving the goal, and that we can design systems to reduce this gulf, with positive effects on the user's interaction. The model also helps us to understand how people use unfamiliar systems; in this respect it relates closely to the next topic.

3.5.3   A theory of exploratory learning

Let us look at a particularly simple example of a theory that explains the organization of a particular kind of activity, namely the way in which someone unfamiliar with a system learns how to use it through *exploration*. We have all experienced this kind of activity when faced with the need to operate an unfamiliar domestic appliance or purchase a ticket from an unfamiliar machine. We try different sequences of operation until we find one that does what we want.

The theory of exploratory learning can be expressed as a simple functional model with four parts (Polson and Lewis, 1990):

(1) **Goal setting.** Users start with a rough description of what they want to accomplish – a task.

(2) **Exploration.** Users explore the system's interface to discover actions useful in accomplishing their current task.

(3) **Selection.** Users select actions that they think will accomplish their current task, often based on a match between what they are trying to do and the interface's descriptions of actions.

(4) **Assessment.** Users assess progress by trying to understand system responses, thus deciding whether the action they have just performed was the correct one, and to obtain clues for the next correct action.

In essence, the theory claims that people perform these four steps in sequence. They start by setting themselves a goal, and then repeat the three steps of exploration, selection and assessment until they achieve it.

The theory can be observed in action wherever and whenever people have to deal with unfamiliar machines. For example, we might observe the user of an Automated Teller Machine repeatedly being told by the machine to 'enter amount in multiples of $5' and keying in '4'. The user's **goal** is to withdraw $20. He has **explored** the control panel, has **selected** the WITHDRAW CASH button and has been asked to enter the amount, which he has **assessed** as progress towards his goal. For his next step he has interpreted the request, 'in multiples of $5', to mean dividing the sum he wants by 5 and entering the result: he has **selected** this as his next action. All that happens is that the machine makes the same request again; he

assesses this to mean that he has made no progress. He may try again with '4', or ask the person standing behind him for advice, or try entering some other value, or possibly give up and walk away.

The value of the Exploratory Learning theory lies, first, in the wide range of design problems to which it applies and, second, in its simplicity and ease of use. We will explore its use in Chapter 8 when we look at methods of Cognitive Walkthrough for analysing user interface designs.

3.6   Sociological theory of group organization

Theories such as the model of task performance and the model of exploratory learning help us understand the behaviour of individuals, but they tell us little about the ways people behave together. When faced with questions about group behaviour we can, as we have already seen, find some answers in the results of sociological and anthropological research. But the examples we have seen in Section 3.4 relate to fine-grained activity; we need corresponding theories that will help us understand how groups of people organize their activities around the use of systems.

As in the case of fine-grained theory, it is easiest to understand what this body of sociological theory can offer by looking first at some examples.

An expert system for crime detection

The first of our three examples is of an expert system installed in a police department in Northern England, reported in Ackroyd *et al.* (1992). The work of police detectives in the UK, as in most parts of the world, revolves around solving crimes and preparing prosecution cases in order to gain convictions (Benson, 1993). The purpose of this system was to help them identify possible suspects in unsolved criminal cases. It allowed details of a crime to be entered at a special dedicated computer terminal, and would then search through criminal records and suggest names of people to investigate further.

The system was not popular with detectives, and received very little use. This was an unexpected outcome, because the system performed reliably according to the specification drawn up for it. However, its design did not fit well with the organization of the detective's working day. We have already seen a glimpse of what this day is like in Figure 2.7, and may have noted the many interruptions. During the 90-minute period shown in Figure 2.7, the detective in question is interrupted four times, and can be seen interrupting other members of the police force at least once.

The expert system required its users to leave their desks and go to the terminal room, log in to the system, set up the details of the unsolved case, and then spend enough time at the terminal to scan the names it produced. This opportunity for peace and quiet could have been seen as a godsend by the detectives, but in fact they felt obligated to be at their desks, available to take messages and handle emergencies. Once they sat down at the expert system and had invested the time to set it up, they felt obligated to follow through to the end of the session. They could not satisfy both sets of obligations, and chose to stick to their established work methods.

Detectives' exploitation of online crime records

This second example also relates to police work, and concerns the unexpected usefulness of a system for generating reports of crime statistics. In the police department where it was installed, its main purpose was to provide management with up-to-date statistics so that they could make strategic decisions about resource allocation according to crime trends. After some initial teething troubles had been resolved, it became a useful adjunct to the department's information systems.

One of its unexpected uses was in supporting detectives during certain kinds of interviews. Much of the work of police detectives focuses around the preparation of prosecution files. However, they are also responsible for clearing up crimes at a satisfactory rate. From time to time they encounter suspects who are confessing to crimes and are willing to admit to other unsolved crimes as a means of plea-bargaining. Detectives then need a rapid means of accessing records of unsolved crimes using the descriptions provided by the suspect.

The crime-reporting system had never been intended for use by detectives. Its user interface was oriented towards data entry and report generation by trained clerks, and was difficult to learn to use; furthermore, the system terminals were housed in a special data-entry room. However, once the detectives discovered that they could search for crime records matching a particular description, they quickly taught themselves to use the system. Then, when faced with a suspect admitting to a crime, they would continue the interview in the data-entry room, where they would use the crime records as a means of matching up the suspect's other confessions with known unsolved crimes. The suspects, somewhat unnerved by this new style of interview, tended to be more cooperative than usual. The detectives weren't troubled by being absent from their desks – they were getting rapid results. Here was a case, then, of a system whose usefulness greatly exceeded expectations (Harper, 1991).

The collaborative nature of air traffic control

The last of these three examples concerns air traffic control. This is a work process whose objective is to manage traffic through sectors of airspace safely and efficiently. Flight plans are filed with control centres in advance of each flight, and are updated as fresh information is received about the progress of the flights themselves, enabling controllers to guide flights through their sectors by communicating with pilots over two-way radio. Figure 3.9 gives an example of about five minutes' worth of conversation,

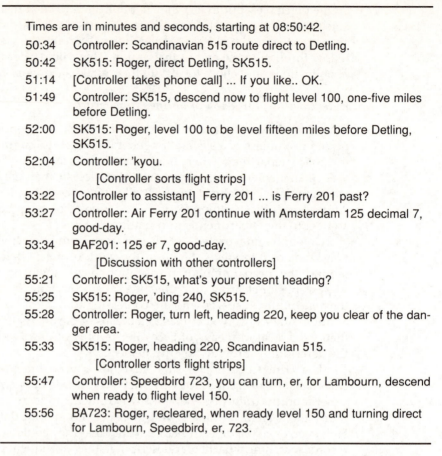

Times are in minutes and seconds, starting at 08:50:42.

50:34   Controller: Scandinavian 515 route direct to Detling.

50:42   SK515: Roger, direct Detling, SK515.

51:14   [Controller takes phone call] ... If you like.. OK.

51:49   Controller: SK515, descend now to flight level 100, one-five miles before Detling.

52:00   SK515: Roger, level 100 to be level fifteen miles before Detling, SK515.

52:04   Controller: 'kyou.
         [Controller sorts flight strips]

53:22   [Controller to assistant] Ferry 201 ... is Ferry 201 past?

53:27   Controller: Air Ferry 201 continue with Amsterdam 125 decimal 7, good-day.

53:34   BAF201: 125 er 7, good-day.
         [Discussion with other controllers]

55:21   Controller: SK515, what's your present heading?

55:25   SK515: Roger, 'ding 240, SK515.

55:28   Controller: Roger, turn left, heading 220, keep you clear of the danger area.

55:33   SK515: Roger, heading 220, Scandinavian 515.
         [Controller sorts flight strips]

55:47   Controller: Speedbird 723, you can turn, er, for Lambourn, descend when ready to flight level 150.

55:56   BA723: Roger, recleared, when ready level 150 and turning direct for Lambourn, Speedbird, er, 723.

Figure 3.9   Transcript of six minutes of an Air Traffic Controller's exchanges with flights traversing a sector in the London area (from Harper *et al.*, 1995).

during which Flight SK515 is guided through a busy air sector in the vicinity of London (Harper *et al.*, 1995).

Controllers work at consoles incorporating radar displays that show each flight in the sector as a trace labelled with the flight's number, altitude and heading direction. They also have racks of paper strips on which details of each flight are printed. These *flight progress strips* are used as a basis for managing the sector; the controller 'works the strips', checking the status of each flight in turn. When flights leave the sector, their flight strips are tossed away.

The introduction of RD3

Traditionally, the design of air traffic control consoles has been seen as a matter of supporting the controller's activities. Therefore when the British Civil Aviation Authority decided to upgrade their system in the mid-

1980s, they undertook a major redesign of the controller's console, and added a number of extra display capabilities, in a system known as RD3. The new system would enable controllers to handle sectors unaided, something that had never been possible before.

Reactions to RD3

When the system was introduced, the reaction of controllers was far from positive; indeed it ranged from indifferent to hostile (Harper *et al.*, 1995). They complained of difficulties in accessing display functions, irrelevance of the functions themselves, unreliability, and confusing layouts. One group of controllers refused to use the new system altogether, regarding it as untrustworthy. Controllers started to revert to the previous system, which they knew and trusted. It appeared that RD3 was doomed to be an expensive failure, and investigations were mounted to find out why, including a sociological study by Harper *et al.* which identified incompatibilities with group work practice (1995).

Findings from sociological studies

The controllers had not been used to working on their own, in the manner proposed for RD3. The previous system had required each controller to work with a number of assistants, who fetched flight strips from the printer, placed them correctly in the racks, liaised with neighbouring sectors, and drew the controller's attention to possible flight conflicts. Controllers also relied on the sector chief, who oversaw several sectors, to keep an eye open for potential conflicts and to deal with special situations when they arose. The whole focus of this team effort was to relieve the controllers of any distractions and allow them to 'work the strips' as reliably and efficiently as possible.

A basic flaw in RD3's design was its lack of recognition for this team structure. The controller was given more responsibility than before, and could no longer operate by 'working the strips'. New display functions were provided to help the controller handle the extra workload, but they made the display more difficult for other members of the team to read and interpret. In particular, the chief could no longer rely on the display when dealing with special situations. These were some of the properties of RD3 that caused the control teams to regard it as untrustworthy, and eventually to refuse to transfer their work onto it.

3.6.1   Modelling users' reasoning about choice of tools

These are three very different stories. Two of them describe design failures, while the other is about a system that scored an unexpected success. It is not easy to perceive an underlying theory of human action, of a kind that might be useful in system design. This is often the case with the results of sociological study, but these examples do provide one useful insight, which we will explore in this final section.

A common theme of all three is the *choice of tools and systems* that users make, and how they reason about this choice. This is a rather different kind of choice from the ones we've discussed previously, such as the telephone caller's choice of response to the answerer's 'Hello', or the exploratory learner's choice of next action. The choice of whether to adopt or abandon an available tool is made by the user over a longer period, during which the tool is experienced in a variety of situations where other issues are at play too, many of them social in nature.

We can see evidence in each of these three examples that users reason about their choice of tools and systems in terms of their goals and obligations. The question they face is, *Will my use of this system, to perform this particular task, help me meet my overall goals and obligations?* This question arises in various circumstances; for example:

(1)   It arises while the user is attempting to perform the task with the aid of the system, where the user asks, *Is this system helping me?*

(2)   It arises while the user is performing the task *without* using the system, and asks, *Would the system have helped me?*

(3)   It arises when the user is faced with a choice of performing the task in one of several ways, and asks, *Which system will help me most?*

As system designers, we are keenly interested in situations of type (3), for it is here that tools compete for the user's acceptance, in the manner described in Chapter 2. To understand how the choice is made, we need to look at situations (1) and (2), because these provide experiences that feed the user's reasoning. We need to be aware of the social forces that contribute to these experiences.

Thus in the example of the expert system, it turned out that detectives were strongly motivated to stick to the daily routine of preparing cases and answering phone calls, because this work produced visible results and maintained their social obligations to their colleagues. While the expert system sometimes helped solve crimes, it didn't help enough to make up for taking detectives away from their other responsibilities. In the second example, use of the unsolved-crimes database offered an unexpected way of clearing up crimes more efficiently than before, an important measure of the detective's performance. The air traffic control system contravened a number of social obligations within the control room, making it difficult for sector chiefs and assistants to support the controller properly, which meant that the controller herself could not do her job properly either.

Sociological theory cannot yet provide designers with the kind of dynamic model they might like to have, one that could answer the question, *Will users accept or reject this system?* This question involves modelling the user's reasoning process, taking into account the complex set of goals and social obligations in his or her work. This is harder to do than, say, modelling the exploratory learning process. However, sociological studies can teach us a lot about the context of work and its social systems (Button, 1993). They can provide many useful insights about users' needs for interactive systems.

3.7 Conclusion

We have looked at three basic types of theory in this chapter. The first type derives from psychological research, and contributes to our detailed understanding of how people perform tasks. The second type is based primarily on anthropological research and provides equally detailed models of how the social context affects human behaviour. The third set of theories, based on both psychological and sociological research, focuses on how people organize larger units of activitiy.

Taken as a whole, these theories contribute to our understanding of the Human Virtual Machine. They leave a great deal unexplained, and this limits the degree to which we can predict the outcome of system design. As more research is done into human behaviour, gaps in the Human Virtual Machine can perhaps be gradually filled in.

The next set of chapters will start to explore ways in which we can apply these theories to the design of interactive systems. We will see instances of the theories' usefulness, and we will also see instances of design problems where the theory is inadequate. In these latter cases, we tend to rely more on building and testing prototypes. The lessons learned from these experiments can, in some cases, provide a basis for developing new theories and thus filling gaps in the Human Virtual Machine.

Exercises

(1) What are the differences between explanatory theories, empirical laws and dynamic models? Give examples of their uses in design.

(2) Using the Keystroke-Level Model, calculate how long it would take to type the command s/hello/goodbye/ <RETURN> to substitute the text 'goodbye' for 'hello'.

(3) With a group of colleagues, try the exercise of Figure 3.4, and compare your performances with those derived from the Human Virtual Machine. Discuss explanations for any major differences.

(4) According to Fitts' Law, how fast can a user select a function key on the side of a keyboard, measuring 1 cm square?

(5) Set up two targets in opposite corners of a computer screen. Measure the time you take to alternate between the targets 20 times, and compare this with the time calculated with the aid of Fitts' Law.

(6)   Try answering just 'Hello' to a series of telephone calls you receive, and note any answers that don't fit into one of Schegloff's nine categories in Figure 3.6.

(7)   Consider how the desktop system described in Section 3.2.1 might affect patients' satisfaction with the consultation service. What kinds of complaints might arise, and how might the theory of Greatbatch *et al.* help explain the complaints?

(8)   In the zig-zag line example of Figure 3.4, the motor subsystem is involved in signalling reversal of direction *and* in correcting the end position. We might therefore expect correction to take longer, because the motor subsystem is 'busy' signalling reversal. Why do you suppose the reversal cycle doesn't slow down the correction process? Hint: try to trace the involvement of the subsystems shown in Figure 3.3.

(9)   Classify each of the following statements according to whether it is an explanatory theory, an empirical law or a dynamic model:

   (a) To recall the details of an event, people try first to reconstruct the context in which the event occurred, and then replay the context.

   (b) People retain their ability to recall specific events in their lives for a maximum of five years, with few exceptions.

   (c) In order for one fact to be easier to retrieve from memory, another fact has to become more difficult.

(10) Suppose the Flight Tracker and Ramp Planner, in the example of Section 3.4.1, had been in separate soundproofed cubicles. Write the dialogue between the Flight Tracker and the pilot as it might then have taken place. What changes would you suggest making to the equipment installed in the Flight Tracker's cubicle?

Further reading

Card S. K., Moran T. P. and Newell A. (1983). *The Psychology of Human Computer Interaction*. Hillsdale, NJ: Lawrence Erlbaum Associates

   A pioneering work on a major body of cognitive psychology research into the design of interactive systems. Chapter 2, on the Human Information Processor, remains the best summary of models of human performance.

Greatbatch D., Luff P., Heath C. and Campion P. (1993). Interpersonal communication and human–computer interaction: An examination of the use of computers in medical consultations. *International Journal of Interacting with Computers*, **5**, 193–216.

   A lengthy but rewarding discussion of how computers in the doctor's office affect doctor–patient conversation.

CHAPTER 4

Design processes and representations

Chapter objectives:

The design of an interactive system involves a number of interlinked design processes, and a number of different representations of the design and of the user's activity that it supports. This chapter introduces:

- The roles of the various design processes and representations
- The relationships of the processes and representations to each other
- The basic form of each process
- Examples of each of the main representations.

4.1 Introduction

Designing an interactive system involves us in a great variety of tasks. At one point we may find ourselves sketching part of the user interface, for example. Next we are interviewing a prospective user. Then we are building a model to determine speed of operation, after which we must incorporate our design changes into a prototype, which we must then test on our users. And so on, sometimes for months or even years. If all goes well, everything comes together at the end in the form of a completed design.

This chapter offers a preliminary view of how all these activities are able to make their respective contributions to design. It points out how the activities form sequences that we can treat as individual *processes*, in the sense defined in Chapter 2. It also highlights the dependence of design on *representations* of systems and of users' activities. It shows how these representations enable the results of one design process to contribute to another in an orderly way.

The chapter's overall purpose is to provide a framework into which the methods described in later chapters can be seen to fit. The aim is not to prescribe a new way of doing things, although it may seem new to some readers. Rather it tries to explain how each existing method makes its contribution to design. The chapter starts with some preliminary words on design processes and representations, and then discusses each of the principal processes in turn.

4.2   Understanding design

We can find many accounts of design in the literature, e.g., in Rogers (1983) and in Ferguson (1992). These accounts identify the activities that take place, including:

- Analysis of alternative solutions to determine whether they are practicable
- Conducting investigations to fill gaps in knowledge
- Drawing up draft specifications
- Making performance and cost estimates
- Building and testing prototypes
- Modifying the design and revising the prototype if necessary.

Every design project involves some or all of these activities. However, each design discipline tends to rely on them to a different degree and goes about them differently.

Interactive system design is no exception here. There is a relative shortage of scientific knowledge, and correspondingly few analytical tools, which means we rely a great deal on building and testing prototypes, even in the early stages of design. At the same time, we are constantly introducing interactive systems to new application domains about which little is known. This means we must spend time studying people in the new domain and analysing the results of our studies.

4.2.1   The multiple processes of interactive system design

For these and other reasons, interactive system design is likely to involve not one process but several concurrent processes. Figure 4.1 characterizes the way these processes interconnect. While specifications are being drawn up, data have been collected from user studies and are being

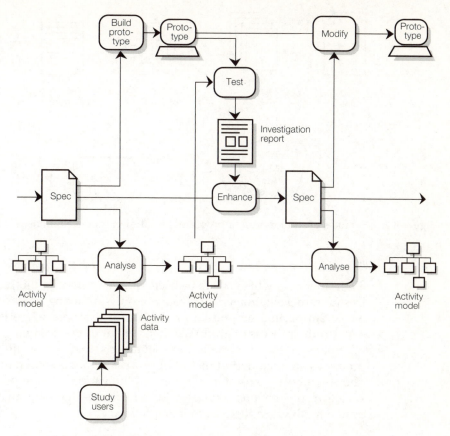

Figure 4.1   Some of the processes and representations of interactive system design.

analysed, possibly a prototype is being built in readiness for user testing, and so on. The processes move forward in parallel, but their results are likely to come together when a new specification is drawn up or a new prototype is built.

The five processes described in outline in this chapter are *user study, model building, specification, analysis of the design* and *evaluation of prototypes*. Each of the processes is expanded in subsequent chapters of this book.

4.2.2   Design representations

The other purpose of this chapter is to introduce some of the important **design representations** that link the processes together. As we saw in Chapter 2, processes arise when activities develop multiple dependencies, and system design is a good example of such an activity. It is often necessary to pass information about the design from one process to another. This information may describe some aspect of the design or of the

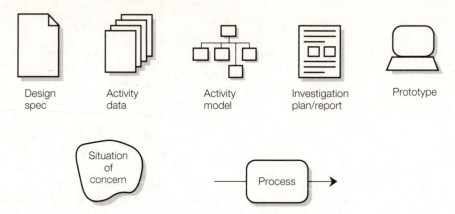

Figure 4.2   Symbols used to represent processes and design representations.

environment in which it is to be used, or it may identify things to be done. Design representations play a role not only in linking processes together but in supporting individual processes; for example, a specification can support the process of gradual enhancement of the design.

Some of the important representations that act as links between processes are included in the set of process symbols shown in Figure 4.2. These symbols are used in diagrams of the various design processes presented in this chapter, and also in the process diagrams that introduce design methods in the chapters that follow.

4.3 Studying the user

Interactive systems address situations of concern through their support for people's activities. If we want to design a system, therefore, we need to understand the activities it is to support. Ultimately we will need to build *models* of the activities, so that we can understand the system's impact on the situation of concern. The first stage, however, is to conduct studies and gather data.

The key to understanding activities is to study the people who perform them – the potential *users* of the system. In effect, we learn about people's activities by studying the people themselves. From these studies we will collect data that will form the input to analysis and model-building (Figure 4.3).

A lot hinges on the results of data collection and analysis. According to the outcome, the design problem may start off in quite different directions, and the design itself may be based on widely different models of the user's activities. If user studies aren't conducted with adequate care, the outcome of the design project can be in jeopardy.

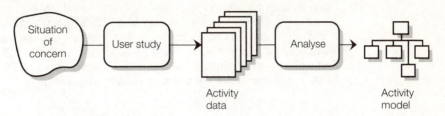

Figure 4.3   The process of user study, leading to the collection of activity data for subsequent use in analysis and model-building.

An example of such a design project was described in Section 3.6.3. We saw there how an air traffic control system was built without adequate input from user studies, and when introduced to service was rejected as unreliable by the air traffic controllers. The underlying problem was the lack of fit between the system's functions and the controllers' responsibilities. Although the system supported individual tasks adequately, it caused breakdowns in teamwork that threatened air traffic safety.

User studies can generate a variety of forms of data. In Figure 4.4 we see several examples:

(a)   A fragment of a transcript of an *interview*, in which the interviewee is describing his day at work.

(b)   A sequence from a *verbal protocol* transcribed from a video recording of an airport control-room Ramp Planner responding to a pilot's request.

(c)   A fragment of the *dialogue* between user and system, in which the application in question is a text editor; here again, the data were gathered by videotaping.

(d)   Part of an answer to a *questionnaire*.

The aim of user studies is not, of course, just to collect data about people's activities, but to assist the design of supporting systems. Raw data are not particularly useful to designers, in and of themselves. They hide the structure of the activity, and make it difficult to test the validity of system designs.

It would not greatly help the designer, for example, to be in possession of a word-by-word transcript of an entire day's conversations of an airport Ramp Planner, like the example of Figure 4.4(b). At best, the designer could look through the transcript for evidence of problems; but if she were to notice a problem, such as momentary uncertainty about the availability of a particular gate, her next questions would probably be, 'Why did this happen?' and 'How often does this kind of thing occur?' To answer these questions, she would have to read through the whole set of transcripts, extracting and analysing the appropriate data.

(a) I thought about doing the price list ... this was like, I thought, *shall I go and do the price list for today*, had a look at it, deleted some files, thought about a problem I have with how it runs, thought about an improvement I could make, thought, *no, that's too much, I'll do it later*, and then didn't do it, yeh? And that took me from about 13:15 ... it's probably about 13:20 ... to about 14:00 ... and then I went and had a meeting with Carol.

(b) Pilot: San Tomás Ramp?
Atlantic two eighty six?

Julie: Two eighty six.
This is operations.

Pilot: I understand gate fourteen is occupied?
Do you have any instructions for it?
(0.3)

Julie: Uh: : m, (0.1)
Should have left ten minutes ago.
Hopefully:,
(1.0)
They have pulled the passenger stairs.
They should be leaving momentarily.

Pilot: O:kay. Thanks.

(c)   The user decides to make the change [from **geart** to **great**] by using the Substitute command to substitute the characters **grea** for the characters **gear**.

USER: **s**   Invokes the Substitute command

SYSTEM: **ubstitute**   Completes the command name and waits for the first argument to the Substitute command.

USER: **grea** RETURN   Types the new text to be substituted and terminates it with RETURN.

SYSTEM: **(for)**   Prompts the user for second argument of Substitute.

USER: **gear** RETURN   Types the old text to be replaced and terminates it with RETURN.

SYSTEM: **[OK]**   Asks the user to confirm that the command is stated correctly before executing it.

USER: **RETURN**   Types RETURN to confirm. The system then makes the substitution every time it can on the current line.

SYSTEM: **1**   Responds by printing the number of substitutions it made – in this case only one was made.

system: **#**   Prompts for a command.

Figure 4.4   Examples of data gathered during user studies: (a) a fragment of an interview, in which the subject is reconstructing his day; (b) a verbal protocol of a videotaped exchange between a pilot and Julie, an airport Ramp Planner, from Goodwin and Goodwin (in press), using the notation shown in Figure 3.1; (c) a dialogue fragment, showing the user correcting a mistake in a document; from Card *et al.* (1983).

22. In my opinion the information centre is

OF SOME HELP		VERY HELPFUL		ABSOLUTELY INDISPENSABLE
1	2	3	(4)	5

23. In my opinion the software vendors are

OF SOME HELP		VERY HELPFUL		ABSOLUTELY INDISPENSABLE
1	2	(3)	4	5

24. In my opinion the people in the department who are knowledgeable about computer applications are

OF SOME HELP		VERY HELPFUL		ABSOLUTELY INDISPENSABLE
1	2	3	4	(5)

(d)

Figure 4.4 *Continued.* (d) a questionnaire response, from Kenneth E. Kendall/Julie E. Kendall, *Systems Analysis and Design*, 2e, © 1992, p. 144. Reprinted by permission of Prentice-Hall, Englewood Cliffs, NJ.

The purpose of building models of people's activities, as described in the next section, is to perform the analysis of raw data in advance of system design. Once these models are available, questions can often be answered quickly and accurately.

4.4 Modelling the user's activity

As we examine the different processes of interactive system design, we become aware of the crucial role played by *models* of people's activities. A task or process model provides insights into the range of supporting functions that the system may need to provide. It can also provide explanations for unexpected results when the system is installed and used. These are some of the areas in which models can help answer designers' questions.

Models of human activity are especially invaluable in making predictions of the *usability* of system designs. They enable us to assess the system's usability in terms of one or more *usability factors*; the table of factors shown in Chapter 2 is repeated in Figure 4.5. Designers' questions are

- The **speed of performance** of the activity, which affects **how many people** are needed to perform it
- The **incidence of errors** while performing the activity
- The users' ability to **recover from errors** that occur
- The magnitude of the users' task in **learning to use the system**
- The users' **retention of learned skills**
- The users' ability to **customize** the system to suit their way of working or the situation of use
- The ease with which people can **reorganize activities** supported by the system – their own activities and other people's
- Users' **satisfaction** with the system

Figure 4.5   Usability factors, repeated from Chapter 2.

likely to focus on one or more of these factors, such as speed of operation or incidence of errors; for this reason, the most helpful type of model is likely to be one that assists in making predictions about particular usability levels. In other words, it will be a dynamic, 'runnable' model of the user's activity. We saw specific examples of runnable dynamic models in the last chapter, in the form of Fitts' Law, the Keystroke-Level Model and the model of exploratory learning.

In building models from data collected during user studies, we tend to focus on modelling either tasks or processes. We would model the simple text-editing activity of Figure 4.4(c) as a task, perhaps as shown in Figure 4.6. A complex activity, involving several people over a period of time, would be modelled as a process. Figure 4.7(a) shows several concurrent processes handled by an air traffic controller, based on the example of Figure 3.9, and Figure 4.7(b) shows the task structures forming one of the processes.

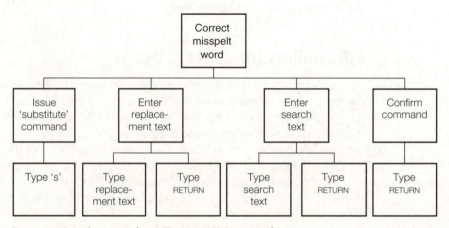

Figure 4.6   Representing the steps from Figure 4.4(c) as a task.

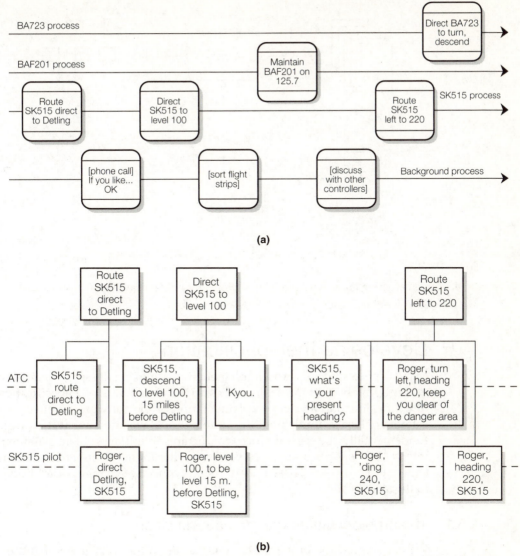

Figure 4.7   Representing activities as processes: (a) the air traffic control activities shown in Figure 3.9 represented as four processes, three of them concerned with handling individual flights, the fourth with background tasks; (b) the tasks making up one of these processes.

We do not usually attempt to develop an activity model from scratch. Rather we choose an existing form of model, according to the nature of the activity and the types of usability questions we expect to encounter. We may choose a generalized form, such as a task model. Sometimes we simply wish to revise an existing model by means of further analysis of new or earlier data. We analyse the data collected during study, abstracting out the data needed to construct the chosen type of model. This process is shown in Figure 4.8.

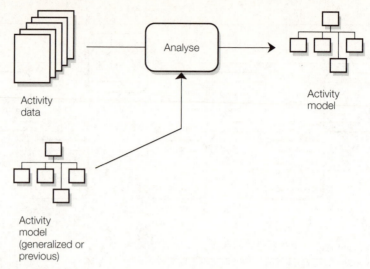

Figure 4.8   Constructing an activity model based on study data, drawing on a previous model or a generalized form of model.

4.5 Developing the specification

Many aspects of design and implementation hinge on the *specification*. For example, analysis of the design relies on the availability of a specification of the design, and so does implementation of the software. In effect, we cannot analyse or implement the system unless we know what it is. More fundamentally, the central process of turning an initial problem statement into a final specification involves many iterations of enhancement, as shown in Figure 4.9. These enhancements consist of changes or additions to the specification.

4.5.1 The problem statement as a specification

We may regard the problem statement as an initial, very general specification of the form of solution. Consider the following problem definition:

> Design an online patient registration system, to be integrated with the current hospital information system, allowing rapid entry and easy update of patient details.

This includes a brief specification of the form of solution, in the words 'an online patient registration system, to be integrated with the current hospital information system'. It also specifies key usability aspects of the two main activities supported, 'rapid entry and easy update of patient details'. Problem statements include, in embryonic form, the functional and performance *requirements* that the system must attain.

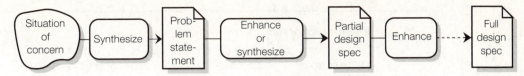

Figure 4.9   Steps in the development of a design specification.

4.5.2   The requirements document

The development of the design specification is a gradual process, as Figure 4.9 suggests. However, there is an important transition at the point when the **requirements** for the system are defined. This is a watershed point in the design process.

Once the system's requirements have been specified, the system is defined sufficiently to show that the original situation of concern can be resolved. In other words, the specification can be *validated* with respect to the initially stated need, as shown in Figure 4.10.

At the same time, the specification now defines a technically feasible design strategy. It has reached a point where the design task can be handed to a competent system designer for completion. There are no major gaps in the specification that might cause this designer to produce something incapable of resolving the situation of concern. It isn't necessary for the designer to look back over the watershed to find out about the situation of concern; the requirements document says all that is necessary for the design to proceed.

The way the solution is spelled out in the requirements document depends on a number of factors. It depends, for example, on the context in which design will be performed – will the system be developed as a product, or in-house by a user organization, or by a software contractor? It also depends on who is expected to read the document; for example,

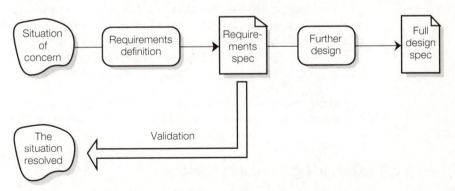

Figure 4.10   The requirements document as a watershed in the specification process, allowing validation in terms of the original situation of concern.

1.1   Patient registration

1.1.1   The system must support the entry of patient information on arrival at the hospital, including name, address, name of physician, date and time of arrival.

1.1.2   The system must allocate a patient ID to be quoted in all transactions while the patient is registered at the hospital.

1.1.3   Patient registration should take a trained operator no more than five minutes.

1.2   Patient record update

1.2.1   The system must enable subsequent update and correction of patient information by nursing staff on the ward.

Figure 4.11   How requirements might be defined in an outline requirements document.

whether it is intended for internal consumption, for those bidding for a contract, or for those to whom a contract has been awarded. Figure 4.11 shows how requirements for a patient registration system might be defined in an 'outline requirements document' made available to prospective contract developers.

4.5.3   Subdivision of the design

In a project of any complexity, the specification won't be developed by a single process. There will be many parallel specification processes, each focusing on a different part of the overall design task. For example, there will probably be a separate design team for each of the major internal software modules. At an early point, not long after the requirements are defined, the system is divided into components, and these are designed more or less separately until it is time to integrate their specifications together.

This subdivision of the design is shown in Figure 4.12. Each design subprocess is given an initial specification to work from. This specification is, in effect, a problem statement for the design of the component. In the case of the patient registration system of Figure 4.11, requirement 1.2.1 might give rise to a separate design problem, as follows:

Modify the user interface to the ward information system, to allow easy update and correction of patient information by nursing staff.

4.5.4   Designing the user interface

The user interface is a particularly important component of any interactive system, for it is the part with which the user interacts directly.

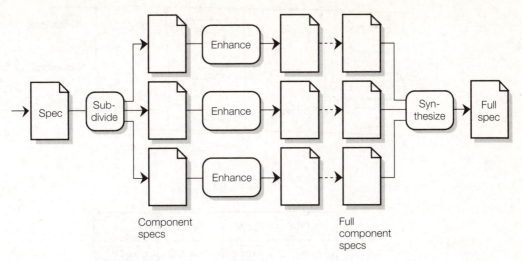

Component
specs

Full
component
specs

Figure 4.12   Subdivision of the specification process, and subsequent synthesis of the components.

Generally speaking, the user interface has the most direct impact on the system's usability; indeed we may have difficulty saying anything definite about usability levels until we have designed it. We may need to build and test prototypes, because there are often aspects of the system's usability that cannot be measured analytically. This need for *evaluation* is discussed in the next section.

Designing the user interface is quite unlike designing the internal software for the system. We are concerned with supporting the cycle of interaction, not just the cycle of execution of software. The cycle of interaction is a cognitive process, and we need to understand it well enough to ensure that the user interface will support it. This involves five basic design activities:

- Adopting a **style of interaction** appropriate to the task performed and the person performing it;

- **Conceptual design**, ensuring that the users have a *mental model* of the system that is adequate to support them in deciding what steps to perform and in understanding the system's responses;

- Performing **analyses** of usability;

- Making decisions about specific aspects of the design, based on **design guidelines**;

- Documenting the user interface, with the aid of appropriate **notations**.

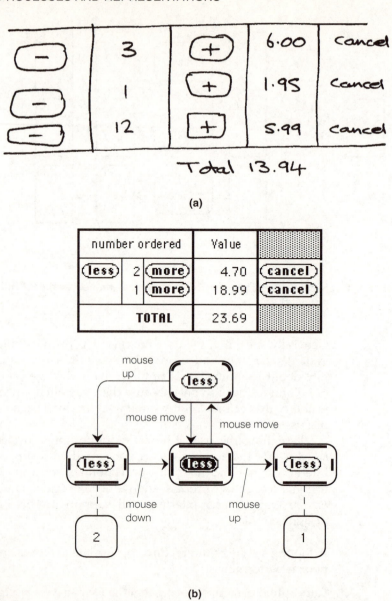

Figure 4.13 Multiple representations of a user interface: (a) rough sketches; (b) detailed drawings of appearance and behaviour.

As in other areas of the design, we may find we need *multiple representations* of the user interface. Thus we may sketch out various aspects of the design for analysis purposes, as shown in Figure 4.13(a), and then construct careful drawings of user interface behaviour and appearance, as shown in Figure 4.13(b).

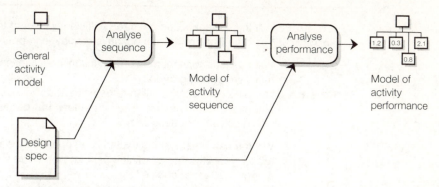

Figure 4.14   Stages of analysis, in which a general model of users' activity is transformed into a model of the users' sequence of steps, and from there into a quantified performance model.

4.6   Analysing the design

One of the roles of specifications is to help us perform **usability analyses** on our designs. This is often the hardest part of the design cycle. We may be able to think quite easily of a number of different forms of solution, but we will probably find it hard to judge which is the most usable. To overcome this kind of difficulty we must tackle the analysis in a systematic way.

4.6.1   Analysis of the organization of activities

We cannot usually go straight to the analysis of usability levels. First we need to know how people's activities will be reorganized. Once we know the sequence in which things will be done, we can make predictions of speed of operation, incidence of errors, and so on.

Therefore the first stage of analysis will often be concerned with understanding the system's impact on the organization of activities. We try to build a model of how people will perform their activities when they have the system to support them. We base these models on general models of the activities, derived from user studies. This is shown on the left in Figure 4.14.

We will usually perform this kind of analysis by constructing a plausible sequence of operation, using a **walkthrough** technique. We work step-by-step through the performance of a task or process, trying to predict the actions that the user will take. A method of *cognitive walkthrough analysis* is described in Chapter 8; it involves repeatedly answering the three questions shown in the example of Figure 4.15.

Walkthrough analyses often tell us a great deal about the design, e.g., about ease of learning and likelihood of user errors. But if we want more precise, quantitative measures of usability we will need to conduct

Q1:	Will the correct action be made sufficiently evident to the user?
Answer:	Yes. The **Patient details** option is displayed in the main menu.
Q2:	Will the user connect the correct action's description with what he or she is trying to do?
Answer:	No. The user cannot tell that the **Patient details** option allows alterations to the details. The label **View/edit patient details** would correct this deficiency.
Q3:	Will the user interpret the system's response to the chosen action correctly, that is, will the user know if he or she has made a right or a wrong choice?
Answer:	Yes. The result is a display of the patient's details, with the first field highlighted for editing if necessary.

Figure 4.15   Cognitive walkthrough analysis.

further analyses of our model of the activity's organization, as shown in the right-hand side of Figure 4.14.

4.6.2 Analysing performance levels

Once we have a model of the user's likely sequence of usage, we can use it as a basis for making predictions of performance levels. In particular, we can often make predictions of speed of operation. We analyse our model of the activity sequence, attaching performance predictions to the steps in the sequence. An example, showing the analysis of changing a patient's records, is given in Table 4.1.

Table 4.1   A keystroke-level analysis of the performance of a task in which a patient's records are updated, using the method described in Section 3.2.3.

Action	Cognitive operation	Time (secs)
–	mental preparation (before command)	1.35
PA	2 keyboard characters	1.00
RETURN	1 keyboard character	0.50
–	response time	5.00
tab	1 keyboard character	0.50
tab	1 keyboard character	0.50
DISCHARGE	9 keyboard characters	4.50
RETURN	1 keyboard character	0.50
	Total	13.85

4.7 Empirical evaluation

Analytical methods allow only partial evaluation of the design. We need to supplement them with empirical methods, in which prototypes are tested in order to answer questions about the design.

Empirical evaluation is a relatively complex undertaking, as Figure 4.16 makes clear. It amounts to an *investigation* of design properties or questions about the design; often these are couched in terms of the design requirements. A prototype must be built from details given in the current specification, and tests must be carried out. The results of the test may confirm that the design is adequate, or may give rise to further enhancement.

When we look at the evaluation process in more detail we see a number of recognizable activities (see Figure 4.17). These include the collection of activity data, which may be performed as in user studies, and the analysis of the data, which usually follows a similar pattern to pre-design modelling and analysis.

Two activities that acquire special importance in the context of empirical evaluation are the planning of the investigation and the documenting of the results. At the outset we need to identify the requirements around which the investigation is to take place, and state our objectives:

It is a requirement that the ward information system should allow easy update and correction of patient information by nursing staff. We have designed a menu-based user interface that runs on the existing ward terminals. We intend to conduct a three-week field trial of the system to confirm that it can be learned easily and used effectively by nurses.

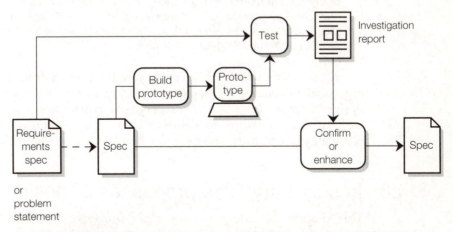

Figure 4.16   The general form of the evaluation process, in which a design specification is investigated to see if it complies with requirements, by building and testing a prototype and writing an investigation report.

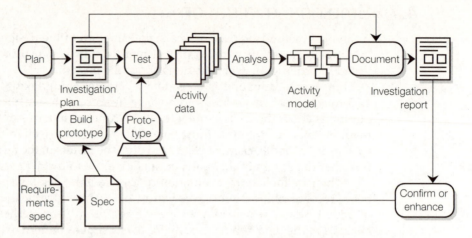

Figure 4.17   The evaluation process in greater detail, showing the role of the investigation plan and of the activity model constructed from collected data.

This abstract of the investigation plan doesn't spell out the details of how the evaluation will be conducted; a more lengthy document will be needed for this purpose, specifying the experimental method, the prototype to be used, the choice of subjects, the type of data to be collected, and so on. The main purpose of the abstract is to identify the purpose of the evaluation, and to link the outcome to this purpose. At the end, therefore, we may write another abstract summarizing the investigation report:

> It is a requirement that the ward information system should allow easy update and correction of patient information by nursing staff. We have designed a menu-based user interface that runs on the existing ward terminals. We have conducted a three-week field trial of the system confirming that it can be learned without difficulty by nurses on the job, but identifying a need to make updating less error-prone.

An outcome such as this, confirming the overall design but suggesting enhancements, provides the necessary input to the next round of design iteration. The plan and report play a crucial role in the evaluation; without them, the purpose of the evaluation can become lost, and the outcome may not be fully understood when the design is enhanced.

4.8 In summary: The processes of design

This chapter has identified the main processes of interactive system design, and has provided examples of some of the representations these processes use. How are the design processes themselves carried out? This question will be answered in the chapters that follow:

- Chapter 5 will cover the methods by which we study users and collect data in preparation for model-building and analysis, both before design and during evaluation.

- Chapter 6 will explain how activity models of different kinds are built and used in design.

- Chapter 7 will explain the role of requirements, and describe how a set of requirements is gradually compiled and validated.

- Chapter 8 will present several methods for analysing a design in terms of usability factors.

- Chapters 9 and 10 will describe methods of conducting empirical evaluations.

- Chapters 11 through 15 cover a range of user interface design methods.

We will see many of the same representations and design activities, introduced in this chapter, surfacing in the pages to come.

Exercises

(1) By examining each of the process charts, make a list of all of the roles of (a) activity models, (b) specifications.

(2) Why is it good practice to introduce a representation linking every step in a process to the next step? What might go wrong if this were not done?

(3) What would it mean to try to design an interactive system without making any use of: (a) specifications; (b) prototypes; (c) activity models; (d) activity data; (e) investigation plans and report?

Further reading

Lammers S.M. (1986). *Programmers at Work*. Redmond, WA: Microsoft Press

A set of interviews with leading software designers. Many of them are advocates of reliance on the prototyping process in software development, but there are glimpses of most of the other design processes in their accounts of how they work. The back pages include a number of interesting examples of design representations.

PART II

System design

5   User study methods

6   Systems analysis and design

7   Requirements definition

CHAPTER 5

User study methods

Chapter objectives:

User study methods provide us with the real-life data we need about people's activities, enabling us to design systems to support them. The main points about user study covered in this chapter are:

- The dependence of design on data gathered from thorough, carefully planned studies
- The choice of methods available, including interviews, observation, questionnaires
- How to conduct each of the types of study
- The kinds of data each method produces.

5.1 Introduction

To design an effective interactive system, we must identify the people it is to support – the **users** – and gain some familiarity with their activities. We must focus from the outset on these prospective users, because this is the only way we can really find out about their activities. This is what we mean when we talk of taking a *user-centred* approach to design (Norman and Draper, 1986). We learn about people's activities, how they perform them, and what they need in the way of support, by focusing our attention on the people themselves. In this way we ensure that the design will be based on *real data*, not imagination, about these people and what they do.

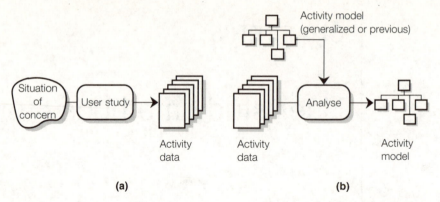

Figure 5.1   (a) The process of user study; (b) the analysis and model-building process that follows it.

We conduct **user studies** as a first step towards building an understanding of users and their activities. We observe them at work, we interview them, we get them to fill in questionnaires, we may collect examples of the materials they work with. As a result, we compile data about them and about their activities, often in large quantities (Figure 5.1(a)). Then we analyse the data, with a view to building a model or abstraction of what we have seen (Figure 5.1(b)).

A number of methods exist for studying users – for carrying out the process shown in Figure 5.1(a). This chapter covers the three main categories of method: interviews, observation and questionnaires. Each study method generates data of a different kind that need to be analysed differently. The outcome is likely to be affected by the method chosen; therefore it is important to be familiar with the full range of methods, to appreciate their strengths and weaknesses, and to know how to use them in conjunction.

5.1.1   When do we conduct user studies?

User studies may be needed at various points during the system's design. There is almost always a need to conduct studies at the outset in order to define the problem. These are often followed up with more studies, targeted specifically at the activities identified in the problem statement, and feeding into the definition of the system requirements.

Studies are also conducted in support of evaluation. As soon as a working version of the system exists, we will want to evaluate it in terms of the requirements it is to meet. We generally do this by conducting user tests, either in controlled laboratory conditions or in real surroundings. The same methods of data collection used prior to design apply also during evaluation, although our choice of method will of course be affected by the circumstances.

5.1.2   How do we ensure quality?

There is little point in conducting studies unless we can rely on the quality of the data they produce. The best ways to ensure quality are to plan the studies carefully and to use reliable methods. It is also important to be thorough, otherwise there is a risk of overlooking important aspects of the user's activity. But we cannot afford to devote unlimited amounts of time and effort to user studies; we must draw the line somewhere.

Accordingly we need to know both how to get a successful study under way, and when to stop it. There is an element of risk in putting the cap on a study and declaring it complete, just as there is in concluding any aspect of design, and we must learn to manage this risk. We will learn this partly from experiencing the analysis that accompanies the collection of data. As we piece together models of the user's activity we see where there are gaps in the data and where there are redundancies. This experience can be fed back into the next study we conduct, and in this way the process becomes more efficient and less risk-prone.

5.1.3   Data collection methods

In the next three sections we will look at a range of methods for collecting the data from which models of the activity are built. The principal methods covered here are interviews, observation and use of questionnaires. These are well-established techniques that have been described elsewhere at length; an excellent chapter on task observation methods can be found in Diaper (1989b) and a classic text on fieldwork has been written by Strauss (1987).

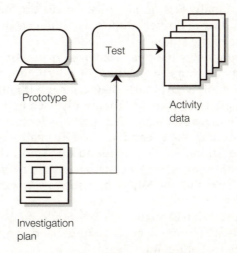

Figure 5.2   The central testing process of evaluation, in which data are gathered using similar methods to those applied during user study.

Several of the methods described here are useful also in evaluation of systems after they have been built, either as prototypes or as the final product (Figure 5.2). Chapter 9 will discuss how these methods can be adapted to collecting data during evaluation.

5.2 Interviews

Interviews provide a particularly rapid and congenial way of gathering data. They require less prior planning and preparation than issuing a questionnaire, for example, and the data are available immediately after the interview in the form of recollections and notes. An interview is a social event that can, if conducted sensitively, gather vital data while helping to make the prospective user feel positive towards the proposed system. By the same token, however, interviews can backfire or give misleading results, as caricatured in Figure 5.3. This makes it imperative to take care in their preparation and conduct.

5.2.1 The basic method

Several issues need to be resolved prior to holding the interviews themselves. First of all, the *interviewee list* must be drawn up, and this involves making decisions about the breadth of the study and the amount of time that can be devoted. According to the breadth of study, the range of users' activities covered will vary. Second, the *length of interview* must be decided; this will normally lie between half an hour and an hour. Longer interviews, possibly stretched across several sessions, are needed when major innovations are being planned, because these demand a deeper investigation. As we shall see, a *structure* will normally be defined for the interview. Finally, a *schedule* must be set up for the individual interviews; scheduling and rescheduling will often be an ongoing activity during the course of the study.

Interviews may be **structured** or **unstructured**, that is, they may be designed around a fixed set of questions with simple answers, or they may be allowed to take their course without constraints. Heavily structured interviews are not commonly used in pre-design studies unless specific information is needed, perhaps to support a minor design change. Equally, it is rare to conduct a totally unstructured interview, starting with the question, 'So what is it you do?' and bringing the conversation to a close an hour later. An essential degree of structure is needed simply to make sure that the following issues are covered in the time available:

(1) **The interview's purpose.** This should be explained at the outset, allowing plenty of time to get acquainted and to establish the right atmosphere for the rest of the interview.

The Bad Interview

A = Systems analyst
B = Accounts Manager being interviewed

A: Good morning. I'm from the Information Systems Department. We sent you a memo telling you I would be coming to see you.

B: Yes I did agree with Mr Poppit, manager of the Information Systems Department, that I would be free for a discussion with one of his staff.

A: Well I'm the one doing the job. You see we want to computerize a lot more of the work of your department. You have an awful lot of staff and we feel that we could do a lot of their work by computer.

B: What did you say? Take away some of my staff? My staff are badly over-worked as it is.

A: No, you don't understand. Let me explain. We are going to set up a data-base of all customer accounts and keep them on disk. Of course, we'll do an updating run before we use the database to input to the invoicing run and monthly reports. Here, let me show you this database layout. (Shows complex diagram and immediately launches into a detailed description of the structure of the database using technical jargon. After some minutes, **B** starts looking at his watch – a gesture that becomes increasingly frequent and obvious as the meeting goes on.)

B: This is all very well, but you know my department is probably the most important one in the company. We control all financial matters very care-fully, and we...

A: (interrupting) Oh, don't worry about that! The computer is much more accurate than humans. (Lights cigarette.) In fact, that's going to be a problem after the new system has been installed. Unfortunately we will still have to rely to some extent on human beings. I mean your people will still have to provide the input data to the system but they'll have to be a lot faster than they are at present.

B: I'd like you to know that my department won the group award last year for courtesy and efficiency. Furthermore we always...

A: (interrupting) Yes, but we're talking here about the new upgraded com-puter with 48 MIPS, which will certainly be a lot faster than any of your staff. Just you wait and see.

B: No, I will not wait and see (Looks at his watch again). I am going to speak to Mr Poppit personally...

Figure 5.3 A caricature of a poorly-conducted interview; from Bingham and Davies (1992).

(2) **Enumerating activities.** In interactive system design, understanding the activities of the prospective user is almost always a prime focus. These can be uncovered by asking a general question, e.g., 'What are your basic responsibilities?' and following this up with more specific questions to fill obvious gaps in the initial answer.

(3) **Work methods.** A second part of understanding the user's activities is finding out how they are performed. This is often the hardest and lengthiest part of the interview because work methods usually involve extensive skills and knowledge, and the interviewer may be unfamiliar with these.

(4) **Tracing interconnections.** People never work entirely in isolation, and the interview needs to discover important interconnections with other people and other parts of the organization.

(5) **Performance issues.** The interview should attempt to uncover issues relating to the current performance of tasks and processes, because these provide a measure of the 'usability' of the current support system and the need for improvement. This is often a sensitive topic because of obvious links to the interviewee's productivity and job security.

This general framework may be varied according to the breadth of focus. It is also common to spend more time during the first few interviews gaining an overall impression of the organization, and the interview schedule should be set up to start with people who can provide this impression, e.g., people with longer experience of the work or the organization.

5.2.2 Effective interviews

The interviewer's other main concern, after resolving basic matters of structure, is to be alert to various factors that contribute to the effectiveness of the interview. Part of the interviewer's technique is concerned with handling these factors. We will look at some of the major factors and techniques here.

Following up on exceptions
Perhaps the most important factor, capable of influencing the collected data most strongly, is the existence of *exceptions*, that is, non-routine aspects of the work. For a variety of reasons, interviews are always in danger of focusing on the routine and ignoring the non-routine. Yet it is often the non-routine aspects of work that cause system failures, and handling exceptions is often a major source of workload and therefore a drain on productivity.

Surprising though it may seem, when we ask people to describe what they do or how they do it, they tell us about their typical activities and leave out the atypical (Eldridge *et al.*, 1994). It takes skill and sensitivity on the part of the interviewer, and an eye for clues, to uncover exceptions. Figure 5.4 shows a classic example, drawn from an actual interview, of how this can happen. A user who at first considers her job to be so routine that 'there's not much to say about it', suddenly launches into a detailed account of how she handles atypical events and, in doing so, uncovers important aspects of the work.

The interviewer in Figure 5.4, Eleanor Wynn, was skilful enough to notice a key phrase, 'set a fire under somebody', in the subject's answer to

E (interviewer): Did you describe your job to me already? Have we gotten that far?

G (user): I'm in the Collections department. I'm the Lead Collector. You've met Jerry and Christine? OK, they're in my group.

There's not much to say about it. We just collect past-due balances, and we do a lot of things that – you do a lot of customer care, you do a lot of check refunds, and you're cleaning their accounts, and a lot of it is not even delinquent accounts, but *problem accounts*, they have the money ... and it's just not the fact that you convince the customer that they *owe* the money, number one, which, you know, is a big step right there, but then to get it through their system, you have to understand what they have to do to get a check cut, and you have to understand their system a little bit. You have to be able to ... know how to set a fire under somebody to get that moving, if it needs to be prioritized. And that, at times – people don't understand how hard that can be.

E: What is involved in that, 'setting a fire under somebody'?

G: Well, see, I have to – you begin to immediately move it upward, up through the management, okay? You start with a clerk, okay? They definitely cannot solve the problem. It's out of their hands. Okay, you ask whose hands is it in? Who can make the deci – the buyer.

Okay, you call the buyer, the buyer says, 'Um, the reason why I'm not paying this is, I said I would pay *twenty* dollars and seventy-*three* cents for a carton, not twenty-*four* dollars and seventy-*two* cents, which you bill me on this five thousand dollar shipment of paper.' So then you say, 'That's all I need to know, let me get back with you.' You get back, you go through your billing system, you try to find out, you know ...

In the meantime, let's suppose time is running out and you do not have time to get a billing adjustment through. So you got sit there and think, *How can I get this person to pay this invoice*. It's wrong, they got the wrong PO, they billed them wrong, Accounts Payable doesn't want to do nothing with it. So you call them back up and say, 'I'm not asking you to pay something that is not due. What I want you to do is to pay *according to your PO*. Pay that invoice short, okay?' Then he says, 'I will not pay the invoice short because I've had too many problems with that. Unless I get a typed invoice from you, specifically.'

So you sit there and think, I can't go through the billing system, it's too late. I can type them an invoice, set the system going through the billing system at the same time, coordinate that so when he pays the check short, there will be a balance on the account. When the credit issues through I'll have the billing department hold that credit, deliver that credit to me, not deliver it to the customer 'cuz the customer will wonder *Why am I getting the credit* if they think they're already gonna receive a bill, right? Then I would just clean up their account later. But in the meantime ...

E: So you kind of short circuit it?

Figure 5.4   Uncovering the atypical during an interview; from Suchman and Wynn (1984).

G: Yeah. So in the meantime I have got to type them an invoice telling them that this is an invoice for the amount of supplies, send that out there, send copies to everybody, prepare a billing adjustment, send that on its way and get the appropriate signatures, call up the buyer, call up the sales rep, tell them to meet together, tell him to present the invoice to him. Then he will release it to Accounts Payable.

Once Accounts Payable gets it, then you get a-hold and she'll say, 'I have your invoice here, but it cannot be cut for two weeks.' Your cutoff is one week. Okay. You say, 'May I speak to your supervisor please', in a nice way because you don't want to offend them, to think, *May I speak to your supervisor please.* You know, you don't want to say, make em feel like, *because you are so incompetent*, you know. What you want to say is, Well fine, thank you, I understand that's your job, you know. Just, you have to do a job like I do, I just want to speak to your supervisor so that maybe we can work out something, that I need that check a little bit early, if we can work out *some way* in your system working with our system so that we can get this out early. So they transfer you to their supervisor and she comes on and says, 'That's it, I can not do it. I can get the check out, but maybe two hours later than you need it.' So you're getting closer, okay?

E (laughing): Yeah!

G: So then you go to Jennie: you tell my manager to call this manager, and you tell her what the situation is. She calls, maybe she can't get them. So then *she* goes to Chuck, which is our Controller here. And when you get a call from the Controller of XYZ Corporation, you know it's gone up quite a bit. And then *he* will call the supervisor there and tell her, 'If you can't get that check out to me by that date will you please let me know so that I can call somebody who can get it out. Either if I have to talk to your controller, or whoever.' And it's amazing how many times that – you don't have that all the time, but you have situations where you're working with about five or six people, and you're coordinating—just to get a check cut.

Figure 5.4   *Continued*

the first question. By following up this comment she gained important information about the subject's problem-solving skills. Had she chosen instead to follow up on the phrase, 'we just collect on past-due balances', she might have learned much less.

Knowledge of the domain

A second factor about interviews, mentioned above, is the amount of skill and knowledge on which people draw in performing their work. Few activities are simple enough to be explained fully in the space of a one-hour interview. Activities that draw on years of training or experience will rarely make sense without in-depth study, and this needs to be done outside the interview, reading background material or learning the technicalities from 'domain experts' – people with experience in the work who are willing to spend the time to explain it.

5.2.3 Recording the interview

It is standard practice to make audio recordings of interviews that contribute to a user-needs study. People are unlikely to object to being recorded, but it is essential to gain their permission, and advisable to raise the matter with them when scheduling the meeting rather than confront them with it when the interview is about to begin (Kendall and Kendall, 1992). If they become uncomfortable about recording or ask to speak 'off the record', it is best to agree to their request rather than risk antagonizing them.

The main reason we tend to audio-record is to allow specific points and choices of words to be checked afterwards. Usually we will take notes on paper as well, but sometimes this is awkward, e.g., when clambering around a construction site or sitting together having lunch; in these situations audio-recording is a necessity.

5.3 Observation

We rely on observational techniques to capture descriptions of the way activities are performed. This is especially valuable in studies with a task focus; we will almost always prefer to observe the task's performance rather than rely on after-the-fact accounts gained from interviews. However, we need to choose a method that doesn't interfere with the task's performance, e.g., that doesn't involve stopping the performer of the task after every few steps. Two techniques – video recording and concurrent verbal accounts – are particularly effective for recording task activities. For studies of larger units of activity, the methods available include passive observation, ethnographic field study and action research.

5.3.1 Video recording

We often use video recording to collect data about task performance and work practice. Video has the advantage of capturing very fine-grain data, thus allowing us to perform very detailed analyses if we should so choose.

An example of a transcript from video-recorded data is shown in Figure 5.5. It shows two equity dealers, Robert and John, engaged in a brief transaction, after hearing that another bank is 'on the bid' for the same stock. The data were collected as part of a study of the feasibility of using speech-recognition technology to record deals. The study showed conclusively that speech played such a complex role in the dealing room, and deals were placed in so many different ways, that no automatic recognition scheme could be made to work (Heath *et al.*, 1993).

Video-based observation is somewhat intrusive. However, the wide use of video recording in the home and at work means that a camera may now be quite acceptable as an aid to observation – even in equity dealing rooms.

There is an associated cost in video recording – the cost of transcribing the material into textual form. This task of generating a written *protocol*

A: *Han:son, twenty of an eighth, forty by fifteen:, (Shearson) on the bi:d.*
R: ((Sitting down))
     (0.2)
J: Are we going to hit 'em?
     (2.3)
R: ((Peers at screen))
     Erm:: (.) *yes::,*
R: (0.9) *who's that?*
     (3.0)
R: Bernie? ((Picks up phone))
     (3.0)
R: We want to sell (forty:) ....

Figure 5.5   Transcript of video recorded data, from Heath *et al.* (1993). For an explanation of the transcription symbols used, see Figure 3.1.

describing all the events taking place on the video record is extremely time-consuming. In comparison with audio, video material demands a much more highly trained transcriber, commanding significantly higher pay.

5.3.2   Concurrent verbal accounts

One way to reduce the magnitude of the transcription task is to ask the user to speak while performing the task, explaining what he or she is doing. This generates an audio recording which can be transcribed, resulting in what is known as a *concurrent verbal protocol*. An example is shown in Figure 5.6.

This method can usefully be combined with video recording; it then helps considerably in overcoming one of the problems with video-based observation: determining what is happening on computer screens. Usually it is quite hard to read video images of screens because of flicker and lack of resolution. The user's explanations in the verbal protocol can often be used to resolve ambiguous images.

5.3.3   Passive observation

In many cases we do not know, at the outset, what tasks to study. The initial purpose of observation is rather to gather data on a broad range of activities, with a view to identifying activities for further study. These broader-ranging studies demand a rather different approach. Their emphasis must be on capturing the goals of activities rather than their precise methods of performance, and to understand the underlying purpose of the work.

The term **passive observation** is applied to studies where the observer attempts not to influence the performance of activities. Passive observa-

1. *The user [U] is trying to check out a book from a library, using an online library circulation system. She has used the system once before, several months ago.*

U: So I first need to . . . I'm in 'Check out/in Mode' and that's what I need to be in. So, what do I do? *Laughs nervously.* Ummm. *Studies screen. Moves mouse pointer up to activity log, where previous user's name is displayed.*

2. *User moves focus down to command-entry field.*

U: OK, I think I need to do something down here, where it says, 'Enter Bar-Code or Command', because they're talking about the number on the book. *Pauses.* I don't know – seems to me I have to enter my user name in here sometime – how's it going to know who it is?

2. *User clicks on command-entry field.*

U. I'm just going to try typing in here the number on the book and see what happens. *Types '0104' and presses* ENTER *key.*

3. *System beeps and displays alert box: 'No current patron, command ignored'.*

U. 'No current patron, command ignored'. All right. So I *do* need to tell it who I am.

Figure 5.6   Concurrent verbal protocol as recorded while a system is under test.

tion may include actions such as asking the purpose of work or discussing its relationship to other work. It would not, as a rule, involve participation by the observer in the work; this would be considered *action research*, described in the next section. We have already encountered an example of data collected largely from passive observation of a police detective in Chapter 3. The complete day's transcript, shown in Figure 5.7, will be referred to in subsequent examples and exercises.

5.3.4. Ethnographic field study

It is rare to conduct extensive periods of wholly passive observation, because of difficulty in later determining the activity's meaning and structure. We cannot tell, for example, that one activity is the continuation or result of another, and we may not know what the subject is focusing on.

Therefore it is common to supplement observations with data gathered from interviews so as to produce a richer record. A term for this kind of real-world study is **ethnography**. We have already encountered a smaller-scale example of ethnography in the video-based observation of equity dealers quoted in Figure 5.5. Ethnography is the basic method of much research in anthropology and sociology. A good example of a full-scale ethnography, focusing on service engineers, can be found in Orr (1990).

9:00   Come on duty, fill in duty diary.
9:03   Attend regular morning parade.
9:24   Make telephone inquiry regarding an ongoing investigation.
9:26   Read through crime file regarding a fraud case (Case A).
9:28   Go to the uniform department (i.e., uniformed patrol officers' department) to discuss a case with a uniformed officer.
9:50   Break in canteen.
10:10   Back in office, chat with an investigator.
10:13   Telephone a hospital about the location of a female suspect in fraud Case A; they know nothing of her.
10:25   Read through the female suspect's file.
10:35   Make further telephone inquiries about Case A.
10:47   Visit the communications room to make sure a message has been passed on to a uniformed colleague.
10:54   Make a telephone inquiry about a rape case, trying to contact a doctor.
11:03   Answer telephone for colleague, take details to pass on.
11:05   Another officer asks the detective to accompany him in making an arrest; they discuss the case but decide not to proceed with the arrest.
11:13   More telephone inquiries regarding Case A; phone home.
11:40   Answer phone to take details for another officer.
11:45   Another uniformed officer comes in to discuss a case.
11:50   Telephone inquiry regarding Case A.
12:05   Lunch.
12:58   Back in office, make telephone inquiry.
13:00   Conversation with another detective about a rape case.
13:08   Leave office and travel to see a complainant.
13:16   At complainant's address; take details of complaint about quality of repairs to roof.
13:32   Leave to travel to next inquiry.
13:40   Visit bank about a suspect in another fraud case (Case B).

14:02   Leave bank for next inquiry.
14:10   Visit house of alleged offender in Case B.
14:13   Travel back to police station.
14:22   Read through files for fraud Case B.
14:31   Make telephone inquiry to record-keeper of nearby police station regarding location of suspects in another case.
14:34   Uniformed officer comes in to explain that another officer has found some stolen property that probably relates to an arrest of shoplifters the previous week. The property was incorrectly sent to Lost and Found instead of reporting it to Criminal Investigation Department (CID).
14:38   Go and collect stolen property from Lost and Found and bring back to CID offices.
14:42   Answer telephone for another officer.
14:44   Discuss another case with fellow detective.
14:49   Make telephone inquiry.
14:51   Read court prosecution file for shoplifting case (Case C).
15:05   Start writing out contribution to Case C file in longhand.
15:11   Court offices call to discuss another case.
15:20   Go to Custody Office to check details of the custody records for the two arrested shoplifters.
15:25   Tea break.
15:42   Continue writing Case C statement.
16:05   Go to uniformed department to leave note for officer who recovered the stolen property.
16:15   Continue writing statement.
16:28   Answer telephone for another officer; then take statement to typing pool.
16:35   Look through crime file to see if a record has been entered of a purse reported stolen last week.
16:41   Phone the uniformed officer responsible for the stolen purse report and discuss who will complete the report.
16:45   Complete the report on the stolen purse for the officer.
17:00   Off duty.

Figure 5.7   The activities of a complete day's work by a police detective, gathered primarily by passive observation; from Thornton and Harper (1991).

5.3.5 Action research

The term 'action research' is applied to methods of studying activities by taking part in them. Action research can overcome one of the main drawbacks of passive observation, the so-called 'Hawthorne effect'. This effect is named after studies of workers at a Western Electric Company plant in Hawthorne, IL, in which it emerged that workers' productivity was improving simply in response to being studied. In action research, the observer becomes a member of the group under study.

The study by Dalton of middle managers is an example of action research (Dalton, 1959). Dalton was interested in studying some very sensitive issues relating to the reward and promotion systems in a manufacturing company. He arranged to be taken on by senior management as an 'employee' (he refuses to divulge in his book what the job was in order to protect his informants in the company). He was able to melt into the surroundings and as a result to make very close observations of his 'colleagues'.

We rarely need to adopt the undercover-agent tactics of Dalton in order to perform action research; most organizations and groups are glad to welcome an analyst as an active member while the study is under way. Usually there are simple administrative duties that we can perform part of the time, leaving the rest for interviews and periods of observation.

5.4 Questionnaires

Questionnaires provide a means of reaching a larger catchment area and thus gathering enough data to perform statistical analyses. They help us to determine, for example, whether there are certain needs that are experienced very widely. We can also obtain data about satisfaction levels with existing support systems and thus discover whether these systems need improvement.

5.4.1 Questionnaire design issues

Questionnaires demand very careful design if they are to produce reliable data. Again, a number of books are available offering detailed guides to questionnaire design (Kendall and Kendall, 1992; Preece *et al.*, 1994). Figure 5.8 shows a stage in the design of a questionnaire for obtaining users' reactions to an automatic currency-changing machine. The questionnaire incorporates a 'semantic differential' table at the bottom to gain ratings on a number of the machine's properties.

One of the prime sites for locating this automatic *bureau de change* machine is in British airports and railway stations so that travellers can obtain the main European currencies quickly without having to find the nearest bank. The figure contains part of a hypothetical questionnaire that will be given out in selected airport departure lounges where a prototype of the Eurochange machine is being evaluated. The questionnaires will be given to people after they have completed their transactions.

EUROCHANGE QUESTIONNAIRE

Background information

Departure lounge   Flight   Destination

How often do you make European flights? (please tick one box)

- less than once a month
- 2–4 times a month
- 4–8 times a month
- other (please specify)

Do you normally get your foreign currency at? (please tick one box)

- own bank
- any convenient bank
- special bureau de change
- airport bank

Please indicate the reasons for using this machine: (you can tick more than one box)

- did not know where airport bank was
- long queues at airport bank
- last minute need for extra currency
- wanted to try out machine
- shortage of time – had to go directly to departures

The Eurochange machine is a useful addition to airport services: (please tick one point)

strongly agree   neutral   strongly disagree

The Eurochange machine should be more widely available at European airports:

strongly agree   neutral   strongly disagree

Rate the Eurochange machine on the following dimensions:

	extremely	quite	slightly	neutral	slightly	quite	extremely	
predictable								haphazard
easy								difficult
simple								complicated
confusing								clear
fast								slow

Comment

It is likely that some people will be confused by the use of three different rating scales one after the other. The semantic differential scale may be particularly foreboding and people may avoid answering the questions associated with it for that reason. The only way to ascertain whether this is true would be to try the questionnaire with a small number of people (that is, do a pilot study), so that such problems are detected and rectified before the questionnaire is put into general use. You may also have anticipated other potential problems concerned with the wording of the questions or the layout of the questionnaire. Readability is particularly important if the questionnaire is to be completed online. Notice also that in the first question about the number of European flights, 4 appears in two categories. So if you wanted to answer 4 which category would you tick, 2–4 or 4–8 times a month? This is a common error and one that can be very confusing for respondents.

Figure 5.8   A stage in the design of a questionnaire; from Preece *et al.* (1994).

Four important points to be considered in questionnaire design are:

(1) **The need to make things easy for the subject.** Questionnaires make demands on people's time and concentration; it is only fair to reduce these demands to the minimum. We should ask as few questions as we reasonably can, and make them simple and consistent in wording.

(2) **The need for unambiguous questions.** If people do not understand a question, we cannot be there to clarify it, and we may have to ignore the answers to it that we receive. A well-known mistake is to ask people to rate their satisfaction with a system on a scale from 1 to 5, but to forget to explain which end of the scale means 'good' and which means 'bad'.

(3) **The need to gather precise data.** Vague answers may tell us something individually, but we cannot carry out statistical analyses of answers that, for example, rate the performance of a system variously as 'sluggish', 'awful', 'mostly OK', 'smooth' and 'what I expected'. We need to design our questions to elicit numerical answers wherever possible; questions about subjective issues, such as performance, should be answered with a value on a numeric scale.

(4) **The need to support the intended analysis.** If we do not know how we will analyse the data, we are likely to find we have too much data of one kind and not enough of another. For example, we may find we know which people were dissatisfied with their training courses, but we don't know what courses they took. It may help to run through the main analyses with dummy data before committing to the final form of the questionnaire.

Generally speaking, it is wise to test-run any questionnaire on a small group in order to ensure that these issues are addressed. Once we have issued the questionnaire 'for real', it isn't usually feasible to reissue it a second time in order to correct a mistake or omission.

5.4.2   Questionnaires by electronic mail

With the rapid spread of electronic mail, increasing numbers of subjects can be reached by this medium. This makes it possible to conduct questionnaires more quickly and inexpensively, with the added advantage that the data collected are already online.

Several points should be kept in mind regarding the use of e-mail to conduct questionnaires:

• **Subjects' time and attention.** Many people allocate only an hour or so per day to their e-mail, and answering the questionnaire must fit into such a work schedule. The questionnaire will normally have to compete with items of e-mail of much greater personal importance to the subject. It needs to be short and snappy.

To: all-staff
From: SystemsGroup
Subject: Four quick questions about the library
———

Folks:

We need your help in sorting out the library borrowing system. Please could you answer the following four quick questions? You'll find it easiest to FORWARD the message back to us (SystemsGroup), adding your answers in the spaces provided.

1.   How many books do you borrow from the library in an average month?
     (answer 0, 1, 2, etc. on the NEXT LINE)

2.   How convenient do you find the current check-out system?
     (answer 1 for very inconvenient,
          2 for rather inconvenient,
          3 for in-between,
          4 for quite convenient,
          5 for very convenient):

3.   Would you be willing to use a pen-like bar-code reader to check books out? This would involve carrying a library card with you.
     (answer 1 for no,
          2 for maybe,
          3 for yes):

4.   Any other comments:

We guarantee that the information you provide will be treated with complete confidentiality. No individual responses will be disclosed to people outside the Systems Group.

Figure 5.9   An electronic-mail questionnaire. Note (a) its brief, attention-grabbing wording; (b) its design for ease of reply; (c) its reassurances about confidentiality of data.

- **Making it easy to reply.** Most electronic mail systems are restricted to plain, unformatted text, and so it is not possible to provide the convenience of a form with check boxes or with items to be circled. Instead the subject must go to the trouble of composing a reply. One way to make this easier is to design the questionnaire so that it can be edited and forwarded back to the sender (see Figure 5.9). This has the advantage of encouraging the subject to follow a standard reply format, which makes processing of the data easier.

- **Lack of subject anonymity.** Some questionnaire surveys depend on offering the subject complete anonymity. This is especially important, for example, in organizational surveys of user satisfaction. Electronic mail cannot offer anonymity because every message provides the name of the sender.

5.5 Conclusion

We have looked at three main categories of study method: interviews, observation and questionnaires. The list is by no means exhaustive. In the next chapter we will encounter the method of *user participation in design*, which achieves some of the effects of interviews by including users in the design team – a kind of 'action research in reverse'.

Any or all of these methods may be applied to understanding people's activities. It is quite common, for example, to combine interviews and ethnographic observation. The use of a combination of methods provides opportunities to check the data for consistency. If time and resources permit such an approach, it will often pay off in terms of the quality of the data collected, and the thoroughness of the analysis that follows.

Exercises

(1)   What are the respective advantages and disadvantages of interviews, observation and questionnaires?

(2)   What is the Hawthorne effect?

(3)   Which of the methods described would you use in studies to support solving the following design problems?

(a) Design an interactive system to enable a taxi dispatcher to handle customers' calls more efficiently.

(b) Design an in-cab system to enable taxi drivers to signal their positions and take incoming job requests.

(c) Design a drafting system to enable an architect to prepare detailed drawings more efficiently.

(d) Design a system to improve the distribution and exchange of electronic mail and documents within a worldwide sales team.

(4)   Enumerate the main points that an interview should cover, and the main factors contributing to an effective interview. How many mistakes can you spot in the caricature of Figure 5.3? How many of the main points did the interviewer cover in Figure 5.4?

(5)   Make a list of the important facts about the current billing system emerging from the interview in Figure 5.4.

(6)   If you were continuing the interview of Figure 5.4, what would be your next question? Which of the other people mentioned would you want to interview?

(7)   Discuss the possible use of observation to discover the kinds of information revealed in Figure 5.4. How would you organize this observational study?

(8)   Suppose you were considering equipping the detective of Figure 5.7 with a word processor that would reduce text-entry time by 25 per cent.

(a) Estimate how much time would be saved in the course of the detective's day, and express this as an overall percentage improvement in efficiency.

(b) How would your efficiency estimates have differed if you had observed the detective only during the morning? Or only from 15:00 onwards?

(9)   Design an electronic mail questionnaire to find out more about a current situation of concern at your place of work or study, regarding one of the following: transportation, parking, site security, lunch arrangements, handling telephone messages.

(10)   Design a questionnaire to study the following aspects of an answering machine's design:

(a) Support for listening to messages

(b) Users' awareness of advanced features

(c) Callers' satisfaction with the machine's design.

Further reading

Diaper D. (1989b). Task observation for human–computer interaction. In *Task Analysis for Human–Computer Interaction* (Diaper D., ed). Chichester: Ellis Horwood

An excellent survey of task-analysis study methods.

Kendall K. E. and Kendall J. E. (1992). *Systems Analysis and Design*. Englewood Cliffs, NJ: Prentice-Hall

A text oriented towards more traditional information systems design, with comprehensive coverage of study and analysis techniques, laid out in a clear and simple style with plenty of examples.

Preece J., Rogers Y., Sharp H., Benyon D., Holland S. and Carey T. (1994). *Human–Computer Interaction*. Wokingham: Addison-Wesley

A comprehensive text on HCI. Chapter 30 covers the basic techniques for collecting usage data.

CHAPTER 6

Systems analysis and design

Chapter objectives:

The analysis of the results of user studies, and the synthesis of a design, are two closely coupled activities. To describe them collectively we use the term **systems analysis and design**. This chapter explains:

- How the analysis and design activities fit together
- How task and process models support systems analysis and design
- Methods of task analysis and design
- Systems analysis methods, including software systems analysis and participatory design.

6.1 Introduction

As we have seen in the last two chapters, interactive system design involves a great deal more than just synthesizing a set of software components. There is a crucial analytical process as well, involving the assessment of design choices and the checking of decisions. There is also a need to study and model the user's activities. Each of these processes plays a key role in interactive system design, and we need to be proficient in all of them. As Gerald Weinberg has put it, we need to operate as *systems analysts/designers* (Weinberg, 1988). A collective term for these central activities, therefore, is **systems analysis and design**.

This chapter presents some methods for systems analysis and design. It starts by explaining the basic processes and how they fit together. It introduces the basic distinction between task-oriented and process-oriented approaches. The remainder of the chapter is devoted to some specific modelling and analysis techniques: task analysis, software systems analysis and user-participative design.

6.1.1   The processes of systems analysis and design

Although there are several different approaches to systems analysis and design, they all draw on the same set of fundamental design processes, and in this sense are not so very different from each other. As we look at each approach, we will find that it involves the following three activities:

- **Model building**, in which the data collected during user studies are analysed and incorporated in a model of users' activities, which can then act as a focal point for further analysis and for design;

- **Synthesis or enhancement of a solution** to support the activities depicted by the model;

- **Analysis of the solution** in terms of the model, in order to determine usability and identify needs for enhancement.

Chapter 4 has already introduced each of these processes. They are shown again diagrammatically in Figure 6.1.

The interlocking fashion in which the three processes contribute to design is shown in Figure 6.2. The basic cycle of design generates a series of gradually enhanced specifications, each one incorporating details and refinements derived from the analysis of its predecessor. At each step in this cycle, analyses are carried out with the aid of an activity model constructed from data gathered during studies. Each analysis involves making predictions of the likely performance of the solution; these predictions take the form of models of the system's usage, from which usability measurements can be taken.

One thing that takes time during interactive system design is the construction of models from data collected during studies. Therefore although we may cycle rapidly through a succession of possible solutions, we tend to reuse the same model. We may make small changes to the model to reflect the ways we think new technology will be used, but we try to retain its overall structure. Only when we find that the analysis is not giving us the answers we need will we try constructing a different kind of model. The choice of type of model is thus one of the more important decisions we make during the early stages of design and analysis.

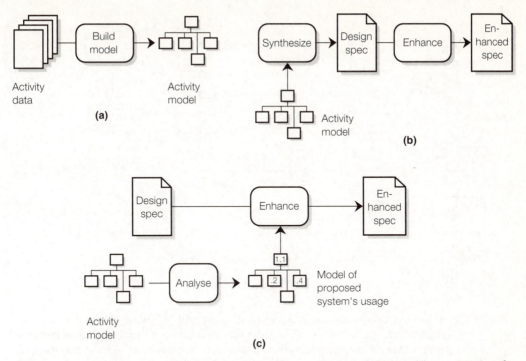

Figure 6.1   The three essential processes of systems analysis and design: (a) constructing the model of the user's activity, based on data from user studies; (b) synthesis of the solution and subsequent enhancement; (c) analysis and enhancement of the solution, using the activity model derived in (a).

6.1.2   The place of prototyping and evaluation

The central process of synthesis and gradual enhancement focuses on a representation of the interactive system. Usually this representation is a specification of the design, as shown in Figure 6.2.

It is not usually possible to test the design fully by analysing the specification; some aspects of usability can be measured only by building and testing a working system. Therefore a prototype is built according to the specification, and is tested in the field or in the laboratory. When the specification is enhanced, the prototype can be modified too, and tested again. This process of *evaluation*, shown in Figure 6.3, will be discussed in Chapter 8.

In the process of Figure 6.3, the specification is still the main representation of the design; but this isn't always the case. A common alternative is to build a prototype and treat *this* as a definition of the system. The design is enhanced principally by evaluating the prototype and making improvements to it. When the evaluation shows that the originally stated needs have been met, the prototype's design can be transformed into a

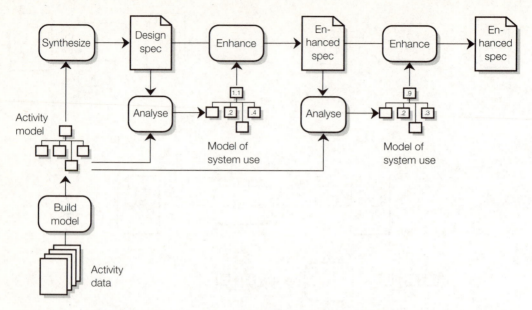

Figure 6.2   The three processes of systems analysis and design, showing their interconnections. Here the focus is on developing the specification through gradual enhancement. At each stage an analysis is performed, generating an activity model
predicting how the system will be used; from this model, usability measures can
be extracted to assist the next enhancement of the design. Analyses are based on
an underlying activity model constructed from data gathered during user studies.

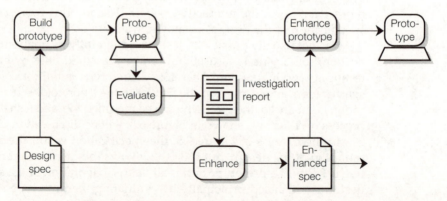

Figure 6.3   How prototypes are built, based on specifications, in order to evaluate in terms
of usability factors that cannot be measured through analysis. The evaluation
process is shown here in simplified form.

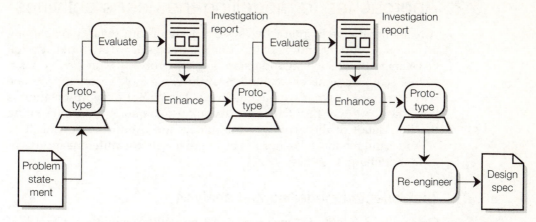

Figure 6.4 How the prototype itself can become the focal point of design. The specification is updated periodically to reflect enhancements to the prototype. As in Figure 6.3, a simplified form of evaluation is depicted here.

specification. This process is shown in Figure 6.4. It is sometimes known as the **rapid prototyping** approach.

The rapid prototyping approach was used in the development of the highly successful Lotus 1-2-3 spreadsheet product (see Figure 6.5). The Lotus team made sure that the prototype was engineered to product-quality standards, and in this way were able to ship the product on the pre-announced date, an unusual achievement at that time.

1-2-3 began with a working program, and it continued to be a working program throughout its development. I had an office in Hopkinton, where I lived at the time, and I came to the office about once a week, and brought in a new version. I fixed any bugs immediately in the next version. Also, people at Lotus were using the program continuously.

This was the exact opposite of the standard method for developing a big program, where you spend a lot of time and work up a functional spec, do a modular decomposition, give each piece to a bunch of people, and integrate the pieces when they're all done... In any case, our method meant that once we reached a certain point in the development, we could ship if we wanted to. The program may not have had all the features, but we knew it would work.

Figure 6.5 The prototype as the principal representation of the solution – the development of Lotus 1-2-3 as described by Jonathan Sachs in Lammers, 1986, pp. 166–7.

6.2   Approaches to modelling the user's activities

A recurring theme in interactive system design is our reliance on gaining an adequate understanding of the user's activities. If we attempt to design a system without such an understanding, we probably won't get very far. As we acquire the necessary understanding, we look for an appropriate way to represent what we have learned. The choice of representation is important. We will find that some techniques are suited to representing the fine detail of the activity, while others are useful in showing how activities interconnect. We need to be familiar with the different approaches to modelling.

6.2.1   Task-oriented modelling and analysis

One set of methods is concerned with modelling activities in terms of tasks, and is known widely as **task analysis**. To perform task analysis we generally confine the scope of the study to activities that relate to a particular overall goal, such as the goal of purchasing a rapid-transit ticket, discussed in Chapter 2 and revisited in the next section. We may deliberately ignore activities that don't relate directly to achieving the goal, such as buying a newspaper before or after buying the ticket, or talking to the counter clerk about the weather. By focusing on a specific user goal we can often build a fairly precise model of the user's activity; this in turn enables us to apply quite precise analysis methods.

6.2.2   Process-oriented methods

The other set of methods we shall discuss focuses beyond individual user goals: it includes methods for modelling sets of tasks, work processes and cooperation within groups of users. Some of these methods date back to before interactive computing became widespread; a general term for them is **systems analysis**. We shall use this term here in a broader sense than it is normally used, to apply to all methods of modelling and analysis that do not focus just on task performance. Several other writers have advocated the same broader view of systems analysis that we take here (Mumford, 1983; Weinberg, 1988).

6.2.3   Activity models, normative and descriptive

In the next few sections we shall be looking at a number of different ways of building and using models of human activity. These models vary not only in their choice of structures and abstractions, but also in whether they attempt to state what people normally do – the 'norm' – or describe what people have actually been observed to do. We call these two types of model **normative** and **descriptive**.

Table 6.1   Building a descriptive model of a task's performance (first two columns) and using a normative model to make speed predictions (last two columns).

Action	Observed time	Cognitive operation	Predicted time (secs)
–		mental preparation (before command)	1.35
NAME	4.12	4 keyboard characters	3.35
space	4.53	1 character	3.85
NEWMAN	7.07	6 characters	6.85
–		mental preparation (before confirming)	8.20
space	9.35	1 character	8.70
55	10.69	2 characters	9.70
–		mental preparation (before confirming)	11.05
RETURN	12.96	1 character	11.55
-	15.44	response time	14.05

A simple example of a normative model is the Keystroke-Level Model introduced in Chapter 3. It models the normal use of keystroke-level devices such as computer keyboards, and provides predictions of typical speeds of operation. It predicts, for example, that after we type a line of data we will pause for a second or two before confirming with a RETURN or ENTER key.

A descriptive model of keystroke-level behaviour could be built in order to describe a particular observed sequence, such as the entry by a doctor of patient details. We would record the doctor's actions, perhaps with the aid of video, and then map them onto the Keystroke-Level Model's set of operators. This sequence is shown in the two left-hand columns of Table 6.1.

We can also build normative models of specific cases; this is how we use models to make predictions about the use of specific system designs. Thus we could use the Keystroke-Level Model, as we did in Chapter 3, to predict the time taken by the doctor to record the patient's details. This is shown in the two right-hand columns of Table 6.1.

6.2.4   How we use models of activities

The way we often go about building and using models is shown in Figure 6.6. We start with a normative model, such as a simple sequential representation of the task. We conduct user studies in order to collect data, and then try to cast chosen sequences of data into descriptive models, in each case identifying the components and structure of the task. We look for a number of instances of each task so that we can check for consistency. We now have a general model of the activity, on which we can base predictions.

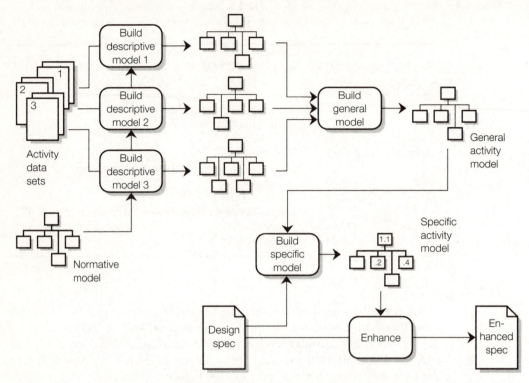

Figure 6.6 How we use models in design. Several descriptive models may be built from different sets of collected data, drawing on a normative model of human activity. These descriptive models are combined to form a general model of the observed data. This is then used to build a specific model of how the activity might be performed with the aid of the system.

During design, we use the general model to make predictions of the usability of specific solutions. We might start by modelling the system currently in use; this would tell us about possible areas for improvement. For example, we could generate keystroke-level models in order to estimate speed of operation. We could generate a series of these normative models as the design progressed. Each model would be based on the original general model.

We may also conduct evaluative tests on users to check the accuracy of our predictions. In other words, we may check our normative models against descriptive models based on observed behaviour. We may need to do this if it is crucial to achieve a certain level of usability improvement. This was done in the case of New England Telephone's design for a new telephone operator's workstation, after the normative models had suggested that the new workstation would be slower than the old one it was replacing. In this case the predictions were shown to be correct, and the new workstation was abandoned (Gray *et al.*, 1992).

6.3   Methods based on task models

The importance of task-level models lies in their support for detailed usability analysis. We depend especially on this kind of analysis when we design the user interface. If we can identify specific tasks that will figure frequently in the use of the system, we can build task models that permit predictions of performance to be made.

6.3.1   Hierarchic task models

Hierarchic task models are valuable in dealing with the variability in task performance and in supporting different levels of detail of analysis. Until now we have treated the performance of tasks as a simple sequence of steps. In hierarchic task representations, we divide tasks into **subtasks**, shorter sequences that serve an intermediate **subgoal** along the way to achieving the overall goal of the task. We can take this process of hierarchic subdivision to a succession of levels, thus modelling the task to a degree of detail that matches the analysis we wish to perform.

An example from Chapter 2 illustrates what is gained when task hierarchy is added. This is the example in Figure 2.8 of handling an order as a single task. It is shown again in Figure 6.7(a).

There are several intermediate subgoals in this task, brought out in Figure 6.7(b). The first three steps are concerned with the subgoal of checking the order to make sure it can be filled; if it cannot, for reasons of unavailibility or invalidity of the customer's credit card, then the remaining steps need not be performed. The next four steps have the subgoal of mailing the product, and the final two steps complete the task. The advantage of separating the task into subtasks is to allow the design of supporting systems to offer new ways of performing parts of the task; for example, we might devise a mechanical conveyor system to assist in fetching and mailing the product.

Figure 6.7(c) shows one of the subtasks, 'credit-card check', expanded to show more detail. It shows, for example, the 'request validation' subtask broken down into individual keystrokes. A detailed model of this kind would enable precise performance analysis. It also shows that there are alternative subtasks, 'notify acceptance' and 'notify rejection', one or other of which is to be performed depending on the outcome of the 'request validation' subtask.

The indication of variable steps and sequences is an essential part of task modelling, for there is always a degree of variation in the way tasks are performed. Hierarchic task diagrams sometimes indicate the sequence, so that variability is made plain to anyone using the model. This technique, pioneered in the notation of Hierarchic Task Analysis (Annett and Duncan, 1967), is shown in Figure 6.8.

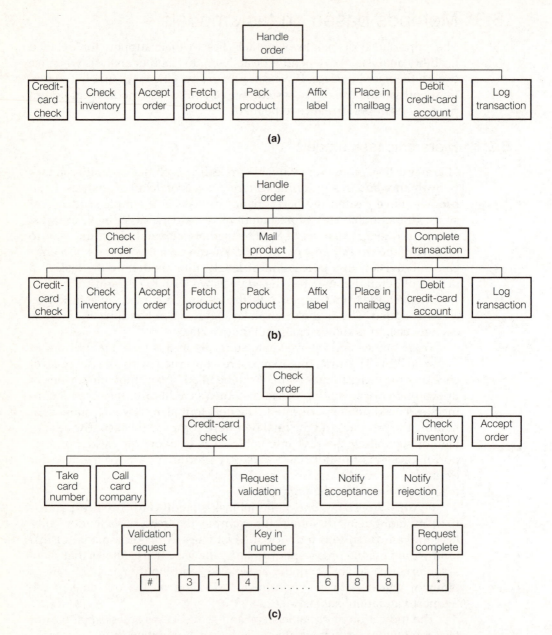

Figure 6.7   Representing the mail-order task: (a) the simple task sequence as shown in
Figure 2.8; (b) the task divided into three main subtasks; (c) detail of the 'check
order' subtask, showing individual keystrokes and alternative steps.

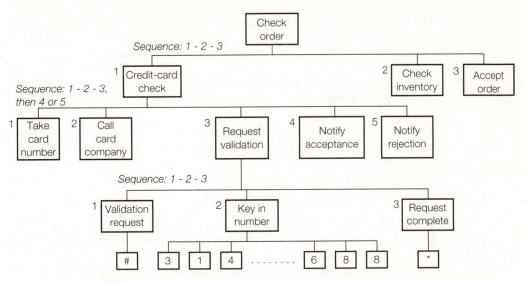

Figure 6.8   Using the technique of Hierarchic Task Analysis to label a task model with descriptions of sequences.

6.3.2   Analysing the task model

A hierarchic task model can yield information of many kinds during analysis. In system design, we are often interested in the efficiency with which tasks are performed; the task model enables us to make predictions about the speed with which variants of the same task will be performed. We can see how individual actions and subtasks contribute to the overall goal and identify time-consuming sequences that appear to make little contribution. We can judge whether the sequence of steps is well suited to the chosen system design, and possibly devise a different set of steps that improves performance. We may perform analyses for other purposes, e.g., to help develop training manuals; some of these applications of task analysis are discussed in Diaper (1989a).

We often use task models in situations where the exact sequence of steps is uncertain. In these cases, we don't rely on the model to give us guaranteed performance figures; rather we use it in making *comparative* predictions. We choose a possible sequence of steps, and make predictions of the performance of different support systems. In this way we can use task models even when the method of use is quite uncertain.

6.4   Task analysis and design: An example

The problem of designing a rapid-transit ticket dispensing machine, introduced in Chapter 2, provides an opportunity to apply task analysis. In Chapter 2 we arrived at a one-sentence problem statement:

> Design a cash-operated machine for quick, easy purchase of rapid-transit tickets by passengers.

Let us look at how we apply simple methods of task analysis and design to this problem. We will take the design through two iterations of the design cycle.

6.4.1   First attempt: Studying the activity

Before entering the stages of systems analysis and design, let us review how we might conduct the user study. We would undoubtedly want to focus primarily on how people purchase tickets. We could spend an hour or two at a station ticket counter, observing and recording the sequence of steps in each purchase. A more efficient method might be to videotape the transactions, but this would involve getting the approval of counter clerks and travellers. We might want to confirm the model by observing the activity performed under other circumstances – the most obvious being the use of existing ticket machines.

6.4.2   Modelling the activity

This study might suggest a task model based on the following five steps:

- Stating the destination
- Specifying the journey type, e.g., one-way or round trip
- Receiving a quoted fare, e.g., $6.25
- Paying the money
- Receiving the ticket and any change due.

We can see immediately that there is an intermediate subgoal of determining the fare. Rather than build a simple two-level model, therefore, we would represent this subgoal as part of a three-level model, shown in Figure 6.9.

6.4.3   Synthesizing an initial solution

The task model is useful in the initial stages of synthesizing a form of solution. We might be inclined to propose a simple five-step machine, requiring the user always to perform the same actions: choose a

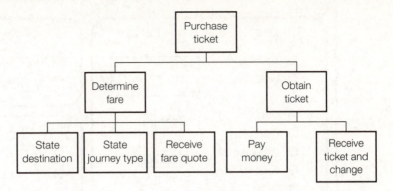

Figure 6.9   A three-level hierarchic task model of the ticket-purchase activity.

destination, choose a journey type, receive a fare quote, pay money, and take the ticket and change.

However, the task model consists of two subtasks, and poses a question: are both subtasks performed every time? If not, should the machine support one without the other? We may decide the answer is, yes – regular travellers need to perform only the second subtask because they know the fare. Furthermore, travellers who are uncertain of their plans may just want a fare quote, not a ticket.

The machine still needs to support the complete ticket-purchase task, but we have identified a possible functional requirement to support fare-quotation and purchase separately. This leads us to propose a solution that contains, in effect, two interconnected machines:

(1)   **A fare-quoting machine** supporting the following steps:

(a) **Specify journey** by specifying destination and journey type.

(b) **Receive fare quote** and retain essential details for ticket purchase, e.g., fare and journey type.

(2)   **A ticket-dispensing machine** supporting the following steps:

(a) **State essential details**, for example, fare and journey type (this step may be omitted if a fare quote has already been given).

(b) **Pay money**.

(c) **Receive ticket and change**.

This might lead to a solution of the form shown in Figure 6.10. The panel on the left provides buttons for indicating the destination, and has a display to show the fare quote and a keypad for entering the fare. On the right are buttons for indicating journey type, slots for inserting money, and a button to print the ticket and return change.

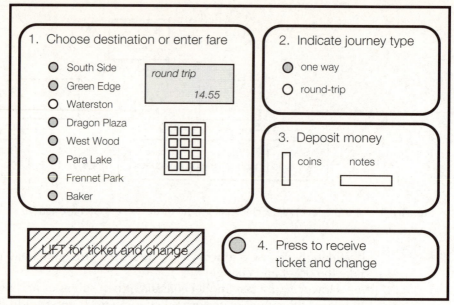

Figure 6.10   Rapid-transit ticket-purchase machine.

6.4.4 Specifying the initial solution

Once we feel confident that we have an initial solution to the problem, we will want to write it down in the form of a specification. One of the first things we need to specify is the set of **requirements** that the ticket machine is to meet. Requirements define what is to be designed and built; their purpose is to make it clear that the originally stated need will be met (that is, the situation of concern will be resolved), and to ensure that the designer understands how to proceed with the design. A preliminary set of requirements, covering just the essential functions of the ticket machine, might read as follows:

(1) A means should be provided for choosing the destination station.

(2) Means should be provided for entering the fare, rather than the destination, if this is known.

(3) A means of choosing the journey type should be provided.

(4) Means should be provided for insertion of coins and bills.

(5) Provision for printing the ticket.

(6) A hopper should be provided to receive the ticket and change.

This set of requirements would not be sufficient to perform any real analysis of the design. It would need to be supplemented with details of the user interface, e.g., by providing a drawing as shown in Figure 6.10. The next chapter will take up the subject of requirements, discuss how they are documented, and explain more fully the role they play in design.

6.4.5   Analysing the initial solution

A design such as this would undergo many cycles of analysis or testing, followed by enhancement and revision of the specification. At this stage, it is worth noting two simple forms of analysis we might apply.

One question we might wish to answer is, how easily will passengers learn to use the machine? Will they be able to master it at the first attempt, under the time pressures of catching a train? To answer these kinds of questions we would use analysis techniques based on the theory of exploratory learning, described in Chapter 3 and restated in Figure 6.11. We would step through the performance of each task that passengers are likely to perform. We would check whether they are likely to discover the appropriate action to perform (step 2 in Figure 6.11); whether they would perceive a match between the discovered action and the subgoal they are trying to achieve (step 3); and whether they will be able to tell that they have performed a correct or incorrect action (step 4).

Another important form of analysis to perform is to check the speed of operation of the machine by experienced travellers. This analysis could be conducted by building a more detailed task model and applying a keystroke-level analysis technique. We would probably then discover that keying-in the fare is somewhat slower than choosing the destination, for it involves pressing several keys instead of one button. Such a result might cause us to question the requirement for a keypad which, after all, has been included to save time!

Techniques for conducting these two kinds of detailed analysis are described in Chapter 8.

1   **Goal setting.** Users start with a rough description of what they want to accomplish – a task.

2   **Exploration.** Users explore the system's interface to discover actions useful in accomplishing their current task.

3   **Selection.** Users select actions that they think will accomplish their current task, often based on a match between what they are trying to do and the interface's descriptions of actions.

4   **Assessment.** Users assess progress by trying to understand system responses, thus deciding whether the action they have just performed was the correct one and to obtain clues for the next correct action.

Figure 6.11   The elements of the theory of exploratory learning, from Chapter 3.

6.5 Systems analysis methods

The term *systems analysis* can be applied to any method of model-building and analysis that contributes to system design as a whole. We commonly associate the term with the requirements-analysis methods used in the software applications industry. In the next section we will look briefly at the core component of these methods, *software systems analysis*. If we are concerned with the interactive properties of the system, however, we need to apply other methods, often in conjunction with software systems analysis. Section 6.7 therefore looks at methods of relating system designs more directly to users' needs, by ensuring that users participate in the analysis and design.

6.5.1 The need for systems analysis

The need for systems analysis arises whenever the scope of study extends beyond simple tasks. It arises, for example, when we start looking at processes consisting of a collection of separate tasks, spaced out over a period of time. An example of such a process might be a journalist's search for material to form an article. The journalist needs a *system* to support this process, capable of retaining and organizing each piece of information gathered.

The need for systems analysis also arises when we need to support a group of users, because a system will be needed to organize support for their separate activities. In particular, when the scope of study extends to cover entire organizations, systems analysis techniques play an essential role. Thus it is the expansion of the activity in these two dimensions – time and user population – that creates the need for systems analysis.

6.5.2 Viewpoints

We can build a variety of different kinds of models to support systems analysis. The particular kind of model we choose depends, to a large extent, on the *view* we take of the environment into which the system is being introduced, and of the technology from which the system is to be constructed.

A traditional view of systems is to treat them in terms of the *data* that flow through them and are transformed by them. This view underlies many of the techniques in software systems analysis. Often it is coupled with modelling the processing steps by which the data are transformed, and the functional units that perform transformations at various stages in the processes. More recently, software designers have begun to take an *object-oriented* view of systems. According to this view, the system's functions are regarded less in terms of processing and more in terms of the collections of data, or objects, to which they apply.

In contrast to these viewpoints, which show the influence of the underlying software technology, are views influenced more by the nature of users' activities. The task viewpoint is one of these, and has already been discussed. We can also view activities in terms of work processes, roles, responsibilities, stakeholdings, and various other factors that organize or motivate people's activity. The sociological analysis concepts introduced in Section 3.6 offer an example of one particular viewpoint on users' activities.

6.6   Software systems analysis

On the grounds that computers primarily process data and transform them into information, we can take the view that the system we design is a data processing system, and the methods we use should focus on users' needs relating to data. This is by far the most common view taken by the developers of software applications. A wide variety of methods have been developed over the years, and a number of different names have been applied to them, including *systems analysis*, *software requirements analysis* and *software systems analysis*; we will use the last of these three.

Software systems analysis methods are very effective in some respects, as we shall see. They help to ensure a thorough, methodical approach to system design, and thus contribute to the integrity and reliability of the system (Davis, 1990). Their other great attraction is the way they help in *costing the software's development* by helping to break it down into recognizable modules. A number of these methods have been incorporated in computer-based tools (otherwise known as *CASE tools*, for Computer Assisted Software Engineering), which have made the methods more easily accessible to designers. However, the focus of these methods on handling data rather than supporting users' activities can be a problem when designing the interactive aspects of systems.

6.6.1   Data modelling

The primary focus of methods in software systems analysis is on modelling data: their flow, their interrelationships, their different forms. We build a model of the way data are used within the organizational unit we are studying. This is usually done stage by stage, adding detail as we go.

We will look at a particular approach to data modelling which focuses on *data flow*, identifying the places where data are processed or stored and the interconnecting paths along which the data flow. In data-flow modelling we try to represent the organization's needs in terms of processing and storage components and their data inputs and outputs. We connect these together, first as we observe things being done at present, and then as we perceive they could be done in the future. We represent these structures diagrammatically, using what are commonly known as *data-flow diagrams* or DFDs.

6.6.2   Data-flow diagrams

Figure 6.12 shows a data-flow diagram based on the mail-order example of Figure 2.6. By convention, complete entities (for example, organizations) are shown as boxes, individual processes are shown as circles, data stores are shown as pairs of parallel lines, and data flows are shown by arrows. In Figure 6.12(a) we see the entire organization shown as a single process, while in Figure 6.12(b) we see it expanded into its major processing units. We can see that the analysis has led to the identification of additional databases not shown in Figure 2.6, such as product data and pending orders, and has grouped some of the tasks together.

We build data-flow diagrams from the results of our studies. We start by determining the organization's inputs and outputs from and to the external world, perhaps learning about these from our interviews with senior management. Then we follow the progress of the inputs through the organization, and the creation of outputs. Information about these comes from further interviews with those responsible for specific processes. For example, Figure 6.12(b) might be constructed on the basis of interviews with people in order-processing, shipping and accounting.

After the basic processes of the organization have been added to the data-flow diagram, each process can be expanded in detail. This may be useful later, when analysing opportunities to redesign the organization's processes.

Data-flow diagrams do not provide a complete description of the information system. They need to be supplemented with details of the data themselves; for example, in the wholesaler example we would want to find out about the contents of the various databases and represent how the data are stored. Techniques such as *entity-relation diagrams* may be used for this; they are described in Sommerville (1994).

6.6.3   Analysis

The main use of models such as data-flow diagrams is to examine their functional behaviour, that is, to determine whether the system they represent will process data correctly and efficiently. We inspect each of the functional units of the diagram, looking for possible sources of error or inefficiency, such as inputs that provide insufficient data for outputs. As in any kind of systems analysis and design, functional analysis can be applied both to the existing system and to new designs for computer support.

A second form of analysis is, as we have seen, analysis of development cost. If we can reduce the system to a set of relatively standard modules, we can make estimates of the amount of effort involved in their design and implementation. Sophisticated models and tools exist for software development cost-estimating (Boehm, 1981).

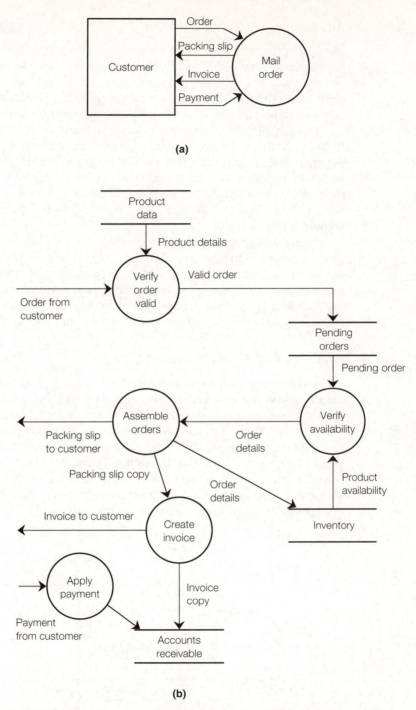

(a)

(b)

Figure 6.12   Data-flow diagrams for the mail-order operation of Figure 2.6: (a) the entire operation shown as one process, (b) each process within the organization shown separately.

An example: The Commission

We will shift our focus to an example at this stage. It concerns a large international financial institution, which we will call *The Commission*. This example will be useful later in studying participative design methods and contrasting them with software systems analysis. We will also refer to this example in our discussion of requirements definition in the next chapter.

The role of the Commission is to make loans to its member countries. It has a Board of Directors who approve these loans, a President who manages the organization and presides over meetings of the Board, and teams of economists who conduct missions to member countries and make recommendations to the Board for loans. On the basis of interviews with senior Commission staff we might draw the data-flow diagram shown in Figure 6.13.

Figure 6.14 shows an expansion of this simple diagram into a diagram of the Commission's main functions: collecting background data while not on mission, conducting missions, preparing recommendations (all of these performed by teams of economists), approval of recommendations (by the Board), gaining acceptance of loan offers (by the Commission's Secretary) and servicing of the loan (by the Commission's Treasurer).

6.6.4 Analysis of the Commission study

What would the diagram of Figure 6.14 suggest as a focus of analysis? One possible focus might be the *member-country database*, because this clearly plays a central part in the Commission's operations. We might therefore conduct interviews with the economists who maintain the database and who draw on it when preparing recommendations for loans. We would then be able to define the essential components of the database and compare this definition with the actual databases in use. We might find that economists were using a variety of informal databases, such as files of correspondence, newspaper articles and tables.

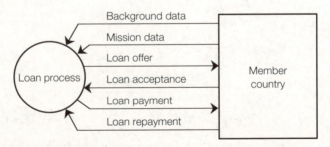

Figure 6.13 Data-flow diagram describing the overall flows between the Commission and a member country.

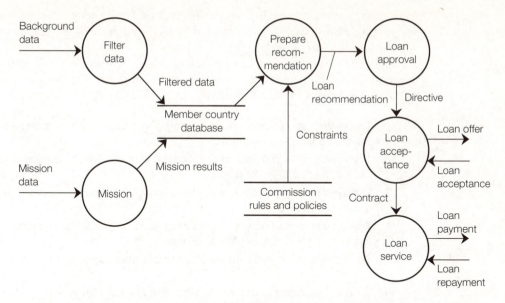

Figure 6.14   First-level data-flow diagram for the Commission, showing basic functional processes, and inputs and outputs from and to the member country.

These kinds of findings can pave the way for design and further analysis. We can start to devise more efficient ways of storing the financial data as they are collected and of accessing them when recommendations are drawn up. In conjunction with this, we may look for ways to design support systems for the other processes and databases of the Commission, thus working gradually towards a new model for the design of a future system.

6.6.5   Allocating functions from the system model

By focusing attention on software modelling, software systems analysis helps us to build a **system model**, that is, an abstract model of how the processing, storage and communication components of the system fit together. This model is crucial to understanding how the system will be built and how it will behave under various operating conditions.

However, we cannot afford to ignore the interactive components of the design. If we have arrived at a system model by means of software systems analysis, we need to know how it affects the user's activities. We need to match the system up with an appropriate set of user roles. This involves deciding which components in the system model will involve user activity and which are to be automated.

In the case of the Commission system, we might decide to automate the *loan service* function and distribute the remainder among the Commission's staff. In other words, functions such as *filter data* and *prepare recommendation* will become interactive functions of the system, supporting people carrying out related tasks. Some functions, such as the *mission* function, may remain purely manual.

Allocation of function is one route towards identifying the interactive functions of the system and the user roles it will support. Via this route we might, for example, be able to identify the main external functions:

(1) The system should support the filtering of economic data for storage in the member country-database.

(2) The system should allow data collected during missions to be added to the member country-database.

(3) The system should provide a source of data for the preparation of loan recommendations.

(4) The system should support the administration of loans, including the approval, offer and acceptance stages.

(5) The system should be capable of automatic loan payment servicing.

We would be making the first steps towards drawing up a set of *requirements* for the system. In the next chapter we will look at requirements definition at greater length.

While it simplifies the task of analysing the technical design, this kind of focus on the system model may make the definition of user roles and

---

The approach carried several assumptions, which were not fully recognized until much later (Jordan, 1968). It seemed to imply that human and machine were competing for functions; if they were, the machine was bound to win. Only those functions that could conceivably be fulfilled by a machine appeared in the listing [of functions], since the question of the allocation of function to human or machine does not otherwise arise. The onward march of technology ensured that more and more functions became at first feasible and, ultimately, more efficient for a machine to fulfil. The approach also implied that the residual human functions were not chosen because they were well-matched to human capabilities and limitations but were incurred by the human because a machine could not be devised to cope with them.

In this approach, the allocation of functions had to be discussed using concepts and a language applicable to machines. Certain human attributes with no apparent machine equivalents, such as job satisfaction, self-esteem, pride in exercising hard-won skills, and a dislike of enforced idleness, thus tended to have little influence on the allocation of functions between human and machine. Another implication of the approach was the notion that every function that can be defined can be fulfilled somehow; the idea that certain functions should be avoided altogether was not seriously entertained.

Figure 6.15   A discussion of some of the drawbacks of designing systems by allocating functions from a list between human and system. From Hopkin (1988).

activities harder. The drawbacks of the function-allocation approach are discussed by Hopkin (1988) and some of his strongest points are reproduced in Figure 6.15. He notes in particular that the approach leads to focusing attention towards functions that systems can carry out, and away from important human attributes such as job satisfaction. He points out the tendency for function allocation to lead to use of technical language as the language of design. These are some of the reasons why we need to introduce other viewpoints when we design interactive systems. The next section describes the participative design viewpoint and explains how it helps to address some of the points made by Hopkin.

6.7 User-participative methods

The methods we will be discussing here originated in socio-technical research in the early post-Second World War period (Emery and Trist, 1960). They gained greater prominence in the 1980s, when several Scandinavian countries enacted legislation requiring employers to involve workers in any decisions that might affect their conditions of work. The new laws covered decisions relating to the introduction of new computer-based systems, and this led to the participation of prospective users in these systems' design. The results were very positive: not only were users more satisfied with the systems they helped to design, but the actual design process appeared to go better. News of these experiments spread, and led to the establishment of *user-participative methods* (sometimes known as *participatory design*) as a recognized way of understanding users' needs and feeding this understanding into design. In this section we will look briefly at user-participative methods and illustrate their use by extending the example of the Commission.

6.7.1 The method in outline

User-participative methods address the same basic issues as the other methods we have covered: they involve study, model-building and analysis; the analysis covers both new and potential future systems. However, the way in which these stages are carried out is very different; they are built into an overall team process whose description here is based on Mumford (1983) and Greenbaum and Kyng (1991):

- **Selection of participants.** The first step is to form the design team. User members of the team should be representative of the whole user community. If the intention is to introduce a departmental support system, for example, then people should be drawn from across the department. Difficulties may arise if the system has a very large potential user community, such as an entire organization, because it is hard then to select a truly representative group. The actual selection of the team members is often better left to the users themselves to avoid the impression that management is selecting 'cooperative' users.

- **Training**. Training is important, not so much to educate the user members to be qualified designers, but to enable them to *feel* qualified. Once the team has been selected, therefore, their training begins. This involves all of the team members, including the user participants, thus ensuring that they share as much common background as possible. Training will usually be organized into an informal workshop, with talks and discussions on a range of topics surrounding the subject matter of design.

- **Facilitation** by a specially designated member of the team is often necessary to manage the dynamics of the design team. When end users are teamed up with computer system designers, the latter tend to intimidate the former. A system designer, being one of 'them', cannot usually facilitate the team meetings; an independent facilitator needs to perform this task and make sure that the end users have an equal say.

- **Tools and techniques** employed during meetings need to be designed with users' participation in mind. End users cannot, as a rule, write computer programs. They need tools that allow them to model aspects of the design and carry out simulations. These tools should not place the end user at a disadvantage in relation to other team members. The tools should not be highly abstract, for example, since end users are often very practical people with relatively little experience of abstract work.

How does such a process cover the essential elements of study, model-building and analysis? For a start, **study** takes place during the meetings themselves: users provide descriptions of their work practices to other team members. **Modelling** may take several forms: for example, work practices may be modelled in the form of *scenarios*, that is, detailed descriptions of actual tasks and processes taken from real life. The team may also build models of solutions, or *envisionments*, using various techniques for mocking up and simulating the real thing. Simple materials such as cardboard and felt pens may be used, or it may be possible to make simple videos. Finally, **analysis** is conducted by all members of the team: users analyse scenarios and solutions in terms of their own experience, while others may apply more formal techniques such as task analysis.

The team needs techniques for exploring innovative solutions lying beyond those easily mocked up with cardboard, pens and video. This is one of the major difficulties in participative design: software designers can perceive opportunities for innovation, but cannot explain them to end users. In these situations, it may be appropriate for a programmer to be asked to build a prototype. The team must be as explicit as possible about the questions that the prototype is to answer.

Finally, we need to recognize the difficulties faced by end users in devoting time to participative design. Their contributions may not receive very much recognition from their management. Meanwhile their normal work must be done; their frequent absence at design meetings makes this difficult. Participative design works best when end users are released from their other responsibilities for the duration of the time they spend on the project.

6.7.2   Participative design at the Commission

We will look at how user-participative methods might be applied at the Commission. These methods could be applied organization-wide, but for the sake of simplicity we will look at a smaller-scale exercise. This focuses on making sure that a shared database, to be introduced as a result of the software systems analysis described above, will address the needs and concerns of a specific 'pilot group' of users. This group has been selected expressly to help spearhead the introduction of the new system. It includes a number of people from different levels of the organization, all of them concerned with countries of the former Soviet Union – the self-styled 'FSU Group'.

Getting started

How do we get participative design under way at the Commission? We form a design team: two senior economists of the FSU Group, two junior 'desk officer' economists from the same group, two designers, a software developer and a facilitator. These eight people constitute a comfortably sized group; it is not too difficult to convene meetings at the odd times when the economists are free from their other duties. We hold a preliminary workshop to go over some of the basic issues in designing with new technology: interaction techniques, usability, software development costs.

We start the design sessions proper with a discussion of possible scenarios to incorporate in a model of economists' work practices. One task that keeps coming up in this discussion, and that we therefore choose as a scenario, is the constant need for information at short notice in preparation for informal meetings with delegates from FSU countries. This becomes known as the 'PCN scenario', for 'pre-contact note'. Figure 6.16 shows how the scenario is described.

Envisioning the PCN system

We move on to discussing how PCNs might be handled with the aid of the new database. There is enthusiasm for the rapid access it will offer to economic data. The team agrees to try to envision what form this access will take.

To create an envisionment, we get hold of some recently prepared PCNs, and mock up the appearance of a computer screen to show how

Scenario for the Pre-Contact Note (PCN), as described by a senior econo-mist:

We get a call from the Public Relations department to say that this high-level official from the Ukraine, Dr Lvov, is due in town next week and wants a meeting. I get assigned to meet with him, and I need to know the latest on the Ukraine's energy crisis. I'm also aware that the Commission has some new export figures, but I don't know the details.

The standard procedure is to request a pre-contact note, or PCN as we call it. There's a desk officer assigned to each of the countries we deal with, and my PA sends this desk officer – Julie Smart her name is – a PCN request, mentioning who the visitor is and when he's visiting. Julie will usually have the PCN back on my desk within forty-eight hours, certainly no later than the day before the meeting. It's usually about three pages long – if it's any longer, I may not have time to read it.

The procedure works well most of the time, but sometimes it breaks down because the desk officer is away on a mission. Then somebody else has to put the note together for her. I've never known the procedure to fail altogether, but things have got a bit hairy at times.

Figure 6.16   A scenario developed in the course of user-participative design at the Commission.

the information might be accessed directly from the database. We use a computer-based tool to create some realistic images (Figure 6.17). At the next meeting these envisionments are circulated to the team. They generate some important sharing of concerns.

Gaining a model of the PCN process
The envisionment of the use of the database triggers some remarks from the junior economists about the feasibility of keeping PCN information

```
> topics
countries policy missions programmes
> policy
FSU-policy-revision-08-13-94
FSU-revised-policy-10-10-94
FSU-policy-minutes-10-27-94
Russian-policy-plan-06-23-94
Russian-policy-plan-06-23-94
Russia-in-2000-07-04-94
Ukraine-policy-04-18-94
> FSU-restructing-95-08-08-94
fetching documemt, please wait...
```

```
              Pre-contact Note
   FSU restructuring policy, 1995-96
   J. Smart, FSU Dept. 8 August 1994

Executive summary
New policy guidelines for FSU
countries were drafted in June and
are currently under consideration
by the Board. They would lead to
easing of loan conditions for FSU
countries complying with the
following broad conditions:
```

Figure 6.17   Envisionments of the screen-based PCN.

online. They raise a number of problems, but keep returning to two particular aspects of the PCN process: the limited timespan during which
data remain valid, and the need to interpret the data according to the
nature of the PCN request.

As one of the junior economists puts it, 'You've got to realize, these
kinds of figures have a half-life of a month or less. When you're putting
together a PCN, your main worry is where to get your data, *any* data that
are sufficiently recent. My worry would be that the database will be full
of numbers well past their sell-by dates.'

The other economist points out that PCNs contain more than just data –
there's an accompanying narrative that helps the reader to interpret the data.
'You don't just type up the figures. You look at who's asking for them, and
why. OK, Dr Lvov's in town, the energy minister. Our figures for energy consumption are out of date. We'll need to add a note to this effect, and include
some indicators on recent consumption trends. On the other hand, if their
banking chief, Glasov, were visiting, we'd need to add some background
about reserve levels. These interpretations are what make PCNs work.'

In the course of these discussions we begin to construct a model of the
PCN process. We can see that it involves collecting up-to-date information, and that this information needs interpretation according to the
nature of the contact. By the end of the discussion, our model of the PCN
process has grown to be quite extensive. We are able to formulate the
problem as follows:

> Design a means of providing immediate economic updates, based on stored
> data, that reflect the recency of the data and the need for interpretation.

Devising a solution: The Economic Update

After several more meetings, we arrive collectively at a solution strategy.
Rather than have the economists access the database directly, we will set
up a system of *economic updates* or EUs, which provide pointers to recent
data about member countries, together with general guidance on how to
interpret them. These EUs cannot take the place of PCNs, with their up-
to-the-minute data and highly specific interpretation. However, they can
provide the nucleus of each PCN. Junior economists won't need to write
every update from scratch; they'll be able to use the latest economic
update, and annotate it with more recent data and with their own interpretations and advice. When all else fails, the EUs can serve on their own
to provide limited update information prior to contacts.

One idea, crucial to the design of EUs, comes from a suggestion by a
junior economist. Why not use the 'hot link' feature found in spreadsheet
packages? This feature allows a link to be made from one part of a spreadsheet to another, in such a way that changes in the latter will immediately be shown in the former. The 'hot link' concept can be incorporated into
EUs so that they always show the current entries in the shared database.

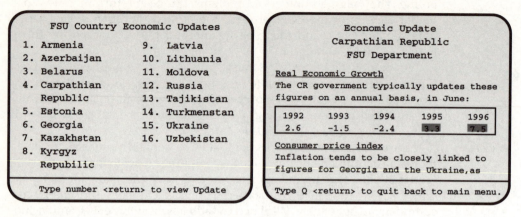

Figure 6.18   An envisionment of a screen-based Economic Update.

A second idea, proposed by one of the other economists to take account of the age and reliability of some of the shared data, is the introduction of 'flags' on items of data to indicate how recent and reliable they are. Showing an item in boldface flags it as reliable; shading its background shows that it may be out of date. Figure 6.18 shows a mock-up of an EU as envisioned by the team.

Specifying the Economic Update system

The team decides, therefore, to recommend that a prototype of the EU system be built and introduced as a pilot system. A preliminary set of requirements are drawn up, as shown in Figure 6.19.

This specification is by no means the last word on the system's requirement; indeed we are still many months from completing the design. The prototype must be tested, reactions must be collected from users, meetings held to hear users' views and suggestions, and another design iteration got under way. However, by the end of the exercise we have a design that we can confidently expect to be well received by the users.

6.7.3   User-participative methods: Pros and cons

User-participative methods are generally better than software systems analysis at dealing with the interactive aspects of system design. They are more effective in gathering data about the activities to be supported, they generate more accurate models of the activities as a result, and the analysis of designs is more 'real' because it is carried out by the users themselves. Finally, when the system is introduced, users are more likely to accept it on its merits, rather than treat it as something imposed upon them.

User-participative methods are not without their limitations, however. They are best suited to in-house development, and least suited to a

1   The system should support the preparation of Economic Updates (EUs) based on the contents of the Shared Database.

2   An EU should consist of one or more extracts from the Shared Database, together with explanatory text narrative.

3   It should be possible to prepare EUs, and include database extracts, with the aid of the standard word processing package used in the Commission.

4   There should be a means of indicating the reliability of items in the extracts.

5   There should be a means of indicating how recently the item has been updated in the database from which it was extracted.

6   The system should support the electronic retrieval of EUs on users' workstations.

7   The data shown in EUs should be extracted from the database at the time of retrieving the EU.

8   EUs should be arranged in directories, one directory per member country, containing EUs on the major sectors of the country's economy.

9   There should be means for those preparing or updating an EU to copy it into the appropriate directory.

10   There should be means for a system administrator to maintain the directories and expunge obsolete EUs.

11   A support team should be set up to provide assistance to those preparing and retrieving EUs.

12   Training courses in EU preparation and retrieval should be provided.

Figure 6.19   An initial set of requirements for the Economic Update system.

product development context, as Grudin has explained (Grudin, 1992). They run up against the usual problems with user involvement, problems of confidentiality and representativeness. Also, the outcome of user participation can be affected by limits to users' understanding: by difficulties in dealing with advanced-technology solutions, and by their lack of facility with analytical tools. Like any approach to systems analysis and design, participative methods need to be reserved for the kinds of problems that can make good use of them.

6.8 Summary

This chapter has covered some issues central to the design of interactive systems. It has taken the story, begun in Chapter 2, from the stage of preparation of a problem statement to a point where the solution is beginning to take shape.

The main purpose of this chapter has been to explain how analysis contributes to design, and how the two complementary activities – analysis and synthesis – can be coordinated successfully. As we have seen, there is no single method for doing this. The choice of method will depend in part on the scope of the human activity to be supported; supporting a single task demands a different approach from supporting one or more processes. Within the domain of designing for process support there are several methods of systems analysis and design, including software systems analysis and participative design.

As the illustrative cases have shown, systems analysis and design assists in defining the solution. An important stage in definition is the specification of *requirements*, for these play an important role in linking the solution back to the original objectives of design, and onwards towards design and implementation. We have seen two preliminary examples of sets of requirements. The next chapter focuses more specifically on the roles requirements play in interactive system design.

Exercises

(1) Explain the main differences between (a) task analysis and systems analysis, (b) software systems analysis and participative design.

(2) What are (a) descriptive models; (b) normative models? Provide examples, such as models of reading a newspaper, placing a collect call.

(3) Build a task model of using an ATM to check your account balance and withdraw $50 in cash.

(4) Build a task model of setting a digital clock and alarm after the settings have been lost due to unplugging it.

(5) Build a task model of using a microwave oven.

(6) Observe an actual ticket counter at a station, and build task models to describe some of the transactions that take place.

(7) Extend the data-flow diagram of Figure 6.12(b), (a) to allow customer details to be kept in a database, (b) to take account of items being out of stock.

(8) Figure 6.14 suggests other places to focus design attention besides the member-country database. What are they? Discuss how you might organize studies and design in these areas.

(9) What systems do you know of that exhibit the features described in Figure 6.15?

(10) You are embarking on a redesign of a mail-order company's information system. Describe how you would organize a participative design exercise to conduct the systems analysis and design.

Further reading

Card S. K., Moran T. P. and Newell A. (1983). *The Psychology of Human Computer Interaction*. Hillsdale, NJ: Lawrence Erlbaum Associates

Chapter 12 of this classic book includes seven pages of 'advice to the designer' that amount to a principled approach to task analysis.

Kendall K. E. and Kendall J. E. (1992). *Systems Analysis and Design*. Englewood Cliffs, NJ: Prentice-Hall

Includes detailed examples of data-flow modelling.

Sommerville I. (1992). *Software Engineering*, 4th edn. Wokingham: Addison-Wesley

Includes some introductory material on data-flow modelling.

Weinberg G.M. (1988). *Rethinking Systems Analysis and Design*. New York: Dorset House

A refreshing and entertaining rethink of many of the concepts of software engineering and design, based on the essential point that systems analysis and design cannot be treated separately but must be tightly integrated.

CHAPTER 7

Requirements definition

Chapter objectives:

A set of requirements defines the system that is to be designed, built and put into service. It helps answer questions such as, 'Will this system provide adequate support to users?' and 'How can it be built?' In this chapter we cover:

- Who reads requirements documents
- How requirements are used during validation and verification
- The role of requirements in defining a usable functional form
- How a set of requirements is gradually refined
- Validation of requirements by analytical methods and by prototype testing.

7.1 Introduction

The preceding chapters have viewed interactive system design in terms of the studies and analyses that contribute to it. In this chapter we will take a different point of view, and track the development of the *specification*, a process shown in Figure 7.1. We will focus on a particular 'watershed' specification that defines the *requirements* that the system is to meet, and that enables us to keep the design on track towards resolving the situation of concern.

Whenever something is designed there is a preliminary task of defining the requirements that are to be met. Requirements definition is always

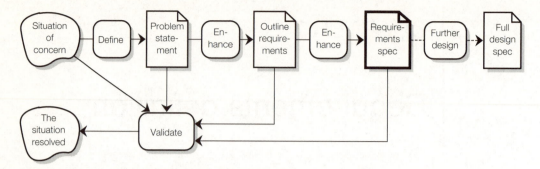

Figure 7.1   The development of the specification. The requirements document retains a direct link with the original situation of concern. Beyond this point it serves as a reference document for design.

an important task, for it helps to ensure that the outcome does indeed solve the original design problem. It is a task normally considered to precede the design activity itself. We can therefore adopt the viewpoint of a system designer who receives a set of requirements, and ask ouselves what role they might play in design, and how they might help. These questions are addressed in the first part of this chapter.

It is important also to look at how requirements themselves are defined. This is the focus of the remainder of the chapter. There are aspects of interactive system requirements that demand special treatment in order to ensure the levels of usability that users need. These aspects make it quite hard to separate requirements definition from interactive system design. By the end of this chapter we will see that it is often necessary to design, build and evaluate a working prototype in order to define the requirements that interactive systems must meet. It is necessary to engage in many aspects of interactive system design in the process of defining the system's requirements.

7.2 How requirements serve design

Requirements define what is to be designed, built and put into service. Their role is to do so in such as way as to demonstrate that the defined needs will be met (that is, that the initial situation of concern will be resolved) while making it clear how the design and implementation can be achieved.

Requirements provide answers to two generic questions that surface many times, in many forms of wording, during the early stages of interactive system design. These two questions are, 'Will it provide adequate support to the user's activities?' and 'How can it be built, given the constraints on cost and resources?' By defining the system's requirements, we try to dispel any uncertainty surrounding these two questions. We try to demonstrate that the system will indeed provide adequate user support to resolve the situation of concern. We also try to show that there is a worked-out design strategy that can be achieved within cost limits and with manageable levels of risk.

Requirements can be viewed as *targets* that the design must meet; indeed Tom DeMarco has suggested calling them just this (DeMarco, 1979). If we can produce a design that we are sure will meet its requirements, hitting home well within the target area, then we can pass on this design to be implemented and put into operation. If we can see that it will miss the target, or if we are simply not sure, then handing it on is unwise – we need to work on the design some more. Requirements enable us to feel confident that the original design problem, defined in the problem statement, will indeed be solved.

7.2.1   Support for validation

As interactive system designers, therefore, one of the things we rely on most in requirements is their *validity*. We assume that all we have to do in order to meet the original need is to design a system that meets all of the stated requirements. We don't expect to find, after doing a first-rate job of the design, that the people who asked for the system are unhappy with it or that the users cannot get their work done with it.

Suppose, for example, we were to design and build an Air Traffic Control system according to the first requirement in Figure 7.2. We wouldn't want to find out later that the users had no need for the required extra strengthening supports, and were most unhappy at having to learn an unorthodox keyboard layout. This would be an indication that the requirement was invalid. Its effect was to hinder, rather than help, the task of resolving the orginal situation of concern.

7.2.2   Support for verification

Another thing we need as system designers is a set of requirements that we know how to design to. While the design task may stretch our design capabilities, it should not leave us wondering how on earth we are going to do the job.

Suppose we encounter the second requirement shown in Figure 7.2, for example, asking for inclusion of 'decision making assistance'. What does this mean? How long will it take to design? How will we know whether our design is adequate? Challenging though it is to be asked to provide such a feature, the likelihood is that this will grow into a design headache. Even if we can come up with a design we think suitable, we will not be able to *verify* that it meets such a vague requirement.

We expect, therefore, to be able to translate a set of requirements into a set of relatively *routine design tasks*. The second requirement in Figure 7.2

- The alphanumeric keyboard for the Air Traffic Control system should provide 60 keys, laid out in three separate groups of 5 × 4 keys so as to allow for extra strengthening supports between the groups.
- Decision making assistance should be provided. Computer-generated proposals will be generated by upstream ATC expert systems and artificial intelligence, still to be developed.

Figure 7.2   Two Air Traffic Control system requirements, based on real-life specifications. The first is *invalid*: air traffic controllers do not need extra-strength keyboards, and the unusual grouping of keys will make the system less usable in the hands of trained typists. The second is *unverifiable*, describing functions so ambiguously that it will be impossible to tell whether the requirement has been met.

cannot be turned into a routine design task, at least not as it is currently stated. In contrast, the first requirement in Figure 7.2 can be met without difficulty; the problem here is that the requirement is invalid in relation to the original needs. What we look for, as designers, is a set of requirements that are both valid and verifiable.

7.3 Defining requirements

Now that we have seen what system designers expect of a set of requirements, we can change hats and look at the task of *defining* the sorts of requirements that designers need. The requirements definition task will be our main concern during the rest of this chapter. It is a task that begins with a problem statement. It ends with a set of requirements that define the solution in a way that is valid in terms of the originally stated need, and that can be reduced to a set of routine, verifiable design tasks.

What is involved in producing such a requirements definition for an interactive system? Before we look specifically at the steps involved, let's remind ourselves of who will read the requirements that we will write. We need to make sure we define the requirements with this readership in mind.

7.3.1 Who reads requirements documents?

Interactive system requirements are a matter of concern to many people; to designers, developers, marketeers, trainers and users, to name just a few. These are some of the *stakeholders* in the system's development (Rouse, 1991). It is challenging to write a single requirements document that will address the concerns of all of these stakeholders.

Client and developer

We can usefully divide our stakeholders into two main groups, those who have a major stake in the system's *use* and those who have a stake in its *development*. We will consider the first group – including users, marketeers and the people who pay for the system – to represent the **client**, a term we introduced at the end of Chapter 2. Those in the second group, including designers and implementers, collectively represent the **developer**. The requirements we write will be read by both sets of people. Clients will read them to make sure they are getting what they need, and developers will read them so that they know what to design and build.

Contexts

Both client and developer can take on widely different identities. In particular, the whole development process may take place in any one of the following contexts:

- In a **product organization**, where the primary client is usually a marketing group and the developer is a combined team of product software designers and builders.

- In a **user organization**, developing the system for their own internal use; here the client is usually a representative group of management and users, and the developer is an in-house software support unit.

- As a **contract development**. The client is a user organization who prefer not to develop the system themselves. They therefore appoint an outside contractor to develop the software. They may define the requirements themselves or ask the contractor to define them; a quite common route is to commission a third organization (perhaps a management consultancy) to prepare the requirements document. Software development – and sometimes requirements definition – may be put out to competitive bidding.

As we can see in Figure 7.3, the way in which requirements are stated in these three contexts can vary considerably – if indeed they are stated at all. But why is this?

Requirements in the contract development context

By far the biggest issue is whether the system is to be developed *under contract*, because in this context the requirements document plays several crucial roles in the contractual process. It defines what the software contractor is to deliver, it provides the contractor with a basis for quoting a price and timescale for the development, it provides both developer and client with a means of confirming that the system does what it should, and if there is any disagreement it plays an important part in resolving the dispute.

Product organization:
I have a very small team working at the definition stage and then I expand it to implement the design, if necessary. The bigger the team that is required to implement the design of a program, the more disciplined you have to be about breaking the design into manageable pieces and defining the interfaces. You don't have to do many structured-programming reports, documenting every step, unless the program is so big that it has to be done by more than two or three people.

(a)

User organization:
Settlement in CREST is a process which runs continuously throughout the business day. Settlement continuously reviews all unsettled transactions on the queues to check whether they are *ready* to settle. These are matched pairs of settlement instructions due for settlement today. For each pair, it then checks whether there are adequate *resources* to settle the instructions (or whether the instruction has a high enough priority to command those available).

(b)

Contract development:

4.3.7   The system MUST automatically update individual staff salaries at their increment date.

4.3.8   The facility to enter annual leave, attendance on training courses, etc., in advance. This information MUST be automatically transferred to the roster screens covering relevant dates.

4.3.9   Duties or time-off booked/requested MUST be highlighted on the planned roster so that it is clear which parts of the roster are less amenable to change.

4.3.10   The facility view time-out already booked, by ward.

(c)

Figure 7.3   Quotes showing how requirements are stated in different contexts. (a) Requirements non-definition in a software product organization: John Page quoted in Lammers (1986); (b) in-house development of a stock settlement system, where the focus is on informal explanation of requirements (CREST, 1994); (c) precise operational requirements for a nursing system for resource management, to be developed under contract (North-West Regional Health Authority, 1990).

Requirements in other contexts
In non-contractual situations the requirements definition plays a relatively low-key role. In a user organization, for example, or in a small product organization, the requirements definition may not exist as a written document; instead there is just an understanding of what is to be designed

and built. Nevertheless the requirements always exist, if not on paper at least in the minds of client and developer. It is usually better if they are written down, especially if there is any risk that things will go wrong.

Whatever the context, requirements need to be defined in a way that satisfies both client and developer. This is often difficult to achieve, because clients are often non-technical people who want things defined simply and in their own terminology, whereas developers are more technical and often want more in the way of detail. It is important not to let the developer's needs dominate, because this results in a document that the client cannot digest.

7.4 Defining requirements for interactive systems

To a first approximation, defining the requirements for an interactive system is like defining requirements for any system. It involves turning the initial problem statement, which defines the overall purpose of the system, into something that spells out each of the functions that the system must provide. This simple view of requirements definition is illustrated in Figure 7.4.

According to this view, defining interactive system requirements is a matter primarily of defining a **usable functional form** for the system. The functional description included in the problem statement, which may amount to just the words, 'Design an interactive system to support ...', must be expanded so as to define all of the major interactive functions that the system is to provide. At the same time, the level of support defined in the problem statement, which may have been worded as simply, '... faster than at present', must now be defined with much more precision and completeness. An adequate specification of the system's functionality and usability is needed.

How do we go about defining a usable functional form for an interactive system? In this section we will touch briefly on the main things we must do: arrive at an initial functional form, identify users, understand their usability demands, set usability targets, and consider alternative functional forms that may enable these requirements to be met more easily and routinely. We will also note the need to validate requirements, both analytically and through prototype testing.

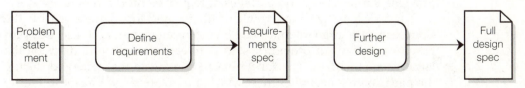

Figure 7.4   A simplified view of the definition of requirements and their subsequent role.

---

1   General

1.1   The system should provide access to Economic Updates (EUs) based on the contents of the Shared Database.

1.2   Each EU should consist of one or more extracts from the Shared Database, together with explanatory text narrative.

1.3   EUs should indicate the reliability of items in the extracts.

1.4   EUs should indicate how recently an item has been updated in the database from which it was extracted.

1.5   The data shown in EUs should be extracted from the database at the time of retrieving and viewing the EU.

2   Preparation of Updates

2.1   It should be possible to prepare EUs, and include database extracts, with the aid of the standard word processing package used in the Commission.

2.2   There should be means to transfer an EU from the word processing system into the appropriate directory (see 3.1).

2.3   There should be means to expunge obsolete EUs from directories.

3   Retrieval of Updates

3.1   EUs should be arranged in directories, one directory per member country.

3.2   The system should allow the selection of a particular EU for display on the user's workstation.

4   Support

4.1   A support team should be set up to provide assistance to those preparing and retrieving EUs.

4.2   Training courses in EU preparation and retrieval should be provided.

Figure 7.5   Starting point of the requirements exercise: initial functional requirements for the Economic Update system, as determined in the course of the participative design sessions described in Chapter 6, rearranged here under four separate headings.

7.4.1   Continuing the Commission example

We will orient our discussion around an example from the last chapter, the Economic Update system for use at the Commission, and follow its progress through the various stages of requirements definition.

This system, we may recall, is to be developed in-house by the Commission, a large international financial organization. It has been proposed as a means of providing staff with easier access to updates on the latest economic data. The functional requirements that emerged during the participative design exercise in Chapter 6 are shown again in Figure 7.5, arranged according to category of function.

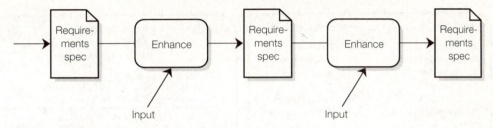

Figure 7.6   Enhancing the requirements specification.

We will treat this list of requirements as our starting point. We will take the solution through several stages of development, each one representing an enhancement to the specification as shown in Figure 7.6. We will look at the kinds of input that inform each stage of enhancement.

7.4.2 Defining the functional form

We are concerned from the outset to find a set of functions that will provide adequate support to the users' activities. This set of functions defines the basic functional form of the system. We have already seen in Chapter 6 how we can arrive at a functional form such as the one described in Figure 7.5. In outline, this process depends on two essential contributions:

- **Building a model of the supported activities.** If we want to support the user's activities, we need to know what these activities are. We need to model them in a form that allows us to simulate how they might be performed with the aid of a system. These simulations will tell us if functions are lacking, or if other functions are superfluous. In this way, we will gradually reconcile the functional form with the activity model.

- **Selecting a form of solution.** We are likely to start by considering ways of adapting existing forms of solution, since these involve less design effort than inventing something new. But if all attempts at adaptation fail, we will try to synthesize a solution of our own.

In the case of the Economic Update system, we have focused initially on supporting the activities of senior economists. Our choice of solution form, shown in Figure 7.7, is based on a simple menu of document files.

7.4.3 Identifying the users

Who will be the users of the new system? In the simplest cases of requirements definition, the system's functionality corresponds closely to the functions of the system currently in use, and the same people continue to perform much the same tasks. However, these cases are rather rare, for the simple reason that they don't usually result in any real improvements or

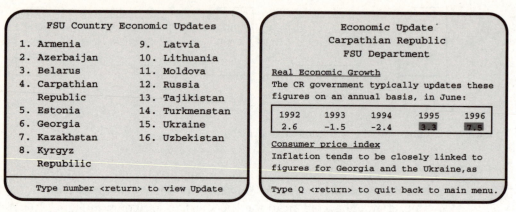

Figure 7.7   Design for the Economic Update system resulting from participative design.

cost savings. Whatever was wrong with the old system remains wrong with the new one. To solve the stated design problem, it is usually necessary to introduce extra functionality. We must then decide whom this new functionality is for.

In the Economic Update system, introduction of the shared database has brought with it a variety of new forms of functionality. In particular, it offers people at the Commission a means to generate lists of stored documents on any topic, and to select individual documents for display, in a manner that amounts to browsing. These functions, described under the **Retrieval of Updates** heading, clearly belong to the economist user. Requirement 2.1, under **Preparation of Updates**, also describes a function for the use of economists, namely the preparation of EUs on word processors. But what about requirements 2.2 and 2.3, concerning transfer of EUs into and out of the system's directories? Are authors to be responsible for adding EUs, for example? And who is authorized to remove updates?

We must always determine who is to perform new duties, because there are always extra costs associated with these duties' performance, such as costs of equipment and training. There may be additional labour costs too. At the Commission, if there is a continuing large volume of EUs to be added to and removed from the system, it may be necessary to employ someone specially to perform these tasks. If the tasks are to be performed by existing members of staff – by EU authors, for example – these people's productivity may be affected.

Once we have identified who the system's users are, we may be inclined to modify the requirements accordingly. Where we know that the user's identity affects the course of the design we should make this clear. In our document-retrieval example we would probably make it clear which functions the economist user would perform, as shown in Figure 7.8 (the changes are shown in italics for clarity).

2   Preparation of Updates

2.1   Preparation of EUs will be performed by economists.

2.2   It should be possible to prepare EUs, and include database extracts, with the aid of the standard word processing package used in the Commission.

2.3   There should be means *for those preparing updates* to transfer an EU from the word processing system into the appropriate directory (see 3.2).

3   Retrieval of Updates

3.1   The system will be used for retrieval by all members of the Commission's professional staff.

3.2   EUs should be arranged in directories, one directory per member country.

3.3   The system should allow the selection of a particular EU for display on the user's workstation.

4   Support

4.1   There should be means *for system administrators* to expunge obsolete EUs from directories.

...

Figure 7.8   Amending the retrieval functional requirements of Figure 7.5 to show the identity of the user. Changes are shown here in italics.

7.4.4   Setting performance requirements

Once we have addressed the question, 'Who will use the system?' we are faced with the next question, 'What levels of support must the system provide?' We need to define *performance requirements*, that is, to set targets for the levels of performance that the system will enable. The 'performance' we are concerned with here is largely the performance of users' activities, and is equivalent to the system's usability.

Every computer system must meet performance requirements, but in interactive systems these requirements are of special importance, because they define what it means to design a system that supports the user's activity properly. In the conventional approach to system design, much more emphasis is placed on defining *functional requirements* of the kind shown in Figures 7.5 and 7.8. By this convention, usability requirements are treated under the general heading of 'non-functional' or 'non-behavioural' requirements, where it is difficult to relate them to specific user activities.

The main usability requirements we consider in every requirements exercise are ease of learning, reduction of errors and speed of operation. Of these, speed of operation is often given highest priority because it has the greatest effect on efficiency and cost savings. However, if people never succeed in learning to use the system properly they will never achieve their intended speed of task performance, and if they make lots of errors they will spend valuable time correcting them. These kinds of requirements are hard to deal with later, once the software's design is under way. We need to consider them at the requirements definition stage.

Identifying learning problems

Let us look at the kinds of usability requirements we might need to set for the Economic Update system. We will start with ease-of-learning requirements because, as we saw, there is not much point in defining speed-of-operation requirements for a system that nobody understands how to use.

Targets for ease of learning can be defined in terms of the amount of training required. Walk-up-and-use systems like automated tellers are designed with a target of zero training; space shuttle control systems, on the other hand, assume training periods of many months. At which end of the scale are our users of the document retrieval system? In particular, how much training can we assume the executive user will undergo?

It is highly unlikely that a senior economist in the Commission will have a lot of spare time in which to learn how to retrieve documents online. We might decide therefore to set a requirement for very brief training, perhaps none at all. By setting arbitrary performance requirements, however, we are in danger of missing the main point. The questions we should ask are, first, how important is ease of learning? And if it is really important, what ease-of-learning targets can we reasonably ask the system's designers to achieve? Using routine design methods, how close can our designers get to a zero-training design without impacting other aspects of usability, such as error rates and speed of operation? If we think it is possible to reduce training time to 15 minutes, say, by dint of careful design, but if five minutes seems out of the question, then we should set a 15-minute requirement.

```
> list topics
EUs policy misssions
> list EUs
Armenia-94          Latvia-94
Azerbaijan-94       Lithuania-94
Belarus-94-95       Moldova-94
Carpathia-94        Russia-94-A
Estonia-94          Russia-94-B
Georgia-94          Tajikistan-93
Kazakhstan-94       Ukraine-94
Kyrgyz-94           Uzbekistan-94
> show Carpathia-94
```

Figure 7.9   An earlier version of the Economic Update system, showing the file-based method of access, using named files.

---

5   Performance

5.1 *The economist user should be capable of using the system efficiently and effectively for retrieval after 15 minutes' training.*

Figure 7.10   Starting the list of performance requirements by addressing ease of learning.

Reviewing the functional form in terms of ease of learning

In conjunction with setting realistic usability levels, we should *review the functional form.* When the user is learning to operate the system, certain forms of solution will be easier to understand than others. If ease-of-learning targets are proving hard to achieve, we may need to consider a different solution strategy.

It may be, for example, that an earlier version of the Economic Update system has been designed around directories of named files, as shown in Figure 7.9. This design might demand a lot more of the novice user than 15 minutes' training. A review of usability may have led us to adopt the menu-driven design shown in Figure 7.7. The overall functionality of the system is unchanged, but we can now be more confident that the system can be designed to meet requirements for ease of learning. We should record the outcome of this review in the requirements definition (see Figure 7.10).

Setting speed-of-operation targets

Other aspects of usability need to be dealt with in a similar manner, including speed of use. We can rarely afford to ignore this aspect of performance, because speed of operation has a particularly direct impact on the system's cost-justification. If the system enables people to do their work faster it will usually save money. Speed of operation may be important for other reasons besides; in a power-plant control system, for example, it will affect the plant's safety.

To determine meaningful speed-of-operation requirements we need to focus on those activities that can be speeded up significantly by the system. We need to pay special attention to high-cost activities, that is, activities that involve a lot of people, a lot of time or a lot of wages paid.

In the case of the Economic Update system, an obvious place to look first is at the economist's browsing, retrieving and document-reading activities. We must deal with the question, 'Is on-screen reading as fast as reading on paper?' There isn't a clear answer to this question, but it is likely that some readers will prefer to use the screen while others will prefer paper, if only because navigation through an on-screen document is sometimes time-consuming. Thus we might address the issue of speed of operation in a roundabout way by adding a requirement for hardcopy output.

We may also see places where it is important to define actual performance times. Consider the case of Requirement 2.3, for example – the

---

3   Retrieval of Updates

...

3.3 The system should allow the selection of a particular EU for display on the user's workstation.

3.4 The system should allow selected EUs to be printed.

4   Support

...

5   Performance

5.1 The economist user should be capable of using the system efficiently and effectively for retrieval after 15 minutes' training.

5.2 The system should permit documents to be added to the database from word processors in no more than three minutes of the author's time.

Figure 7.11   Adding requirements relating to speed of operation. Note the inclusion of a hard-copy function to address users' need for speed of reading.

requirement for a means of transfer of new documents prepared on word processors. We might have decided that the authors of documents themselves should copy their documents onto the system, to ensure that they are made available as soon as possible. However, this copying operation should not involve a lot of the authors' time; we want them to carry it out right away, not put it off until they have half an hour to spare. So we should set a limit, perhaps three minutes, to the amount of users' time involved in copying each document onto the system. In Figure 7.11 we see the inclusion of additional requirements relating to speed of operation.

7.4.5 Requirements for other layers of technology

Requirements definition involves doing more than just defining a usable functional form. It involves recognizing that interactive systems involve many *layers of technology*. The user interface is a particularly important layer, and we tend to concentrate on defining its requirements; but there are other layers supporting it, as Chapter 2 pointed out. They include application software, operating system, networked resources and hardware. The requirements document may need to state requirements for any or all of these other layers.

The layers of technology don't just support the interactive system, they often surround it, in the form of other systems already in place. The new system will need to be *integrated* with these other systems. Often it is these systems, more than anything, that constrain the design. They dictate many of the conventions and abstractions that the interactive system must abide by, and they limit the levels of usability that can be attained.

1 General

1.1 The system should provide access to Economic Updates (EUs) based on the contents of the Shared Database.

1.2 Each EU should consist of one or more extracts from the Shared Database, together with explanatory text narrative.

1.3 EUs should indicate the reliability of items in the extracts.

1.4 EUs should indicate how recently an item has been updated in the database from which it was extracted.

1.5 The data shown in EUs should be extracted from the database at the time of retrieving and viewing the EU.

2 Preparation of Updates

2.1 Preparation of EUs will be performed by economists.

2.2 It should be possible to prepare EUs, and include database extracts, with the aid of the standard word processing package used in the Commission.

2.3 It should be possible to include tables of data by specifying an appropriate portion of the Shared Database.

2.4 There should be means for highlighting items to indicate reliability.

2.5 There should be means to distinguish items that have not been updated in the Shared Database since a particular date.

2.6 There should be means for those preparing or updating an EU to transfer it from the word processing system into the appropriate directory (see 3.2).

3 Retrieval of Updates

3.1 The system will be used for retrieval by all members of the Commission's professional staff.

3.2 EUs should be arranged in directories, one directory per member country.

3.3 Within each directory, EUs should be indexed by the major sectors of the country's economy.

3.4 The system should allow the selection of a particular EU for display on the user's workstation.

3.5 The system should allow selected EUs to be printed.

4 Support

4.1 A support team should be set up to provide assistance to those preparing and retrieving EUs.

4.2 Training courses in EU preparation and retrieval should be provided.

4.3 There should be means for system administrators to expunge obsolete EUs from directories.

Continues

Figure 7.12 Requirements for the Economic Update system, after iterating through the requirements process.

5   Performance

5.1   The economist user should be capable of using the system efficiently and effectively for retrieval after 15 minutes' training.

5.2   The system should permit documents to be added to the database from word processors in no more than three minutes of the author's time.

Figure 7.12   *Continued.*

By the time we have considered all of these issues and have factored them into the solution, our requirements document will have changed considerably. Figure 7.12 shows some of the changes that we might need to make to our Economic Update system. As in this example, there is always a tendency to address issues by adding requirements, and so the requirements document tends to grow in size. We need to track this inevitable growth, and make sure the solution doesn't become overloaded with requirements to a point where design is no longer feasible. If this happens, it is time to review the form of solution.

7.5   Validating requirements

The requirements process involves maintaining contact with both the requirements for the solution and the original definition of the problem. This means checking that the two are consistent, ensuring that the requirements are valid with respect to the problem. We have already seen instances of validating requirements in the examples quoted above. It is important to understand how validation is carried out; in particular, we need to distinguish between *analytical* and *empirical* methods of requirements validation.

7.5.1   Analytical methods of validation

As much as possible, we try to validate requirements as we go. To defer validation may mean that a whole set of requirements are found to be inconsistent with the original problem, and must be discarded. We look for validation methods that are quick and easy to apply, preferably as soon as we have written the requirements down. We are interested in methods that are by nature analytical – methods that enable us to analyse the solution and make predictions about its performance.

Consider the two solutions shown in Figures 7.7 and 7.9. Can we analyse these in terms of ease of learning, for example, or speed of operation? There are tools and methods for performing such analyses, some of which are described in Chapter 8. For example, the Cognitive Walkthrough method helps to identify problems that first-time users will encounter due to lack of training; it might tell us that the menu-based interface of Figure 7.7 is somewhat error-prone. Another technique, based on Keystroke-Level Modelling, helps us to estimate speed of operation by experienced users. These methods do not provide all the answers about usability, but they do often enable us to make more informed decisions when we are faced with important choices.

7.5.2   Building and testing prototypes

One of the biggest problems in interactive system design is the difficulty in performing thorough validation of requirements by analytical methods. The available methods tend to run out of steam, leaving us with many questions that we cannot answer. When this happens, construction and testing of prototypes provides the only way to ensure that the problem is being solved and the users' needs are being met.

The Economic Update system we have been discussing would almost certainly be tested in prototype form before committing to designing and building the real thing. We would want to be sure, for example, that executives could indeed learn to use the system effectively in 15 minutes, and that new documents could indeed be stored in less than three. There are probably a number of other questions relating to functionality and performance that a prototype would help us to answer. We would almost certainly find, during testing, that some requirements had not been met, and we would have to decide whether to relax the requirement or look for a way to address it properly.

The use of prototypes to validate requirements introduces a delay between taking decisions and learning whether they were wisely made. Even with the most rapid prototyping techniques, it will usually take us several weeks, if not months, to design, build and test a working prototype and to analyse the results of the test. The requirements process must be organized differently to take account of these delays. The well-known spiral development process, proposed by Barry Boehm, is intended to help in managing the prototyping activities that take place during the requirements process (Boehm, 1988).

7.5.3   On documenting the prototype's design

The final issue we must consider, and it is an important one, is the fate of the prototype's design. After we have built the prototype, tested it and confirmed that the requirements are valid, what then? Do we consign the prototype's design to the wastebasket, and leave the system designers to come up with their own design? Or do we document the prototype and include it in the requirements document?

There are arguments to be made for both courses of action – for excluding and for including details of the prototype. On the side of exclusion, there is the point that prototypes are often developed using totally different software from the ultimate system. The prototype might be built in HyperCard, for example, or in Visual Basic; the final system might be programmed in C++ to run in the X Windows environment. In such cases it will be inappropriate to demand that the system's developers should follow every detail of the prototype's design. They need a more abstract definition that they can specialize in terms of the chosen software 'platform'. It is also the case that the design of a prototype often involves making arbitrary decisions, on the choice of typefaces, for example, or on the placement of objects on the screen. If we are not careful, these decisions become cast in concrete. Years later, there is still a funny-looking object on the screen that was included in the design at a late stage in the development of a prototype.

The argument in favour of including details of the prototype's design rests on the need to ensure adequate usability in the final system. Many aspects of usability are hard to define in words. For example, how do we specify the ease with which users can recover from errors? How do we set targets for ease of customizing? These are often very important factors in the system's overall usability. However, they are impossible to assess by purely analytical methods. The only way to be sure that they are being met is to build and test a prototype – and even then we may have our doubts. If the prototype's design is discarded, and another team of designers is invited to design the system afresh, we will be even more doubtful of a successful outcome.

7.6 Requirements and innovation

Many of the complexities surrounding the requirements process arise because interactive systems tend to involve novel design ideas. When a new system is developed there may not be any other system quite like it, and so the functional requirements must be defined largely from first principles.

Of course there are exceptions to this rule; we don't adopt an innovative approach every time. There are well-established interactive systems and tools such as automated teller machines, airline check-in terminals and telephone operator switchboards, and these have relatively standard functional forms. In cases where we are seeking a small improvement, the existence of this well-established solution makes the functional requirements quite easy to write down. Also, these systems' performance requirements are relatively easy to identify. For example, the speed-of-operation requirements for a telephone assistance workstation include the requirement that collect calls will be handled in a certain amount of time (Gray *et al.*, 1992). A reasonable target for this task's performance is 25 seconds.

Innovative system design problems tend to dominate the field of interactive system design, however. They may not be startlingly novel. Our Economic Update example is a typical innovation, a fairly familiar application that nevertheless demands working out the requirements and the design from first principles. A problem such as this inevitably leads us into a highly iterative requirements process and into prototyping and testing. Furthermore we are very likely, in documenting the requirements for such systems, to decide to include details of the prototype's user interface. We are concerned with a problem that our software designers have probably never tackled before. In designing the prototype, we have solved some hitherto unsolved design problems, and we naturally want to share our knowledge with the system's designers.

What we see here is a requirements activity that overlaps the design activity. This, too, is a feature of innovative projects. The decisions we make in drawing up requirements are, for the most part, design decisions. They involve making predictions about the impact of the system, and making changes to requirements in order to achieve the impact we want. They involve us in activities such as the study of users' needs, the choice of user interface styles and structures, and the use of analytical methods. They lead frequently to the construction and evaluation of prototypes because the available analytical design tools are rarely adequate. When we have completed the requirements definition, and have handed it to the system's designers, they continue in the same vein. What we have achieved, during the requirements process, is a reduction of the original problem to something that can be designed by routine methods, within the available time and resource limits, and with manageable levels of risk.

7.7 Verification against performance requirements

We have focused here on the process by which requirements for interactive systems are defined. Before we finish, let us return to the earlier topic of how requirements serve design. Let us look once more at what it means to verify the design – to check that it meets requirements. In effect, verification tells us whether we are making progress towards solving the design problem.

An especially clear indicator of design progress is provided by performance requirements. They constantly play the role of design targets, a role identified at the start of this chapter. At each step in the design they help measure whether progress is being made, in a manner illustrated in Figure 7.13. If the design is found to fall short of meeting requirements, a further iteration will be needed; the analysis of the design indicates where it may need to be changed. If the design meets its targets, it can be considered ready for implementation. In this sense, performance requirements plays a key role in helping to manage the design process.

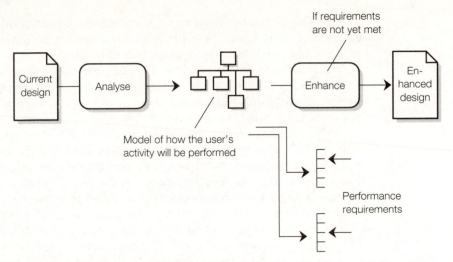

Figure 7.13 How performance requirements assist design by setting targets and determining when the design's performance is adequate.

7.8 Conclusion

This chapter has explored some of the main issues in requirements definition for interactive systems. The issues include support for validation and verification, contexts of use, the focus on finding a usable functional form, and the separate roles of functional and performance requirements. The chapter has brought out the role of prototypes in assisting in the definition of requirements in innovative projects. It has explained why, in these projects, there is an inevitable degree of interweaving between requirements definition and design.

Depending on the context of development, varying emphasis is likely to be placed on explicit definition of detailed requirements. Requirements tend to be most evident in the contract development context, where they define what is to be delivered and paid for. They are least visible in the context of innovative product development, where they are sometimes not written down at all. But whatever the context, requirements are always implicit to the design process. In the next three chapters we shall see how requirements provide the yardsticks against which we analyse and evaluate the design.

Exercises

(1) Define what is meant by requirements for an interactive system, and explain the difference between functional and performance requirements.

(2) Why are requirements especially important in projects performed under contract?

(3)   (a) Define the requirements you would draw up if you were buying a camera.

(b) Define the requirements you would set yourself before planning a two-week vacation.

(c) Discuss why these two requirements exercises are so different.

(4)   In the Economic Update example, consider the ease-of-learning requirements of the author, and suggest an appropriate performance requirement.

(5)   Suppose it is important that the Economic Update system should make documents accessible to executives as quickly as possible. How would you go about defining the relevant requirements?

(6)   Explain the difference between validation and verification of requirements.

(7)   Under what circumstances would you use analysis rather than prototype evaluation to validate requirements? Think of a problem in which analytical methods would be adequate.

(8)   Define performance requirements to accompany the ticket machine's functional requirements given in Section 6.4.4.

(9)   Individual functional requirements have some of the features of problem statements. Why is this? Why is it important that this should be so?

(10) Do you agree with John Page, quoted in Figure 7.3(a), that his design teams should avoid writing down requirements? If not, what argument would you use to try to change his mind?

Further reading

Davis A. M. (1990). *Software Requirements Analysis and Specification.* Englewood Cliffs, NJ: Prentice-Hall

An extensive survey of techniques for defining software requirements. Provides a valuable example of analysis (pp. 100–11) and specification (pp. 262–8) of outline requirements for a small but non-trivial application. However, the emphasis is on requirements for software design, not application design. Annotated 100-page bibliography.

Howes N. R. (1988). On using the User's Manual as the requirements specification. In *IEEE Tutorial on Software Engineering Project Management* (Thayer R. H., ed.), pp. 172–7. Washington, DC: IEEE Computer Society Press

An interesting paper on an alternative to conventional software engineering approaches to requirements definition.

Sommerville I. (1994). *Software Engineering*. 4th edn. Wokingham: Addison-Wesley

A comprehensive text on software engineering, with some discussion of the user interface and examples of interactive application requirements.

PART III

System evaluation

8   Usability analysis and inspection

9   Prototyping and evaluation

10 Experiments in support of design

Case study A:
Evaluation and analysis of a
telephone operator's workstation

CHAPTER 8

Usability analysis and inspection

Chapter objectives:

We are likely to be concerned about questions of usability at every stage in the design of an interactive system. Usability analysis tools enable us to answer these questions on paper, without building and testing a prototype. Here we look at:

- The kinds of usability analyses needed during design
- The two-stage approach to analysis in which a walkthrough stage precedes the analysis of performance
- Specific analysis techniques: GOMS, Cognitive Walkthrough and Heuristic Evaluation.

8.1 Introduction

We perform analyses when we are faced with the question, 'How well will this design do the job?' It is a question that arises in many forms of words during the course of designing interactive systems; for example:

Will the operator be able to handle emergency telephone calls faster than before?

Have we simplified the design of this ticket machine to a point where people will use it successfully on their first attempt?

Is the small size of this screen target going to result in a significant number of errors in selecting it?

If the user invokes this command by mistake, will he or she find the escape route?

Will the word-processor user remember that there are three different ways of changing the properties of a formatting style?

Is it so difficult to change the layouts of menus that hardly any users will bother?

Once the system is set up to support work-groups of a particular size and structure, how much effort is involved in changing the system to support changes in the group?

How many of the people who try the system will actually continue to use it?

These are questions about *usability* – the system's ability to support the user's activities. They arise constantly during design, right from the problem definition stage through requirements specification to detailed design. It is quite common to encounter usability questions even during the system's implementation and introduction to use. In this chapter and the next we will be looking at methods of answering these questions.

Before we start, we should note that questions about interactive system designs cover many other issues besides usability. There are other levels of technology involved, as Chapter 2 pointed out. Questions about the software's performance are especially likely to arise, as will questions about hardware cost and performance, maintenance, safety, and so forth. But these questions are not exclusive to interactive systems, and so we won't be concerned with them here. Good software-engineering textbooks, such as Sommerville's (1994), are available covering methods of analysis and evaluation in each of these areas.

8.2 Answering usability questions

Questions about usability are rarely straightforward to answer. None of the questions listed above, for example, would be at all easy to answer off-the-cuff. Usability is a system property that we can rarely determine by a quick calculation. On the contrary, it involves conducting an analysis or experiment. Depending on the complexity of the design and the desired accuracy of the answer, we may be in for an exercise lasting anywhere from ten minutes to six months. Before we enter into this exercise we need a clear idea of the form of answer we want and how we are going to derive it.

8.2.1 Two approaches to measuring usability

Broadly speaking, measurements of usability can be conducted in either of two ways:

- **Analytically**, by performing a simulation of how the user's activities will be performed;

- **Empirically**, by building a prototype and testing it in the hands of users.

These are two very different approaches to answering questions about usability. Analytical techniques can sometimes be carried out quite quickly and informally, using 'back-of-envelope' methods. They don't involve real users, and so there's much less organizing to do. Nevertheless they can on occasions involve a considerable amount of work – see, for example, the analyses reported in Card *et al.* (1983) and Diaper (1989a).

Empirical measurements, on the other hand, almost always involve a lot of prior planning, and rely on careful conduct and analysis of the experiment (Hix and Hartson, 1993). Users need to be 'signed up' as subjects, and testing must be arranged at times when the users are available. Thus even the simplest investigation can take several days to conduct, and will need to be planned with care. But the results usually justify the time and effort invested, because it is possible to address aspects of usability that lie beyond the scope of analytical methods.

This chapter is devoted solely to *analytical methods*, and to methods of *usability inspection* aimed at discovering flaws in the design that will affect the system's usability. The next two chapters cover empirical methods of usability evaluation.

8.3 Analysis as a two-stage process

The point was made earlier that usability analysis involves more than just a single quick calculation. The basic reason for this is that we are concerned with the performance of a human activity, and our analysis must therefore be applied to each step in the activity's performance. We cannot do a split-second usability analysis any more than we can instantly account for the money we spent during a week's vacation.

Rather, we are likely to perform the analysis in two stages. First we determine the sequence or method by which the activity is performed; then we analyse the steps in the sequence to determine usability measures. These two stages are shown in Figure 8.1.

As we can see, each stage of analysis operates on a *model* of the user's activity, and results in a refinement of the model. We start with a general model, perhaps just indicating the goal of the activity. From this, and from a description of the system's functionality, we build a model of a sequence of actions. From the activity sequence model we build a model that identifies usability properties, such as the time taken to perform each step, or the steps where errors may occur.

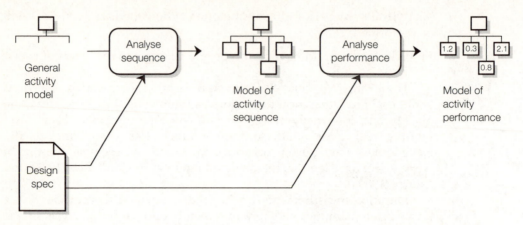

Figure 8.1 Stages of analysis, building successively more refined and specific models.

8.3.1 Determining the sequence by walkthrough

The first stage of analysis, in which we build a model of the activity sequence, is an important one. If we get the sequence wrong, this invalidates our usability analyses. But how do we determine the sequence?

Sequence analysis relies largely on **walkthrough methods**, by which each step in the sequence is determined from the state of the interaction after the previous step, and from the user's current goal. Thus if the user's goal is to correct the spelling of a word in a document, her first step is likely to be to find the word in question. With the word in view, her next step may well be to select the word. With the word selected, her next step is probably to retype it. We have just 'walked through' the sequence, building a model of how we expect the activity to be performed (Figure 8.2).

It's important to realize that, in many interactive contexts, there is no single walkthrough sequence – the activity may be performed in a wide variety of different ways. For example, the sequence by which someone edits a six-page technical report can vary considerably; the sequence by which someone else reads the report will be almost entirely unpredictable. Sometimes it is necessary to model a number of alternative sequences in order to check for possible usability problems. These may take the form of **benchmarks**, that is, activities that will be used to compare the performance of different design solutions.

8.3.2 Determining the sequence empirically

It may be easier and more reliable to determine the sequence of operation empirically, by studying users. This is preferable if, for example, the activity involves special skills and is performed by highly trained operators.

Suppose we were interested in how a patent officer might conduct

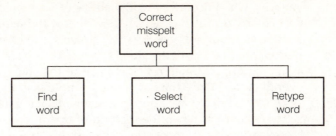

Figure 8.2   Task model of correcting a misspelt word, generated by walkthrough.

searches for previous patents that may relate to a current patent application. We wouldn't attempt to work this out on our own with the aid of walkthrough methods. After all, what do we know about searching through patent archives? So we would conduct a user study, observing patent officers at work and interviewing them about their methods. Then we would build a model of the sequence, or sequences, of activity performance.

8.3.3   Folding in the usability analysis

Once we know the sequence of the user's activity we can perform a more detailed usability analysis. This may take the form of a separate stage of analysis, as in the keystroke-level technique described in the next section.

It is also appropriate, and sometimes convenient, to fold in the usability analysis with the walkthrough analysis. It is often the case that usability is affected by the juxtaposition of steps, not by each step in isolation.

8.3.4   Methods of analysis

The first two methods of analysis discussed in this chapter are variants of the basic walkthrough method. In effect, they each adapt the basic method to the needs of particular kinds of design questions. The first method, *Keystroke-Level Analysis*, provides measures of speed of operation by trained users. The second, *Cognitive Walkthrough*, is tuned to assessing users' learning problems in systems that they walk up and use. By way of contrast, we conclude the chapter with a non-walkthrough method, *Heuristic Evaluation*, but we will see that even this method involves consideration of sequences of operation.

8.4   Analysis techniques based on the GOMS model

The theory of the human information processor, outlined in Chapter 3, has given rise to a number of tools and techniques known collectively as methods of *GOMS analysis*. One particular GOMS technique, keystroke-level analysis, was introduced at the start of Chapter 3. GOMS techniques are particularly useful in cases where we know the sequence of operation and want to find out how quickly the sequence can be performed by an experienced operator. With the aid of GOMS we can walk through the sequence, assigning approximate times to each of the steps, and thus calculate an overall performance time. It sounds simple, and in many instances it is.

GOMS is not always appropriate for analysing designs. It does not give accurate answers when the method of operation isn't known or the user is inexperienced. Its most effective use by far is in predicting speed of performance, because here it can draw on a large body of empirical laws and results, some of which were summarized in Chapter 3. In addition GOMS can sometimes be used to predict errors or choice of method.

8.4.1   The GOMS model

The GOMS model of task performance has four parts. Each part relates to one of the letters in the acronym, which stand for 'Goals, Operators, Methods and Selection rules'. These are the four kinds of variable that affect the outcome of the analyses. Thus:

- The **Goal** defines the end-state that the user is trying to achieve; for example, the goal may be to change to boldface the two words 'The cat' of the sentence 'The cat sat on the mat'. Top-level goals are subdivided into subgoals, and each of these is then analysed separately. Thus we can divide this task into two subtasks: selecting the two words, and setting the selected text to boldface.

- **Operators** are the basic actions available to the user for performing a task, such as moving the mouse pointer, clicking the mouse button, pressing a key.

- **Methods** are sequences of operators, or procedures, for accomplishing a goal. A method for selecting the words 'The cat' is to move the pointer to 'The', hold the mouse button down, move to 'cat' and release the button. A method of setting the selected words to boldface is to hold down the CONTROL key and press 'B'. These two methods are both employed in the sequence shown in Figure 8.3.

- **Selection rules** are invoked when there is a choice of method. The user interface doesn't always offer a choice. However, there is an alternative to the boldfacing method shown in the bottom half of Figure 8.3, involving the use of a pull-down menu to select the **Bold** reformatting command, and this is shown in Figure 8.4.

GOMS models of task performance can support analysis in a number of ways. They are at their simplest and most effective when predicting speeds of task performance in those cases where the method of operation

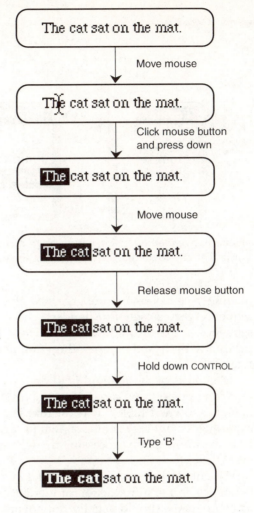

Figure 8.3   A method for selecting the words 'The cat' and changing them to boldface.

is known, that is, when selection rules are not an issue. This is done through *Keystroke-Level Analysis*, a technique described in the next section. Another kind of analysis concerns method selection: by estimating the speed of alternative methods we can compare them, and judge whether the user is likely to prefer one to another.

8.4.2   Keystroke-Level Analysis

The purpose of the Keystroke-Level Model is to predict the user's speed of execution of tasks. It can be used in situations where the user's method of performing the task is known: for example, it could be applied to

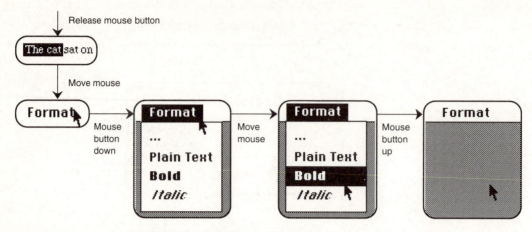

Figure 8.4   An alternative method, using a pull-down menu, for changing the selected words 'The cat' to boldface after selecting them. Courtesy Apple Computer.

dialling a telephone number, since this tends to follow a standard sequence very closely (lift handset, check for dial tone, press buttons in sequence, wait). It could not be applied to the task of drawing a freehand portrait with the aid of a painting program, since everyone does this differently.

The basis of the method is to divide each task-performance method into components, and assign execution times in seconds to each component, as shown in Table 8.1. These times have been derived from repeated experiments, but they can be shown to correspond to predictions derived from the information processing model and from extensions to it, such as Fitts' Law.

Use of the Keystroke-Level Model involves applying certain rules, or heuristics, in the introduction of **mental preparation** components. These **M**-components should usually, but not always, be introduced before keystrokes or pointing operations that are not part of a sequence. The rules proposed by Card *et al.* (1983) are given in Figure 8.5.

Keystroke assignments are simple and quick to apply to sequences of actions, but some practice is needed in order to apply the rules for placing **M** operators correctly. Two worked examples follow, and Case Study A describes a more detailed application of GOMS modelling. A number of worked examples can also be found in Card *et al.* (1983).

A simple keystroke-level comparison

We can use keystroke-level analysis to compare the two methods of selecting a pair of words and setting them to boldface, shown in Figures 8.3 and 8.4. The method of Figure 8.3 is analysed in the following table. Here the rules of Figure 8.5 have been applied to remove unneeded **M** operators

Table 8.1   Performance times for keystroke-level operators; from Card *et al* (1983).

Operator	Description and remarks	Time (sec)
K	PRESS KEY OR BUTTON.	
	Pressing the SHIFT or CONTROL key counts as a separate	
	K operation. Time varies with the typing skill of the user;	
	the following shows the range of typical values:	
	Best typist (135 wpm)	.08
	Good typist (90 wpm)	.12
	Average skilled typist (55 wpm)	.20
	Average non-secretary typist (40 wpm)	.28
	Typing random letters	.50
	Typing complex codes	.75
	Worst typist (unfamiliar with keyboard)	1.20
P	POINT WITH MOUSE TO TARGET ON A DISPLAY.	1.10
	The time to point varies with distance and target size	
	according to Fitt's Law, ranging from .8 to 1.5 sec, with	
	1.1 being an average. This operator does *not* include the	
	(.2 sec) button press that often follows. Mouse pointing	
	time is also a good estimate for other efficient analogue	
	pointing devices, such as joysticks (see Chapter 7).	
H	HOME HAND(S) ON KEYBOARD OR OTHER DEVICE.	.40
$\mathbf{D}(n_D, l_D)$	DRAW n_D STRAIGHT-LINE SEGMENTS OF	
	TOTAL LENGTH l_D CM.	$.9n_D + .16l_D$
	This is a very restricted operator; it assumes that drawing	
	is done with the mouse on a system that constrains all	
	lines to fall on a square .56cm grid. Users vary in their	
	drawing skill; the time given is an average value.	
M	MENTALLY PREPARE.	1.35
$\mathbf{R}(t)$	RESPONSE BY SYSTEM.	t
	Different commands require different response times. The	
	response time is counted only if it causes the user to wait.	

(the number of the rule applied is shown in the right-hand column). A value of 0.50 seconds has been chosen for **K** operators, since these are mostly random keys:

Select words			
Reach for mouse	**H**	0.40	
Point to word 'The' with mouse	**P**	1.10	
Double-click and hold down mouse button	**K**	0.60	(1)
Move mouse to word 'cat'	**P**	1.10	
Finish selection by releasing mouse button	**K**	0.60	(1)

Begin with a method of encoding that includes all physical operations and response operations. Use Rule 0 to place candidate **M**'s, and then cycle through Rules 1 to 4 for each **M** to see where it should be deleted.

Rule 0.   Insert **M**'s in front of all **K**'s that are not part of text or numeric argument strings proper (e.g., text or numbers). Place **M**'s in front of all **P**'s that select commands (not arguments).

Rule 1.   If an operator following an **M** is *fully anticipated* in an operator just previous to **M**, then delete the **M** (e.g., **PMK** → **PK**).

Rule 2.   If a string of **MK**'s *belongs to a cognitive unit* (e.g.,the name of a command), then delete all **M**'s but the first.

Rule 3.   If a **K** is a *redundant terminator* (e.g., the terminator of a command immediately following the terminator of its argument), then delete the **M** in front of it.

Rule 4.   If a **K** *terminates a constant string* (e.g., a command name), then delete the **M** in front of it; but if the **K** terminates a variable string (e.g., an argument string) then keep the **M** in front of it.

Figure 8.5   Rules for placing **M** operators. From Card *et al.* (1983).

Set to boldface:

Press CONTROL	K	0.60	(2)
Type 'b'	K	0.60	(2)
Release CONTROL	K	0.60	(3)
Total		5.60 secs	

Note that no **H** operator is included before the CONTROL-b action, which can be given with the left hand only.

In comparison, the sequence of Figure 8.4, in which the **Format** pull-down menu is used, involves the following operators:

Select words (unchanged from previous example)

Reach for mouse	H	0.40	
Point to word 'The' with mouse	P	1.10	
Double-click and hold down mouse button	K	0.60	(1)
Move mouse to word 'cat'	P	1.10	
Finish selection by releasing mouse button	K	0.60	(1)

Set to boldface:

Point to Format menu with mouse	P	1.10	
Press and hold down mouse button	K	0.60	(1)
Move down to Bold	P	1.10	(1)
Release mouse button	K	0.60	(1)
Total		7.20 secs	

Thus the use of the keyboard 'short cut' does indeed reduce the task's performance time, by over a second and a half. This is due mainly to avoidance of two **P** operators.

Keystroke-Level Analysis: A second example

As a further example of a design problem where GOMS modelling is useful, consider the design of a method for generating hard-copy plots of data. This is a problem of choosing an efficient sequence of operation for a set of existing programs. The original plots are produced on the screen with a program called *plotgraph*, running in the UNIX environment, and the plots are printed by using the UNIX *xwd* and *xpr* utilities.

The first stage of analysis is to walk through the operating sequence, identifying each of the steps:

(1)   Type the following to plot the data:

   plotgraph <4-digit number> <3-digit number> <return>

The program takes an average of five seconds to produce the plot.

(2)   Type the following to run *xwd*:

   xwd –out abc <return>

The cursor changes within one second to a cross in readiness for selecting the window containing the plot.

(3)   Select the window by pointing anywhere within it. The window image is dumped on the file *abc*, which takes six seconds.

(4)   Type the following to print the image file:

   xpr –device ps abc / lpr <return>

The *xpr* program responds within one second.

The Keystroke-Level predictions for task performance times are as follows. A time of 0.30 seconds is assigned to **K** operators. Again, numbers in the right-hand column refer to the rules in Figure 8.5.

(1)   Run *plotgraph*:

Mentally prepare	**M**	1.35	
Type *plotgraph*	**9K**	2.70	
Type terminating SPACE	**K**	0.30	(4)
Type 4-digit number	**4K**	1.20	
Mentally prepare	**M**	1.35	
Type terminating SPACE	**K**	0.30	
Type 3-digit number	**3K**	0.90	
Mentally prepare	**M**	1.35	
Type terminating RETURN	**K**	0.30	
System response	**R**	5.00	
Subtask 1: *plotgraph*	Total	14.75 secs	

(2)   Run *xwd*:

Mentally prepare	**M**	1.35
Type *xwd* command	**12K**	3.60
Type terminating RETURN	**K**	0.30 (4)
System response	**R**	1.00
Subtask 2: *xwd*	Total	6.25 secs

(3)   Select window:

Reach for mouse	**H**	0.40
Point to window with mouse	**P**	1.10
Click mouse button	**K**	0.30 (1)
System response	**R**	6.00
Subtask 3: window selection	Total	7.80 secs

(4)   Run *xpr*:

Mentally prepare	**M**	1.35
Type *xpr* command	**24K**	7.20
Type terminating RETURN	**K**	0.30 (4)
System response	**R**	1.00
Subtask 4: *xpr*	Total	9.85 secs

Adding together the subtotals, we arrive at the following total time for each printout:

Subtask 1: *plotgraph*	14.75 secs
Subtask 2: *xwd*	6.25 secs
Subtask 3: window selection	7.80 secs
Subtask 4: *xpr*	9.85 secs
Total	38.65 secs

The significance of this time prediction depends on the number of plots to be generated. Suppose we need 300 plots? This will take over three hours at the workstation. How can this be reduced?

A simple method of speeding up the task is to set up an alias, such as *p*, for the command *plotgraph*. This takes eight **K** operators, or 2.40 seconds, out of the first subtask, and reduces the overall time for 300 plots by 12 minutes. The search for other means of saving time is left as an exercise for the reader, but we can already see that the task must take at least 13 seconds each time, or over an hour for 300 plots, just in terms of the system's response time. It is the remaining two hours that we can hope to reduce.

8.5   Analysis by Cognitive Walkthrough

Cognitive Walkthroughs provide a method of analysing designs in terms of *exploratory learning*. They can be applied to designs for systems that will be used by people without any prior training, perhaps in a walk-up-and-use manner. They are also useful in the analysis of systems whose designs have been changed or extended, because these changes and extensions may be encountered by users who have never been taught how to use them. In either case, the user must learn how to use the system by exploring its user interface. Cognitive Walkthroughs answer questions of the form, 'How successfully does this design guide the unfamiliar user through the performance of the task?'

We tend to use Cognitive Walkthroughs, then, when we want to assess operation by users who are exploring the system's user interface and learning as they go. Particular measures we will be looking for concern users' success rates in completing tasks, and their ability to recover from errors. We should not expect to measure users' speed of task performance. We need a fairly complete description of the user interface in order to conduct Cognitive Walkthroughs, because we need to cover all possible routes that the user may take. However, we don't need to know the user's sequence of operation, because the analysis itself helps us to discover what the sequence is likely to be.

8.5.1   The underlying model of exploratory learning

Analysis by Cognitive Walkthrough involves simulating the way users explore and gain familiarity with interactive systems, with the aid of the simple step-by-step model introduced in Chapter 3:

(0)   The user starts with a rough plan of what he or she wants to achieve – a task to be performed;

(1)   The user explores the system, via the user interface, looking for actions that might contribute to performing the task;

(2)   The user selects the action whose description or appearance most closely matches what he or she is trying to do;

(3)   The user then interprets the system's response and assesses whether progress has been made towards completing the task.

The analysis involves simulating steps 1, 2 and 3 at each stage of interaction, by asking questions of the form:

Q1:   Will the correct action be made sufficiently evident to the user?

Q2:   Will the user connect the correct action's description with what he or she is trying to do?

Q3:   Will the user interpret the system's response to the chosen action correctly, that is, will the user know if he or she has made a right or a wrong choice?

The result of performing a Cognitive Walkthrough is usually to discover problems in these three areas, that is, where the questions receive a 'No' answer. Solutions to these problems are fed into the next iteration of design.

8.5.2 Cognitive Walkthrough: An example

To illustrate the use of Cognitive Walkthroughs, let us analyse the use of the rapid-transit ticket machine described in Chapter 6. The preliminary user interface design for the machine is reproduced in Figure 8.6.

We will work through an analysis of the machine's use by a first-time user. Let us suppose this user wishes to purchase a round-trip ticket to Dragon Plaza. We will add a complication: the traveller has only ten dollars in cash, but doesn't know this at the outset.

Our first step in the walkthrough is to answer the task-definition question:

Q0:   What does the user want to achieve?

Answer: Purchase a round-trip ticket to Dragon Plaza.

Now we can enter into the walkthrough analysis itself. The initial display is as shown in Figure 8.6. We start by asking question Q1 about this display:

Q1:   Will the correct action be made sufficiently evident to the user?

Answer: There are two possible correct actions, press the 'Dragon Plaza' button or press 'round-trip'. The design doesn't make this clear, for it instructs the user to choose the destination before indicating the journey type. This doesn't impede the user's progress, but it hides an available option. Thus we have identified **Design Flaw**

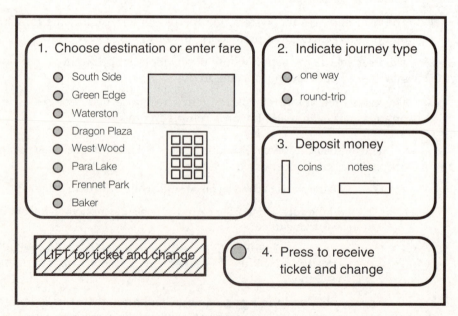

Figure 8.6   The design for a rapid-transit ticket machine, as developed in Chapter 6, to be analysed by Cognitive Walkthrough.

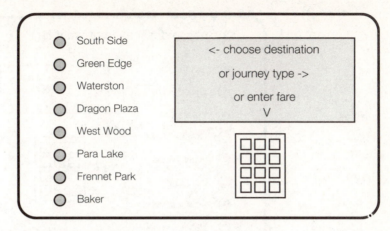

Figure 8.7   Making the range of methods more obvious to the user

**no. 1: Option to indicate journey type first is not made suffi-
ciently evident.** One possible way to rectify this flaw might be to
provide a prompt via a larger display (see Figure 8.7).

The user is thus likely to be aware of only one correct action, pressing
the 'Dragon Plaza' button. Following the walkthrough analysis sequence,
we will now ask questions Q2 and Q3 about this action:

Q2:   Will the user connect the correct action's description with what
             he or she is trying to do?

Answer: Yes, the instructions for panel 1 and the button label will enable
             the user to make the connection.

Q3:   Will the user interpret the system's response to the chosen action
             correctly, that is, will the user know if he or she has made a right
             or a wrong choice?

Answer: The machine will respond by lighting up the button pressed, as
             shown in Figure 8.8. This should appear to the user as confirma-
             tion of a correct action.

The user must now indicate the journey type, using panel 2. We apply
the same walkthrough steps as before:

Q1:   Will the correct action be made sufficiently evident to the user?

Answer: Yes. The correct action is to press the 'round-trip' button in panel
             2, and the instructions labelling this panel make it clear that this
             is the next step.

Q2:   Will the user connect the correct action's description with what
             he or she is trying to do?

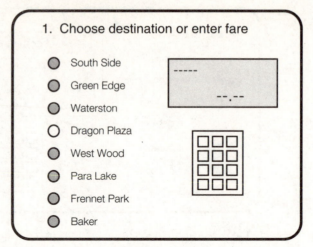

Figure 8.8   Confirming the user's choice of destination with a lighted button.

Answer: Yes, the instructions and the labels on the buttons make the connection very clear.

Q3:   Will the user interpret the system's response to the chosen action correctly, that is, will the user know if he or she has made a right or a wrong choice?

Answer: Yes. The machine will respond by lighting up the 'round-trip' button and by displaying the journey type and fare, as shown in Figure 8.9. This provides confirmation of this and the previous action. If the user should press the 'one-way' button by mistake, this too will be made clear.

We'll now proceed to the next action, depositing money.

Q1:   Will the correct action be made sufficiently evident to the user?

Answer: Yes. Again, the user's main source of assistance is the numbered sequence of instructions. According to this sequence the next step is to deposit money.

Q2:   Will the user connect the correct action's description with what he or she is trying to do?

Answer: Yes, a request to deposit money is consistent with purchasing a ticket.

Q3:   Will the user interpret the system's response to the chosen action correctly, that is, will the user know if he or she has made a right or a wrong choice?

Answer: Unclear. We need to know what kind of response the machine will provide to a correct action, that is, to depositing the first portion of the fare. If the machine merely swallows the money, the

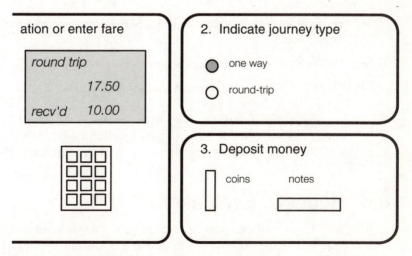

1. Choose destination or enter fare

- South Side
- Green Edge
- Waterston
- Dragon Plaza
- West Wood
- Para Lake
- Frennet Park
- Baker

round trip

17.50

2. Indicate journey type

- one way
- round-trip

3. Deposit money

coins   notes

Figure 8.9   The machine's response to selecting the journey type.

user will be little the wiser. According to Figure 8.9, there is no means of indicating receipt of the money, and thus no means for the user to keep track of the amount deposited. This could be considered **Design Flaw no. 2: No display of total money received**. A solution might be to extend the display as shown in Figure 8.10.

The completion of the walkthrough of the normal ticket-purchase sequence is left as an exercise for the reader. Let us conclude this example by instead introducing the slight complication we've held in reserve – the

ation or enter fare

round trip

17.50

recv'd   10.00

2. Indicate journey type

- one way
- round-trip

3. Deposit money

coins   notes

Figure 8.10   Improving the design to show the amount paid so far.

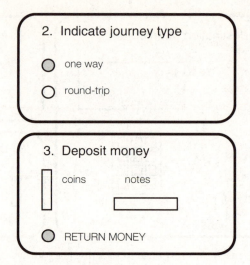

Figure 8.11   Adding the capability to retrieve money deposited.

passenger who has only ten dollars, and who discovers this only after depositing all of it.

Q1:   Will the correct action be made sufficiently evident to the user?

Answer: No, because there is no action that the user can take to retrieve the money deposited. We have discovered **Design Flaw no. 3: No means of retrieving money deposited**. The design should include a 'return money' button as shown in Figure 8.11.

This initial analysis has been very useful, in pointing out three design flaws:

- The option to indicate the journey type before the destination is not made clear.

- No display is provided of the amount of money deposited.

- There is no means to retrieve money deposited.

The analysis will not stop there, however. A design such as this will need to be subjected to a full range of walkthrough analyses, covering all of the likely tasks that users will want to perform, under all likely conditions.

8.6 Heuristic Evaluation

The two methods discussed so far, GOMS analyses and Cognitive Walkthroughs, both have the disadvantage that they can be applied successfully only to certain kinds of design problems. We need methods of analysing designs in situations where the method of operation is not fully predictable, and where the user is not a complete novice. Indeed, a great many designs fall into this category. The method discussed in this section, *Heuristic Evaluation*, can be applied in these cases.

As its name suggests, Heuristic Evaluation is not a pure analysis technique. It might be thought of as 'analysis by a team of analysts using a variety of informal models'. A more useful descriptive term applied to Heuristic Evaluation is *Usability Inspection*: an inspection is carried out, and a list of problems that could affect usability is drawn up. Then, as with Cognitive Walkthroughs, the designer revises the solution to address the problems.

8.6.1   The method of evaluation

For its effect, the Heuristic Evaluation method relies on two techniques in combination.

First, it employs a **team of evaluators** rather than relying on one person to carry out the analysis. This has a number of advantages: in particular, a team of external evaluators can be more impartial than the designers themselves; and through a process of *aggregation* a compilation is made of the problems identified by each evaluator, with the result that a small team of perhaps four evaluators can produce a comprehensive list.

Second, a set of **design heuristics** is used to guide the evaluators. Heuristics can be thought of as general-purpose guidelines; the set recommended by Nielsen and Molich (1989) is shown in Figure 8.12. Any one of these heuristics is likely to apply only some of the time; for example, 'Be consistent' is sometimes inapplicable, as Grudin has pointed out (1989). The important role of the heuristics is to guide the analysis that the evaluators apply. 'Prevent errors', for example, would focus the evaluator on searching for errors, perhaps by scanning the design for features that the user might misinterpret. 'Provide short cuts' would suggest looking for frequently performed tasks that involve lengthy sequences of actions. Ultimately the evaluator will fall back on performing informal walkthroughs in response to many of the heuristics.

Simple and natural dialogue	Provide clearly marked exits
Speak the user's language	Provide short cuts
Minimize user memory load	Good error messages
Be consistent	Prevent errors
Provide feedback	

Figure 8.12   Usability heuristics used to guide a team of evaluators (from Nielson and Molich, 1989).

A number of advantages are claimed for the Heuristic Evaluation method (Nielsen, 1992). They include low cost, in comparison to other methods; intuitive to perform; no advance planning required, since the evaluations can be conducted by team members in isolation; and suitable for use early in the development process. Disadvantages are its focus on problems rather than solutions, and its tendency to encourage designers to strengthen the overall solution proposed rather than break away from it (Nielsen and Molich, 1990).

It should be added that Heuristic Evaluation is intrinsically **less repeatable** than analysis methods that are strongly theory-based. If the same design is offered to two evaluators, they may well deliver two quite different sets of design problems. If different descriptions of the same design are given to the same team, again, different lists of problems may be handed back. Through the use of a number of evaluators, however, and the aggregation of problems, the lack of repeatability is brought under control.

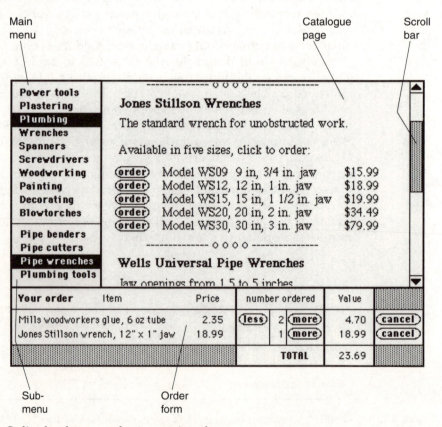

Figure 8.13   Online hardware catalogue user interface.

Example: Heuristic evaluation of an online hardware-store catalogue

The use of Heuristic Evaluation can be appreciated from a brief example of evaluating a design for an online catalogue for use by customers of a hardware store. Its purpose is to allow customers to place orders so that they can pay for them and collect them from a pick-up counter. A typical display layout is shown in Figure 8.13.

The catalogue is laid out as a two-level menu, the first level (shown in the top left of the screen) allowing the user to choose between broad categories of hardware, the second level (below the first) allowing access to individual types of product. To select a menu item, the user points to it with his or her finger.

Details of the products available are shown in the main window. Each item has an **order** target that can be selected by pointing. The scroll bar on the right can be used for moving up and down the list of available products.

When the user points to the **order** target, an entry is made in the bottom panel. The number ordered is set initially to 1, but may be altered with the **less** and **more** targets. As items are added, and the numbers ordered are changed, the total value of the purchase is shown at the bottom of the 'Value' column. The **cancel** target can be used to cancel the order for an item.

Here are some of comments that evaluators might make about this design, and the related heuristics:

Evaluator A: The menus aren't labelled, so it's hard for the user to know their purpose, or to understand the hierarchy (*Simple and natural dialogue*).

Evaluator C: I think the user will tend to confuse the menus, they look too much alike (*Simple and natural dialogue*).

Evaluator A: Why display the menus all the time anyway? While the user is searching the product descriptions, the menus aren't needed (*Simple and natural dialogue*).

Evaluator B: It would be good to have pictures of the products, that's what conventional catalogues have (*Speak the user's language*).

Evaluator D: The panel at the bottom is too small – people will order more than just two different items. They won't be able to remember all the items they've ordered (*Minimize user memory load*).

Evaluator B: The targets for ordering items are different from the menu targets, which are different again from the scroll-bar target. Shouldn't they be more alike? (*Be consistent*).

Evaluator C: How does the customer confirm the order? There's no button for doing this.

Evaluator A: What if the user accidentally cancels an order? They're going to have to go back to the catalogue to order it again (*Prevent errors*).

Evaluator B: It's more normal to show price and value alongside each other, and to place the number ordered on the left (*Speak the user's language*).

Some of these problems are relatively loosely connected with the heuristics. We should expect this, because there are always specialized considerations to take into account in any design problem. There are a number of special heuristics to consider in the design of menu-based dialogues, for example. We will return to the subject of heuristics and guidelines in Chapter 15.

8.7 Conclusion

A range of analysis methods are available to the designer of interactive systems. In this chapter we have looked at GOMS analysis techniques, Cognitive Walkthroughs and Heuristic Evaluation. There are other methods in addition to these, some of which are found in Nielsen (1993) and Preece (1994).

To be realistic, however, the choice of analysis method is often likely to be very restricted, because most of the available methods are themselves of restricted applicability. GOMS, for example, demands a definition of the methods of operation, while Cognitive Walkthrough applies primarily to analysis of learning by exploration. Although the designer will sometimes have the opportunity to use two or more methods of analysis and compare the results, the opposite extreme can also arise: no suitable method of analysis can be found. In these situations, evaluation must be postponed until a prototype can be built and tested. The next chapter discusses this use of prototype evaluation as an alternative to analysis.

Exercises

(1) What is the difference between analytical and empirical methods of assessing usability? Why are some assessments made analytically and some empirically?

(2) Why is it usually necessary to perform a walkthrough analysis before attempting to apply some performance analysis techniques? Why is this not needed in the case of Cognitive Walkthroughs?

(3) Conduct a Cognitive Walkthrough analysis of performing the following tasks with the aid of the ticket machine of Figure 8.6: (a) travelling as far as possible for $10; (b) buying a round-trip ticket for $14.55; (c) after selecting a round-trip ticket to West Wood and depositing $10, deciding to buy a one-way ticket instead.

(4) Online library catalogue systems often pose problems for first-time users because they must offer a wide range of functions. Conduct a Cognitive Walkthrough analysis of an online catalogue to which you have access.

(5)   Calculate the time for scrolling a Macintosh or Microsoft Windows window. Ignore the value of **R**, the system response time, in calculating times for the following tasks: (a) moving to the end of the displayed document; (b) moving up one screen-full; (c) moving from near the end of the document to near the beginning, and then stepping down two screens-full.

(6)   What difference will faster or slower typing make to the second example of Section 8.4.2?

(7)   Suppose, in the example of Figure 8.4, the CONTROL-b formatting command is changed to CONTROL+SHIFT+b; in other words, the user must hold down CONTROL and SHIFT with the left hand, and type 'b' with the right. What effect will this have on the overall task performance time? Does this still represent a 'short cut'?

(8)   In the second keystroke-level analysis example, how much time would be saved in generating 300 plots by (a) reducing the plot-file name to one character instead of three? (b) invoking *xwd* and *xpr* by using a two-character command macro in place of each command, such as *xx* in place of *xwd -out abc*? (c) rewriting the *plotgraph* program to generate hardcopy directly?

(9)   Make a note of the sequence of operations and displays from one or more Automated Teller Machines (ATMs) that you use, and perform cognitive walkthroughs.

(10) Conduct a keystroke-level analysis of the ticket machine of Figure 8.6. This will involve estimating the time taken for some of the special operators involved, for example, inserting money and taking ticket and change. Determine approximate values by timing yourself using a similar machine. From your analysis, work out how many commuter passengers the machine can handle per hour.

Further reading

Card S. K., Moran T. P. and Newell A. (1983). *The Psychology of Human Computer Interaction*. Hillsdale, NJ: Lawrence Erlbaum Associates

Chapter 8 provides a full description of the Keystroke-Level Model, with a number of worked examples.

Desurvire H. W., Kondziela J. M. and Atwood M.E. (1992). What is gained and lost when using evaluation methods other than empirical testing. In *People and Computers VII* (Monk A. *et al.*, eds.). Cambridge: Cambridge University Press

A comparative study of several usability analysis methods.

CHAPTER 9

Prototyping and evaluation

Chapter objectives:

Empirical evaluation, in which a prototype is constructed and tested by users, is an essential part of interactive system design, because available analytical tools are limited in scope. This chapter looks at the following aspects of building prototypes and conducting evaluations:

- Why evaluations need to be carried out during the iterative design process, rather than just at the end
- The choice of methods of evaluation available, and how to choose between them
- Conducting the evaluation as a true investigation, with specific learning objectives, and the steps this involves
- How to write concise plans and reports of evaluations
- How we go about building prototypes, and the tools we use
- Methods of informal evaluation
- Methods of iterative field testing.

9.1 Introduction

This chapter continues our discussion, begun in the last chapter, of how to make informed choices between design alternatives, and how to check

189

the soundness of these and other decisions made in the course of design. As we have seen, analysis tools can be effective in testing interactive system designs, but these tools are in short supply. We will often find ourselves making a decision that we cannot immediately check for validity. But we cannot afford to leave such a decision unchecked for long, for it will affect further decisions. We risk building more and more of the design on an untested – and possibly unsound – design decision.

When the need arises to check design decisions or compare alternatives, and this cannot be done with available analytical tools, the problem is solved *empirically*, by building and testing a prototype. Since the system is interactive, testing must be carried out with people as subjects, either under controlled conditions or out in the field. These kinds of tests are generally known as *evaluations*. In this chapter we shall discuss how we can apply prototyping and evaluation effectively during the design process. The discussion is continued in Chapter 10, which covers methods of quantitative evaluation under controlled conditions.

9.2 Evaluation in support of design: The formative approach

We treat prototyping and evaluation as we have already treated the use of analytical tools – as activities performed in support of design. We carry them out in order to solve the design problem as efficiently and effectively as possible. This means incorporating them into the iterative processes of design in such a way that the momentum of the design work is maintained and progress is assisted towards a successful conclusion.

Figure 9.1 shows in outline how evaluation assists the process of enhancing the system's design. At intervals a prototype is built, based on the current state of the design. The prototype is tested on users, and the results are fed into the next stage of enhancement of the design. The overall approach has been called *formative evaluation* because it is oriented towards helping *form* the solution to the design problem (Hix and Hartson, 1993).

9.2.1 Evaluating against requirements

The purpose of formative evaluation is to inform the design process – to check design decisions that have already been made and to assist in making the decisions that lie ahead. Most of the time the designer is facing questions of the following two kinds:

- Which should we adopt of the design alternatives under consideration?

- Are there any problems with the design we have already adopted?

These questions can be applied to the design problem as a whole, but there are advantages to be gained from applying them more narrowly. By

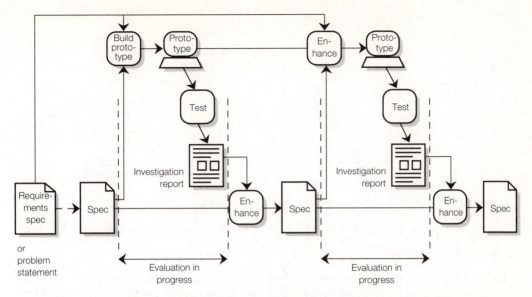

Figure 9.1   The evaluation process in outline. By building and testing a prototype, with reference to the requirements or problem statement, we are able to report results that influence the next stage in the development of the design's specification.

focusing the evaluation on a specific area of the design we can learn about the decisions we have made in that area, and can discover whether these decisions were sound. We learn where the source of the problem lies.

In particular, it can be helpful to focus evaluation on specific *requirements* that have been set earlier in the course of design. Rather than evaluate against the entire set of specified requirements we evaluate against just one or two. Ideally we focus on *performance requirements* so that we can test the design against defined targets.

For example, we might evaluate a mail-order system in terms of the requirement, 'The system should enable the availability of the ordered item to be checked in 25 seconds.' This evaluation would be relatively easy to carry out, and it would provide feedback about the specific parts of the design supporting availability checking. By the same approach we could compare two alternative solution strategies for this function.

9.2.2   The summative approach, and its drawbacks

In order for evaluation to influence the design it must be carried out at frequent intervals. But conducting an evaluation can be time-consuming. Unlike analytical methods for checking designs, which often yield valuable feedback from an hour or two's analysis, evaluations can take months to organize, conduct, analyse and write up. These lengthy exercises can bring all other design activities to a halt; during the 'evaluation in progress' periods in Figure 9.1, the design enhancement process simply

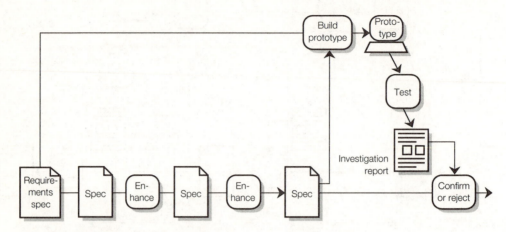

Figure 9.2   Summative evaluation, in which a single evaluation exercise is performed at the end of the iterative enhancement process, when it is too late to influence the design.

stops and waits for the evaluation to deliver its results. If we are not careful, our design process will be reduced to fits and starts.

In the face of tight deadlines and impatient design teams, the formative approach to evaluation is sometimes abandoned. Instead the design is prototyped and evaluated at the end, as shown in Figure 9.2. The result is to test the design as a whole, and to learn whether or not it meets overall usability requirements – a *summative* approach. There is a strong likelihood that the design will fail this test – up until this point, remember, it will have been tested only on paper. If indeed it fails by a wide margin, rectifying the problem may be too big a task for the time available. Effort will have been poured into conducting an evaluation that cannot really influence the design. For these reasons, summative evaluation is less effective than the formative approach (Hix and Hartson, 1993).

We need to ensure that evaluation is performed in a formative manner, during rather than after design. This means ensuring that each evaluation exercise is performed quickly enough to maintain design momentum. We need to consider ways of shortening the evaluation time, from months down to weeks or, better still, to a few days' investigation.

9.2.3   Methods of formative evaluation

In this chapter we shall be looking at three principal ways of reducing the amount of time and effort involved in the evaluation of interactive system designs. The three methods discussed, and their typical durations, are as follows:

A   **Learning from designing and building prototypes.** Before we can evaluate a design we must design and build a prototype incorporating a working user interface; in the course of doing this we are very likely to discover problems in the design that were not apparent on paper. The duration of this evaluation approach depends on the time taken to produce the prototype – usually a few weeks to a few months.

B   **Running informal user tests of the initial prototype.** As soon as we have a working prototype, we can test it ourselves or offer it to willing users for them to try out. This kind of early evaluation almost always exposes unexpected properties and design flaws. The duration of each exercise is typically a few days to a few weeks.

C   **Conducting a series of field tests** of progressive enhancements of the same prototype. Rather than build a separate prototype for each evaluation, we can leave the system in the field for continued testing by users, and can introduce minor changes in order to test users' preferences and performances. The duration of an entire field test is usually measured in months if not years, but individual evaluations can be completed more quickly, typically in a few weeks.

A fourth approach will be covered in the next chapter, because it is rather different from the other three:

D   **Testing a component of the design under controlled conditions.** Typically this is done in a *usability lab*, and provides more accurate results than the other methods. Duration: typically several weeks, sometimes one or two months.

9.2.4   Choosing between the methods

When we encounter a design question, or reach a point where we need to check the design, we will select an appropriate method of evaluation from amongst methods A, B, C and D above. The methods are not mutually exclusive, and so we can apply several, perhaps even all four – although this will hardly speed things up.

Some questions may be answered simply by building and quickly testing a prototype, following methods A and B. The more difficult choices are:

- whether to mount a full-scale field test (C), and

- whether to evaluate under controlled conditions (D).

Typically we will need to conduct a full-scale field test of any system destined for a **critical application**, that is, for an application on which people depend for essential services, for health and safety, for conduct of business and performance of work. This covers a great many of the interactive systems designed today. In addition, field testing is essential for systems that will support *collaborative activities*, involving more than one concurrent user, because these activities are very hard to simulate during informal or laboratory tests.

It is appropriate to conduct a controlled investigation when faced with a crucial decision, perhaps over a central component of the user interface such as a menu structure; an experiment can be designed to determine the effect of the component on task performance. Evaluation under controlled conditions is also essential for systems that must comply with standards. As more and more national and international standards for usability are introduced, this becomes an increasingly important issue; only controlled evaluations can provide the kind of statistically valid results needed to confirm compliance.

9.3 Conducting the investigation

Whichever method of evaluation we choose, the success of the exercise will depend on careful planning, execution and analysis. It will depend on having a clear perception of what we hope to learn from the exercise. We can usefully treat evaluation as a matter of conducting an *investigation* aimed at discovering the information needed at a particular stage in the design. In this section we will look at some of the basic activities common to all such investigations, including the basic sequence of stages, the design of the investigation, the analysis of data, and the documentation of results.

9.3.1 The basic stages of evaluation

In any evaluation that goes beyond simply designing and building a prototype, the basic course of events is likely to run as follows:

(1) We identify the usability properties to be measured, stating particular requirements that the design should attain.

(2) We make ready the prototype to be used for the evaluation.

(3) We design the experiment: we locate the users who will test the system, we define the activities the users should perform, and we schedule the tests.

(4) We run the tests and collect data; each user is briefed suitably beforehand on the testing procedures.

(5) We analyse the data to establish how the conditions of testing have affected the performance of activities.

(6)   We draw conclusions about any improvements needed in the design.

These six stages provide a useful basis for any investigation carried out during interactive system design. They include, in Stage 4, activities whose methods we have already covered in Chapter 5.

These six stages form only a framework, however. The central stages (3, 4 and 5) will need to be filled in by a process of *experimental design*, and special attention will need to be given to the *analysis* to be performed during Stage 5. Let us look briefly at these two closely related tasks.

9.3.2   Experimental design and analysis

When we conduct an experiment we always hope to obtain a clear-cut result that we can rely upon with some confidence. We want to be sure that the eventual product will perform just as well as the prototype we have tested. In graphical terms, the kinds of results we hope for are as shown in Figure 9.3(a) – user satisfaction is clearly higher in one case than the other, task performance time is clearly down.

Figure 9.3 also shows some of the kinds of results we hope to avoid by careful design and analysis. We would prefer not to find, for example, that we can detect no difference to speak of between the two designs, as shown in Figure 9.3(b). This can occur if the designs are tested on an unsuitable mix of tasks; see Card *et al.* (1983), Chapter 4, for an interesting case where this happened. This kind of result is especially troublesome if the measured performance value lies close to a requirement.

We can obtain misleading results from experiments if we conduct them carelessly. For example, we might inadvertently test one design on

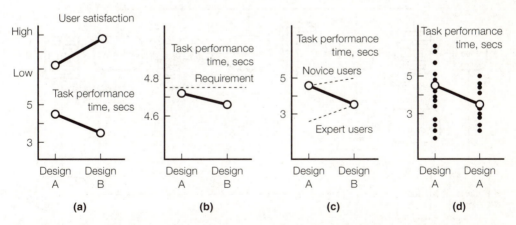

Figure 9.3   The dependence of evaluation on good experimental design and analysis: (a) the results we want; (b) indistinguishable results, close to the requirement, caused by poor choice of task mix; (c) poor experimental design leading to misleading results; (d) a large spread of performance figures, making the result insignificant.

novice users and the other on experts. Our data may suggest we have improved the design when in fact we have made it worse, as shown in Figure 9.3(c). This is a case of poor experimental design.

A problem we always face is variation in the performance of users. We will always see a spread of performance figures, even when we test users on the same design under carefully maintained conditions. The values we compare are usually **mean values** therefore, calculated by averaging all of the measurements taken. However, a large spread of values, as shown in Figure 9.3(d), can lead to a result that is not statistically significant – we cannot place any confidence in it. Careful analysis, using methods such as those described in Chapter 10, will help us to determine the significance of our averaged results.

9.3.3   Documenting the planned investigation and its result

It is important to document the planned investigation and its results, because we need to integrate the investigation into the design enhancement process. From an adequately documented plan we can tell that the investigation is aimed at acquiring the knowledge we need, and from an adequate report we can discover what we need to confirm the usability of the current design or to suggest changes. The roles of the investigation plan and report are shown in the expanded process diagram of Figure 9.4.

Plans and reports can take many forms and can go into matters in varying amounts of detail. To document the investigation thoroughly, the plan and report would need to cover each of the stages listed in Section 9.3.1. This kind of full-scale documentation is often needed by those closely involved in conducting the investigation or in making use of its results.

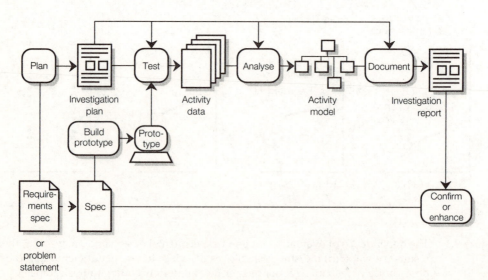

Figure 9.4   The roles of the investigation plan and report in the basic process of evaluation.

9.3.4   Documenting with the aid of pro formas

For more general use, e.g., when discussing alternative evaluation strategies, it is useful to encapsulate plans and results in shorter documents. Two crucial components of the plan and report are (a) the requirement or requirements on which the evaluation focuses, and (b) the knowledge gained. Thus it is important, before we plan an evaluation in detail, to be able to summarize its aims in words such as, 'There is a requirement that users of the ticket machine should need no prior training, and we intend to run tests on first-time users to confirm that they can operate it successfully.' At the end of the evaluation, we should be able to state the same requirement and conclude, '... and we have found that 95 per cent of first-time users have no difficulty in operating it successfully.'

We can construct useful two-sentence **pro formas** that document evaluation plans and reports in this way. The first sentence states the requirement:

> It is required of the ticket machine that first-time users should be able to operate it successfully without prior training...

The second sentence of the **pro forma plan** summarizes the proposed evaluation:

> ... We intend to carry out laboratory tests of the machine to confirm that at least 95 per cent of users can complete normal purchases without difficulty.

In the case of the **pro forma report**, the second sentence summarizes the investigation's results:

> ... We have carried out laboratory tests of the machine in which over 97 per cent of users completed normal purchases in less than 60 seconds.

Thus the two pro formas for this particular investigation would be written as shown in Figure 9.5(c). Figures 9.5(a) and 9.5(b) show other examples of pro forma plans and reports.

Pro formas have other uses. In particular, they can be used in conjunction with the use of analytical tools; it is sometimes useful to write pro formas summarizing the results of these analyses. Consider, for instance, the keystroke-level analysis of the graph-plotting program described in Section 8.4.2. We could summarize its outcome as follows:

> It is a requirement of the plotting package that sequences of hard-copy plots should take minimum time to prepare. We have established a set of performance-time predictions for the steps in the graph-plotting task, and have shown that each plot will take the user roughly 40 seconds to generate.

Pro formas can also be used for documenting the results of research; see Newman (1994).

It is a requirement of the large-screen drawing tool that it should maintain and augment normal informal meeting practices. We propose to confirm that it meets this requirement in informal user tests.

It is a requirement of the large-screen drawing tool that it should maintain and augment normal informal meeting practices. We have conducted informal user tests that confirm the usefulness of the tool but indicate that the complexity of the user interface deters some potential users.

(a)

It is a requirement of the video environment that physically separated colleagues should be able to work together effectively and naturally. We intend to mount an ongoing field test of the environment to determine its effectiveness in support of distributed work.

It is a requirement of the video environment that physically separated colleagues should be able to work together effectively and naturally. We have conducted a field test extending over several years that has generated a number of findings, identifying the need to support the full range of shared work and to meet users' desire for both privacy and unobtrusive awareness.

(b)

It is required of the ticket machine that first-time users should be able to operate it successfully without prior training. We intend to carry out laboratory tests of the machine to confirm that at least 95 percent of users can complete normal purchases without difficulty.

It is required of the ticket machine that first-time users should be able to operate it successfully without prior training. We have carried out laboratory tests of the machine in which over 97 percent of users completed normal purchases in less than 60 seconds.

(c)

Figure 9.5   Examples of pro forma plans and reports: (a) for an informal test of a large-screen shared drawing tool, (b) for an ongoing evaluation of a video environment, (c) for controlled tests of a rapid-transit ticket machine. Examples (a) and (b) are based on research reported by Pedersen *et al.* (1993) and Gaver *et al.* (1992) respectively.

9.4 Prototyping

The construction and testing of prototypes is common in almost every field of engineering design. In fields with a strong basis of engineering science, however, many design decisions can be checked analytically, without reliance on prototypes. For example, traffic engineers can test the design of signalling systems for road intersections by means of analytical models of vehicular flow (McShane and Roess, 1990); aircraft designers can conduct on-paper analyses and simulations of the designs for wing sections and flying controls (Vincenti, 1991). In these established fields of engineering design, it is appropriate to keep prototyping in reserve until the design is more or less complete (Rogers, 1983). It then serves to 'prove' the design and to identify areas where minor design changes are needed.

Things are very different in interactive system design. Here prototyping takes on some special properties, which in their turn justify building prototypes at a much earlier stage in the design. In this section we will look briefly at some of the demands that this places on prototypes, and at the kind of tools available to assist us in building them.

9.4.1   Prototyping in interactive system design

In interactive system design, prototyping is often dominated by the need to design and implement a *complete user interface*, and to do this under *tight time constraints*.

The completeness of the user interface

Even when we are just evaluating a component of the design we will want to test it under realistic conditions. We need to make sure our users can perform tasks as they would in real life – as *externally valid tasks*. To do this we need to provide them with a full set of interactive functions.

Consider the earlier example of evaluating the mail-order system's means of checking availability (see Section 9.2.1). If our users cannot perform a full order-entry task, but are restricted to using only the availability-checking command, they will no longer be testing it in the context of 'normal' operation. Problems that they might otherwise encounter, such as in handling a customer's question while availability-checking is in progress, will not occur. We need a prototype that supports the full user interface.

Software engineering under tight timescales: The need for tools

Prototyping is also affected by issues of reliability, performance and ease of maintenance of the software, in other words by issues of *software engineering*. This is an important issue in full-scale field tests, where users come to depend on the prototype in their work. Simply because it is a prototype, we cannot allow the system to be so slow as to affect users' productivity, or to be so unreliable that they lose valuable data and waste time.

Software engineering requirements can usually be met by using appropriate methods and devoting suitable care to design and construction. However, the methods take time to learn and to apply, and during evaluation there is little time to spare. The prototyping task therefore depends heavily on the availability of simple *tools* to assist the designer, especially in designing and implementing the user interface.

Both of these aspects of prototyping, completeness and timescales, need to be taken into account. Furthermore we need to allow for the large amounts of effort that can go into user interface work: Myers and Rosson

(1992) have estimated that nearly half of the entire software development effort relates to the user interface. We therefore need to make sure we have access to prototyping tools that assist in its development.

9.4.2   Prototyping tools

What sorts of facilities should we look for, in terms of user interface support, when we choose a prototyping tool? What kinds of things will make user interface prototyping easier? Hix and Hartson (1993) identify a number of desirable features, including:

- Ease of developing and modifying screen layouts

- Ease of linking screens together and modifying links

- Support for a range of types of user interface

- Support for a variety of input devices

- Means of calling external programs and accessing external text, graphics and other media.

A number of prototyping tools and toolkits are now available, including Visual Basic and Tcl/Tk. We will look briefly at how one of the best known, HyperCard, provides some of these features.

9.4.3   An overview of HyperCard

HyperCard was developed for the Apple Macintosh, and was the forerunner of a number of similar tools for user interface prototyping on PCs and other standard platforms. It allows the development of systems of quite substantial interactive power. A number of successful products have been

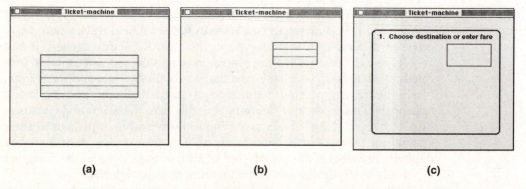

      (a)   (b)   (c)

Figure 9.6   Creating a display layout in HyperCard: (a) creating a box; (b) re-sizing it and placing it in position; (c) adding graphics and a text label. Courtesy Apple Computer.

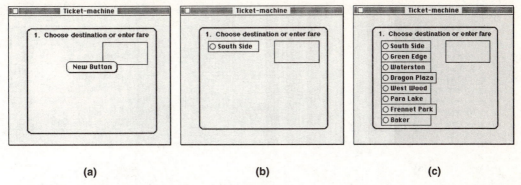

(a)   (b)   (c)

Figure 9.7   Adding buttons to the card: (a) the button is created in a standard form with 'New Button' as a label; (b) it is changed to a radio button, the label is changed and the button is placed in position; (c) further buttons are added for the remaining stations. Courtesy Apple Computer.

implemented and shipped as HyperCard programs. The basic features of HyperCard can be appreciated from a simple example, showing how the rapid-transit ticket machine of the last chapter might be prototyped.

HyperCard provides the first of Hix and Hartson's features, support for screen layout design, by providing a set of tools for composing layouts on separate **cards**. Starting with a blank card, the designer can add one or more **boxes**, that is, rectangular regions that can contain typed-in text. In Figure 9.6(a) we see a box being created in response to a menu command, and in Figure 9.6(b) it is re-sized and positioned. This box will serve as the ticket machine's display. HyperCard also provides a set of graphics tools, which the designer can use to add the border and label shown in Figure 9.6(c).

To turn a card into an interactive display, the designer adds **buttons** to it. In Figure 9.7(a) we see a new button being created, again by a menu command, and in Figure 9.7(b) it has been repositioned and changed to a 'radio button' with a round target; its label has been changed to the station name, 'South Side'. A separate button is created for each of the stations, as shown in Figure 9.7(c). While they are being created and modified, HyperCard gives the buttons rectangular outlines, but these are removed when the prototype is run.

The facility to link screens together provides a means of making the prototype machine's appearance change in response to user actions, as the machine would in actual use. Figure 9.8(a) shows a second card that has been created by copying the first card and making some minor changes to its appearance; for example, text has been typed into the 'display' box. By returning to the first card and double-clicking on the 'South Side' button, the designer can bring up a panel including a **LinkTo** command, shown in Figure 9.8(b). Then the designer switches to the second card, as shown in Figure 9.8(c), and clicks on the button labelled **This Card** to complete the link.

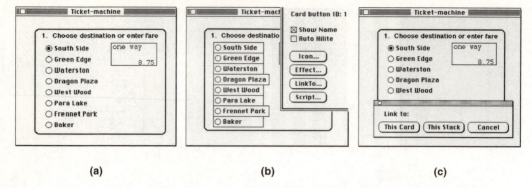

(a)   **(b)**   **(c)**

Figure 9.8   Creating a HyperCard link: (a) the linked-to card is defined; (b) the link-from card
is selected, and the linking button is double-clicked to bring up a control panel,
on which the **LinkTo** option is chosen; (c) the linked-to card is selected, and the
This Card option is selected to complete the link. Courtesy Apple Computer.

Even with just two cards and one link the prototype is capable of
being tested. The designer switches into 'run' mode, clicks on the 'South
Side' button and sees the display change as the second card replaces the
first (Figure 9.9). People with little or no programming experience can
construct prototypes in this way.

9.4.4 HyperCard programming: The HyperTalk language

More cards and links will be needed in order to complete the prototype.
This could be achieved by following the same set of steps a number of
times. However, HyperCard also provides a simple programming language, HyperTalk, that allows programs to be invoked when buttons are
pressed or cards are displayed. These programs are known as **scripts**. For

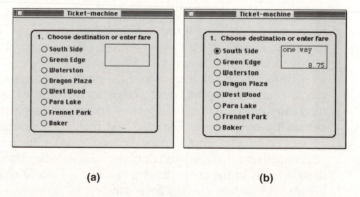

(a)   **(b)**

Figure 9.9   Testing the prototype: (a) the first card, (b) clicking on the 'South Side' button
causes the second card to replace the first. Courtesy Apple Computer.

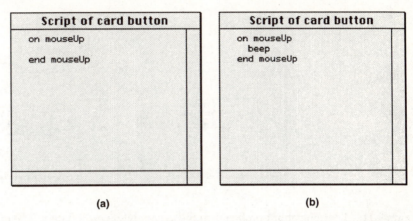

```
Script of card button

on mouseUp

end mouseUp
```

```
Script of card button

on mouseUp
   beep
end mouseUp
```

(a)   (b)

Figure 9.10 Making a very simple change to a button's script, using the HyperTalk language: (a) when a button is created it is provided with an 'empty' script that is run on the up-stroke of a mouse-click over the button; (b) adding a 'beep' to the script. Courtesy Apple Computer.

convenience, HyperCard equips each new button with a script whose contents are empty, as shown in Figure 9.10(a).

A very simple example of HyperTalk programming might be the addition of audio feedback when a button is pressed. This would be added by selecting the button and choosing the '**Script...**' option, visible in Figure 9.8(b). The button's current script is displayed as shown in Figure 9.10(a), and the designer can modify it as shown in Figure 9.10(b). The button will now beep when the user clicks on it.

The designer would almost certainly use HyperTalk to program the behaviour of the ticket machine's display. This would reduce the number of separate cards needed in the prototype.

9.5 Learning while prototyping

Many aspects of an interactive system come under scrutiny as the prototype is being built. Even though the user interface may have been designed in some detail before prototyping began, many aspects will have been left undefined, and we will 'discover' these as the prototype takes shape.

It is very common, for example, to omit details of screen layouts from specifications. Even simple properties like the dimensions of boxes to receive typed-in text may be left undefined, for it is quite difficult to determine how wide such a text box should be to accommodate, say, a 24-character customer name. When the prototype is under construction, we can very easily create a text box, type 24 characters into it, and set the size accordingly.

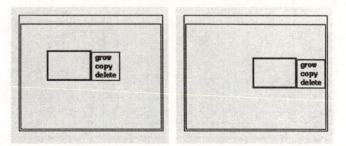

Figure 9.11   Learning about problems in the design while prototyping. The menu prevents
the box from being positioned at the extreme right-hand edge of the window.

During prototyping we also learn about problems in the design of the
interaction. We will find parts of the user interface that cannot be reached
from other parts, or buttons that are obscured from view just when the
user needs to press them. Figure 9.11 shows a typical problem that might
emerge during prototyping: a moveable selection object has a menu
alongside it for invoking functions on the object itself. But the menu prevents the object from being positioned at the extreme edge of the screen.
We will need to find an alternative solution.

A complete study of a prototyping exercise, identifying some of the
lessons learned along the way, is included towards the end of this book in
Case Study B.

9.6 Informal testing of prototypes

We have discussed the lessons to be learned during the design and construction of prototypes. Now we look at the kinds of informal investigations we can conduct as soon as we have a working prototype. This form
of evaluation has been discussed by Hix and Hartson (1993) and others in
the context of rapid prototyping. In this section we discuss the goals of
informal testing and look at how the basic investigative framework is
adapted to this style of evaluation.

9.6.1 Goals of informal testing

We undertake early, informal testing in order to find out whether we are
proceeding in the right direction. By this time we have selected our

solution strategy, and have made some progress with the design. We need to know, as soon as possible, whether we have made the right choice, and are on course to achieve a solution to the overall design problem. We will probably have tested our design analytically; however, as Gould points out, we miss things during analysis and simulation, and we rely on prototype testing to bring these things out (Gould, 1988).

We are interested, therefore, in checking whether we are covering the main points in the problem statement. Have we designed a system that supports the identified activity? Does it meet the primary performance targets? Can it be operated by the designated users? To a first approximation, our problem statement defines what we need to test.

Suppose, for example, we have designed a hand-held tool for storing voice notes, similar to the device shown in Figure 2.10. Here is our problem statement, worded as in Section 2.7.3:

> Design an interactive hand-held consumer product to support the quick and easy storage and retrieval of voice notes.

To determine whether we are on-course to solve this problem, we need to answer a number of questions as early as possible, e.g.:

- How successful is the tool at recognizing message-category names? How is the recognition rate affected by the number of categories in use?

- What kinds of errors does it make due to ambient noise?

- Is it affected by the pitch of the user's voice?

- Is it fast enough in operation to be preferable to a microcassette recorder?

- Is it easy to learn to use?

The problem statement does not cover all of the kinds of knowledge we seek at this early stage. We will have encountered questions during early design and prototyping, and we need answers to these. We will want to know about users' general reactions to the design, and we will be alert to any other factors that crop up unexpectedly during testing. We plan and conduct our investigation so as to ensure that we get feedback in all of these areas.

9.6.2 Conducting the investigation

Informal testing is more likely to be effective if conducted according to the general six-stage framework laid out in Section 9.3.1. Thus we should pay attention to the following points:

(1) **Identifying key properties**. We focus on properties identified in the problem statement or in early requirements documents, and write an investigation plan such as the following:

> It is a requirement of the voice message taker that it should support quick and easy storage and retrieval of voice notes. We intend to run initial tests of the message taker with a number of users, testing users' reactions and identifying problems in use.

(2) **Developing the prototype**. The prototype should offer appropriate levels of functionality, performance and robustness. We can often skimp in some of these areas, and especially in robustness, which is one of the most difficult properties to guarantee in an early prototype. We need a prototype that simply has the functions to support the tasks of interest, has the performance to allow a realistic test, and has enough robustness to survive each test without serious failure.

(3) **Experimental design**. We need access to a small number of users with an interest in helping us evaluate the design. If potential users have participated in the design, they will be obvious candidates for the testing exercise. We need to set our users a suitable range of benchmark tasks to perform, and these should be chosen to exercise the prototype's functionality as fully as possible.

(4) **Collecting data.** Several of the techniques discussed in Chapter 5 are appropriate for data collection. Direct observation and recording of video and concurrent protocols are especially effective in informal tests.

(5) **Data analysis.** There may be little need for in-depth analysis of the data gathered – the good and bad features of the design may be obvious right away. More importantly, we need to ensure that all of the design team take part in the analysis; as Shneiderman points out, the effect on designers of seeing their systems fail is a powerful one, and we need to make sure this happens (Shneiderman, 1992). We may also take simple performance measurements. For example, we might make rough comparisons of users' speed of accessing messages with the voice-notes tool and with a microcassette recorder.

(6) **Drawing conclusions.** The primary outcome of informal testing is a list of design changes. We will also note users' reactions, and will identify successful aspects of the design so as to ensure that these are not discarded. We write a report, and perhaps summarize it in a pro forma:

> It is a requirement of the voice message taker that it should support quick and easy storage and retrieval of voice notes. We have conducted tests on six users, and have received a largely positive reaction, but have identified problems with navigation through the voice-notes database, with perceived modes, with methods of message interruption, and with lack of response to voice input.

This example is based on the study conducted by Stifelman *et al.* (1993). It outlines the areas in which further enhancement will be needed.

A great many accounts of informal evaluations can be found in published reports. The case in Section 9.8 at the end of this chapter describes the evaluation of a large-screen drawing tool, as featured in Figure 9.5(a).

A good example of a design exercise followed up with an informal evaluation can be found in Bly and Minneman (1990). Here a preliminary study of group design work led to the definition of requirements for a prototype, and from there to informal testing by members of the design team. A quote from this study is given in Figure 9.12: we see two users discussing a problem of specifying a rectangular box by its diagonal. User A has missed the fact that this is insufficient for a tilted box, and suddenly gets the point.

9.7 Iterative field tests

The primary aims of conducting a field test are to expose the prototype to a wide variety of realistic forms of usage, and to give evaluators a chance to observe this usage thoroughly. Both of these require time – users must adapt to the new system, and evaluators must gather sufficient data to do a proper analysis. This is why field tests need to be treated as extended evaluation exercises, lasting many months and sometimes stretching into years.

9.7.1 Participative evaluation

Users *participate* in extended field tests. An illustration of this can be found in one of the earliest documented examples of an extended field test of an interactive system, conducted in-house by Apple Computer. In a published interview Larry Tesler of Apple describes how the results of the tests fed into the system's design:

> It turned out that good ideas and good criticisms came from everywhere. We had to come up with some objective ways to decide. That's why we established the methodology which involved user testing. We had a procedure for proposing changes, reviewing the changes, narrowing it down to a few choices, with certain criteria like consistency and parsimony. And then we actually implemented two or three of the various ways and tested them on users, and that's how we made the decisions. Sometimes we found that everybody was wrong. We had a couple of real beauties where users couldn't use any of the versions that were given to them and they would immediately say, 'Why don't you just do it this way?' and that was obviously the way to do it. So sometimes we got the ideas from our user tests, and as soon as we heard the idea we all thought, 'Why didn't we think of that?' (Morgan *et al.*, 1983)

We see here confirmation of field tests' participative nature. They succeed by drawing users into the investigation rather than placing them on the sidelines, and in this respect draw on the same principles as the participative design techniques described in Chapter 6. When we mount such

B: Well, that's okay, it looks like
A: Which is
B: this.
A: Which is, if you take your
     blue box
B: uh huh
A: and note that its corner Top
     Left, if you will. Bottom
     Right, so it's a diagonal
     line

B: Right.
A: between these two. What
     you've given me from the
     starting point — oooh, is the
     inside-out version. I'm sorry,
     you're right.
B: So I get this, 'cause I wanted
     mine to be stretchy. Well,
     only you'd draw it better than
     I just did.

Figure 9.12   Two users solving a problem with the aid of a shared drawing tool, during an
informal test; from Bly and Minneman (1990).

an investigation we try to engage our users' support, and in return we commit to supporting the users' activities. This in turn affects quite considerably the way we conduct the evaluation.

9.7.2 Stages in field testing

Let us look in some detail at how the six stages of evaluation are affected by conducting the investigation in the field:

(1) **Identifying key properties**. Whereas this comes first in most evaluation exercises, in extended field tests we are more likely to delay this step until we have developed the prototype, identified our users and installed the system. Then we will conduct a series of investigations according to the properties that are of current concern.

    As we saw in the quote above, investigations often involve changes to the prototype. These changes must be kept within bounds. We must avoid constantly changing the system 'under the user's feet'. The initial introduction of the system will be a major upheaval for users, and further major upheavals will risk alienating them.

(2) **Making ready the prototype.** We need a full-scale prototype, engineered to adequate levels of reliability and performance. Weaknesses in the software system will cause failures, and these in turn will lose us our users' support. We also need a prototype that can be modified as the field test proceeds; difficult though this may be, we need to leave room for unanticipated changes to be made along the way.

    It is often difficult to estimate when to plan the installation of the prototype, because problems with the design will be discovered during prototyping itself, and rectifying them may cause the schedule to slip. If possible, generous amounts of slack time should be built into the evaluation plan.

(3) **Experimental design.** In comparison with other evaluation methods, field testing can involve investing a very large amount of effort in identifying users and planning their tasks. Unless the design project has been organized as a participative or in-house exercise from the start, it will be necessary to find a suitable user organization and gain their commitment to the evaluation. This alone can take months to achieve, for it normally involves high-level management approval.

    The user group must be identified and introduced to the project, and their commitment too must be secured. We try to avoid groups whose work is highly critical to the organization, but this may not be possible if the system itself is designed to perform a critical function. Sometimes the only solution here is to foot the bill for running the new and old systems in parallel.

    The overall design of the evaluation will be strongly affected by the choice of activities to be supported by the prototype. These activities should match, as closely as possible, the kind of activity for which the system has been designed. They should also provide opportunities to conduct experiments and vary the way in which the activity is supported.

(4) **Running the tests.** Our users will need to be thoroughly trained before any tests are run; the evaluation plan should allow time for this training. We will also need to ensure that the system is adequately primed with data; a new mail-order system, for example, will need to be loaded with customer and product databases. Some of the tests may be scheduled to take place soon after the system is brought online, in order to measure users' learning rates and identify problems in familiarization. Other tests will be delayed until users are fully familiar with the system and have started to adjust their work practices.

(5) **Analysis.** Ongoing field tests offer opportunities for before-and-after investigations. We will be able to measure improvements in task performance times and reductions in errors as users gain familiarity, and we may observe similar effects as changes are made to the design. To make the most of these opportunities we should use appropriate methods of analysis, as described in the next chapter.

(6) **Drawing conclusions.** Some of our analyses will point to a need for immediate changes in the design; others will be of a more general nature, perhaps to be considered in future projects. We will undoubtedly learn a great deal about the users and their activities; ultimately, these findings may be among the most useful results emerging from the evaluation.

Reports on field tests are frequently published in the literature; see, for example, the articles by Schroeder *et al.* (1984) on electronic mail systems, Gaver *et al.* (1992) and Dourish *et al.* (1994) on video communication systems, and Harper (1991) on police information systems. We will conclude with a short case study of an in-house field test.

9.8   Case study: Evaluating a meeting support tool

To illustrate real-world evaluation, we will review a project in which a meeting-support tool called *Tivoli* was evaluated (Pedersen *et al.*, 1993). This was a case of a design whose impact was too far-reaching to measure in a brief informal test. Nor could the system have been evaluated adequately by controlled experiments, for the principal target in the system's design was to support meetings, in the manner shown in Figure 9.13. In the designers' words, the requirement was 'to support and augment its users' informal meeting practices'. They wanted to find out if Tivoli could meet this requirement, because their longer-term goal was to support meetings at a distance, with Tivolis in use at two or more sites concurrently. How did they go about measuring the system's initial success?

Figure 9.13   The Tivoli electronic whiteboard in use (Pedersen *et al.*, 1993).

9.8.1   Setting up the experiment

Tivoli was developed in the research lab, and this itself provided an adequate real-world environment in which to test it – many meetings were taking place at the lab every day. It was unnecessary to identify specific user groups or to sign up users to carry out specific tasks. Instead the Tivoli system was installed in ten different locations where meetings frequently took place. No specific action was taken to train users: the intention was that users should 'walk up and figure how to accomplish what they could on an ordinary whiteboard'.

9.8.2   The pro forma plan

The purpose of the investigation, then, could be defined as follows:

> It is a requirement that Tivoli should enable users to maintain and augment informal meeting practices in non-distributed situations. We propose to confirm this by means of extended user trials in a number of meeting rooms.

Data were gathered about the usage of Tivoli by direct contact with its users. Many of these users had participated in the design of Tivoli. The initial evaluation of the system that took place roughly a year after its introduction consisted basically of an analysis of the views collected from users.

9.8.3 Results

The basic conclusion was that successful meetings could indeed be conducted. Tivoli was used frequently in 'brainstorming' meetings where its ability to assist in reorganizing collected points was put to good use. It worked well enough for the next stage of design, a multi-site 'Tivoli 2.0', to be undertaken.

The main unexpected discovery was that usage of Tivoli tended to be by one person at a time, rather than by all members of a meeting as a group. In other words, one person would act as scribe. The reason for this lay in the design of the user interface, which had erred in favour of increased functionality rather than simplicity. In a typical meeting, some users would have gained significantly greater Tivoli skills than others, and these people would naturally gravitate towards the role of scribe, while the rest would play the role of non-user participants in the meeting.

This outcome from the evaluation was fairly clear-cut: most of the essential meeting practices were supported, but the equality of participants was affected. A pro forma report of the investigation might run as follows:

> It is a requirement of Tivoli that it should maintain and augment normal informal meeting practices. We have conducted informal user tests that confirm the usefulness of the tool but indicate that the complexity of the user interface deters some potential users, and leads to a meeting practice in which all use is by one meeting member.

9.9 Conclusion

This chapter has presented methods for developing prototypes and testing them informally and under real-world conditions. We have seen how these evaluations can assist the design process, and how they can help maintain its momentum by fitting in with the timescales of design. By conducting evaluation in this way, rather than at the end of the design process, we can ensure a formative effect on the design's progress.

Informal evaluation methods, and evaluations conducted in the field, provide many useful qualitative results. Indeed these are the only methods that can tell us about user satisfaction, ease of customizing, adaptation of work practices, and other such aspects of the system's usability. They can also provide us with quantitative measures, for example, of task performance times. Under real-world testing conditions, however, we may not be able to control all of the factors affecting users' performance. It is for this reason that we may turn to controlled experimental methods to supplement what we have learned from real-world testing. The next chapter describes these methods.

Exercises

(1) What are formative evaluation and summative evaluation, and why is the former to be preferred to the latter?

(2) What are the two main forms of design question that evaluation helps answer?

(3) What are the four main methods for conducting evaluations? Discuss whether it makes sense (a) to apply them exclusively, that is, to use one method without involving any of the others, (b) to apply two or more of them together.

(4) We often focus evaluation exercises on specific requirements.

   (a) Why do we do this?

   (b) What kinds of questions are answered by focusing on functional requirements?

   (c) What kinds of questions are answered by focusing on performance requirements?

(5) Why do we sometimes conduct evaluations of just a component of the design? When we do this, should we implement just the appropriate component of the user interface? If not, why not?

(6) (a) Make a list of the six basic stages in evaluation.

   (b) Discuss each stage in turn in terms of what might go wrong if you were to omit it.

(7) Discuss the usefulness of the data collection methods described in Chapter 5 in support of evaluations.

(8) Write pro forma plans and reports for the other examples in Chapter 8 besides the graph-plotting example.

(9) How would you deal with the examples in Chapter 8 *without* using analytical tools, that is, solely by empirical evaluation? Which methods would you use in each case? Describe in detail how you would conduct (a) an empirical test of users' problems in using the ticket machine of Section 8.5.1 for the first time; (b) an empirical evaluation of the online hardware store catalogue of Section 8.6.1.

(10) What are the main differences between the methods for conducting informal user tests and full field tests?

(11) (HyperCard programmers) Complete the implementation of the ticket-machine prototype. Write a pro forma report on what you learn during the exercise.

Further reading

Hix D. and Hartson H. R. (1993). *Developing User Interfaces: Ensuring Usability through Product and Process*. New York: Wiley

A general and highly readable introduction to user interface design. Chapters 9 and 10 provide thorough coverage of most aspects of prototyping and evaluation in support of user interface design.

Whiteside J., Bennett J. and Holtzblatt K. (1988). Usability engineering: Our experience and evolution. In *Handbook of Human-Computer Interaction* (Helander M., ed.), pp. 791–817. Amsterdam: North-Holland

An excellent, thought-provoking survey of the major issues in usability and how to measure it.

Bly S. and Minneman S. (1990). Commune: A shared drawing surface. *Proc. COIS '90, Conference on Office Information Systems*, Cambridge, MA, April 25–27, 1990, pp. 184–92

An example of a carefully conducted exercise in study, analysis, design and evaluation in which some of the originally identified user needs were indeed seen to be addressed when the system was evaluated.

CHAPTER 10

Experiments in support of design

Chapter objectives:

Some design questions can be answered properly only by conducting carefully controlled evaluations. The resulting data then need to be analysed to determine the result and to establish the level of confidence that can be attached to it. This chapter presents:

- The reasons why we conduct controlled experiments in support of design
- Methods for designing experiments that will deliver useful results to the design team
- The kinds of problems we face in analysing the results
- Some simple analysis methods that illustrate the approach we take to establishing confidence in the results of experiments.

10.1 Introduction

Chapter 9 discussed three approaches to the empirical evaluation of designs for interactive systems: learning through prototyping, informal evaluation and field testing. We come now to a fourth and last approach, in which we evaluate by conducting *controlled experiments*, that is, where we control carefully the conditions under which the system is used. We do this so that we can take accurate measurements and thus compare the performance of different designs.

The methods we use here are different from the methods of field testing and informal evaluation described in Chapter 9. In particular, controlled experiments are often planned with a view to exploring very specific *hypotheses*, for example, the hypothesis that one system is faster in use than another. An experiment of this kind needs careful planning and conduct if it is to show whether the hypothesis can be accepted. Careful analysis is needed to determine how much confidence can be attached to the result.

This chapter describes in outline how such evaluations are carried out, and describes some simple statistical methods of data analysis. In such a short chapter it is not possible to offer a thorough treatment of statistical methods; the aim here is to indicate the nature of the process that we go through in conducting an experiment and then in establishing a level of confidence in the experimental result. For those who want to take these methods further, some good introductory texts are available (Keppel and Saufley, 1980; Klugh, 1986; Howell, 1989).

10.2   The purpose of controlled experiments

The basic reason for engaging in controlled experiments is to take accurate measurements of usability levels, more accurate than can be achieved during informal testing or field evaluation. Sometimes a great deal hinges on performance, and a small improvement may offer substantial benefits. Sometimes we can see that the design of a central component will affect the performance of many tasks. In these cases we need accurate estimates of the likely effects on task performance. We can conduct these high-precision evaluations if we can exercise adequate control over the conditions of testing.

10.2.1   Evaluation when usage is predictable

As we have seen in the last chapter, the basic purpose of evaluation is to help us make choices between design strategies and to check that we are on target to meet usability requirements. More specifically, evaluation addresses design questions of two main kinds:

- Is Design A preferable to Design B on the grounds of usability?
- Does the chosen design strategy meet requirement R?

These questions can be answered qualitatively, without resorting to calculating usability values, by the methods described in Chapter 9. This may be appropriate when the circumstances of system use are unpredictable.

If the situation of use is more predictable, however, a more precise evaluation may be feasible. One such situation arises when a well-established system is being upgraded in a way that preserves users' task structures. A similar situation arises if a small but important component of the user interface is changed, for example, a frequently used menu. Then we have an opportunity to measure the effect on usability more precisely. Furthermore, we may have a real need to know the precise effect on usability, because the success of the whole design may hinge on it.

An example: Upgrading a CAD package

Consider the following example, in which a controlled evaluation might be preferable to evaluation in the field.

We are upgrading a software drafting package for computer-aided design (CAD), and need to offer our prospective users more efficient ways of preparing drawings than they already have. The current user interface makes heavy use of pull-down menus of the kind shown in Figure 10.1(a).

We might decide to investigate the use of *pie menus*, that is, menus of the kind shown in Figure 10.1(b) in which the options are arranged in a circle around a selected spot (Callahan *et al.*, 1988; Hopkins, 1991). But this would represent a significant change in the design of the user interface. Before making a commitment to this change, we would like to know whether pie menus will offer a substantial performance improvement over pull-down menus. We would like to compare the performance of the current pull-down design with that of a design based on pie menus.

We might consider evaluating the new design by means of a field test. However, a field test of the new design would involve a large-scale software development exercise, which we might wish to avoid. Furthermore, we would have difficulty obtaining an accurate answer, since we would have less control over the tasks performed and the conditions surrounding each test. We would be more likely to gain our answer by conducting laboratory tests on users performing a carefully chosen selection of typical drafting tasks.

Controlled evaluation of user interface components

As in this example, it is common to apply carefully controlled methods of evaluation to *components* of the user interface such as menus, icons, screen layouts and so forth. These components receive heavy use, thus influencing overall performance significantly. By conducting a controlled experiment we factor these other influences out. We can measure the effect of changing the component on the performance of users' activities.

Designing an experiment

Accordingly, we could evaluate the pie-menu design against the current pull-down design by running an experiment. In this experiment we could set two groups of users to perform the same task, or set of tasks, one group using the current system, the other using the new system with pie menus. We would want to ensure that no other factors were affecting

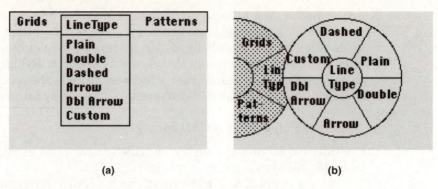

Figure 10.1   Two alternative designs for menus in a CAD package: (a) the current pull-down menu design; (b) an alternative design based on pie menus.

performance of the task, and that the task itself was representative of CAD system use. Provided we paid sufficient attention to these and other aspects of experimental design, the performance data collected could be used as a basis for a decision on whether to adopt pie menus.

As we can see, this example raises some important issues in experimental design, some of which have already been touched on in the last chapter. There are issues to do with eliminating extraneous factors that might affect the result. There is the issue of recruiting subjects for the experiment and choosing appropriate tasks for them to perform. And there is the matter of how to analyse the data collected. These issues need to be addressed in conjunction, because they are not entirely independent. The next section covers some basic material that helps tie these issues together.

10.3 Populations and samples

Experimental design introduces some new concepts and terminology. We draw on methods from experimental science, particularly from psychology. Some of these methods may seem a little out of place in the context of evaluating designs. It is important to understand the basic principles on which they build, however, if we want to apply the methods successfully.

10.3.1 Populations

As much as possible, we design experiments to reproduce the same effects as will occur when the system is installed in the real world. In other words, we use a realistic prototype, we recruit subjects who perform like real users, and we give them realistic tasks to do.

The one thing we cannot reproduce in an experiment is the entire **population** of the real-world phenomena we are investigating. We cannot test our system on the entire population of people who will use it, unless these are a small and very stable group. We cannot test it on the whole 'population' of tasks our users will perform, unless these are a small and very repetitive set. In many cases we have no idea of the populations of potential users and tasks.

There is another even larger population involved in the evaluation of systems, made up of all of the possible *performance values* that our users might achieve when carrying out their tasks. In theory, we would like to measure all of these performance values, or **scores**, in our experiment. For example, we would like to have complete data on how fast the existing CAD system enabled users to perform their tasks in the past, and we would like to know how fast our new pie-menu version will be every time it is used in the future. Then we could take the average, or **mean**, of the scores with the old system, and the mean of the scores with the new system, and compare the two **population means**. This would give us a reliable result.

But all of this is out of the question. Not only is it too late to measure the performances that have taken place in the past, but it is too *early* to measure the performances that will take place in the future. We can take measurements only during the conduct of the experiment. Somehow we must transform these measurements into a useful result.

10.3.2   Samples and sample means

During the experiment, therefore, we gather just a few measurements, a tiny fraction of the entire population of scores. We call this set of scores a **sample**. We try to ensure, through careful design of the experiment, that our sample is representative of the population. In particular, we try to draw our samples *randomly* from the population, so that they are not biased in one direction or clustered in a particular region. Then we can calculate the mean of the sample, which we call the **sample mean**. If the sample includes an adequate number of scores, taken in a truly random manner, then the sample mean should lie close to the population mean that we would like to know but cannot measure. Stated in reverse, the unknown population mean is likely to lie somewhere near the known sample mean we have calculated.

10.3.3   Confidence levels

It is not enough to know that the population mean 'is likely to lie somewhere near' the sample mean. A lot may hinge on the result of the experiment, and we need to know how much confidence we can place in it. How sure are we that our sample is representative of the population? Could we possibly have gathered a sample whose mean differs considerably from the population mean? What is the likelihood that this has happened?

Suppose, for example, we work in a company with a large order-entry department. Errors in data entry are causing problems and losing the company money. The error rate needs to be reduced by at least 10 per cent. We therefore design an improved user interface and invite users to test it in a controlled experiment. Our sample of error rates shows a reduction of 15 per cent. The data entry manager is delighted, and initiates a major upgrade of the software, costing several hundred thousand dollars. But this decision is based on just a sample. A true population mean might conceivably show that the new interface causes only a two per cent reduction in errors, or perhaps even an increase. We know there is a low probability of this, but with hundreds of thousands of dollars about to be spent, we would like to know just what this probability is.

So when samples are taken and sample means are calculated, further calculations are then performed to work out what level of confidence can be attached to the result. Our concern is always that we have been misled by a promising-looking sample mean, and that the population mean actually lies on the wrong side of some critical value, for example, below 10 per cent reduction in error rates. The calculation tells us the probability, p, that this is the case. Normally we consider a value of $p < 0.05$ (that is, a chance of less than 5 in 100) to represent an adequate level of confidence.

We try to design experiments to achieve results that justify such confidence levels. We set targets for the level of confidence we want to achieve. If our samples enable us to achieve such a target, we consider them to be **significant**. The targets set at the outset of experiments are often stated separately from the probabilities attached to the outcome, in the form of α values; for example, they may set significance targets of $\alpha = 0.05$ or $\alpha = 0.02$. These simply mean that we are aiming to achieve p values below 0.05 or 0.02.

Now let us look at how experiments are designed to achieve significant results.

10.4 The design of two-sample experiments

The experiments we conduct in support of design frequently involve comparisons of two solutions. We may need to compare a new design with an existing one, as in the case of the CAD package or the order entry system. We may need to know which of two proposed designs performs better, independent of any current solution. To find out, we collect performance data from tests of the two designs in question, and compare the sample means, as illustrated in Figure 10.2. We call this a *two-sample experiment*.

Two-sample experiments are not the only kind that arise in the course of design. These experiments address only the question, 'Is Design A preferable to Design B?' As mentioned above, we also encounter questions of the form, 'Does Design A meet requirement R?' As we shall see, however, the methods that we use for two-sample experiments can be adapted to the single-sample case. They then enable us to compare the performance of a design with a stated requirement (see Figure 10.3).

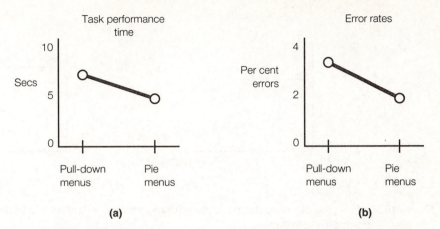

Figure 10.2   Results of two-sample experiments. The circular symbols represent sample means, in this case the mean scores determined from testing a pull-down menu design and a pie-menu design, and measuring (a) task performance time, and (b) number of errors made when selecting from menus.

Occasionally we encounter more complex evaluations, perhaps involving three or more samples. Methods for these experiments would take a lot more explaining than there is room for here. By the end of this chapter we will have identified some of these more complex cases.

10.4.1   Measurements in the context of task performance

When we conduct controlled experiments we try to ensure that our data are relevant to real-world use by giving our subjects realistic tasks to perform. The choice of these *externally valid tasks* is an important part of experimental design.

We try to choose tasks that have similar characteristics to the population of tasks performed in the external world. At the same time, we try to make sure that the tasks will exercise the designs so as to bring out any differences in their support for the tasks. Thus we would not ask CAD package users simply to make as many menu selections as possible in two minutes, because this is a most unlikely thing to find people doing in the real world. Nor would we ask them to enter 500 numbers into a table – even though this does happen in the real world – because users entering text make relatively little use of menus. This task is not sufficiently *sensitive* to changes in the menu designs.

Part of the difficulty in task choice lies in the limited range of tasks we can ask users to perform. Under the tight timescales of design evaluation we have no time to test them on a wide range of tasks. Inevitably we can collect data about only a small subset of the full task population.

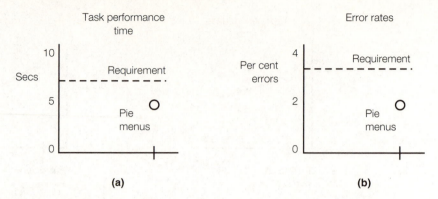

Figure 10.3   How we can treat comparisons with requirements as simplified forms of two-sample experiments.

10.4.2 The variables in the experiment

When we plan an experiment, we identify the quantity we want to measure, for example, the speed of performance of a task or the number of errors made. We call this the **dependent variable** because its value is dependent on the conditions of the experiment, for example, on the nature of the system used in support of the task. Experiments are usually concerned with measuring how the experimental conditions affect the dependent variable; they are conducted by changing the conditions, that is, by altering the **independent variables** that determine the conditions. In many evaluations of designs we select a usability factor – speed of performance, incidence of errors, and so on – as our dependent variable. We modify the independent variable by introducing changes in the system's design.

An example of altering the independent variable and measuring a dependent variable has already been seen in Figure 10.2(a). Here the design was varied from a pull-down menu version to a pie-menu version (the independent variable) and measurements were made of task performance time (the dependent variable). In Figure 10.2(b) we see the same variation in the independent variable, but with measurements of a different dependent variable, error rates.

In the evaluation of interactive systems it is very common to treat the design solution as the independent variable and a usability factor as the dependent variable. Other independent variables may be used; for example, we may measure the effect on error rates of varying the amount of prior training given to users. However, these kinds of experiments are less directly helpful in making choices between design decisions or checking designs against requirements.

10.4.3 Nuisance variables

In designing the experiment, a great deal of effort goes into making sure that *only* the independent variables are affecting the dependent variable. Typically this means making sure that *only* switching between one design and another can affect task performance times. We will never succeed in eradicating other influencing factors entirely, because there is an inevitable degree of variation among our subjects. What we must guard against, however, are so-called **nuisance variables** that vary alongside the independent variables we are controlling, and cause uncontrolled variation in the dependent variable.

In our test of the speed of operation of pie menus, for example, we might fail to maintain the same menu hierarchy as before. Indeed it might be impossible to squeeze all of the items from a pull-down menu onto one pie menu – we might have to replace one long pull-down menu with several pies. Unfortunately it is known that changes in menu hierarchy affect task performance time (Miller, 1981). By dividing up the existing menus we are interfering with the experiment – we are **confounding** the result, to use a common term.

Once we have realized that we are dealing with a nuisance variable we can neutralize it in one of a number of ways. One way is to take steps to hold it constant, for example, we can be very careful to keep our pie-menu structure the same as the pull-down structure. Another method is to spread the effect of the nuisance variable randomly over the subjects, so that its effect disappears in the averaging of results. In the pie-menu example, this would involve designing a new menu hierarchy with the same overall depth and breadth as the old one – not an easy task. It is usually preferable to deal with nuisance variables by holding them constant, if this is at all feasible.

10.4.4 The stages of the experiment

These principles of experimental design are reflected in the way we go about conducting controlled evaluations under laboratory conditions. We can see their influence on each of the six basic stages:

(1) **Identifying the variables.** We identify the usability factors to be measured and treat these as our dependent variables; our independent variable is typically represented by the alternative designs we are testing. At this stage we should also define the tasks that our users will perform; they should be externally valid, and sensitive to the proposed changes in the independent variable.

(2) **Making ready the prototype.** We need to ensure that the prototype can support the performance of the selected tasks. We may not need a full implementation of the user interface, however. If we are comparing two proposed designs, we may build the prototype so that we can vary

properties of the design independently. We may also introduce tools for taking precise measurements.

(3) **Recruiting the subjects.** We need to decide at an early stage how many subjects we will need. Using more subjects will probably provide a better estimate of the true population mean, but will expand the scale of the exercise too. We will draw our subjects from a suitable pool of people with appropriate backgrounds, for example, by employing students or by recruiting members of the user organization. We may need to consider what the subjects should be paid for taking part in the experiment.

(4) **Running the tests and collecting data.** We must schedule the experimental sessions according to their length and to the availability of subjects. We use precise methods of measurement, such as a stop watch or a time-stamped video recording, or methods built into the software.

(5) **Analysing the data.** The calculation of sample means is usually a simple matter, as we have seen. The analysis of confidence levels is more complex; some simple methods are described in the latter part of this chapter.

(6) **Drawing conclusions.** According to the results of Stage 5, we may now have evidence that one solution strategy is preferable to another, or we may have results indicating that our chosen strategy meets our performance targets.

Steps 1, 3 and 4, in which the actual experiment is organized and carried out, typically involve much of the effort. Some of the techniques are similar to those described in Chapter 9 for other types of evaluations. Data gathering can often be carried out using the techniques described in Chapter 5. For a more thorough discussion of planning and running evaluations, see Hix and Hartson (1993).

10.5 Establishing confidence levels

Thus far, this chapter has been concerned primarily with explaining the nature of populations, samples and confidence levels, and in laying out some of the issues in designing successful experiments. Now our discussion turns to methods of testing for significance and establishing confidence levels. A few simple techniques are presented in order to give the flavour of how these calculations are done. To cater to readers with varying backgrounds, the explanations are given both in terms of the mathematical formulae involved and as simple step-by-step worked examples. Although some readers may prefer to stop at this point in the chapter, they are strongly recommended to read further and catch a glimpse of how these important analyses are done.

10.5.1   Normal distributions

The challenge in conducting experiments lies, as we have seen, in learning about unseen populations by taking small samples. One of the assumptions we can make about our population concerns the shape of the **distribution** of its constituent scores. This is extremely helpful, for it helps us to be much more precise about the range within which the population mean is likely to lie.

In many of the situations we study, populations of scores will tend to have a so-called **normal distribution**. Most of the scores lie near the population mean, tailing off symmetrically on either side, as shown in the bell-shaped curve of Figure 10.4(a). Sometimes it is possible to collect scores for large populations and verify that they follow such a distribution; for example, Gray *et al.* (1993) conducted a study of telephone

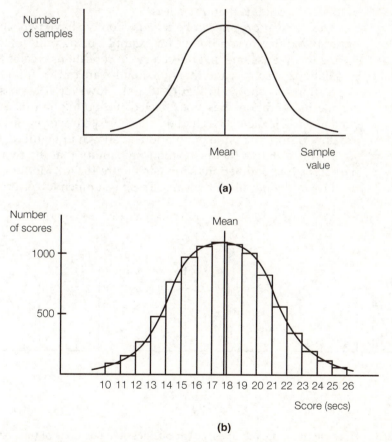

Figure 10.4   The normal distribution curve: (a) the shape of the normal distribution; (b) how a histogram of scores tends to follow the normal distribution curve; the chart shows the distribution of task performance times we might find in a population of 75 000 scores.

operators in which they collected data on task times for 78 240 calls, as described in Case Study A, which follows this chapter. To find the distribution of such data, we count the number of scores lying in each of a number of intervals, for example, the number of calls lasting between 10.00 and 10.99 seconds, the number from 11.00 to 11.99, and so on. We will probably arrive at a histogram like the one in Figure 10.4(b), closely following the path of the bell-shaped curve.

When we conduct an experiment in which we believe that the population has a normal distribution, we can make some useful estimates of probability on this basis. Suppose the population has the distribution shown in Figure 10.5; we can calculate the probability that it lies at any of the three positions, in relation to the sample mean, shown in Figures 10.5(a), 10.5(b) and 10.5(c). The further away the population mean lies, the fewer scores are likely to lie in the 'tail' of the curve, to the left of the sample we have taken. As a result, the probability of such a sample being part of this population is that much less.

The same approach can be taken when we have two samples, taken under two different conditions, for example, using pull-down menus and pie menus. We assume that the change in conditions creates two different populations of scores, and that our samples are drawn from two different populations, as shown in Figure 10.6(a). However, it is possible that the change in conditions has not affected the population of scores at all – changing to pie menus has had no effect. In other words, our two samples are drawn from the same population, as shown in Figure 10.6(b).

In this example there is a good probability that the two samples are part of the two populations shown in Figure 10.6(a), for the sample means lie close to the population means. There is a much lower probability that

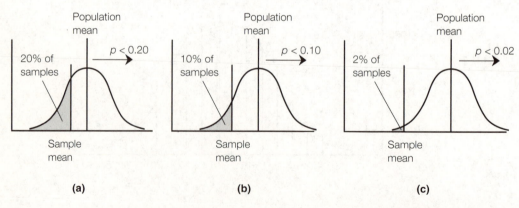

Figure 10.5   How we place probabilities on various possible positions of the population distribution. Here the population mean is seen in three positions increasingly far from the sample mean. As the area under the curve to the left of the sample mean decreases, so does the probability (shown as values 0.20, 0.10, 0.02) that the population curve lies in or beyond this position.

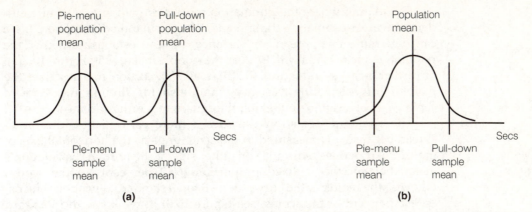

Figure 10.6   Alternative hypotheses we might offer to explain samples taken under two different conditions: (a) the two samples come from two different populations; (b) the two samples are part of of the same population.

the samples are part of the single population shown in Figure 10.6(b), for their means lie out in the two tails of the curve, where the population has relatively few scores.

10.5.2   Population variance and standard deviation

Although normal distribution curves all have roughly the same bell-like fall-off on either side of the mean, some distributions spread further than others, because there is more variation among the scores. It is possible that a sample may belong to a narrow population or a broad one, as shown in Figure 10.7. This in turn affects how far the population mean is likely to lie from the sample mean we have measured.

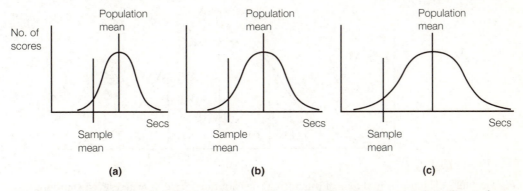

Figure 10.7   Samples with different variances. The probability that the sample is drawn from the population is the same in each case, but the increased variance of populations (b) and (c) implies that their population means may lie further from the sample mean.

Calculating where the population mean lies with any level of confidence involves estimating the spread of the population distribution. If we can determine this spread, or **variance**, we can establish whether the population mean is likely to lie near the sample mean, as in Figure 10.7(a), or further away, as in Figures 10.7(b) or 10.7(c). Section 10.6 describes the method for calculating variances, and also for finding the *standard deviation*, s, of a sample by taking the square root of its variance.

The **standard deviation** provides a more convenient indicator of spread because it is measured in the same units as the horizontal axis of the curve. It defines a distance on either side of the normal distribution's mean that encloses a fixed proportion (68.2 per cent) of the scores. Likewise the region of the curve from −3 to +3 standard deviations encloses 99.8 per cent of the scores (see Figure 10.8). If we know the standard deviation of a population we can calculate the percentage of scores enclosed within any range along the horizontal axis. This is how, for example, we could calculate the size of the 20 per cent, 10 per cent and 2 per cent regions shown in Figure 10.5.

We cannot calculate variances and standard deviations of populations, of course, any more than we can determine population means, for we do not have access to the full set of scores. However, we can make the useful assumption that the population's standard deviation is closely related to the standard deviations of samples from the same population. This means that if we take two samples under different conditions (for example, using two different designs) and find that they have different standard deviations, then they probably come from populations with different standard deviations too. This is illustrated in Figure 10.9.

We are starting to see here how small samples can provide us with the basis for making estimates of the likely nature of much larger populations.

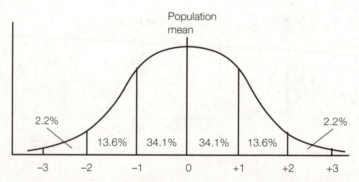

Figure 10.8   The horizontal axis of the normal distribution curve, marked off in standard deviation units. The regions 1 standard deviation in width on either side of the mean enclose 34.1 % each of the scores, that is, 68.2 % altogether. The regions 2 standard deviations wide enclose 47.7 % each, or 95.4 % total; 3 standard deviations enclose 49.9 % on each side, or 99.8 % total.

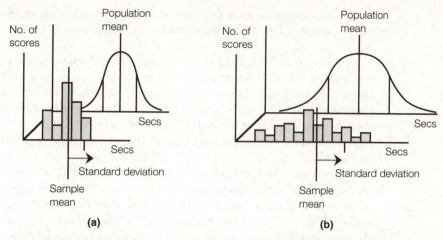

Figure 10.9   How sample variances can inform us about population variances. The two samples in (a) and (b), shown as histograms, contain the same number of scores. However, sample (a) has relatively small variance compared with sample (b), indicating that the population variances are likely to differ in the same way.

According to where we think the population mean lies, we can calculate the probability that our sample was drawn from this population. According to the sample's standard deviation we can make assumptions about the population's variance and standard deviation. These are the calculations that enable us, in the design context, to set confidence levels on measurements of usability.

10.5.3   The null hypothesis

During this chapter we have seen how experiments can produce data that have different possible explanations. Thus our samples of speed of operation of the CAD package, indicating a reduction in task times, may indicate that the new design does indeed increase speed of use (as in Figure 10.6(a)), or that we have simply drawn two very different samples from a single, unchanged population of task times (as in Figure 10.6(b)). In the data entry case, the 15 per cent measured reduction in errors may be caused by the change in user interface design, or alternatively the new user interface may have had no effect, and the difference is simply due to sampling errors.

Every controlled experiment can have two such outcomes. Whatever the scores in our samples, we can explain them in two different ways, by two different *hypotheses*:

> H_0 Our deliberate change in the experimental conditions has had no effect; any difference in sample means is due entirely to variations among the population;

H_1 Our change in the experimental conditions has had an effect on scores, which is reflected in the difference in sample means.

Explanation H_0 is known as the **null hypothesis**. It is an explanation we hope to reject. If we cannot reject it, we must conclude either that the change in conditions is having no effect on scores, or that our experiment was insufficiently sensitive to pick up the effect. On the other hand, if our calculations show that the null hypothesis is false, we can accept H_1 – the **experimental hypothesis** that claims that the change in conditions has had an effect.

This is how we go about calculating confidence levels. We establish a null hypothesis that states the converse of the result we hope to find. In other words, if we want to show that task time has improved, we state a null hypothesis that it has not changed at all. We set a target of demonstrating that the null hypothesis is false, for a particular level of significance α. If we succeed, we can accept the alternative hypothesis, and can set an upper limit, p, to the probability that the null hypothesis holds true. This represents the confidence level of our result.

10.5.4 Some simple methods of statistical analysis

In the remainder of this chapter we will work through some simple methods for calculating confidence levels in the results of experiments. The purpose of introducing these methods is to show that certain simple kinds of experiments can produce results that are quite easy to analyse. Some of these types of experiment are very useful in the evaluation of designs; they can help answer the kinds of questions mentioned at the start of this chapter, concerning relative usability levels and meeting requirements. It can be useful to know how to calculate answers to such questions and to attach confidence levels.

It is important to understand, however, that statistical methods cover a wide spectrum, and go far beyond these methods in terms of power and complexity. Sometimes it is necessary to use more complex statistical methods in support of design evaluations, because the relationship between the experimental variables is itself more complex. The conclusion to this chapter identifies some situations where this can occur.

So the methods here should be regarded as methods that are suitable for use in simple experimental cases and that are themselves fairly easy to perform. If it is feasible to design experiments to comply with these cases, then the calculations can be carried out in the ways described. But if the conditions of the experiment change, then it will be unwise to attempt to use these methods. Advice should be sought from someone experienced in experimental design and analysis.

10.6 Basic calculations of variance and standard deviation

We will start with some simple calculations that provide building blocks for the analyses that tell us how to treat scores from experiments. They enable us to calculate the sums of squares of differences, the variance of samples, and standard deviations.

Each of these is a very simple calculation, which will be shown as a formula into which data values can be substituted. To clarify how the substitutions are done, each calculation is also shown as a worked example, in the style of a recipe.

10.6.1 Sums of squares of differences from the mean

The first three steps in almost every analysis of experimental data are to calculate the mean, and then to find the sum of the squares of the scores' differences from this mean, and from there to proceed to find the variance and standard deviation. Sums of squares themselves are not particularly meaningful, but we need to calculate them frequently and therefore rapidly.

To compute the mean $\overline{X}$ of a set of scores $X_1, X_2, \ldots X_N$, we add them together and divide by the number of scores, N. The Σ symbol, sigma, is used to represent the summing calculation:

$$\overline{X} = (\Sigma X_i) / N$$

To compute the sum of squares of differences, SS, we perform the following calculation:

$$SS = \Sigma (X_i - \overline{X})^2$$

Each of the differences, $X_i - \overline{X}$, is squared before computing the sum.

An alternative computational formula can be used, involving fewer steps:

$$SS = \Sigma X_i^2 - \overline{X}^2 / N$$

In other words, we can calculate SS as the sum of the squares of the scores, minus the square of the sum of scores divided by N.

Worked example: Sum of squares of differences

In this first example we will calculate the mean and the sum of the squares of differences for the following five values:

   3.4, 7.6, 4.5, 6.2, 5.3

To compute the mean we add together the five values and divide by 5. This gives a value of $(3.4 + 7.6 + 4.5 + 6.2 + 5.3) \div 5 = 27 \div 5 = 5.4$.

The sum of squares of differences is calculated as the difference between two components:

- The sum of the squares of all of the scores: $3.4^2 + 7.6^2 + 4.5^2 + 6.2^2 + 5.3^2 = 156.1$.

- The square of the total, divided by the number of scores, that is, $27^2 \div 5 = 729 \div 5 = 145.8$.

Subtracting the second from the first, $156.1 - 145.8$, gives us the sum of squares $SS = 10.3$.

From the following table we can see that the basic method, in which individual differences are calculated, arrives at the same result:

Score	Difference from mean	Difference squared
3.4	−2.0	4.00
7.6	2.2	4.84
4.5	−0.9	0.81
6.2	0.8	0.64
5.3	−0.1	0.01
27.0		$SS = 10.30$

10.6.2   Degrees of freedom

There are **degrees of freedom** in calculated values such as sums of squares. They arise from the fact that scores are *free to vary* independently of each other; thus each of the five scores in the above worked example is free to take any positive value, whatever the value of the other scores. When we use calculated values in other calculations we may need to eliminate the degrees of freedom, which we do by simple division. This division by the number of degrees of freedom is built into most of the methods described below.

The rules governing the number of degrees of freedom in a calculation are complex, and do not need to be understood here; they are explained in the recommended texts. We will simply note the number of degrees of freedom in each calculation, as we perform the divisions.

10.6.3 Variance and standard deviation of a sample

The variance of a set of N scores, s^2, is calculated by dividing the sum of squares by the degrees of freedom, in this case $N - 1$:

$$s^2 = SS / (N - 1)$$

The standard deviation, s, is the square root of the variance:

$$s = \sqrt{(s^2)}$$

A step-by-step calculation of variance and standard deviation is shown in the worked example.

Worked example: Variance and standard deviation

We will continue with the same set of scores as in the previous example (3.4, 7.6, 4.5, 6.2, 5.3) and compute the variance. We have already calculated the sum of squares $SS = 10.3$. The variance is then the sum of squares divided by the degrees of freedom, that is, by one less than the number of scores, $10.3 \div 4 = 2.575$.

Now we can calculate the standard deviation by taking the square root of the variance. Our answer is $\sqrt{2.575} = 1.605$. We can confirm, in the following table, that this lies within the range (0.1 to 2.2) of the magnitudes of individual differences from the mean:

Score	Difference from mean
3.4	−2.0
7.6	2.2
4.5	−0.9
6.2	0.8
5.3	−0.1

10.7 Comparisons of two samples: The *t* test

Many design experiments involve two sets of small samples in which measurements are taken of a single dependent variable, typically measures of task performance supported by two different designs. The means of the two samples indicate the difference in performance. In these experiments, the *t* **test** provides a simple method of estimating the confidence with which we can reject the null hypothesis.

The method involves calculating a value *t* from the sampled scores, and comparing this with the *critical* value of *t* indicating that the null hypothesis is true, for a particular significance value α and number of degrees of freedom. If the calculated *t* value exceeds the critical value, we will have shown that the null hypothesis is false, for this value of α. The critical values of *t* need not be calculated: they can be looked up in the values given in Table 10.1.

To calculate the *t* value we must first calculate a combined variance for the two samples. As in the single-sample variance method described above, we calculate the sums of squares and divide by the degrees of freedom. In this instance we add together the sums of squares SS_1 and SS_2 from both samples, and use a value of $N_1 + N_2 - 2$ for the degrees of freedom:

$$s^2 = (SS_1 + SS_2) / (N_1 + N_2 - 2)$$

From this variance we compute the *standard error of difference*, s_{ed}:

$$s_{ed} = \sqrt{(s^2 (1/N_1 + 1/N_2))}$$

To complete the calculation of *t* we evaluate the following expression:

Table 10.1   Table of *t*. Each entry represents the value above which the null hypothesis may be rejected, for a given number of degrees of freedom and significance value. Significance values are shown both for two-tailed tests of pairs of samples, and for single-tailed tests of one sample against a required value. Source: the figures were computed by the authors.

Degrees of freedom	$\alpha = 0.10$ $\alpha = 0.05$	$\alpha = 0.05$ $\alpha = 0.025$	$\alpha = 0.02$ $\alpha = 0.01$	$\alpha = 0.01$ $\alpha = 0.005$	(two-tailed) (single-tailed)
1	6.314	12.706	31.821	63.656	
2	2.920	4.303	6.965	9.925	
3	2.353	3.182	4.541	5.841	
4	2.132	2.776	3.747	4.604	
5	2.015	2.571	3.365	4.032	
6	1.943	2.447	-3.143	3.707	
7	1.895	2.365	2.998	3.499	
8	1.860	2.306	2.896	3.355	
9	1.833	2.262	2.821	3.250	
10	1.812	2.228	2.764	3.169	
11	1.796	2.201	2.718	3.106	
12	1.782	2.179	2.681	3.055	

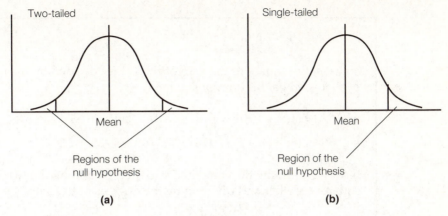

Figure 10.10   Two-tailed and single-tailed null hypotheses.

$$t = (\bar{X}_1 - \bar{X}_2) / s_{ed}$$

Table 10.1 can be consulted to determine whether this value lies above or below the critical value. If it lies above, we can reject the null hypothesis with a level of probability less than the α value shown at the head of the column. We use the 'two-tailed' probability values because we are testing for differences in either direction between the two samples. In effect, we are trying to reject a null hypothesis which would place the difference at either extreme of a distribution curve (Figure 10.10(a)).

Worked example: A **t** *test on two samples*

Suppose we have conducted tests of two designs, each on three subjects. This would normally be too small a sample, but we are using it here to simplify the calculation. Our two sets of three scores are shown in the table:

	Design A	*Design B*
	12	8
	10	3
	6	5
	28	16
means	9.33	5.33

Before we can calculate *t* we need to find the sums of squares SS_1 and SS_2. We will use the second, faster method described above. For each sample, we compute the sum of the squares of the scores, and

continues

continued

subtract the square of the sum of the values divided by the number of scores, to get the sum of squares:

- $SS_1 = (12^2 + 10^2 + 6^2) - (28^2 \div 3) = 280 - 261.33 = 18.67$
- $SS_2 = (8^2 + 3^2 + 5^2) - (16^2 \div 3) = 98 - 85.33 = 12.67$

Next we compute the combined variance, by adding the two sums of squares together and dividing by the degrees of freedom, $3 + 3 - 2 = 4$:

$$\text{combined variance} = (18.67 + 12.67) \div 4 = 31.33 \div 4 = 7.83$$

From this we can compute the standard error of difference. We compute $1/N_1 + 1/N_2$, where N_1 and N_2 are the number of samples, in each case 3, and multiply this by the combined variance. In other words, we multiply $(1/3 + 1/3)$ by $7.83 = 2/3 \times 7.83 = 5.22$. We take the square root of this value to obtain the standard error of difference:

$$s_{ed} = \sqrt{5.22} = 2.285$$

Our t value is then the difference between the two means, $9.33 - 5.33$, divided by this standard error of difference, that is,

$$t = (9.33 - 5.33) \div 2.285 = 4 \div 2.285 = 1.75$$

We have 4 degrees of freedom, and so we consult this row of Table 10.1. The entry for $\alpha = 0.05$ (two-tailed) is 2.776, and our value of t is well below this, so we have failed to reject the null hypothesis. Our result is not significant, for $\alpha = 0.05$.

10.8 Using *t* values to derive confidence intervals

A simplified form of t test may be used to test a sample in relation to a required value. It follows much the same sequence of steps as before. This kind of test is useful when evaluating a system in terms of a performance requirement. We can easily compute the mean of any performance data we gather, but how much confidence can we place on this mean value?

The method we use involves calculating the two extreme positions at which our population mean may lie. We call the interval between these positions the *confidence interval*. We want this interval to lie entirely above a stated minimum performance level or entirely below a stated maximum. For example, if we have a requirement that collect calls should be handled in 25 seconds or less, our confidence interval should lie entirely below the 25-second mark. Figures 10.11(a) and 10.11(b) show confidence intervals that lie clear of the requirement, and Figure 10.11(c) shows a case in which the requirement falls within the interval.

The case shown in Figure 10.11(c) is the case we wish to avoid, and this forms our null hypothesis: the confidence interval contains the required score. In order to reject the null hypothesis we use a simplified version of the t test method above. We calculate the variance by the usual formula; our degrees of freedom are equal to one less than the number of scores:

$$s^2 = SS/(N-1)$$

and then compute a *standard error of the mean*, s_{em}, as follows:

$$s_{em} = \sqrt{(s^2/N)}$$

In the final stage we can calculate the confidence interval as follows, using a value of $t_{p,df}$ read from Table 10.1 according to the desired probability p and the degrees of freedom df:

$$X_{min} = \overline{X} - (t_{p,df} \times s_{em})$$
$$X_{max} = \overline{X} + (t_{p,df} \times s_{em})$$

In other words, we can decide on the maximum acceptable probability level, and compute the corresponding confidence interval. We use the single-tailed values for p since we are attempting to show that our values lie entirely on one side of the required value, as shown in Figure 10.10(b). Provided this is the case with X_{min} and X_{max}, we can reject the null hypothesis.

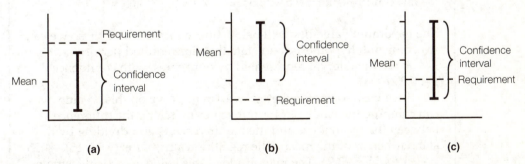

(a)   (b)   (c)

Figure 10.11   The use of confidence intervals to test a sample of scores against a required score: (a) the confidence interval lies beneath the requirement; (b) it lies above; (c) the requirement lies within the interval, the condition of the null hypothesis we wish to reject.

Alternatively we can compute a value of t in terms of the mean score $\overline{X}$ and the required score R, as follows:

$$t = (\overline{X} - R) / s_{em}$$

Table 10.1 can be consulted to determine whether this value lies above or below the critical value. If it lies above, we can reject the null hypothesis with the level of probability shown at the head of the column, using the 'single-tailed' probability values.

Worked example: Checking against a performance requirement

Suppose we have tested a system for frequency of user errors, using four subjects, and have recorded 13, 6, 8 and 11 errors in the four tests, to arrive at a mean of $(13 + 6 + 8 + 11) \div 4 = 38 \div 4 = 9.5$. Our requirement is that no more than 15 errors should occur under these conditions.

We calculate the sum of squares of differences by the usual method:

- $SS = (13^2 + 6^2 + 8^2 + 11^2) - (38^2 \div 4) = 390 - 361 = 29$

Our variance is this value divided by the degrees of freedom, $4 - 1 = 3$, i.e., $29 \div 3 = 9.67$. Our standard error of the mean is found by dividing this variance by the number of scores, and taking the square root: $\sqrt{9.67/4} = \sqrt{2.418} = 1.55$.

If we are willing to reject the null hypothesis with a probability of $p < 0.05$, our critical value of t is $t_{.05,3} = 2.353$, using the single-tailed α values in Table 10.1. The extremes of the confidence interval are therefore:

minimum value = $9.5 - (2.353 \times 1.55) = 9.5 - 3.65 = 5.85$

maximum value = $9.5 + (2.353 \times 1.55) = 9.5 + 3.65 = 13.15$

The maximum value lies well below our requirement of 15, so we can reject the null hypothesis, and state that our required performance lies above the interval represented by our scores, with confidence $p < 0.05$.

If we wish to know whether we can improve on this p value, we can compute the value of t for our scores by taking the difference between the mean score and the required score, and dividing by the standard error of the mean. The resulting value of t is $(9.5 - 15) \div 1.55 = -5.5 \div 1.55 = -3.95$. The magnitude of this value exceeds the single-tailed value in Table 10.1 for $\alpha = 0.025$. Therefore we can improve on our confidence level, from 0.05 to 0.025.

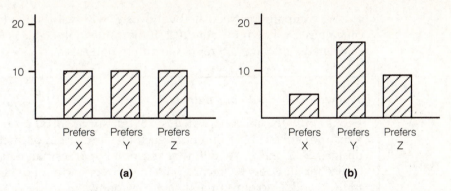

Figure 10.12   Testing the significance of categorical data: (a) the null-hypothesis condition, (b) the data to which we apply the chi square calculation.

10.9   Chi-square analysis of categorical data

Another simple form of analysis helps us to deal with experimental data that fall into two or more *categories*. We may need to categorize data if, for example, we have conducted a survey of 30 users to find out which they prefer out of three designs, X, Y and Z. We define as our null hypothesis an equal preference for all three, that is, the frequencies in each of the categories will be the same (Figure 10.12(a)). In our analysis, we attempt to reject this null hypothesis by analysing the differences in the scores (Figure 10.12(b)).

The **chi square** (χ^2) calculation involves finding the difference between the observed and expected frequencies, f_o and f_e. We then square the difference and divide by the expected frequency. The results of the divisions are summed to give a value of chi square:

$$\chi^2 = \Sigma \left((f_o - f_e)^2 / f_e \right)$$

Table 10.2   Values of chi square. Source: the figures were computed by the authors.

Degrees of freedom	$\alpha = 0.05$	$\alpha = 0.01$
1	3.84	6.63
2	5.99	9.21
3	7.81	11.34
4	9.49	13.28
5	11.07	15.09
6	12.59	16.81
7	14.07	18.48
8	15.51	20.09
9	16.92	21.67
10	18.31	23.21

We compare the calculated value of χ^2 with values in a table of critical values, as shown in Table 10.2. If the value in the table is *less* than our calculated value, we can reject the null hypothesis.

Worked example: A chi square test

Let us apply the chi square analysis to our survey of 30 users, in which we are trying to find out which they prefer out of three designs, X, Y and Z. We define as our null hypothesis an equal preference for all three. We record preference frequencies of 6, 14 and 10 for X, Y and Z, so our initial data are as follows:

Design	Frequency expected under null hypothesis	Observed frequency
X	10	5
Y	10	16
Z	10	9

We compute the squares of the differences between the observed and expected data, and divide these squares by the expected values. By summing these quantities we calculate chi squared. These calculations are shown in the following table:

Design	Expected frequency	Observed frequency	Difference	Difference squared	Divided by expected
X	10	5	−5	25	2.5
Y	10	16	6	36	3.6
Z	10	9	−1	1	0.1

$$\text{Total} = \chi^2 = 6.2$$

We have 2 degrees of freedom in this calculation (3 categories − 1 estimate), and so we consult the corresponding row of Table 10.2. We find a value of 5.99 for $\alpha = 0.05$. This is less than the calculated value, so we can reject the null hypothesis with $p < 0.05$.

10.10 Illustrations of the methods: Testing the ticket machine

To offer further examples of the use of these methods, we will analyse two sets of data that might result from controlled evaluations in support of the design of the rapid-transit ticket machine of Chapters 6 and 8. Let us suppose that we need answers to two questions:

(1)   Will it be faster to use the machine than to buy tickets over the counter? The answer to this question will be crucial in the cost justification of the machine. A certain level of increase in purchase time may be acceptable, for example, 30 per cent, but no more than this.

(2)   How frequently do the one-way and round-trip journey types occur? This question might arise if we were considering designing the machine to reset automatically after each purchase to a particular journey type, for example, to round-trip.

The first question involves the use of a t test, while the second makes use of a chi-square analysis.

10.10.1   The question of speed of operation

To answer the first question, we might conduct tests at a real station counter from which members of the public are excluded. We could then measure the times taken by a set of six subjects purchasing tickets at the counter, and by another set of six using the ticket machine. To avoid the influence of learning difficulties we might give each of the second set of subjects prior training in the use of the machine. We would certainly make sure each set of subjects purchased the same kind of ticket and had the same money available. However, one of the second set of subjects might fail to turn up, so we would be reduced to five. The performance times (in seconds) might be as follows:

Counter purchases:	28, 35, 23, 26, 30, 32	sum: 174; mean: 29
Machine purchases:	32, 41, 37, 40, 30	sum: 180; mean: 36

These mean times – 29 and 36 seconds – suggest that machine purchase takes about 24 per cent longer than counter purchase. However, we need to be sure that we can reject the null hypothesis, which states that the difference in method of sale has no effect on purchase time. We therefore perform a t test, as follows:

(1)   The sum of squares $SS_1 = (28^2 + 35^2 + 23^2 + 26^2 + 30^2 + 32^2) - (174^2 \div 6) = 92$

(2)   The sum of squares $SS_2 = (32^2 + 41^2 + 37^2 + 40^2 + 30^2) - (180^2 \div 5) = 94$

(3)   The combined variance $s^2 = (SS_1 + SS_2) \div (N_1 + N_2 - 2) = (92 + 94) \div 9 = 186 \div 9 = 20.67$

(4)   The standard error of difference $s_{ed} = \sqrt{(s^2 (1/N_1 + 1/N_2))} = \sqrt{(20.67 \times (1/6 + 1/5))} = \sqrt{(20.67 \times 0.367)} = \sqrt{7.59} = 2.75$

(5)   The value of t is the difference between the two means, divided by s_{ed}, that is, $(29 - 36) \div 2.75 = -7 \div 2.75 = -2.55$

Table 10.1 gives a critical value of 2.262 for $\alpha = 0.05$ and 9 degrees of freedom. Our value of t exceeds this in magnitude, so we can reject the null hypothesis. We could report the following result:

It is required of the ticket machine that purchases should take no more than 30 per cent longer than counter purchases. We have carried out comparisons of counter and machine purchases which show that the machine takes 24 per cent longer, $p < 0.05$.

10.10.2 The question of preferred journey type

This second question is typical of the kind of knowledge-seeking queries that arise early in design. We would like the ticket machine to be as rapid as possible in operation, and one way of speeding it up is to reduce the need to select the journey type. If a particular journey type is very frequent, we should design the machine to select it automatically after every purchase. If no journey type predominates, we may design the machine to maintain the same journey type unchanged so as to assist passengers who are buying several tickets at a time. We cannot make this decision unless we know the relative frequency of journey types.

To answer the question, we could take random samples of ticket purchases made over the counter. We would count the number of journeys of each type. The data gathered from 50 samples might be as follows:

Round-trip ticket:	31
One-way ticket:	19

These frequencies suggest that over 60 per cent of passengers will purchase round-trip tickets. We can use the chi square method to determine the significance of the data. Since we took 50 samples, we define our expected null hypothesis values to be 25 in each category, and perform the calculation of chi square as before:

Design	Expected frequencies	Observed frequencies	Difference	Difference squared	Divided by expected
Round trip	25	31	6	36	1.44
One way	25	19	−6	36	1.44
				Total = χ^2 =	2.88

In this case we have only one degree of freedom, so we compare our chi square value of 2.88 with the first row of Table 10.2. We see that the result is not significant, even to a significance level of $\alpha = 0.05$ for it lies below the critical value of 3.84. On this basis, we could not justify taking a design decision about resetting the journey type. We should reword our pro forma report as follows:

It is a requirement of the ticket machine that it should reset to the most frequently selected journey type, if this significantly outnumbers other types. We have sampled purchases currently made by passengers, but have not been able to establish a clear-cut preference.

The failure of this experiment can be attributed to an insufficient sample size. If we had taken 100 sample frequencies, and had recorded the same ratio of values as before, our chi square value would have quadrupled to 11.52. This exceeds the $\alpha = 0.01$ value in Table 10.2. We would have been able to report our observations with $p < .01$, or with a 99 per cent level of confidence.

10.11 Case study: Evaluating a cockpit display

Before concluding this discussion of laboratory-based evaluation, let us look at a real case of evaluating a cockpit display, in which some of the methods described here were applied.

10.11.1 The design problem: Reducing automation deficit

One of the problems encountered in aviation, both commercial and military, is a loss in pilots' performance when switching off automatic flight control to manual flying. When the autopilot is switched off there is a temporary *automation deficit* in the pilot's speed of task performance, lasting perhaps for a minute. During this period the pilot may be as much as a second slower than normal in performing tasks. In an aircraft flying at Mach 3, one second is long enough to cover a kilometre. There is a great incentive, especially in high-speed military aircraft, to find ways of reducing the effects of automation deficit.

A recent investigation conducted at the US Naval Research Laboratory showed the effects on automation deficit of the design of the pilot's tactical display of targets (Ballas *et al.*, 1992). The designers replaced pilots' normal textual display with a graphical display, and also introduced a touch-screen for selection of targets in place of the usual keypad. They then evaluated the four designs: textual versus graphical displays, each with touch-screen versus keypad selection (Figure 10.13). They had a theory, which we will not elaborate here, that the graphical design with touch-screen input would offer a low automation deficit.

This kind of evaluation is best done in the laboratory. It is expensive to install a new kind of display in a military aircraft, and dangerous to ask pilots to test experimental equipment at high speed. The conditions of the evaluation are much easier to control in the laboratory. Accordingly, the experiment was set up on a prototype system, and 24 subjects were tested, six with each of the four versions of the system.

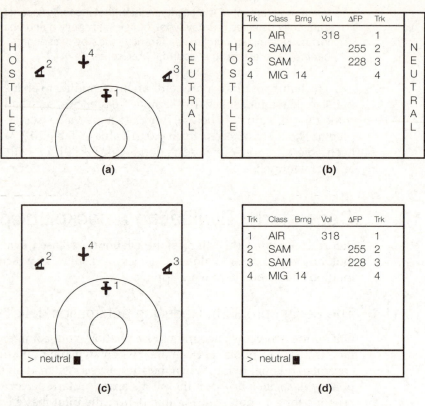

Figure 10.13   The four tactical display designs, from Ballas *et al.* (1992). (a) Graphical display with touch-screen (direct manipulation); (b) tabular display with touch-screen; (c) graphical display with keypad input; (d) tabular display with keypad input (command language).

10.11.2   The experiment

The goal of the experiment was to test the effectiveness of subjects in assessing targets on the display under various conditions. One condition was the 'autopilot' condition – the pilot had nothing else to do but assess targets. The other was a 'manual tracking' condition, in which the pilot had to keep tracking a target on a separate display alongside the tactical display. When the system switched to autopilot, this tracking became automatic. The condition of particular interest was the short period after the autopilot was switched off, and while the pilot was experiencing automation deficit as a result. The investigators took particular care, therefore, to measure speed of target assessment during this period.

Figure 10.14(a) shows the results of the investigation. Task performance times were measured during the period following the switch back

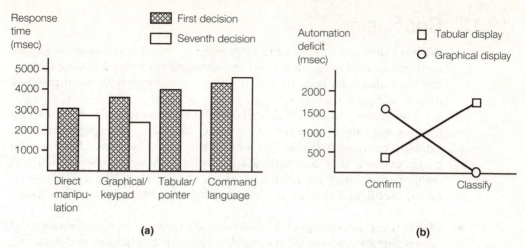

Figure 10.14   Results of the evaluations: (a) task performance times, (b) influence on deficit of task type, from Ballas *et al.* (1992).

to manual tracking. The chart shows the difference in performance times for the first task performed during this period and the seventh task: this provides a measure of the automation deficit. It shows that the deficit was much smaller, at around 250 msec or less, for two of the four designs; the other two had deficits of around one second. The leftmost design in Figure 10.14(a), with a small deficit and a low average performance time, was the design with graphical display and touch-screen selection. The confidence level was $p < 0.002$.

On the face of it, therefore, the investigation was successful, showing a low deficit for the favoured design. But the story did not end there. The tasks that pilots performed were in fact of two kinds, classification and confirmation, the first considerably more complex than the second. On looking closer at the data, the investigators discovered that the automation deficit for confirmation on the graphical display was quite high, a lot higher than for the other low-deficit design (tabular display and keypad). This is shown in Figure 10.14(b): the graphical display and touch-screen were better for the complex task but worse for the simpler task, with $p < 0.02$.

Thus a pro forma abstract for this investigation would state a need for further study:

> It is a requirement of the avionics display that automation deficit should be kept well below one second. We have achieved general confirmation of this by comparing the design with other designs in user trials, $p < 0.002$. However, the results show that the choice of display design for low deficit must take into account the complexity of the task, and this demands further investigation in order to achieve reliable deficit figures.

10.12 Conclusion

We have devoted much of the discussion in this chapter to some simple methods of analysing data from experiments performed during design. We have also seen how to conduct these experiments so as to produce data of adequate quality.

The analysis methods described here represent only a few of those that we may need in order to compute the results of experiments and establish confidence levels. The methods included here have been chosen partly because they are particularly useful in simple experiments, and partly because they are relatively simple themselves. Others that may be found useful, and that are described in the recommended texts, include:

- Methods for determining whether there is a *linear relationship* between the dependent and independent variable. These would help us to determine, for example, whether the time for performing a task was related to the number of entries displayed on the screen, and thus set the number of entries so as to achieve a desired performance time (Figure 10.15(a)).

- Methods for use when two or more independent variables influence the outcome, for example, two aspects of the design are being altered rather than just one. One aspect might concern display layout, the other the type of menu (Figure 10.15(b)). These *multi-factor* methods are especially useful when a larger-scale evaluation is undertaken to test several aspects of the design.

- Methods that can handle three or more conditions, using the so-called *F* test.

- Methods for analysing the results of testing two different systems on the same set of subjects. These 'within-group' experiments are harder to

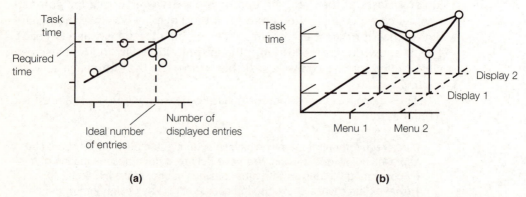

(a)

(b)

Figure 10.15   Experiments that require additional analysis methods: (a) to fit a line to task performance times recorded with different displays, and thus determine the ideal display; (b) to analyse the effects of changing two independent variables.

analyse than the 'between-group' experiments we have discussed in this chapter.

Some of these experiments may turn into small research projects in their own right. Thus the investigation of task performance times and display layouts might discover a more complex relationship than the straight line shown in Figure 10.15(a). In some circumstances it might be appropriate to investigate this relationship. The dividing line between evaluation and applied research is often crossed in the world of interactive system design.

Exercises

(1) What are the two basic questions in interactive system design that controlled experiments help answer?

(2) What is the difference between a sample and a population?

(3) What is meant by an externally valid task?

(4) What are nuisance variables, and how can they be neutralized?

(5) In what ways do the stages of a controlled experiment differ from the stages in a field test?

(6) Take down the last digit of 30 observed car number plates and plot their distribution.

(7) Find the mean, variance and standard deviation of the following sample: 21.6, 18.3, 16.7, 19.4, 20.8, 19.0, 18.3, 22.1, 16.9, 19.7, 18.8, 17.9.

(8) Suppose the times in seconds scored by five subjects when selecting a 3D target using a virtual-reality headset are 4.4, 6.6, 4.5, 6.2 and 5.3. On a conventional workstation screen, another set of subjects' scores are 5.9, 5.7, 7.2, 8.3 and 8.1. Compute the means, and use a t test to determine whether these results are significant for $\alpha = 0.05$.

(9) It is a requirement that users should make fewer than 7 errors per 100 times they set up a machine tool. During tests of the tool, eight subjects recorded the following number of errors: 2, 5, 3, 7, 8, 1, 6, 2. Using t values, calculate whether these indicate that the requirement has been met, for $\alpha = 0.05$.

(10) Three different icon designs (A, B and C) are tested on 12 users. Nine users prefer design A, one prefers B and two prefer C. Conduct a chi square test to determine whether these data are significant, for $\alpha = 0.01$ and $\alpha = 0.05$.

Further reading

Keppel G. and Saufley W. H., Jr. (1980). *Introduction to Design and Analysis: A Student's Handbook*. San Francisco: Freeman

An elementary text on analysis methods, clearly written and mathematically undemanding. Does not cover *t* tests (for which see Howell (1989)), but provides an excellent introduction to methods lying beyond the scope of this chapter, suitable for analysis of more complex experiments.

Howell D. C. (1989). *Fundamental Statistics for the Behavioral Sciences*. Boston MA: PWS-Kent

A good introductory text on statistics. Highly readable, with a wide variety of examples, worked through using both manual and computer-based methods.

Sellen A. J. (1992). Speech patterns in video-mediated conversations. In *Proc. CHI '92 Human Factors in Computing Systems*, May 3–7, Monterey, CA, pp. 49–59. New York: ACM/SIGCHI

An example of how even the best-designed experiments can lead to unexpected results. The investigation was expected to show differences between conversations held in the same room and via video, but most of these differences failed to materialize.

CASE STUDY A

Evaluation and analysis of a telephone operator's workstation

Chapter objectives:

The work of the Toll and Assistance Operator (TAO) is crucially dependent on the support of interactive systems. This case study describes an attempt to design a faster workstation to speed up the TAO's handling of calls. It covers:

- The nature of the TAO's work
- The design of the new workstation
- The conduct of a field trial, from which it emerged that the proposed workstation was slower than the one currently in use
- The use of analytical models to explain the results of the field trial.

A.1 Introduction

Many projects in interactive system design aim to achieve an incremental improvement in support for people's activities, rather than a radical change. They concern mundane applications like order processing, customer service, record keeping, machine tool operation, and so on. These are not, as a rule, projects that get a lot of publicity; they have little of the novelty and mass appeal of virtual reality, say, or multimedia tele-shopping. Nevertheless a lot may hinge on achieving these incremental enhancements, especially if they affect systems in widespread use. If an automated teller machine is made faster and easier to use, for example, this is good news for the bank and its customers, but if the same redesign project backfires and has the opposite result, the effect can be disastrous for business.

In this case study we will look at a real-life case of redesigning the support system for a mundane but essential activity, the handling of calls by Toll and Assistance Operators (TAOs) employed by a phone company. These are the people who answer when we dial 0 (or 100 in the United Kingdom) and who assist in placing collect calls and pay-phone calls. Interactive systems are essential to the TAO's job, for they provide the TAO with billing information and handle the connection of calls, so that the whole process becomes much simpler and faster.

In this particular case, a new workstation was designed for the TAO in an attempt to make call-handling faster still. As we shall see, things did not turn out as expected. The redesigned workstation became the focus of an extensive field trial and some pioneering research in analysis methods; the study became known as 'Project Ernestine' and has since been reported by John (1990), by Gray et al. (1992, 1993) and by Atwood et al. (in press). The work of John, Gray and Atwood represents an outstanding example of how cognitive science can come to the assistance of interactive system design. This case study summarizes their work and links it to some of the methods discussed in the preceding chapters.

A.2 The work of the Toll and Assistance Operator

The work of the telephone assistance operator is familiar to all of us, because we have all had occasion to call for assistance. Very few of us, however, will have sat in the operator's seat and attempted to handle subscribers' calls. Probably the nearest we will ever come to this is answering calls at the office switchboard.

A.2.1 The basic task structure

What is involved in toll and assistance work? Basically the TAO handles a steady stream of subscribers' calls. Frequently the caller will have dialled the call in full, with a preceding '0' to ensure that the call is handled by the operator. In handling each call, the TAO makes sure (a) that the appropriate person pays for the call, (b) that the appropriate rate is charged, and (c) that the call is handed over to the caller as soon as these two aspects have been taken care of, so that the next incoming call can be taken. These three subgoals can be observed in all common categories of call, which include:

- **Collect calls.** In this case the called party (the 'callee') will need to agree to pay for the call, which will be billed to their phone at the normal collect-call rate; the call can be connected as soon as the callee agrees.

- **Person-to-person calls.** These are charged to the caller's phone, at a higher rate than normal calls, but only if the requested person can be brought to the phone; only then is the call connected.

- **Coin-box calls.** These are paid for in cash by the caller, usually at the basic pay-phone rate, and are connected when the necessary amount has been deposited. They are interrupted if the money runs out, and the caller must then deposit more money to have the call reconnected.

- **Call failures.** If the caller reports failure in a call they have just made, the billed party is credited for any charges, and the operator makes the call afresh, connecting the caller as soon as the call is answered.

The same pattern can be found in the remainder of the 20 or so common call categories. Thus although the TAO's tasks vary considerably, they mostly share the common stages of determining who is to pay, establishing the billing rate, and releasing the call. As we shall now see, support for these stages is built into the user interface of the TAO's workstation.

A.2.2 The user interface

The TAO's workstation typically has a screen on which call information and prompts are displayed, as shown in Figure A.1(a), and has a keyboard for entering commands. The TAO wears a headset with earphone and microphone.

As soon as each incoming call is received at the phone-company station, it is routed through to one of the TAO's workstations. Waiting calls do not generate a normal ringing sound (although this is what the caller hears) but instead sound a beep, or 'call-arrival tone', through the TAO's headset, indicating that they are about to be put through. Information appears on the top line of the TAO's display indicating the type of call, and a short while later the display is amended to show that the caller is now connected to the TAO (Figure A.1(b)).

The TAO speaks the appropriate greeting, for example, 'Great Lakes Telephone, may I help you?' or 'Please deposit seventy cents', to commence the interaction with the caller. Various keys are used during the interaction to enter data and to mark stages in the progress of the task. When the call has been connected and is ready to release, this is indicated by pressing a special CALL-RELEASE key. Then the TAO waits for another beep indicating that the next call is coming through.

A.2.3 Sample interaction sequences

During every interaction the TAO maintains a conversation with the caller, and with any other people involved, e.g., with the person called. In the relatively simple task of connecting a credit-card call, the interaction might be as follows:

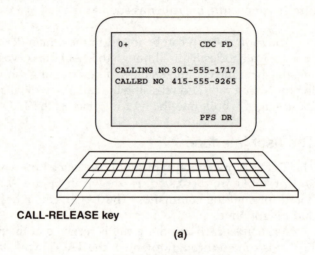

CALL-RELEASE key

(a)

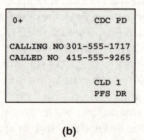

(b)

Figure A.1   A Toll and Assistance Operator's workstation, showing a typical display, (a) immediately after the call-arrival tone indicating that a call is coming through, and (b) when the caller is connected to the TAO. In (b), note the symbol CLD 1 indicating a call connected on the TAO's line 1. Based on Gray *et al.* (1993) and Atwood *et al.* (in press).

> *Caller dials 0-305-555-6748 and waits for operator to answer.*
> *TAO's headset beeps; display shows this is a dialled call and then shows it connected*

TAO: Great Lakes Telephone, may I help you?

Caller: Can I charge this to my credit card, please?

TAO: Card number, please.
> *Presses CARD-NUMBER key.*

Caller: 412-555-6789-4321.

TAO: *Enters 14-digit number;*
> *Waits for display of billing rate, presses RATE-CONFIRM key.*
> *Waits for display of credit-card authorization.*
> Thank you.
> *Presses CALL-RELEASE key.*

A collect call will involve a more complex verbal interaction, perhaps along the following lines:

> *Caller dials 0-817-555-9091 and waits for operator to answer.*
> *TAO's headset beeps; display shows this is a dialled call and then shows it connected*

TAO: Great Lakes Telephone, may I help you?

Caller: Can I make this a collect call please?

TAO: Your name, please.

Caller: Oh, er, John.

TAO: Thank you.
> *Writes 'John' on paper;*
> *Presses COLLECT-CALL key; waits for someone at called number ('callee') to answer.*

Callee: Hello?

TAO: I have a collect call to anyone from John, will you pay for the call?

Callee: Er, can you hold on a minute? ... Yes, we can accept the call.

TAO: *Presses RATE-CONFIRM key to confirm displayed rate.*
> Thank you; go ahead, caller.
> *Presses CALL-RELEASE key.*

The workstation's function keys and displayed messages enable the TAO to handle a wide variety of requests. The time to handle calls varies, but the average time is around 20 seconds.

A.3 The workstation redesign project

The case in question began with the redesign of the TAO's workstation. This was done with a view to increasing its capacity to support TAOs' tasks. Subsequently the new workstation was chosen by NYNEX, the parent company of New England Telephone, as a proposed replacement for their TAO's current equipment.

It was essential that the new system should pay for itself through improvements in efficiency. In other words, the time taken to handle calls for assistance must be reduced so that fewer TAOs could handle the same volume of calls. The problem statement might have been written as in the example in Section 2.7.4, that is, as:

> Design an enhanced workstation that enables a skilled operator to handle a full range of telephone-assistance calls, in an average of 2 seconds less per call than at present.

In this section we will look at the design strategy employed, starting with the underlying cost–benefit analysis.

A.3.1   Cost–benefit analysis

Telephone operators in the USA earn about $25,000 per year on average (US Department of Labor Statistics, 1993). At New England Telephone they work in offices employing about 100 operators; the typical phone company might have 25 such offices. Altogether, therefore, a phone company's TAO wage bill might be in the region of $25,000 × 100 × 25 = $62.5 million per year.

On this basis we can estimate the approximate savings from speeding up performance by two seconds. A two-second saving on a 20-second task is equivalent to a 10 per cent reduction. Therefore if we can design a system that will regularly achieve this kind of improvement, we can save the company 0.1 × $62.5 million, or roughly $6 million per year (Gray *et al.*, 1992).

A saving of $6 million per year may seem a lot, but it is not large in relation to the cost of replacing such a system. The cost of equipment and software to support a thousand TAOs is likely to run to several million dollars, and must be paid off over the space of a few years. There will also be initial costs in retraining TAOs to use the new system.

A.3.2   Designing for improved TAO performance

Clearly the designers would have to achieve a substantial improvement in TAO performance in order to cost-justify the new system. This did not seem difficult, however; the system in current use was already somewhat dated, and there were several obvious ways of improving its usability.

First, the current TAO workstation was a text-only terminal, connected to the central computer by a line running at only 300 baud (that is, at thirty characters per second). A new workstation was proposed with a 1200 baud line and a high-resolution graphical display, capable of supporting a multi-window user interface.

Second, the current keyboard was organized into groups of keys according to function. No attempt had been made to place frequently used keys in more optimal positions. A new keyboard layout was devised so as to minimize the TAO's hand travel. The CALL-RELEASE key, for example, was moved from its position at the left-hand side of the keyboard (see Figure A.1(a)) into proximity with the numeric keypad.

Third, the TAO's task sequences involved a number of inefficient practices. There were instances, for example, of using two or more keystrokes where one would suffice. The sequences were therefore redesigned so as to reduce the number of keystrokes. In some cases it was possible to eliminate as many as four keystrokes.

A.3.3   The phone company's expectations

Taking all of these changes into account, NYNEX expected substantial improvements. For example, they expected the proposed workstation to save nearly a second on every display of a screenful of information, just because of the improved line speed. The reduction in keystrokes was sufficient to save another half-second per call on average. Other savings could be gained from decreased TAO hand movement. An average saving of two seconds seemed eminently achievable.

These expectations were not, however, considered sufficient grounds to go straight ahead with the introduction of the proposed new workstation. Rather they were viewed by NYNEX as justification for a controlled evaluation of the new workstation. As we shall see, this turned out to be a wise decision.

A.4   The field trial

The evaluation of the proposed workstation was carried out as a field trial under controlled conditions. For reasons explained in Chapter 9, the conditions of field tests are usually far from controlled, but New England Telephone were able to overcome most of the usual problems in experimental design, and to run controlled tests of the new workstation handling 'live' customer calls. Instrumentation built into the workstation software enabled collection of accurate data on call-handling times for both the current and proposed workstations.

A.4.1   Experimental design

Twelve of the new workstations were introduced at a New England Telephone location, replacing twelve of the current workstations. These were used over a four-month period by a group of 24 experienced TAOs; the performance times of this 'proposed' group were monitored. During the same period another group of equally experienced TAOs (the 'current' group) continued to use the current workstation, and their performance times were monitored too.

The experiment was designed with considerable care. For example, the TAOs in the proposed and current groups were carefully matched, and

TAOs in the proposed group were retrained strictly according to the company's standard procedures and guidelines. Members of the current group did not know they were taking part in the experiment although they were aware, as all TAOs are, that their performance times were being monitored.

Data were collected on all of the 78 240 calls in the 20 major call categories handled by all 48 TAOs over the entire four-month period. The subsequent analysis was applied to only the 15 most frequently occurring categories, however, and to only 23 TAOs in each group because one member of the proposed group left during the experiment. This still resulted in a substantial sample size of 72 390 calls.

A.4.2   Analysis of results

The initial analysis indicated an *increase* of 6 per cent, or 1.3 seconds, in the average time for handling calls. This unexpected result was statistically significant, with a probability of $p < 0.02$, that is, with a chance of less than 2 in 100 that it was due to factors other than the change of workstation. Further analyses were conducted, showing that the increase applied to virtually all call categories. According to these analyses, the proposed workstation would incur extra operating costs of at least $6 million per year. This was not at all what the phone company had hoped to learn.

The result was so unexpected that NYNEX looked for possible sources of error in the data. The most likely nuisance variable was the increasing experience of the proposed group over the four-month experimental period; during the early months, lack of experience could have affected this group's performance. The results did show the difference between the two groups to be even greater (9 per cent) during the first month, but after that the difference dropped to a value that did not change significantly over the remaining three months.

A fresh analysis was therefore conducted using just the last three months' data. To achieve a realistic estimate of the effect on operating costs, the final analysis also took into account the relative frequency of call categories. The proposed workstation was still significantly slower in this analysis, by 3.4 percent or 0.65 seconds, with a confidence level of $p < 0.05$. This was equivalent to a cost increase of just under $2 million per year. The fact that such high confidence levels were achieved is a tribute to the quality of experimental design here.

A.5   What went wrong with the predictions?

The phone company could perhaps feel relief that the performance problems had been discovered before it was too late, but there were bound to be questions. How could the early estimates of performance improvements have been so far wrong? What was causing the performance degradations measured in the field trial?

The next two sections continue the case history, describing a parallel project in which a detailed analytical model of the performance of TAO tasks was built. This model provided explanations for the performance problems of the proposed workstation.

A.5.1   Operators performed in parallel

The basic reason why the early estimates were wrong is simple. These estimates were made by identifying all of the steps where time savings could be expected, and adding up the savings. They assumed that each task could be treated as a simple sequence of steps. However, if we look at how a TAO task is performed we find many instances where steps are performed in parallel. In these instances, shortening a step may not shorten the overall task.

For example, in the case of a credit-card call the TAO enters the card number as it is being dictated by the caller. Auditory steps are carried out in parallel with motor steps. In the case of collect calls, the TAO presses the COLLECT-CALL key while saying 'Thank you' to the caller, combining motor operators with voice operators. As Chapter 3's Human Virtual Machine would predict, the TAO is capable of performing two or more operators in parallel, since they use different subsystems.

When two such operators are performed in parallel, savings in each operator cannot be added together. Indeed, if one operator always takes longer than the other, savings in the shorter operator will probably have no overall impact.

Suppose the COLLECT-CALL key is always pressed while the TAO is engaged in the longer operator of saying 'Thank you'. Then nothing will be gained by repositioning the key so that it is faster to operate. As illustrated in Figure A.2, the overall time for the collect-call task is limited by the TAO's speed in saying 'Thank you'. Short of leaving out this courtesy altogether, the TAO cannot take advantage of the keyboard's redesign.

A.6   The CPM-GOMS modelling technique

CPM-GOMS is an extension of the GOMS modelling technique described in Chapter 8. We saw there how keystroke-level models of task performance can be constructed as sequences of operators, and how these sequences allow predictions of performance times to be made. In CPM-GOMS, separate sequences are constructed for each category of operator, thus allowing for the possibility that operators will be performed in parallel. Then the *critical path* is traced through the parallel streams of operators, that is, a connected sequence that determines the overall time for the task is found. In Figure A.2(b), for example, the voice operator 'Thank you' would probably be on the critical path; the keystroke would not.

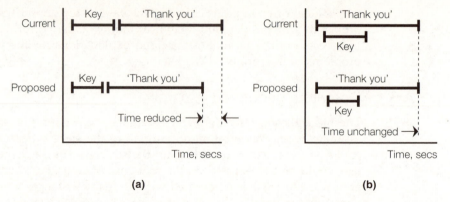

(a)   (b)

Figure A.2   Effect of reducing keystroke time: (a) if motor and speech operators are assumed to be performed in sequence, a time saving can be expected; (b) if they are performed in parallel, there may be no such saving.

A.6.1   An example

Figures A.3 and A.4 illustrate the difference between basic keystroke-level GOMS modelling and CPM-GOMS modelling. Figure A.3 shows a sequential keystroke-level model of the TAO completing a task by pressing the F3 function key, waiting two seconds for a system response, saying 'Thank you' and pressing the F4 key. The times for each of the operators are shown in milliseconds. When these times are totalled, they give a performance time of **3.37 seconds**.

Figure A.4 shows a simplified CPM-GOMS model of these five steps. They are separated into three categories of operator, shown on separate horizontal lines: system response operators, hand operators and verbal response operators. The diagram shows where opportunities exist for operators to be performed in parallel. However, some operators are dependent on completion of others; thus until the TAO has pressed the F3 key the system cannot respond, nor can the TAO begin the verbal 'Thank you' response; likewise the TAO cannot press F4 until the system's response is displayed.

By tracing the dependencies in Figure A.4 we can locate the critical path; this is shown with heavier lines. The performance time for the

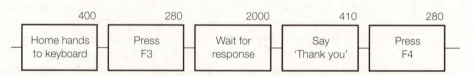

Figure A.3   Sequential GOMS model of pressing two keys and saying 'Thank you'.

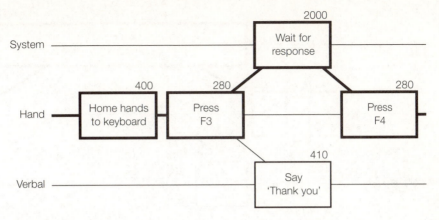

Figure A.4   Parallel model of pressing two keys and saying 'Thank you'.

whole set of operators is determined by the length of this path. If we add up the individual times, we arrive at a new total of **2.96 seconds**. This time, we have taken into account the TAO's ability to say 'Thank you' while awaiting the system's response.

Note that Figure A.4's model of parallel activities, although drawn with time proceeding from left to right, does not show the durations of operators to scale. A more realistic picture of where the time is spent and how operators overlap is shown in Figure A.5. Although this notation gives a clearer picture of the time-sequence of the call, it takes up a lot of space and has not been used by Gray *et al.* in drawing CPM-GOMS models.

A.6.2   Building a CPM-GOMS model

Constructing a CPM-GOMS model is more complicated than the original keystroke-level modelling technique developed by Card *et al.* (1983). The CPM-GOMS method has been described by John (1990) and by John and Gray (1994), and is merely summarized here.

The first stage in model building is much the same as in simple key-stroke-level modelling. In other words, we build the CPM-GOMS model around a known sequence of manual or voice operators (for example, F3 – 'Thank you' – F4), based on observation or prediction of the user's actions. Then we introduce cognitive and other operators by applying a set of rules.

The main difference in the modelling technique is the assignment of operators to different categories according to the human resource on which they rely:

- Perceptual operators – visual
- Perceptual operators – aural
- Cognitive operators

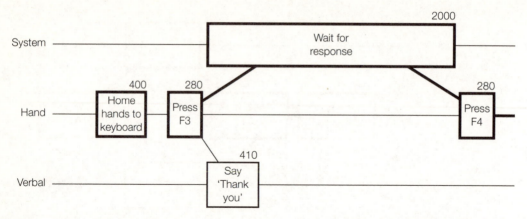

Figure A.5   The same diagram as Figure A.4, drawn with the operators scaled according to their duration. This notation is not used in CPM-GOMS modelling, however, in order to save space.

- Motor operators – left hand movement
- Motor operators – right hand movement
- Motor operators – verbal response
- Motor operators – eye movement

The operators within each category can then be assigned performance times and placed in sequential order; there is no possibility that operators in the same category will overlap, since they rely on the same resources. To complete the picture, two more categories of operator are added:

- System response time – display
- System response time – other

A *schedule chart* is drawn, in which each category of operator is shown on a separate horizontal line.

A.6.3   Schedule chart templates

Three categories of operator can easily be derived from observation or prediction of users' behaviour: left-hand, right-hand and verbal motor operators. The other categories must be added to the schedule chart by applying rules and heuristics. The overall process by which the model is built is shown in Figure A.6.

Some of the modelling heuristics are quite simple; for example, a system response-time operator is added at every point where the user depends on a response generated as a result of a previous operator.

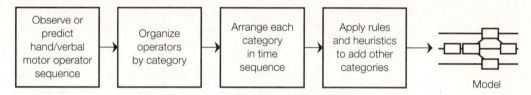

Figure A.6   The process by which CPM-GOMS models are built.

Other model-building heuristics are more complex; typically they involve the introduction of several cognitive, perceptual or motor operators around each observed operator. However, the rules for introducing these operators tend to result in repeating patterns of operators. Each pattern is a miniature schedule chart in itself, a *template* that can be imported into the main chart in its entirety.

Two examples of schedule-chart templates are shown in Figure A.7. In Figure A.7(a) we see how pressing a function key is divided into two hand-operators, down and up, preceded by a cognitive operator that initiates the keystroke and a horizontal hand movement to the key. In Figure A.7(b) we see the sequence of operators involved in perceiving visual information with prior eye movement.

The operators in schedule chart templates are of a finer grain than the operators used in earlier GOMS modelling techniques, and cover a wider range. For example, the home-hands operator **H** used in keystroke-level modelling (see Table 8.1) is split into two operators, a 50-msec cognitive operator and a 350-msec motor operator. The total time, 400 msec, is the same in both modelling techniques, but the CPM-GOMS template allows for overlap of other cognitive or motor operators. Further time estimates for operators have been published by John (1990) and by Gray *et al.* (1993).

A.6.4   Plotting the critical path

When the schedule chart is complete, the critical path is plotted. This is the sequence of linked operators that represents the greatest total time and therefore determines the overall time for the task.

In simple charts the critical path can be found by inspection; for example, in Figure A.7 we can see that the path leads from the initial two cognitive operators ('attend to information' and 'initiate eye movement') to the eye-movement operator, then to 'perceive complex information' and finally to the cognitive operator, 'verify information'. This critical path is 470 msec in duration. The only alternative path lies along the sequence of cognitive operators, and this is only 150 msec in duration.

In more complex cases, computer-based tools can be used to locate the critical path and calculate its length. This method, described in John and Gray (1994) is especially useful in fitting schedule charts to observed data and in testing the performance of alternative designs.

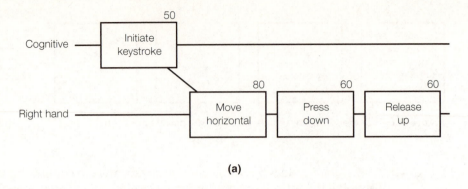

(a)

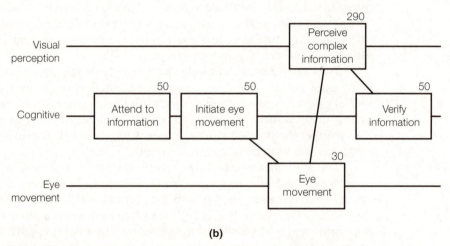

(b)

Figure A.7   Schedule chart templates: (a) pressing a function key; (b) perceiving displayed information. Note, as explained in the text, that the charts show overlap even where operators may not overlap in time. Based on John and Gray (1994).

A.7 Analysis of the TAO workstations

The CPM-Goms technique was used to model the handling of calls with both the current and proposed TAO workstations. The analysis began before the field trial, giving early indications that the trial might not report the expected performance improvements. Subsequently the analysis helped to explain why the proposed workstation was slower.

A.7.1 Benchmark tasks

Calls for assistance do not always follow the same sequence of operators, because callers make requests and provide information in different ways. Thus a credit-card call might involve the exchanges shown earlier, or it might involve only three conversational turns:

TAO: Great Lakes Telephone, may I help you?
Caller: Operator, bill this to 412-555-6789-4321.
TAO: Thank you.

When we are analysing a system that can be used in many ways, we need to choose a smaller number of representative sequences, or *benchmarks* (see Section 8.3.1). In the case of the TAO's tasks, the three-turn sequence shown above is a common form of the credit-card task, and is an appropriate benchmark.

The TAO analysis involved identifying benchmarks for all 15 of the common call categories, and recording the sequence of hand and voice operators. This was done by video recording. Out of a number of recorded calls in each category, one benchmark recording was adopted as the basis for modelling this category of call. All 15 benchmarks were recorded using the current workstation. The aim was then to make predictions of the proposed workstation's performance by analytical techniques alone, and thus attempt to explain the results of the field trial.

A.7.2   Constructing the models

CPM-GOMS models were constructed for each of the 15 categories of call, handled on both the current and proposed workstation. Figure A.8 shows two portions of one of these models, representing stages in handling a credit-card call. Figure A.8(a) is near the start of the call, and Figure A.8(b) is the concluding stage. The full model for this category of call can be found in Gray *et al.* (1993).

The charts shown in Figure A.8 are made up primarily from operators with known durations, for example, cognitive operators of a constant 50-msec duration or keystrokes of different standard forms. Times for these operators were derived from prior research, for example, from the research of Card *et al.* (1983). Other operators, such as speech and system responses, were measured from the videotape.

Models for the proposed workstation took into account the changes in the workstation's design. These changes meant that TAOs would use different sequences of keystrokes; they also affected the amount of hand travel and the length of perceptual operators. The models' construction involved substituting new keystroke sequences in accordance with the procedures for which the TAOs were to be trained. Some operators were left unchanged, for example, where TAOs spoke the same words as before.

A.7.3   Comparison of modelled performance times

The modelled performance times were aggregated for all 15 categories of call, first for the current workstation, then for the proposed design. When the same allowances were made for relative frequency as in the field trial, the predicted loss in performance with the proposed workstation was

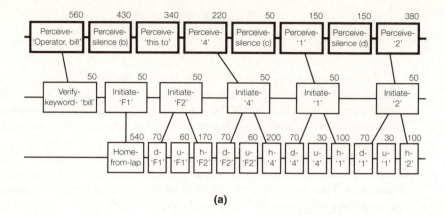

(a)

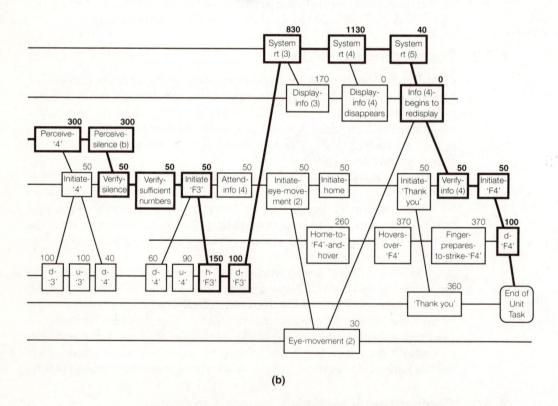

(b)

Figure A.8   Portions of the CPM-GOMS model of a credit-card call: (a) in the early stages of handling the call; (b) the final stage of the same model. Home, down and up strokes are
abbreviated as 'h-', 'd-' and 'u-'. Horizontal lines represent, in (a), from top to bottom, the following operators: perceptual-aural, cognitive, motor right-hand; in (b):
system response, perceptual-visual, perceptual-aural, cognitive, motor left-hand,
motor right-hand, motor verbal, motor eye-movement. From Gray *et al.* (1993).

0.63 seconds. This compared very closely with the difference of 0.65 seconds measured in the field trial.

This was a striking illustration of the ability of analytical modelling to predict usability. But what was the cause of loss of usability in the proposed design? This question could also be answered with the aid of the models, for they predicted how the tasks would be performed with the proposed systems.

As a check on the validity of using the models in this way, an analysis was done to compare the individual call-time predictions with the times measured in the field trial. The average differences between the modelled times and the field trial times were 11.30 per cent for the current workstation and 11.87 per cent for the proposed workstation. These differences were not unexpected, because the benchmark tasks had not been chosen for their close adherence to mean performance times. The comparison suggested that it was valid to use the models of the proposed workstation's usage to explain its poor performance.

A.8 Why the proposed workstation was slower

The reasons for the proposed workstation's failure to live up to expectations fell into three categories:

- Lack of benefit from the keyboard's redesign

- Lack of benefit from the new display

- Effects of redesigning keystroke sequences.

In this final section we will review some of these reasons, which are discussed more fully in Gray *et al.* (1993).

A.8.1 The keyboard's redesign

We will recall that the proposed workstation had a redesigned keyboard in which commonly used keys, such as the numeric keys and the CALL-RELEASE key indicating call completion, were moved closer together. This was expected to produce significant time savings.

The CPM-GOMS model made it clear, however, that few function-key operators were on the critical path, whichever workstation was used. For example, when the TAO types in a credit-card number the critical path is determined by the speed with which the caller dictates the numbers. This can be seen in the chart of Figure A.8.

The close placement of commonly used keys in fact had the opposite of the intended effect, because it discouraged two-handed use of these keys. In the current design, the TAO was able to press the CALL-RELEASE key with the left hand immediately after pressing numeric keys with the right.

With the new keyboard layout, the right hand would be used throughout this sequence, and the model predicted that the hand movements between the keys would increase the overall task performance time.

A.8.2   The new display

The layouts for the display were not changed significantly in the proposed workstation. However, since the new display was to be four times faster in presenting a screenful of information, it was expected to help achieve substantial performance gains. Here, again, the model showed why these gains failed to materialize.

The new display was in fact slower in one respect, because it took over half a second longer to display the first displayed line of text. This time was on the critical path of every task's performance, and therefore added to the time for every category of call.

At the same time, the new display had little effect on speed of perceiving information. As with the current display, text was displayed from top to bottom, and the critical items of information were almost always on the first or second line displayed. This is illustrated in Figure A.1: the TAO needed to read only the first line of the display in order to choose the appropriate response to the caller. The difference in times for displaying these few characters was only a small fraction of a second. The fact that the entire screenful of text could be displayed in much less time offered no advantage to the TAO.

A.8.3   The redesigned keyboard sequences

As we saw earlier, the TAO's keying procedures were redesigned so as to involve fewer keystrokes. In some cases four fewer keystrokes were needed. These changes were expected to reduce task times by up to a second.

The CPM-GOMS models showed, once again, that this design change was not always achieving the desired effect. In some cases there was indeed a resultant saving in time, but in other cases the result was to make task performance slower. The reason for this lay in the way keystrokes were moved from one point in the procedure to another.

Thus in the redesign of the credit-card call procedure, several keystrokes were removed at the start of the keying sequence shown in Figure A.8(a), and instead an extra keystroke was added at the end of the call, just before the final F3 keystroke in Figure A.8(b). But we can see that the keystrokes in Figure A.8(a) are not on the critical path, because the caller is speaking at the time. On the other hand, any keystrokes added prior to the F3 keystroke automatically become part of the critical path, and lengthen the overall time for performing the task.

A.8.4   The limited opportunities for speed-up

The CPM-GOMS models also help us to judge the feasibility of achieving the desired speed-up. They made it possible to categorize the total critical-path time according to the main types of operator, and this showed that most of the TAO's time was spent in conversation (64 per cent), in waiting for system responses (16 per cent) or in waiting for calls to be answered or coins to be inserted (8 per cent). The activities that could have been influenced by workstation redesign – keying and reading – amounted to only 11 percent.

In the case of the credit-card call, for instance, the keying operators that the designers were trying to speed up amounted to only 2 per cent of the overall task performance time. Even if these operators had been removed entirely from the critical path, only a 2 per cent improvement would have resulted.

A.8.5   How a faster design could have been achieved

In the end, we are left wondering if the design team attempted to solve an impossible design problem. Was there any solution strategy that could have led to the required savings in performance time? Or should the problem have been redefined, with a goal of simply maintaining the same performance levels as before?

Gray *et al.* (1993) address this question, pointing out that other workstation designs could have been investigated and assessed against requirements in the same way. They suggest one possible alternative design, employing a personal response system capable of playing prerecorded initial greeting messages such as 'New England Telephone, may I help you?' This could have been integrated with the workstation, and could have selected and played the appropriate message according to the type of incoming call. The TAO would have been saved from carrying out this initial step. A CPM-GOMS analysis showed that this design could have achieved the savings of up to $6 million per year in labour costs that the phone company was seeking. This example illustrates how, as a result of the work described here, telephone-operator workstations can be designed to achieve the specific performance requirements.

A.9   In conclusion

This case study has reviewed a design exercise – the redesign of a Toll and Assistance Operator's workstation – and two follow-on evaluation exercises. The design exercise involved some carefully considered changes to the keyboard layout and display, and to the keying procedures. It was followed by a field trial, also carried out with great care, in which the proposed new workstation was compared for performance with the workstation in current use. This evaluation gave the unexpected result that the new work-station was 0.65 seconds slower than the current one, per call handled.

In parallel with the field trial a second evaluation was carried out. This followed a more unconventional route, employing the CPM-GOMS analysis method as a means of explaining the outcome of the first evaluation. The analysis provided accurate predictions of the outcomes of the field trial, including a prediction of an increase of 0.63 seconds in call-handling time. It also provided a number of explanations for this loss in performance.

The case of 'Project Ernestine' is an outstanding example of providing tools of the kind interactive system designers need in order to meet per-formance requirements. The proposed workstation was in fact designed without the aid of such tools. A requirement was set to reduce call-hand-ling times by a certain amount, but without tools to help them the design-ers were unable to achieve this target. As the CPM-GOMS analysis illustrated, however, the performance of the proposed design could have been predicted quite accurately on paper. The project illustrated the invaluable role of analytical tools in predicting the outcome when performance-critical interactive systems are designed.

Further reading

John B. E. (1990). Extension of GOMS analyses to expert performance requiring perception of dynamic auditory and visual information. In *Proc. CHI '90 Human Factors in Computing Systems*, April 1–5, Seattle WA. New York: ACM/SIGCHI, pp. 107–15

A short paper about the modelling technique and its use in the TAO evalua-tion exercise.

John B. E. and Gray W. D. (1994). *GOMS Analyses for Parallel Activities.* CHI '94 Tutorial notes. New York: ACM/SIGCHI

A set of notes and viewgraphs explaining how CPM-GOMS analyses are per-formed, with several simple examples.

Gray W. D., John B. E. and Atwood M. E. (1992). The précis of Project Ernestine or, an overview of a validation of GOMS. In *Proc. CHI '92 Human Factors in Computing Systems*, May 3–7, Monterey, CA, New York: ACM/SIGCHI, pp. 307–12

Gray W. D., John B. E. and Atwood M. E. (1993). Project Ernestine: Validating a GOMS analysis for predicting and explaining real-world task performance. *Human Computer Interaction*, **8**, 237–309.

The 1992 paper is a short précis of the full account of the project published in 1993.

PART IV

User interface design

11   User interface notations

12   Interaction styles

13   Conceptual design: The user's mental model

14   Conceptual design: Methods

15   Designing to guidelines

Case study B:
Designing a human memory aid

CHAPTER 11

User interface notations

Chapter objectives:

User interface notations are needed to assist in exploring different solutions, to allow analysis in terms of usability, and to communicate with others involved in the design. This chapter is about choosing the right notation to describe user interfaces. Among the points covered in this chapter are:

- Different strategies for describing designs – delineation, enumeration, instantiation and the use of schemas
- State transition charts and other techniques for describing the input syntax of the user interface
- Methods of describing the program's output
- Methods for describing interactive objects
- The use of prototyping tools for describing the user interface.

11.1 Introduction

The design of interactive systems involves a great deal of exploration of alternative solutions. Each solution explored needs to be analysed to assess its usability. These activities lead in turn to a constant need to communicate with other people about the design. All of these aspects of design depend on adequate methods for describing the solutions in question. In this chapter we look at how we choose appropriate methods to describe our designs for interactive systems.

Our particular concern here is with notations for describing the system's **user interface**. As we saw in Chapter 1, the user interface is the part of a tool or system with which the user interacts directly, the part that enables the user to issue commands and enter data, and the part that provides the user with feedback of computational results. The design of the user interface determines how users perform activities; in this way the user interface affects the degree of support that the system provides. The user interface is also the user's only means of accessing the inner functionality of the system. Thus a description of the user interface is essential in understanding both the usage and the internal structure of the system.

The first section of this chapter looks at the way notations serve the design process. The rest of the chapter is devoted to an overview of the main types of user interface notations and representations.

11.2 The use of representations in design

When we describe a system's design in words or pictures we are *representing* it, that is, we are transforming the real system to be built into an abstract form, usually so that we can record it on paper. Sometimes we record the design with the aid of a computer-based tool, for example, a prototyping system like HyperCard, discussed in Chapter 9. Sometimes we make a video to describe it. Whatever way we choose, the notations, wordings, mock-ups and prototypes we use when working on system designs count as *representations* of the systems themselves.

11.2.1 The roles of representations

What are the main roles of representations in design? A hint to the answer was given in the first sentences of this chapter, which identified **exploration**, **analysis** and **communication** as three important design activities that representations support. Ferguson has described these three categories slightly differently, in identifying the need for *thinking*, *talking* and *prescriptive* sketches (Ferguson, 1992). As this chapter proceeds we will encounter a number of examples of each category. At the end we will return to the question of what these three roles mean in terms of user interface design.

Let us look first at what it means to support exploration, analysis and communication.

Supporting exploration
During **exploration** the designer is concerned with understanding what options are available. This may involve sketching out or piecing together new options. Figure 11.1(a) shows a fragment of a system design in its

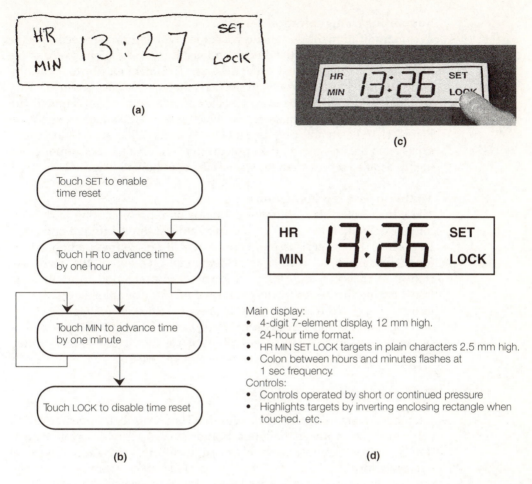

Figure 11.1   Representing the design for a digital clock, by (a) a quick sketch, (b) a schematic representation for use in analysis, (c) a still frame from a video, used in presenting the design, and (d) a precise specification.

early, exploratory stage. The design has been sketched very quickly, with a view to deciding whether it merits further development, and so a representation has been chosen that is quick and easy to draw.

Supporting analysis
During **analysis** the designer makes predictions about the performance of the finished article. It is important to find a representation that makes this analysis easy and accurate. To analyse a system's efficiency we might choose to enumerate the steps in the user's operation of the system as shown in Figure 11.1(b). From such sequences we can conduct walk-throughs and make more accurate predictions of speed of operation or user errors.

Supporting communication

In **communication** the designer is concerned with informing specific people about specific aspects of the design, and needs representations suited to the audience and to the content of the message. The intent may be to invite others to join in explorations or analyses, and notations may be chosen that support these. The aim may be to explain the design to someone unfamiliar with it, such as a marketing manager, in which case a video such as shown in Figure 11.1(c) as a still may be suitable. A crucial line of communication exists from the designer to the implementer, and needs to be supported by highly detailed representations such as the one shown in Figure 11.1(d).

Multi-purpose representations

These three roles place different demands on representations, and so we might expect that designers would need at least three different notations. In practice, however, it is more convenient if one representation can be found that meets all three sets of demands. This avoids the need constantly to *transform* the design from one representation to another. In transforming the design we lose information (for example, we lose layout information if we transform the detailed specification of Figure 11.1(d) into the action sequence of Figure 11.1(b)) and we may make mistakes. A single, general-purpose representation, such as the Object State Transition Charts described below, can overcome these problems.

11.2.2 Representational strategies

Interactive systems are dynamic systems. They vary their appearance and behaviour constantly as the interaction progresses. Any descriptive notation we adopt should be capable of capturing this variation. There are strategies for doing this, and it helps to know about them because each one has its strengths and weaknesses. The four principal strategies are *delineation*, *enumeration*, *instantiation* and *schematization*.

The first strategy, **delineation**, applies only to designs that *don't* vary: it consists of laying out the design in its static form. This is sometimes useful in describing fixed components of interactive systems, e.g., in defining

(a)   (b)

Figure 11.2   Delineation of exact static forms (a) of a screen icon, (b) of a command menu.

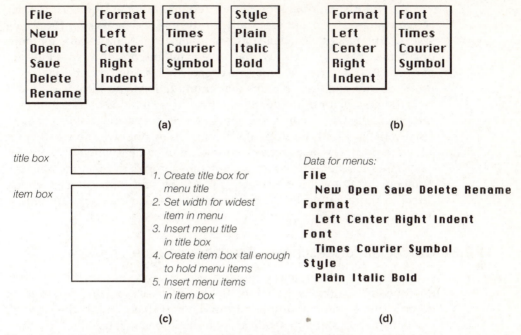

Figure 11.3   Representational strategies for describing text-editing menus: (a) enumeration of all possible forms, (b) instantiation of two possible forms, (c) use of a schema to generate all forms, (d) data used in conjunction with the schema.

the appearance of icons or menus for display on the screen (Figure 11.2).

When designs can take more than one form, we use other ways of describing them. One method is **enumeration**, which means drawing all of the possible forms. Figure 11.3(a) enumerates all of the four menus for controlling a simple text-editing system.

If time or space does not permit the enumeration of all forms, an alternative is **instantiation**: one or more *instances* of forms are given, and the rest are left to be inferred by the reader. Figure 11.3(b) shows two instances of the menus of Figure 11.3(a), from which the variation in length and the similarity in layout can be inferred. These properties of the menus could not have been inferred from the single example of Figure 11.2(b).

The final option is **schematization** – the use of a *schema*. This involves the use of an indirect or abstract representation that is *generative*, that is, capable of generating any or all of the possible forms. A schematic representation of menu construction is shown in Figure 11.3(c); the actual menus of Figure 11.3(a) will be generated if this schema is used with the data of Figure 11.3(d). Schematic representations are used extensively in software design, such as in the notations used for describing programming language syntax.

We will discover uses for all four representational strategies in interactive system design, but especially for the use of schemas, for these have special advantages. Schemas are usually better at handling the extremes of complexity and variability that we encounter constantly in the design of interactive systems. Schemas are capable of bringing out special design properties for analysis, in ways that enumerations and instances cannot. As we shall see, for example, schematic representations of user interfaces can often help us to analyse designs in terms of specific usability factors. Finally, the generative nature of schemas means that we can use them to generate particular instances or enumerations when we want them. We could use the schema of Figure 11.3(c), for example, to generate other sets of menus by using different data. It has to be said that schemas are less direct in representing the forms of designs, and it may take us time to learn how to read them, but this is usually time well spent.

11.2.3   Strategies for describing the user interface

A user interface design has a number of parts, each of which needs to be described. Usually the part that fields the user's actions needs to be described in a different notation from the part that presents the system's reactions. For example, a sequence of user actions will usually be defined in a schema, while a graphical screen layout will probably be described by delination or instantiation. In the remainder of this chapter we will look at examples of notations for these two parts of the user interface. We will look also at ways of describing objects and action sequences.

This will be only a partial list of the many notations and representations available to the designer. There are no real standards in this area. Many of the notations described here can be modified to suit special circumstances, as long as the rules for using them and reading them are carefully restated.

11.3   User actions: Defining input syntax

We need to define the order in which steps may be taken by the user and the alternatives available at each step. A definition of these conventions is essential, because software must be designed and written accordingly to handle the user's inputs, and analysis of the user interface depends on knowing the input sequence. These conventions are known as the *input syntax* of the user interface.

The most commonly used notation for describing input syntax is the *state transition chart* (Newman, 1968; Engelbart and English, 1968). An example is shown in Figure 11.4. Each of the circular symbols, or *nodes*, represents a point in the input sequence where the user can pause or make a choice: it represents one of the unique *states* of the user interface. The nodes are linked together into a *directed graph*; this is achieved by drawing connecting lines, or *arcs*, from each node, representing the user actions

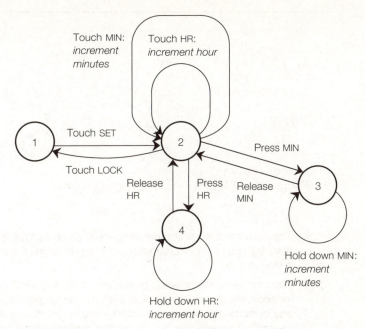

Figure 11.4   A state transition chart, representing the input syntax of the digital clock shown in Figure 11.1.

available to the user when the user interface reaches that state. Arcs may return to the same node that they left, indicating repeated actions such as mouse movements. By labelling the arcs we can show, in a single state transition chart, all possible user actions.

We can also show, on each arc, the effect of the action. This allows us to indicate the software function that is invoked or the output response that is generated. Descriptions of these responses may be appended to the action descriptions, as in Figure 11.4, or the diagram may use special symbols such as boxes or special arrowheads.

State transition charts are not always ideal for describing user interface syntax. They can become very complex, with many hundreds of states, and this hinders analysis and communication. Fortunately there are alternatives. For example, user inputs in the form of lines of text, such as the commands that airline check-in clerks type at great speed, can be described in terms of the overall structure of each command rather than the individual items of data (Figure 11.5).

A more serious problem is presented by user interfaces that permit several independent streams of user action at the same time, for example, systems that support several users. These and other problems in user interface description are still the subject of ongoing research. Often the only satisfactory means of description lies in the construction of working prototypes, which we discuss below.

```
LKI

1. KING. R. L        PAR  Y
2. KIRKSIECK         ROM  Y
3. KIELSZEWSKI       ROM  F        O

P2/F/ES/1
```

(a)

L <text> <return>
P <integer> / { M | F } / <text> / <digit> <return>

(b)

- The command for listing passengers is given by typing 'L' followed immediately by one or more characters of the passengers' names, and the terminating RETURN.

- The command for entering passenger data is given by typing 'P' followed immediately by an integer, and then by the single character 'M' or 'F', by one or more alphabetic characters, and by an integer, each of these three operands preceded by a '/' character, and the whole line terminated by typing RETURN.

(c)

Figure 11.5 Describing text-based interaction syntax. The example in (a) shows interaction with an airline reservation system, taken from Martin (1973). The user has typed the command LKI, followed by <return>, to list passengers whose names begin with the letters KI. A list of three passengers is displayed by the system, and the user then invokes the P command to select a name (the second name, Kirksieck, from the displayed list), and to key in the passenger's sex (female), initials (E.S.) and number of bags (one). In (b) a formal definition of the syntax of the L and P commands is given; alternatives are shown in curly brackets { } separated by vertical bars. In (c) we see the same syntax described informally.

11.4 Appearance: Describing system output

In most user interfaces, output from the system is presented to the user on a display screen, and we need methods of describing the screen's appearance. If the output is in the form of simple text we may be able to use a schematic representation, such as a template describing how each line of output is to appear. More and more user interfaces are graphical, however, and these demand a different approach to output specification, with more reliance on delineation and instantiation.

It is possible in some cases to enumerate all possible forms of a user interface. Figure 11.6 shows a roadside display indicating lane closures; it

Figure 11.6   Enumeration of all allowable forms of a roadside lane-closures display.

enumerates all six allowable closures. It is unusual to encounter a design that can be enumerated fully in this way. Sometimes we can enumerate all forms of a portion of the user interface, such as the set of menus that were shown in Figure 11.3(a).

As with the user's input, the system's output may not be expressible as a static graphical image. For example, the system may respond with voice, with synthesized audio, with an animated sequence or with a video sequence. These forms of output are best represented as *streams* of data, possibly by describing a number of separate instances in the stream. A video can be made to describe the output to be generated. Again, this is an active area of research, and the use of working prototypes may prove to be the best method of documenting the design.

11.5   Describing interactive objects

We naturally want to achieve as complete a description of the system's user interface as possible. However, systems rarely have well-defined boundaries that enable us to decide when a description is complete. There may be a number of separate interactive components, and we must decide which of these are parts of the 'system' and which are not. Ultimately the best way to achieve this is not to try to describe a single user interface to the system as a whole, but to describe the individual user interfaces of the separate **interactive objects** with which the user or users interact.

An example: Interactive objects in an airport control room

To understand this point better, let us look at how the staff of an airport control room deal with traffic in and out of the airport's gates. This is the same control room that was introduced in Chapter 3, and that figured in the transcript of Figure 4.4(b). The controller's support system consists primarily of a workstation that provides access to up-to-date flight information (the Flight Information Display), but there is also a panel of TV monitors showing views of each of the gates, as shown in Figure 11.7(a). Controllers are in communication with pilots through two-way radio, and use telephones to contact the crews at the gates. They keep printouts of the day's arriving and departing flights on their desks for easy reference.

When a gate-assignment problem arises, e.g., when an arriving pilot finds the assigned gate still occupied, the controller 'interacts' with all of

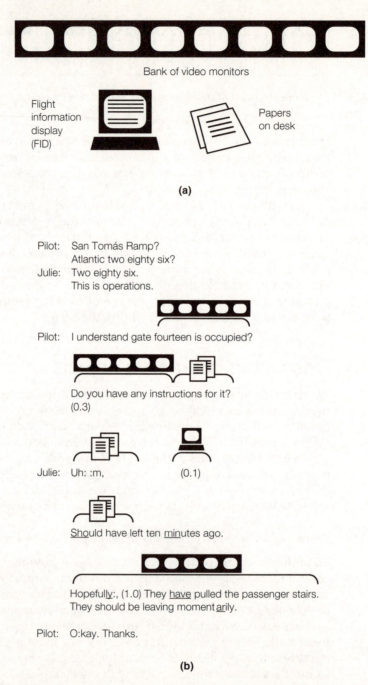

Bank of video monitors

Flight
information
display
(FID)

Papers
on desk

(a)

Pilot: San Tomás Ramp?
         Atlantic two eighty six?
Julie: Two eighty six.
         This is operations.

Pilot: I understand gate fourteen is occupied?

Do you have any instructions for it?
(0.3)

Julie: Uh: :m,   (0.1)

Should have left ten minutes ago.

Hopefully:, (1.0) They have pulled the passenger stairs.
They should be leaving momentarily.

Pilot: O:kay. Thanks.

(b)

Figure 11.7   San Jose Airport control room: (a) layout of controller's information; (b) transcript of controller (Julie) solving a gate-conflict problem, with symbols showing
where she refers to workstation, video monitors and flight schedules (from
Goodwin and Goodwin (in press)).

these objects to resolve the problem. An example is shown in the annotated transcript of Figure 11.7(b). Labels over the controller's speech indicate her focus of attention.

This example makes the point that people interact with many objects
besides the screen in front of them. They shift attention from one object to
another in sequences that we, as designers, have no control over. It is only
by letting users manage this sequence themselves that we enable them to
make full use of their problem solving skills.

Objects in graphical user interfaces

An airport control room is just one example of an environment supporting
many interactive objects. Another example is found in the user interface of
a modern interactive workstation. When we look at the workstation's screen
we see an arrangement like Figure 11.8 involving a variety of separate interactive objects: windows, menus, icons, control panels, and so on. Each of
these objects is capable of maintaining a separate stream of interaction, or
dialogue, with the user. Each has its own user interface for this purpose.

When the user is surrounded by many interactive objects, each with
its user interface and each capable of maintaining a separate dialogue, the

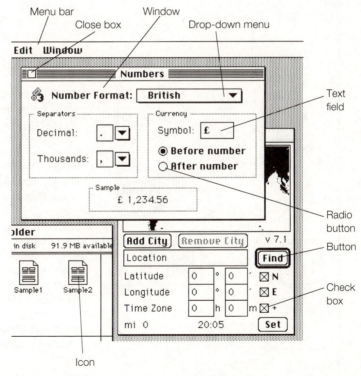

Figure 11.8   Interactive objects on a screen, each capable of maintaining a separate dialogue
via its own user interface. Courtesy Apple Computer.

only simple way to describe the overall user interface is by describing the user interface of each object in turn.

The panel presents an object-oriented notation for this purpose, based on Object State Transition Charts, otherwise known as OSTCs or 'ostrich charts'. The notation makes use of state transition charts to define the input syntax of each object in the user interface. State symbols and transitions are labelled with instances of the object's appearance, and with other aspects of the object's behaviour such as audio feedback.

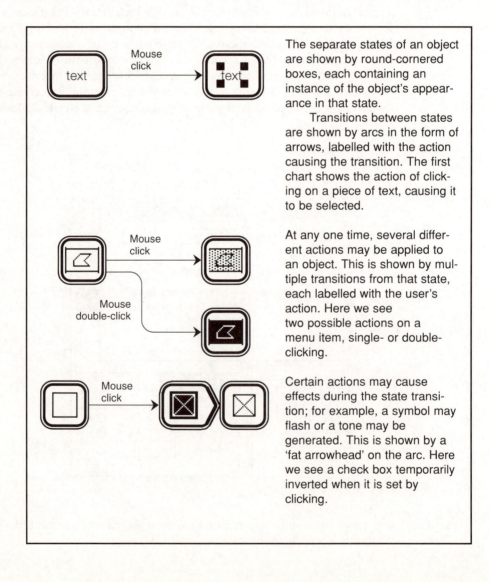

The separate states of an object are shown by round-cornered boxes, each containing an instance of the object's appearance in that state.

Transitions between states are shown by arcs in the form of arrows, labelled with the action causing the transition. The first chart shows the action of clicking on a piece of text, causing it to be selected.

At any one time, several different actions may be applied to an object. This is shown by multiple transitions from that state, each labelled with the user's action. Here we see two possible actions on a menu item, single- or double-clicking.

Certain actions may cause effects during the state transition; for example, a symbol may flash or a tone may be generated. This is shown by a 'fat arrowhead' on the arc. Here we see a check box temporarily inverted when it is set by clicking.

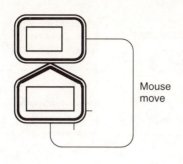

Mouse move

An action may be applied without causing a change of state. The arc is shown returning to the state it left. A 'fat arrowhead' may be used to show the effect of the action.

Here we see the effect of moving the mouse while drawing a box. The changed box shape is shown in the arrowhead. Tick marks on the sides of the arrowhead show the mouse position, which controls the corner of the box.

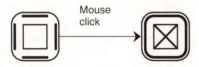

Mouse click

Often a graphical action takes effect only when applied within a certain region of the object. This may be shown by limiting the extent of the thick bars surrounding the object. Here this is done to show the region in which the user must click within a check box.

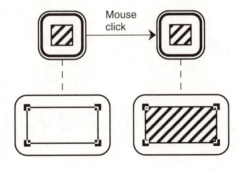

Mouse click

An action on an object may change another object; the two objects are *linked*. Links are shown by dashed lines connecting the objects. The inactive object – the object to which the actions do not apply – is shown with a single-line surrounding outline.

Here a selected box is given a different shading by clicking on a linked object, an item in a menu of patterns.

Several objects may be grouped together to form a composite object. This is shown by enclosing the composite object in a dashed rectangle, and linking it to charts describing the behaviour of each of the component objects.

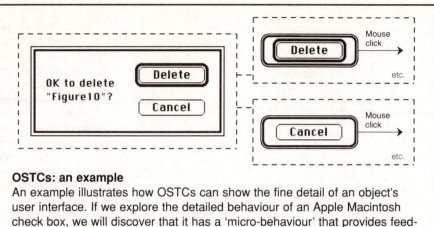

OSTCs: an example

An example illustrates how OSTCs can show the fine detail of an object's user interface. If we explore the detailed behaviour of an Apple Macintosh check box, we will discover that it has a 'micro-behaviour' that provides feedback during mouse-clicks, and that allows the user to have a change of mind. The simple mouse-click action, taking the object from the *unchecked* to the *checked* state, in reality has two additional states. Pressing down on the mouse button takes the check box into an intermediate *selected* state in which it acquires a thick outline. During this state the live zone surrounding the box enlarges, and if the mouse pointer is moved out of it into the outer dead zone, the box ceases to be selected. In this *unselected* state, the release of the mouse button will return the check box to its *unchecked* state. The chart shows the action of checking the box in full detail.

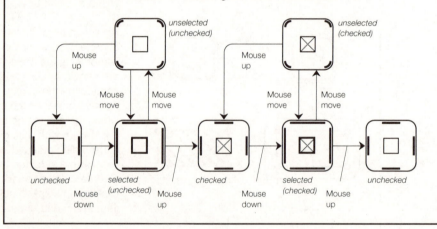

11.6 Describing methods of operation

One of the main purposes of describing interactive systems is, as we saw at the outset, to support the analysis of designs. Many of the analyses we perform are concerned with the system's usability, e.g., with speed of task performance or likelihood of user errors. These analyses often make use of descriptions of the user's method of operation. This section briefly discusses what it means to describe methods of operation.

11.6.1 An example: Extracting methods from Object State Transition Charts

Like any schematic notation, state transition charts are generative: they can describe specific sequences of interaction. We can extract sequences, corresponding to methods of achieving specific goal states, by tracing back from the appropriate state in the chart.

Figure 11.9 shows an example, the user interface for icons in an Apple Macintosh folder. Figure 11.9(a) shows part of the user interface, and Figure 11.9(b) shows the particular method of selecting an icon and retyping its label. A description such as this could be used in making approximate estimates of user selection speeds, using a Keystroke-Level Model as described in Chapter 8.

11.6.2 Describing action sequences with the UAN

Other methods are available for describing methods of operation at this detailed level. One example is the User Action Notation or UAN of Hartson, Siochi and Hix (Hartson *et al.*, 1990). UAN sequences are described in a text format: the sequence of user actions in retyping an icon's name could be described as follows:

~[label]
Mv^
K(new-label)

The syntax of UAN is quite rich, and only a few of its symbols are used here. The notation ~[object] means that the user positions the pointer on an object. The symbol M refers to the mouse-button, and the symbols v and ^ indicate that the button is pressed and released, respectively. The symbol K refers to keyboard input; it may be followed by a literal or a variable string.

Thus we can see that the above sequence of UAN actions starts with positioning on the label to be changed, is followed by pressing and releasing the mouse button, and finishes with the user typing the new label for the icon.

The User Action Notation allows for the definition of interface feedback and interface state. The full description of the label-changing sequence would be as shown in Table 11.1.

The second column shows the feedback provided by the interface. The '!' symbol is used to indicate that an object has been highlighted, and '-!' to indicate de-highlighted. The third column shows the current state of the interface. For a full description of the UAN, see Hix and Hartson (1993).

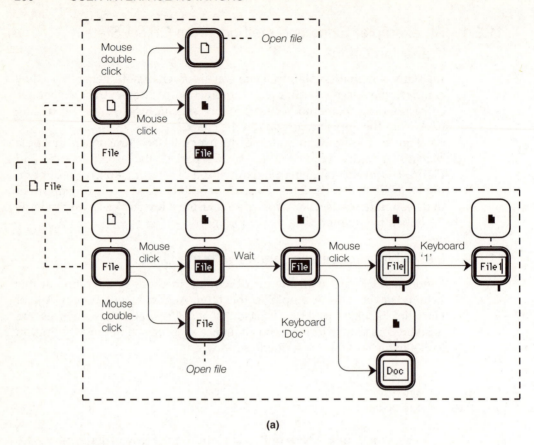

(a)

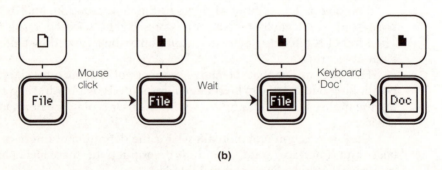

(b)

Figure 11.9   Icon selection and renaming: (a) the user interface described as an OSTC; (b) a
method of operation extracted from the OSTC. Icon designs courtesy Apple
Computer.

Table 11.1   The label-changing example described using the User Action Notation.

User actions	Interface feedback	Interface state
~[label]		
Mv^v	label!	ready for change
K(new-label)	label-!	label changing

11.7 Describing by prototyping

A description on paper has a number of limitations. It cannot show the full dynamic properties of the user interface, and it may not be able to communicate the true nature of the application to people outside the design team. Furthermore, the cycle of enhancement and evaluation is likely to be slowed down by documenting every detail of each stage on paper. For these and other reasons it is common to use prototyping tools to describe ideas for user interface designs. Once described in this way, the designs can be tested directly, without the need to wait while they are implemented.

An example of the use of HyperCard

Chapter 9 described in outline how prototypes may be built in HyperCard. In this section we will look at the kinds of descriptions that such a tool generates.

The example illustrated here is a device to assist memory recall and retrieval (Lamming and Flynn, 1994). It makes use of records of daily events such as meetings, receipt of electronic mail, and so on, from which it helps the user to reconstruct the *context* of some other event that he or she is trying to remember. In other words, it acts as a 'memory prosthesis'. A photograph of the prototype, implemented on a hand-held display device, was shown in Figure 1.1. Its development is described in Case Study B which follows Chapter 15.

Figure 11.10(a) shows a pre-prototype description of the design – a rough sketch, drawn on a whiteboard during a design meeting. At this meeting the decision was made to mock up the design in HyperCard, and the result is shown in Figure 11.10(b). It includes buttons for stepping to previous or following cards in the stack, a couple of text boxes, some icons and other buttons, all created with the HyperCard editor.

Later versions of the prototype allowed the design team to experiment with different ways of displaying events. Figure 11.11(a) shows an early version of this prototype, in which no attempt was made to scale it to fit the hand-held display. In Figure 11.11(b) we see the final form of the design.

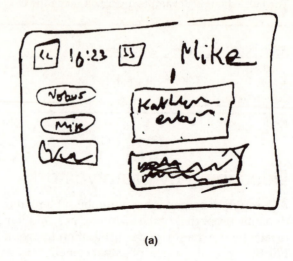

(a)

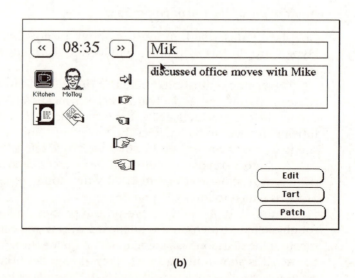

(b)

Figure 11.10   Human memory aid: (a) initial sketches; (b) initial prototype. Courtesy Rank Xerox.

(a)

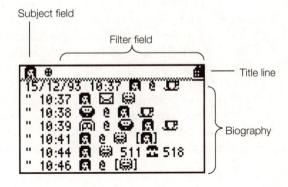

(b)

Figure 11.11   The memory aid: (a) a later prototype and (b) the final design. Courtesy Rank
Xerox.

11.8 Conclusion

These are only some of the wide range of notations available to the user interface designer. When we choose a notation, it is wise to remember some of things we may wish to apply it to, because we don't want the notation to let us down.

First, we make a lot of use of notations during the *exploratory* stages of design. When we have ideas for user interfaces we make a note of them, because other ideas may cause us to forget them. We don't want to spend a lot of time at this stage drawing intricate diagrams, however, and so we need a notation that is quick to prepare and easy to read.

Our notations of user interfaces will be used to support *analyses* of various kinds. Some are simple analyses that we carry out in our heads: will the user be able to tell one object from another, for example? Other analyses involve application of predictive models, as described in the next chapter. The most important property of a notation, in terms of support-ing more powerful methods of analysis, is its ability to help us generate the sequence of actions that the user carries out. Some notations, such as UAN, are intended for this specific purpose.

We also use notations to *communicate* our designs to other people – to other members of the design team, to users outside the team, to imple-menters, to marketing people. There may not be a single notation suitable for all of these people. Screen images may convey a lot more than OSTCs or UANs to people outside the design team.

When none of the available notations is capable of supporting our design activities, we look for new methods. This is how all of the existing methods originated: solutions were devised that existing notations could not describe. We can expect to continue to encounter new solutions that present us with the same difficulty. It is OK to try out a new notation when this happens. But we should remember that notations are used in communicating with other people. A new notation will need to be learned by everybody with whom we communicate about the design.

Exercises

(1) What are the three main roles of notations in design?

(2) Explain the meaning of delineation, instantiation, enumeration and schematization as strategies for describing designs.

(3) Identify as many different types of object as you can on your computer's screen. For each object, (a) which of the four strategies of Question 2 would you use to describe it, and (b) what notation would you expect to find most capable of filling the three roles of Question 1?

(4) Describe the user interfaces of specific examples of two of the following: (a) a pay phone; (b) a VCR's controls for playing videotapes; (c) a VCR's programming controls; (d) an automated teller machine; (e) a telephone answering machine; (f) a fax machine; (g) an on-screen window.

(5) Describe the ticket machine of Chapter 6 as a set of Object State Transition Charts.

(6) Describe the scroll bar of a Macintosh or Microsoft Windows as a set of Object State Transition Charts.

(7) Draw a state transition chart for a digital alarm watch.

(8) In what circumstances would you use static screen images to describe a design, and what kinds of user interface would be most effectively described this way?

(9) Describe the full behaviour of the Macintosh check box using the UAN (you will need to read the description of the UAN in the references).

(10) As described in this chapter, Object State Transition Charts require the regions within which graphical actions take effect to be rectangular. Discuss how the notation might be extended to permit other shapes of region, for example, circles.

Further reading

Coulouris G. F. and Thimbleby H. (1993). *HyperProgramming: Building Interactive Programs with HyperCard*. Reading, MA: Addison-Wesley

An introduction to the use of HyperCard and to writing programs in HyperTalk.

Hix D. and Hartson H. R. (1993). *Developing User Interfaces: Ensuring Usability through Product and Process*. New York: Wiley

Includes a chapter on UAN, in addition to general treatment of user interface design.

Siochi A. C. and Hartson H. R. (1989). The UAN: A task-oriented notation for user interfaces. *Proceedings of CHI '89 Human Factors in Computing Systems*, April 30–May 4, Austin, TX, pp. 183–8, New York: ACM/SIGCHI

A short introduction to the UAN.

CHAPTER 12

Interaction styles

Chapter objectives:

The choice of interaction style is an important decision made early in the design of the user interface. The choice of style will help establish a design strategy, and will orient the design towards certain levels of usability and system cost. In this chapter we explore what styles are available and how the choice is made, covering the following points:

- The basic categories of style: key-modal, direct manipulation, linguistic
- The eight principal styles, their underlying principles, variants of each, and their basic strengths and weaknesses
- How each style lends itself to a specific application.

12.1 Introduction

The last chapter reviewed the range of notations available for describing user interfaces. This chapter now begins the coverage of methods of user interface design: choice of interaction style, conceptual design and the use of guidelines. Choice of style is covered first, because this is a major decision that designers must take early in the course of design.

12.1.1   What are interaction styles?

Interaction styles represent alternative design strategies for the user interface. Each style offers its own cohesive way of organizing the system's functionality, of managing the user's inputs, and of presenting information. Knowledge of interaction styles is therefore of great value to user interface designers, who need ways of organizing these aspects of the system's design. There isn't a continuum of design strategies to learn about, but a relatively small number, each one easily distinguishable from the others.

When we start to design the user interface of an interactive system, we choose an appropriate interaction style. This is an important choice: it affects how the system's functionality is delivered to the user, and thus impacts the system's usability. Our choice of style is closely linked to the choice of interactive technology we adopt, the one tending to influence the other. We need to know what interaction styles exist and what their general properties are, so that we can choose styles on an informed basis.

The purpose of this chapter is to provide an introduction to the more widely used interaction styles. It starts with an explanation of the three main categories of interaction style, and then presents the eight styles shown in Table 12.1. It covers each style by explaining the underlying design strategy and discussing the style's properties, applying each one to addressing the same situation of concern so as to bring out the strengths and weaknesses of each.

Table 12.1   The eight interaction styles presented in this chapter, organized into three categories.

Key-modal	Direct manipulation	Linguistic
Menu-based interaction	Graphical direct manipulation	Command-line interaction
Question-and-answer	Forms fill-in	Text-based natural language
Function-key interaction Voice-based interaction		

12.2   Three categories of style

The main property that sets one interaction style apart from another is the way the system's interactive resources are organized – the 'architecture' of the user interface, to use a popular computer term. In some styles, the system's resources are made available step by step, while in others they are all made available to the user more or less from the outset, and in yet others they are accessed by composing and issuing commands in an appropriate language. It is convenient to distinguish between these three categories of style, which we will call *key-modal*, *direct manipulation* and *linguistic*. Within each category, we will find certain common properties shared by interaction styles and we will find certain notations particularly useful for describing the user interface.

12.2.1   Key-modal interaction styles

The term 'key-modal' is a shorthand way of saying that the user interface is operated mainly with the aid of function keys or an alphanumeric *keyboard*, and that it has a number of different *modes* of behaviour. Four common interaction styles can be considered key-modal:

- **Menu-based interaction.** The user interface presents the user with a display of options, and the selection of an option may generate a further set of options.

- **Question-and-answer.** The system presents a series of questions in text form, and the user enters the answers via a keyboard.

- **Function-key interaction.** The user makes a series of inputs by pressing function keys or using other special-purpose hardware, prompted along the way with displayed information.

- **Voice-based interaction**, often supported by simple telephone equipment. The user is presented with options by a recorded or synthesized voice message, makes choices with the keys on the telephone keypad, and records voice responses.

Each of these interaction styles depends on shifts of *mode*. In other words, the behaviour of the system in response to a particular input (for example, typing YES or pressing the RETURN key) varies according to the stage of the dialogue. A question-and-answer system might ask the question, 'Do you want to continue?' at one point, and later on might ask, 'Do you want to stop now?' The answer YES will have opposite effects at these two points, and we therefore say that the system has multiple modes or is *modal*.

Key-modal user interfaces are used in almost all systems designed for walk-up use, for example, automated tellers, ticket machines and voice-mail systems. A very simple key-modal interface, presented by a door security system, is shown as a state transition chart in Figure 12.1. It has a sensor capable of detecting a badge shown to it, and a set of keys for entering a personal identification number or PIN. It has an illuminated sign that tells the user what to do next.

One reason why key-modal interfaces are so popular for walk-up-and-use systems is that they can provide the user with step-by-step instructions. The system always 'knows' what state of the interaction has

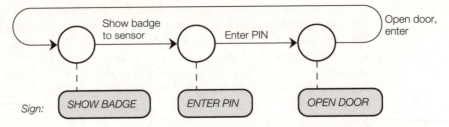

Figure 12.1   A state transition chart showing the operation of a simple key-modal interface for a door security system.

been reached, and hence what actions are now available to the user, so it can present appropriate help. Styles that do not have modes cannot always be as helpful to the inexperienced user.

In the discussion of individual key-modal styles, we will find the state-chart notation useful for capturing the details of the user interface. It identifies each of the modes of the user interface, and shows what user actions are permitted at each step in the interaction. The system's responses can be shown in separate images and labels attached to the nodes of the chart. Figure 12.1, for example, shows each of the messages displayed on a sign beside the badge sensor and keypad.

12.2.2 Direct-manipulation styles

As we saw in the last chapter, the user interface can display a number of objects on the screen and allow the user to interact with each one independently. With the aid of a pointing device the user can apply actions directly to the object of interest. This style of user interface is known as **direct manipulation**. Later in this chapter we will study two widely used styles of direct-manipulation interface:

- **Graphical direct manipulation.** Information is displayed in the form of graphical objects, which the user can query and manipulate graphically with a pointing device.

- **Forms fill-in.** The system displays a set of text fields on the screen, and the user can select individual fields and enter or modify their contents.

A well-known example of a direct-manipulation interface is the Apple Macintosh desktop, shown in Figure 12.2.

As in other categories of style, there are properties of direct manipulation that set it apart and make it easy to distinguish from other categories. These properties are as follows:

- The user is provided with a means of manipulating individual objects, each of which has a *direct display representation*.

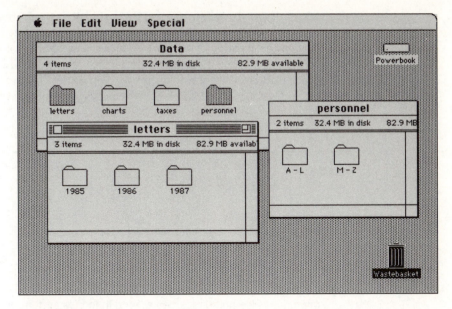

Figure 12.2 An example of a direct manipulation interface: the Apple Macintosh desktop; from Apple (1987).

- The user *applies actions directly to objects* by selecting them, and then entering text or issuing a command via a function key or menu.

- After each user action, *the display of the objects concerned responds immediately* to show any resultant change.

    If the user interface doesn't meet this description it cannot be considered a true example of direct manipulation – it probably belongs in one of the other categories, or in a class of its own.

12.2.3 Linguistic styles

Some styles of user interface require all of the user's inputs to be made on an alphanumeric keyboard, using a particular set of conventions or *language*, and for this reason we group them together as *linguistic* styles. The two principal linguistic styles that we discuss in this chapter are:

- **Command-line interaction.** The user types a command on a keyboard, and the results are displayed back to the user, usually in the form of text.

- **Text-based natural language.** The user types queries and enters information by typing words and phrases in English or another spoken language, and the system responds in the same language.

To use a linguistic-style interface, the user must know the language. This involves knowing both the *syntax* of the language, that is, the rules of grammatical expression, and the *semantics* or meaning of words and phrases. When we design these user interfaces, we must define the syntax and annotate it as necessary to explain the semantics. Figure 12.3 shows the syntax and semantics of the UNIX operating system's *mv* command for moving and renaming files.

NAME

mv – move or rename file

SYNOPSIS

mv [–] [–fi] filename1 filename2
mv [–] [–fi] directory1 directory2
mv [–] [–fi] filename ... directory

DESCRIPTION

mv moves files and directories around in the file system. A side effect of **mv** is to rename a file or directory. The three major forms of **mv** are shown in the synopsis above.

The first form of **mv** moves (changes the name of) filename1 to filename2. If filename2 already exists, it is removed before filename1 is moved. If filename2 has a mode that forbids writing, **mv** prints the mode (see chmod(2V)) and reads the standard input to obtain a line; if the line begins with a y, the move takes place, otherwise **mv** exits.

The second form of **mv** moves (changes the name of) directory1 to directory2, only if directory2 does not already exist – if it does, the third form applies.

The third form of **mv** moves one or more filenames (may also be directories) with their original names, into the last directory in the list.

mv refuses to move a file or directory onto itself.

OPTIONS

–   Interpret all the following arguments to **mv** as filenames. This allows filenames starting with minus.

–f   Force. Override any mode restrictions and the –i option. The –f option also suppresses any warning messages about modes which would potentially restrict overwriting.

–i   Interactive mode. **mv** displays the name of the file or directory followed by a question mark whenever a move would replace an existing file or directory. If you type a line starting with y, **mv** moves the specified file or directory, otherwise **mv** does nothing with that file or directory.

Figure 12.3   An example of a linguistic user interface: the *mv* command of UNIX, as described in the 'man' pages from the online manual. Copyright in this documentation of the *mv* command is owned by Sun Microsystems, Inc. and is used herein by permission. All other rights reserved.

Command-line user interfaces like this one are extremely widely used in interactive systems, particularly in those with an information focus. They are not particularly easy to learn, and normally demand an extended training period. It is partly for this reason that natural-language interfaces are sometimes proposed instead. In theory, a language that mimics the user's spoken language should be easier to learn. As we shall see, however, the use of a natural language style does not always offer the benefits that system designers seek.

12.3 A survey of interaction styles

The next eight sections provide a brief survey of the major interaction styles, grouped according to the three categories: key-modal, direct manipulation and linguistic. It is not possible to cover the styles in all of their many variations during such a brief guided tour. However, it is possible to see how each style supports the designer in achieving particular levels of functionality and performance, and also helps in dealing with the limitations of particular hardware choices. To assist in this, we orient our survey around a specific example, and show how changes in requirements lead to the adoption of different interaction styles.

12.3.1 The example: Purchasing from a hardware catalogue

Let us suppose we wish to design a system to support the task of purchasing items of hardware from a catalogue. Our clients are managers of a hardware store with the aim of increasing turnover and profits, which they hope to achieve by applying interactive technology.

This desire for business improvement is the 'situation of concern' from which we can develop the problem statement and hence the design itself. But there are many ways of addressing this situation, corresponding to the different activities we can support and the levels of support we can achieve. There is an opportunity here to explore a full range of interaction styles.

The activities involved
Some of the solutions we will be looking at involve supporting the customer's activities of identifying products, paying for them, and so on, while other solutions support the sales staff. The entire process to which these activities contribute involves five stages, shown in Figure 12.4.

We can address the situation of concern by tackling different combinations of activities. In each case, we can set different targets for usability and cost. The result is a number of separate design problems that we solve by adopting different interaction styles.

Figure 12.4 identifies the supporting role of the catalogue – the list of all items available for sale. In a conventional hardware store, the

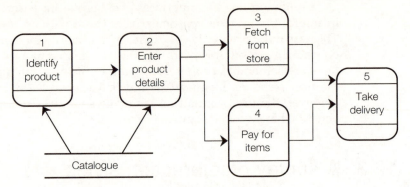

Figure 12.4   Stages in the purchase of items of hardware by customers.

catalogue would be used by staff in answering queries and checking product details, but the customer might never set eyes on it. Making the catalogue available online provides one of the keys to making the operation less expensive to operate. Thus we can provide customers with access to the catalogue so that they can make their selections and take the list to the sales counter to pay for them; or we can provide sales staff with an online catalogue so that they can help customers identify the products they want. We will look at solutions that follow each of these approaches.

How we will conduct the survey of styles
In the sections that follow, each style is explained in outline. The style is then illustrated with the aid of the hardware-store example, starting with a redefinition of the problem based on a choice of supported activities and performance targets, and finishing with a brief description of the solution. We discuss the basic principles underlying the style, some of the common variants, and some of the style's properties.

  We won't attempt to explore each style in detail. To understand how to design user interfaces in any particular style, we need to be familiar with conceptual design methods, explained in the next two chapters. We also need to be familiar with design guidelines appropriate to the style in question, and these are discussed in Chapter 15.

12.4 Menu-based interaction

Menu-based interaction provides a means for inexperienced users to navigate through an extensive system functionality, using simple forms of technology such as alphanumeric display terminals. In the hardware sales example, menu-based interaction might be our first choice of style, offering customers a straightforward means of searching through the catalogue, and allowing the clients to settle for low-cost equipment. Having adopted this style, we could write our problem statement as follows:

Design a low-cost menu-based in-store catalogue system allowing customers with no prior experience to search for products.

A solution might be designed along the lines shown in Figure 12.5. At the outset the customer is shown a list of general categories of product. By typing in the number opposite the category required, she or he makes a selection, and another panel of choices is presented. This interaction style proceeds until the specific item is identified. The customer can then start another search, or go to the counter to purchase the items selected so far.

12.4.1   Principles of menu-based interaction

The basic principle of menu-based interaction design is to offer the user only those actions that make sense in the circumstances. This prevents the user from issuing an inappropriate or unavailable command. Menus are aptly named in this respect: by analogy, they ensure that the customer orders a dish that the kitchen can prepare.

The range of options available may be very large, and this leads to a second underlying design principle. Available options can be divided into categories and sub-categories, through which the user navigates with the aid of a sequence of menus. This is how multi-level hierarchies of menus arise, such as the set of menus shown in Figure 12.5.

12.4.2   Variants of menus

Menu selections can be made in a variety of ways, depending on the input device available. Keyboard-based menu selection is usually done either by typing option numbers as in Figure 12.5, or by typing the initial letter of a command option. Non-keyboard techniques include:

- Pointing with a graphical input device

- Touching a target on a touch-screen

- Pressing a button alongside the displayed option.

The last two of these methods enable the inclusion of menus in *function-key interfaces*, discussed below.

While menus can set an interaction style all of their own, they are also used in support of other interaction styles. They are often used in graphical direct-manipulation interfaces, for example. Here, however, they play only a subsidiary role in organizing the user interface; they don't set the style of interaction.

12.4.3   Hypertext embedded menus and the World Wide Web

The use of graphical selection techniques, supported by pointing devices or touch-screens, allows a more free-form approach to the design of

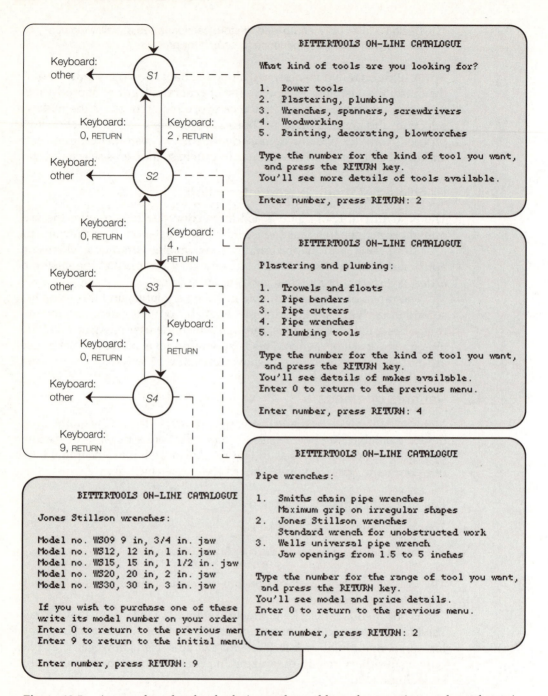

Figure 12.5   A menu-based style of solution to the problem of supporting catalogue browsing and searching. This state transition chart shows four particular panels displayed in sequence when choosing a Stillson wrench. The full interface would involve many more panels.

menus. This technique has been described by Koved and Shneiderman (1986). Recently it has become the basis of interaction with information on the World Wide Web via the Internet network (Berners-Lee *et al.*, 1994).

A Web-style hardware catalogue might be designed as shown in Figure 12.6. The 'menu' is embedded in the text as underlined or outlined items picked out in a special colour, typically dark blue. When the user selects an item the appropriate new page is displayed. Targets at the bottom of the screen allow the user to go **Back** to the previous page, to go **Forward** again after going back, to return to the **Home** page, and to perform other more specialized functions.

The World Wide Web is an example of a system supporting **hypertext** documents, that is, documents written non-sequentially and intended for non-sequential reading (Carmody *et al.*, 1969). Non-sequential reading is facilitated by providing *links* from one place to another. These may simply take the reader to another place in the same sequential document.

In the case of the World Wide Web, however, links can point to other documents, stored at publicly accessible sites all around the Internet. These documents can be accessed by any program supporting the Hypertext Transfer Protocol (HTTP) and capable of interpreting the particular language (Hypertext Mark-up Language or HTML) in which Web documents are encoded. As in conventional menu-based interaction, the overall structure of the information is a directed graph, organized hierarchically so that the user can navigate downwards by clicking on targets, and up again by clicking on **Back**.

12.4.4 Properties of menu-based interaction

Menu-based interaction supports some aspects of functionality better than others. Its strength lies in the way it supports navigation around the system's resources; it helps the user who wants to find a particular function or item of data, or who maybe just wants to know what functions are available. Its weakness lies in its lack of support for complex actions or input, for example, commands with several operands. As we shall see, the second stage in the hardware sales task does involve actions of this kind, and needs to be supported with a different interaction style.

As regards usability, first-time users can normally find their way around menu structures with little difficulty. They are helped in this by the additional information usually displayed along with the menu items themselves. If problems do arise, these will probably occur when users try to access parts of the menu that are not immediately accessible, for example, when they try to reach the list of power-tool products from the list of pipe wrenches. Menu-based navigation is not a particularly rapid way of accessing information when its location is already known to the user. However, in the kinds of browsing applications we have discussed, high-speed access to pages may not be important because the user spends so much time scanning each page retrieved.

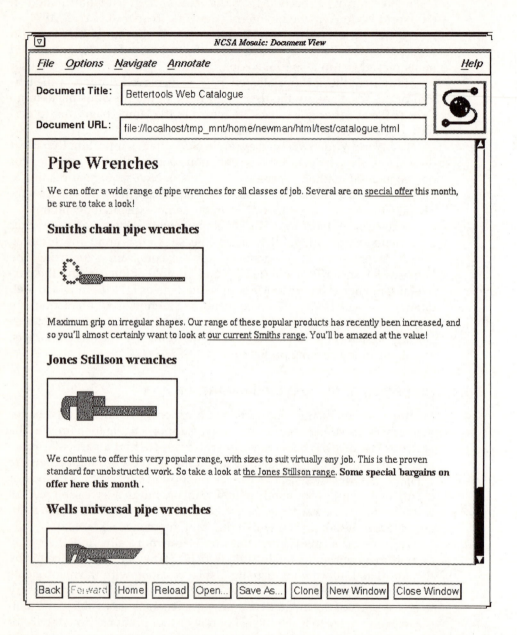

Figure 12.6   A catalogue with embedded menus, based on the style of the World Wide Web. NCSA Mosaic™ is copyrighted by and is property of the Board of Trustees of the University of Illinois.

12.5 Question and answer

There are a number of unsatisfactory aspects to the solution of Figure 12.5. Although it supports the customer in finding the items to purchase, it provides no support at all to the remaining stages in the process, for example, the stages of identifying and paying for the selected items. By demanding that the user should write the product model number on a piece of paper it invites all sorts of errors. When payment is made, details of the order must inevitably be entered for the purpose of generating a receipt. We haven't really addressed the situation of concern. We need to extend the problem statement to cover at least the next stage of the process:

> Design a low-cost in-store catalogue system allowing customers with no prior experience to search for products and record details of the items they wish to purchase.

How does a question-and-answer style of interaction enable us to solve this problem?

To record details of the order, the customer needs both to identify the item and to specify how many are wanted. Equally importantly, she needs to identify herself as the originator of the order, so that when she goes to the checkout counter the clerk can match her up with the right order. The simplest way to achieve this is by issuing numbered tickets on entry to the store (Figure 12.7). By this scheme, the customer need enter just three pieces of information – product number, number of items wanted and ticket number – with each product selected.

A question-and-answer style of user interface is often the best choice for data-entry tasks performed by unskilled users. In this instance the user interface can be extended as shown in Figure 12.8.

Unlike the menu panels of Figure 12.5, the questions and answers of the dialogue will normally remain displayed so that the user can check back to previous questions and their answers:

Figure 12.7   Issuing tickets to enable customers to identify themselves when placing orders on the system.

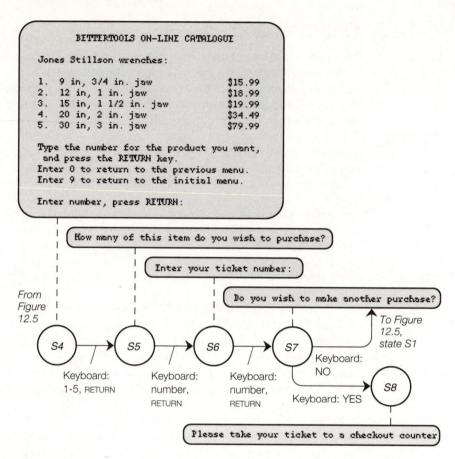

Figure 12.8 Extending the menu-based interface with a three-stage question-and-answer dialogue for entry of product choice, number of items and ticket number.

Enter number, press RETURN: 2
How many of this item do you wish to purchase? 1
Enter your ticket number: 1534
Do you wish to make another purchase? NO
Please take your ticket to a checkout counter.

12.5.1 Properties of question and answer

Question-and-answer user interfaces support a particular range of functionality in which the emphasis is on simple data capture, one item at a time. They allow a limited degree of variation in the sequence, for example, through the use of YES/NO questions. The provision of prompts and explanatory information at each step means that they require little or no prior training.

Question-and-answer interfaces have a number of inherent usability problems, however. They are very slow and unreliable in the hands of a non-typist; they provide no natural means of correcting errors in previous entries; they provide little reassurance in the form of feedback, giving the user little idea of where the interaction is leading; and they often waste time by asking the user unnecessary questions. This is therefore a style to use sparingly, so as not to impact the usability of the system as a whole.

12.6   Function-key interfaces

In systems intended for use in public places, we see increasing reliance on special-purpose input technologies such as push-buttons, function keys and numeric keypads. The systems in which these technologies are used include ticket machines, automated tellers, pay phones, door-entry systems and automated tollbooths, to name just a few examples. They support a particular *function-key* interaction style in which the user's dialogue has many of the properties of menu-based or question-and-answer interaction, but in which different input devices are used as the task progresses.

Figure 12.9 shows a function-key solution to the problems of the hardware sales user interface. It incorporates a graphical display flanked by two sets of function keys (numbered 1 to 6 in the figure) and with a card-reader on the right. We might choose this solution strategy if it should become important to support the payment stage in the process:

> Design an in-store catalogue system allowing customers with no prior experience to search for products and pay for the items they choose by credit card.

The design of Figure 12.9 overcomes several of our two previous designs' limitations in functionality and usability. By allowing credit-card holders to pay for their selected items it saves them from waiting at the checkout counter. It avoids possible breakdowns in the process of Figure 12.8 due to lost tickets or incorrectly entered numbers. It relies less on customers' keyboard skills. These improvements might be crucial to maintaining customer satisfaction.

12.6.1   Principles of function-key interfaces

A wide variety of interaction devices can be incorporated into function-key style user interfaces. The list includes not only function keys, but numeric keypads, credit-card readers, coin and bill slots, vehicle sensors, and magnetic or infrared ID badge detectors. Many of the domestic and personal devices that incorporate microprocessor-based controls – heating controls, digital watches, stereo and TV equipment, and so on – have function-key interfaces.

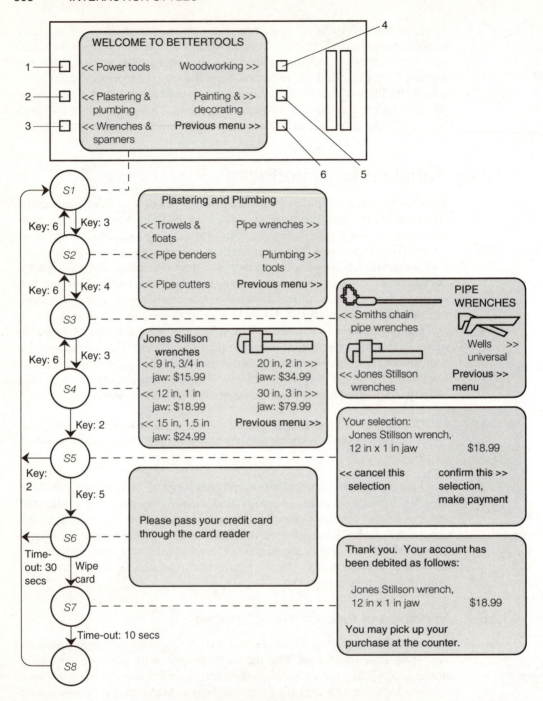

Figure 12.9   A function-key interface incorporating a credit-card reader. This state transition chart shows just one purchasing sequence.

There are some principles, however, that help us to design these interfaces in a systematic way. A basic principle is to manage the *activation* of input devices during the course of the interaction. As a rule the various buttons, keys, coin slots, and so on, cannot be operated in any order, even though they are all phyically accessible to the user. On the contrary, they must usually be operated in strict sequence: thus the Stillson wrench must be selected before the credit-card is wiped. Automated teller machines likewise enforce a strict sequence of operation, and so do ticket machines, door entry systems, VCR programmers and so on. The design of a function-key interface involves managing the activation of devices, a task that is often aided by laying out the state transitions in a systematic way, as in Figure 12.9. It also involves making sure that the user is guided successfully from one active device to the next by means of prompts and messages.

12.7 Voice-based interaction

A voice-based solution enables us to take a completely different approach to hardware sales: ordering by phone. The customer telephones the hardware sales service, and is presented with a sequence of pre-recorded messages that guide him through the stages of the purchase, including identification of products and entry of credit-card information or account numbers. Thus voice-based interaction enables us to address the situation of concern by solving a quite different problem from before:

> Design a phone-based system allowing customers with no prior experience to make credit-card purchases.

Figure 12.10 shows a simple solution employing voice-based interaction. We rely here on the customer having set up an account with the hardware company, thus avoiding the difficult problem of capturing the customer's name and address. We also require the customer to identify products from a printed catalogue.

We could nevertheless offer catalogue searching as an alternative, using a series of voice-based menus such as the following:

> For power tools press one, for plastering and plumbing press two, for wrenches and spanners press three, for woodworking press four, for painting and decorating press five, to hear this list again press zero, to hear the previous list press eight, to stop searching press nine.

USER PRESSES 2

> For trowels and floats press one, for pipe benders press two, for pipe cutters press three, for pipe wrenches press four, for plumbing tools ...

USER PRESSES 4

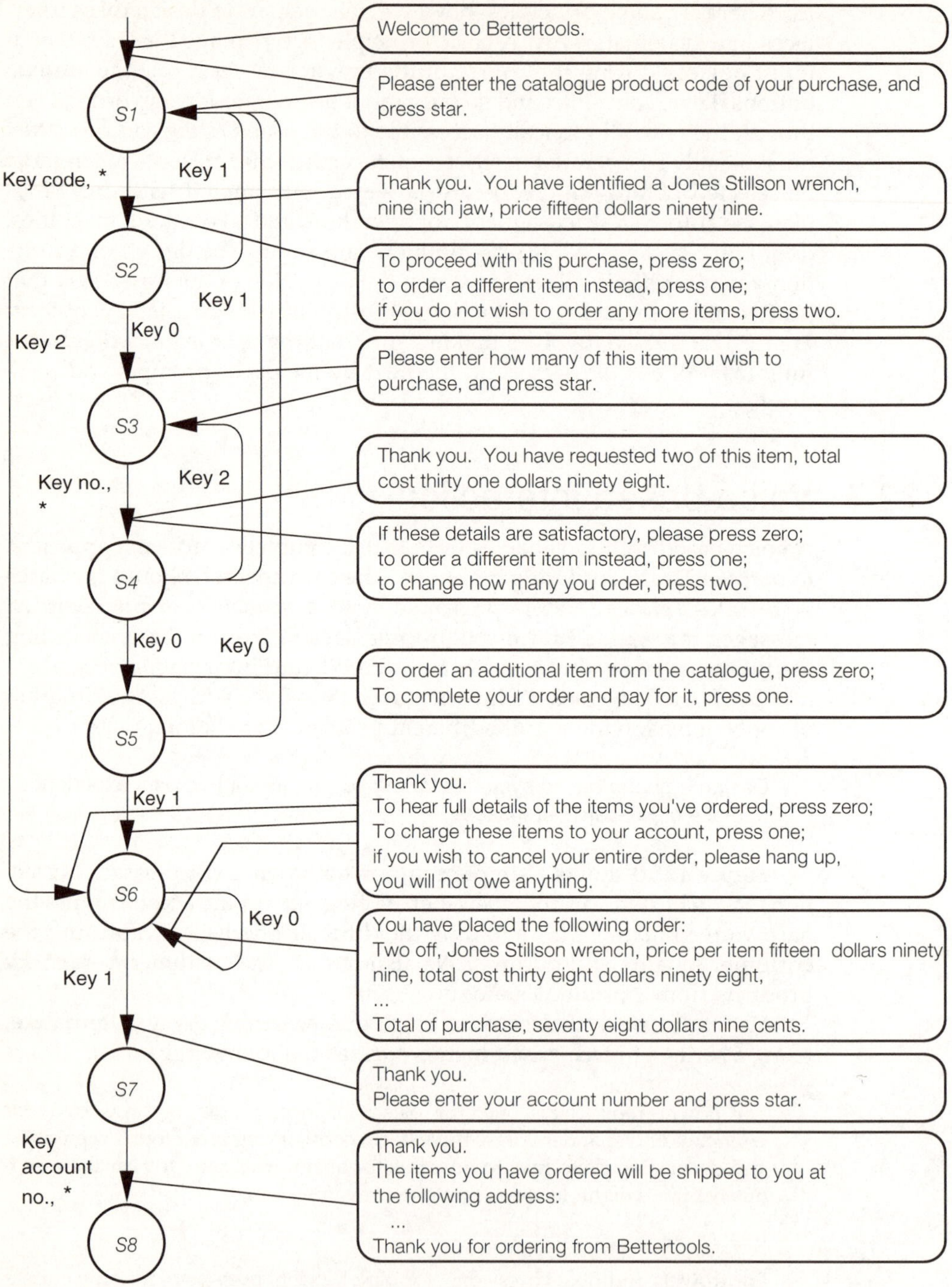

Figure 12.10   Voice-based interaction with an online catalogue.

For Smiths chain pipe wrenches press one, for Jones Stillson wrenches press two, for Wells universal pipe wrenches press three, to hear this list ...

USER PRESSES 2

For a nine-inch wrench, three-quarter-inch jaw, price 15.99, press one; for a twelve-inch wrench, one-inch jaw, price 18.99, press two; for a fifteen-inch wrench, one-and-a half-inch jaw, ...

USER PRESSES 1

Thank you, you have selected a Jones nine-inch Stillson wrench, three-quarter-inch jaw, price 15.99. Please enter how many of this product you wish to purchase, and press star.

USER PRESSES 2 *

The great attraction of voice-based systems is their ability to exploit the existing telephone network, thus reaching many millions of homes and businesses without the need to install any new interactive equipment. The disadvantage is poor usability. Try reciting the voice messages in the above sequence: it will probably take you nearly a minute. The four equivalent displays of Figure 12.9 could be presented, one after the other, in just a few seconds. The voice-based solution makes greater demands on the user's memory: there is no visual representation of the products for the user to peruse.

12.8 Graphical direct manipulation

The styles we have explored thus far have offered various ways of achieving a compromise between functionality, usability and system cost. Some solutions can improve usability through the use of special-purpose function-key terminals, while others can reduce equipment costs by making use of standard terminals or by providing a voice-based interface. One further approach, graphical direct manipulation, is worth considering, because it offers a compromise between the relatively high cost of the function-key terminal and the poor usability of the phone-based interface. We might be tempted to adopt this approach in order to provide a more attractive user interface:

> Design an attractive in-store catalogue system allowing customers with no prior experience to search for products and to record details of the items they wish to purchase.

A graphical direct-manipulation solution is shown in Figure 12.11.

This interface could be operated either by pointing at a touch-sensitive screen or by using a separate pointing device such as a mouse. The design shown in Figure 12.12 has been seen in an earlier version in Chapter 8, and addresses some of the problems identified there by

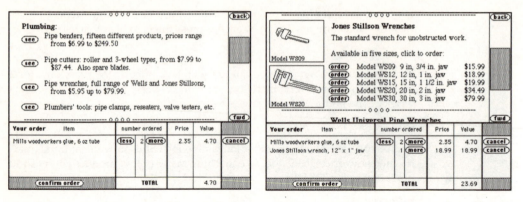

Figure 12.11   A graphical direct-manipulation style of user interface to the hardware catalogue.

heuristic evaluation. It uses fairly large targets that would probably allow the use of a touch screen. It includes a number of interactive objects: targets for selecting catalogue sections, a scroll box and scrolling controls, and several other targets for invoking specific commands. These are shown in Figure 12.12.

12.8.1   Properties of graphical direct-manipulation interfaces

A number of advantages are gained by providing access to the system's functionality via a set of directly manipulated graphic objects. The fundamental advantage is the directness of interaction: when the user wants to see a particular section of the catalogue she points to the title and the section is immediately displayed; when she wants to order an item she selects the **order** button beside the item's catalogue entry, and the item is immediately added to the list of ordered items. Thus not only is the goal easily translated into action, but the action produces an effect that confirms success in achieving the goal. This in turn helps the user to make fewer mistakes, identify more easily those mistakes that are made, and learn the interface more quickly via exploratory learning.

Graphical direct manipulation is well suited to applications that involve editing and problem solving. There aren't very many opportunities to exploit these advantages in the hardware-catalogue example; however, we can see how the **less** and **more** buttons allow simple editing of the number-of-items value, and the **cancel** button supports editing on an item-by-item basis. The system also allows the customer to set a goal of spending a certain amount (say $25) and to use the automatic totalling capability to experiment with different sets of items.

In terms of usability, therefore, graphical direct manipulation scores high for error-reduction and ease of exploratory learning. How well does it score for speed of operation in the hands of a skilled operator? As we have seen in our analyses of graphical interfaces, it is sometimes slower

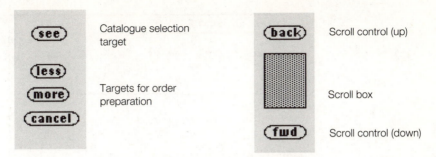

Figure 12.12   Interactive objects of the interface shown in Figure 12.11.

to perform tasks by pointing and clicking than by pressing one or more keys. For this reason, grapical direct-manipulation interfaces sometimes provide keyboard 'short cuts'. However, people browsing through a catalogue are unlikely to worry about an extra second or two in task performance time.

The one property of graphical direct manipulation that might argue against its use in this application is the magnitude of the learning task. Direct-manipulation interfaces cannot usually provide the same step-by-step assistance that key-modal interfaces provide, because they do not progress through an identifiable sequence of modes. The user finds his way by exploring rather than by following instructions. If he gets lost somewhere in a complex task sequence, the system may not be able to help him find his way out. For these reasons, graphical direct-manipulation interfaces are more commonly used for work support than for walk-up use by the public.

12.9 Forms fill-in

Some interaction styles are particularly well suited to the support of work activities: they enable skilled users to achieve rapid task performance and to tackle a variety of complex tasks and processes. The key-modal styles we have looked at earlier cannot support work so well, except in the case of very simple tasks such as key-punching data. The next two styles are specifically oriented towards work support. The first, forms fill-in, is another example of a direct-manipulation interface.

In our hardware sales example we might adopt a forms fill-in interface to support order entry by sales staff, rather than by customers. In other words, we might address the situation of concern by tackling the following design problem:

Design a system to support rapid entry of customer purchases by sales counter staff.

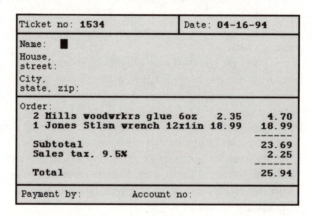

```
┌─────────────────────────────┬──────────────────────────┐
│ Ticket no: 1534█            │ Date: 04-16-94           │
├─────────────────────────────┴──────────────────────────┤
│ Name:                                                   │
│ House,                                                  │
│ street:                                                 │
│ City,                                                   │
│ state, zip:                                             │
├─────────────────────────────────────────────────────────┤
│ Order:                                                  │
│                                                         │
│                                                         │
│                                                         │
│                                                         │
├─────────────────────────────────────────────────────────┤
│ Payment by:          Account no:                        │
└─────────────────────────────────────────────────────────┘
```

(a)

```
┌─────────────────────────────┬──────────────────────────┐
│ Ticket no: 1534             │ Date: 04-16-94           │
├─────────────────────────────┴──────────────────────────┤
│ Name:   █                                               │
│ House,                                                  │
│ street:                                                 │
│ City,                                                   │
│ state, zip:                                             │
├─────────────────────────────────────────────────────────┤
│ Order:                                                  │
│   2 Mills woodwrkrs glue 6oz     2.35      4.70         │
│   1 Jones Stlsn wrench 12x1in 18.99       18.99         │
│                                           ──────        │
│   Subtotal                                23.69         │
│   Sales tax, 9.5%                          2.25         │
│                                           ──────        │
│   Total                                   25.94         │
├─────────────────────────────────────────────────────────┤
│ Payment by:          Account no:                        │
└─────────────────────────────────────────────────────────┘
```

(b)

```
┌─────────────────────────────┬──────────────────────────┐
│ Ticket no: 1534             │ Date: 04-16-94           │
├─────────────────────────────┴──────────────────────────┤
│ Name:    Jane Smith                                     │
│ House,                                                  │
│ street: █                                               │
│ City,                                                   │
│ state, zip:                                             │
├─────────────────────────────────────────────────────────┤
│ Order:                                                  │
│   2 Mills woodwrkrs glue 6oz     2.35      4.70         │
│   1 Jones Stlsn wrench 12x1in 18.99       18.99         │
│                                           ──────        │
│   Subtotal                                23.69         │
│   Sales tax, 9.5%                          2.25         │
│                                           ──────        │
│   Total                                   25.94         │
├─────────────────────────────────────────────────────────┤
│ Payment by:          Account no:                        │
└─────────────────────────────────────────────────────────┘
```

(c)

Figure 12.13   Entering details of a hardware purchase using a forms fill-in style of interface: (a) entering the ticket number; (b) the TAB key confirms the ticket number and automatically fills in the order details; (c) the customer's name and address are filled in.

Such a system would be appropriate for use in conjunction with the solutions of Figures 12.5 and 12.8, combining menu-based searching with question-and-answer entry of order details. The sales clerk could then complete the purchase with the aid of an interactive form. The interface is shown in Figure 12.13 as a sequence of screen layouts.

12.9.1 Properties of forms fill-in

As this example illustrates, forms fill-in provides a means of both entering and retrieving data, often in the course of performing one task. Here we see the entry of the customer's ticket number, leading to the retrieval of order details, followed by the entry of customer data. Forms fill-in also supports the editing of existing entries in fields. Its basic functional limitation lies in its restriction to textual data. More broadly, forms-based interaction tends to limit the range of supported tasks, because each task may require a pre-defined form.

As regards usability, the user of a forms fill-in system must have adequate typing skills and will usually need to be trained in the use of the various forms and templates. We would not normally choose forms fill-in as an interaction style for walk-up-and-use systems. However, some experiments have been conducted into the use of interactive forms to support online application for welfare benefits (Frohlich, 1988).

12.10   Command-line interaction

Many modern-day occupations involve performing a wide range of data-entry and retrieval tasks, some of them highly complex. These occupations – which include banking, airline reservation and check-in, record keeping, and so on – make heavy demands on supporting interactive systems. Most of the interaction styles we have discussed so far are unsuitable, for they cannot deliver the functionality and speed of operation that the user needs. Instead, the tendency is to provide a keyboard-based user interface in which the user types commands as lines of text, using a style known as *command-line interaction*.

The hardware sales application might justify a command-language approach if the decision were taken to have staff handle sales by telephone. We would address the situation of concern as follows:

> Design a system to support rapid catalogue search and customer order entry by telephone sales staff.

The user interface would then need to be designed to support both order entry and catalogue searches; a range of commands would be needed in order for staff to handle orders sufficiently rapidly.

For example, a **find** command could be used to identify a customer, using command-line 'switches' to label the various items of text to search for. The following command might be used to search for customers called 'Thwaites', using the switch '/n' to indicate a 'name' search:

```
find thwaites/n
```

The name on its own might be insufficient to identify the customer – it might return with a number of candidates:

```
find thwaites/n
1. Thwaites, Bertha F.  1215 Colorado Ave, Bu
2. Thwaites, Frank V.   21 Flamsteed Way, Cla
3. Thwaites, Mary P.    660 2nd Ave, Salt Lak
4. Thwaites, Vincent J. 4134 Main Street, Pal
```

The salesperson could narrow down the search by asking the customer for his or her address, but is more likely to request this at the outset to avoid wasting time: 'Could I have your name and address please?' A more complex form of the **find** command would then be used, including the first few letters of the street name indicated by the '/s' switch:

```
find thwaites/n flamst/s
```

This would identify the customer uniquely in this case, printing out the entry for 'Frank V. Thwaites'.

A similar command could be used to search the catalogue; the 12-inch Stillson wrench might be tracked down and displayed as follows:

```
cat still/d 12/s
106041 Stillson wrench   Jones   12 in.   $18.99
```

12.10.1 Properties of command-language interaction

In other words, a command-line style of user interface could support much of the salesperson's interaction with the system. Where might it give trouble? Probably the only part of the order-entry task where an alternative style might be preferable lies in the entry of a new customer's details; it isn't easy to enter a several-line address, for example, in a single command line. Here a forms fill-in interaction style is preferable.

In summary, command-line interaction can support a wide range of functional properties including both the entry and retrieval of data. Like most of the styles covered so far, it relies only on simple technology. In terms of usability, its major drawback is the amount of training involved: command languages usually involve a wide range of commands and formats, simply because this is how they derive their power. In return for this investment from the user, command-line interaction often offers the fastest way of entering and retrieving data.

12.11   Text-based natural language

A computer can be programmed to interpret simple sentences typed by the user in a natural language such as English. It can extract the meaning from the sentence and respond to it, either in the conventional manner of command-line interaction, or by composing a natural-language sentence itself. This is called *natural-language* interaction; it has been the focus of a great deal of research over the past few decades, and is sometimes appropriate for use in interactive applications.

Natural-language interaction may at first sight seem to offer the answer to many problems in user interface design. In particular, it appears to provide us with a way around the problem of training the user to understand the system's language: instead, we train the *system* to understand *our* language. In the case of the hardware-store example, natural language might suggest a means of reducing training costs, and lead us to define the design problem as follows:

> Design a system to support rapid catalogue search and customer order entry by telephone sales staff, with little need for prior training.

It is a mistake to view computer-based natural language as the user's language, however. What natural language really offers is a means of lowering the initial 'learning hurdle' of a command-line interface. It is easier to get started. But the language we ask the user to adopt isn't really English, or some other spoken language. It is a computer language that uses certain natural-language components, thus allowing commands of the form shown in Figure 12.14.

The use of a familiar syntax makes the user interface more approachable. There is nevertheless a lot for the user to learn in order to become an efficient user. Unless the user interface is designed very carefully, the learning 'hump' that follows the initial hurdle may be insurmountable. Problems that must be addressed fall into four categories, mentioned here briefly; for more thorough discussions, see Ogden (1988) or Shneiderman (1992).

The first problem is to overcome the user's unfamiliarity with the *structure of the information* accessible via the user interface. It is not easy for a hardware-store customer, for example, to guess what information is available within a system that offers the following initial display:

```
Please enter your first request
```

By way of contrast, the menu-based and function-key styles presented earlier each made the top-level structure quite clear at the outset.

The second problem is that the user cannot easily determine what *repertoire of functions* the system offers. This is a problem with command-line styles in general, and is one of the reasons why prior training is usually a necessity. An online hardware catalogue might offer functions

```
LIST DESCRIPTIONS AND PRICES OF PRODUCTS WITH MAKER = JONES
AND PRODUCT-TYPE = STILLSON-WRENCH

1.    Model no. WS09 9 in, 3/4 in. jaw        $15.99
2.    Model no. WS12, 12 in, 1 in. jaw        $18.99
3.    Model no. WS15, 15 in, 1 1/2 in. jaw    $19.99
4.    Model no. WS20, 20 in, 2 in. jaw        $34.49
5.    Model no. WS30, 30 in, 3 in. jaw        $79.99
```

Figure 12.14   Natural-language interaction with an online hardware catalogue. The user's input is shown in upper-case.

for listing the products of a particular description, for providing details about one particular product, for asking about special offers, for placing orders for products, and so forth:

```
LIST PRODUCTS WITH PRODUCT-TYPE = WRENCH
PRINT DESCRIPTION OF PRODUCT WITH ITEM-NUMBER = 2
LIST PRODUCTS WITH PRODUCT-STATUS = SPECIAL-OFFER
ORDER PRODUCT WITH ITEM-NUMBER = 2
```

However, the user doesn't know at the outset which of these functions are available, and probably doesn't even know how to find out.

A third problem for the user is to learn the *syntax* that the system expects. Many natural-language systems allow a more informal syntax than the one shown above; for example, the command shown in Figure 12.14 might be restated as the following question:

```
WHAT STILLSON WRENCHES ARE MADE BY JONES?
```

There will always be syntactic forms that the system cannot understand, for example, 'DO YOU HAVE ANY JONES STILLSON WRENCHES?' One of the techniques used in natural-language systems is to restate the user's question in the form preferred by the system:

```
User:     WHAT STILLSON WRENCHES ARE MADE BY JONES?
System:   LIST DESCRIPTIONS AND PRICES OF PRODUCTS WITH MAKER
          = JONES AND PRODUCT-TYPE = STILLSON-WRENCH
          1.    Model no. WS09 9 in, 3/4 in. jaw  $15.99
          ...
```

This helps the user to learn to use the system's language more effectively.

A final problem lies with the system's limited vocabulary. A question such as 'DO YOU HAVE ANY CHEAPER MODELS?' may confuse the system – it may start looking for models made by Cheaper Inc. Like all of the other problems mentioned, this one is eventually solved as the user gains experience with the system, but it can cause a lot of problems for first-time users.

It still isn't clear whether natural-language interaction technology can overcome all of these problems, and compete successfully with other styles in terms of usability. The idea for text-based natural language dates back to a period when text terminals were the only form of interactive device widely available. At that time, it seemed to offer the only means of making interactive computing acceptable to professional and managerial users. Now, as Shneiderman points out, there is a much wider choice of styles available; in particular, there is the alternative of graphical direct manipulation, which has established a very strong following among professional users.

12.12   Choice of interaction style

The choice of an interaction style is one of the most important decisions the designer makes about the user interface. The chosen style provides an architecture that supports the functionality of the user interface; it provides the means of fitting all the functions together into a usable design. If the choice of style is a poor one, fitting things together will become more difficult, maybe impossible. This final section looks at some of the issues we face in choosing an appropriate style of interaction.

12.12.1   Narrowing down the choice

Although the range of styles available to the designer is quite large, the eventual choice often narrows down to one or two, and indeed there may be no freedom of choice at all in the matter. The reason for this lies in the need to address requirements for functionality and usability, and at the same time achieve cost targets for hardware and software. The result is often a heavily constrained design problem, in which most of the available interaction styles can be ruled out immediately.

In the example of the hardware sales system we have seen instances of how requirements place constraints on the choice of style. We saw, for example, that the requirement for an easily learned, walk-up-and-use interface pointed towards the adoption of a key-modal style. We saw that the introduction of a further requirement to combine catalogue-browsing and order-entry functions narrowed the choice to two possible solutions: a function-key design and a combination of menus and question-and-answer. Of these two, only the function-key design could support unassisted purchase by the customer. The only reason for choosing menus and question-and-answer would have been to reduce hardware and software costs.

This process of elimination can often be carried out during problem definition or in the early stages of requirements definition. We start by identifying the range of activities that the system is to support. If these include editing activities, the choice of style will already be focusing on graphical direct manipulation. If there is no editing requirement, but rather an emphasis on data entry, the choice will probably lie between forms fill-in and command-line interaction. By the time we have identified the system's broad functionality, we will probably be in a position to eliminate several of the remaining candidates; for example, we may rule out forms fill-in if there are a number of non-data-entry functions. If there are still several candidates at this stage in the requirements process, they will be narrowed down still further when we consider the levels of usability we must attain, and the limits on cost of equipment.

12.12.2   Style-specific design knowledge

This approach to selecting a style does not guarantee that requirements for functionality, usability and cost will be met; it simply sets the stage for designing a user interface that meets them. A great deal of detailed design work goes into achieving a satisfactory interface. The course taken in this work will be affected by the initial choice of style. In particular, it will depend on the availability of *style-specific design knowledge*.

Much of what we know about user interface design is specific to one style or another. Many of the available solution strategies are still evolving, and our understanding of them is built upon the experiences that we and other people have had with them. Some of these experiences are extremely solution-specific; we saw an instance in Chapter 10, in the experiments with different interaction styles for aircraft pilots. However, a lot of what we know relates more broadly to a collection of solutions, and often it applies to solutions that follow a particular style. This is what we mean when we say that knowledge is style-specific.

Style-specific design knowledge is often shared amongst designers in the form of *guidelines*. Thus we can find guidelines for designing menu-based systems, guidelines for forms fill-in, and so forth. An example, taken from Shneiderman's text on user interface design, is shown in Figure 12.15. These are akin to the design heuristics used in heuristic evaluation, and one way to evaluate a design is in fact to apply a heuristic approach, focusing on style-specific guidelines. Chapter 15 will explore the use of these and other kinds of guidelines in user interface design.

12.12.3   Combining styles and maintaining consistency

Under certain circumstances we can combine together two or more styles in a single user interface. This means we can sometimes consider a wider range of styles, and deal with problems that no single style can solve. However, it also complicates the selection process.

Generally speaking, we combine styles to overcome hard limits on functionality or usability. Thus we needed to combine menu-based and

Menu selection guidelines

- Use task semantics to organize menus (single, linear sequence, tree structure, acyclic and cyclic networks)
- Prefer broad and shallow to narrow and deep
- Show position by graphics, numbers or titles
- Use item names as titles for trees
- Use meaningful groupings for items
- Use meaningful sequencing of items
- Make items brief, begin with keyword
- Use consistent grammar, layout, terminology
- Allow typeahead, jumpahead, or other shortcuts
- Allow jumps to previous and main menus
- Consider online help, novel selection mechanisms, response time, display rate, and screen size.

Figure 12.15   Guidelines for designing menu-based user interfaces, from Shneiderman (1992).

question-and-answer styles in the hardware sales example, because neither style could support both catalogue searching and order entry on its own. We might need to combine graphical direct manipulation and function-key styles in order to overcome the performance limits of direct manipulation: this is what 'keyboard short cuts' achieve.

We cannot mix interaction styles with complete freedom, however. The reasons for this relate to the user's need for consistency, and especially for consistency in the *structures* that the system presents and the *sequences* by which tasks are performed. Structures can change their appearance or behaviour according to the interaction style: a hardware item that appears as a line of text in a menu can appear as a picture in a graphical direct-manipulation interface, and even as a three-dimensional working simulation in a virtual-reality environment. The user must learn how to deal with information according to the style of presentation.

A change of style can also affect task-performance sequences. The sequence for changing a piece of text to boldface is different if performed with key combinations than if performed graphically, as we saw in Chapter 8. The user's selection of a sequence of operations is made more complex by the availability of a choice of methods. These issues relate to the user's *mental model* of the system, and are discussed in the next two chapters.

Exercises

(1)   Summarize the pros and cons of the eight styles described in this chapter.

(2)   Make a list of the interactive tools and systems you have used recently, or that you have seen others use, and identify the interaction style of each one.

(3)   List the three basic properties of direct-manipulation styles.

(4)   Security systems usually have time-outs to avoid, for example, leaving the door unlocked indefinitely. Extend Figure 12.1 to show the time-outs you consider appropriate for this design.

(5)   Why are user interfaces that rely entirely on a small set of function keys likely to have several modes?

(6)   Apply heuristic evaluation to the voice-based design of Figure 12.10, and modify the design to overcome any problems identified.

(7)   Conduct a Cognitive Walkthrough analysis of the direct-manipulation interface of Figure 12.11.

(8)   Under what circumstances or for what reasons might the World Wide Web represent an appropriate strategy for addressing the hardware-store situation?

(9)   What style best describes the user interface of an answerphone, as used by the receiver, and as used by the caller? Discuss what other styles could be used.

(10)   Another situation of concern we might explore is a doctor's general practice that needs to provide a better service to patients. Think of different ways of addressing this situation, and explore the interaction styles that might suit each problem you define.

Further reading

Mayhew D. J. (1992). *Principles and Guidelines in Software User Interface Design*. Englewood Cliffs, NJ: Prentice Hall

A comprehensive survey of the major styles of user interface, discussing HCI research that has contributed to understanding of each style and presenting design guidelines.

Shneiderman B. (1992). *Designing the User Interface: Strategies for Effective Human–Computer Interaction*, 2nd edn. Reading, MA:Addison-Wesley

A book on user interface design that addresses both the practitioner's and the researcher's needs. All of the principal interaction styles are covered, and are copiously illustrated with examples.

Newman W. M. (1988). The representation of user interface style. In *People and Computers IV* (Jones D.M. and Winder R., eds.), pp. 123–43. Cambridge: Cambridge University Press

CHAPTER 13

Conceptual design:
The user's mental model

Chapter objectives:

It is crucial that the user should understand how to use an interactive system. Conceptual design is concerned with achieving this understanding, by helping the user build a mental model of the system. The nature of this mental model is the first topic in conceptual design, and we therefore cover in this chapter:

- What is meant by the user's mental model
- How the user relies on it in the course of system usage
- The various forms that mental models can take
- How the mental model supports the user's cycle of interaction.

13.1 Introduction

In this chapter we continue our exploration of user interface design methods. The issue at stake here, and in Chapter 14, is the user's understanding of the system – a vitally important issue since lack of understanding is a serious barrier to effective use. We will be looking at *conceptual design* techniques, aimed specifically at assisting users in understanding systems better.

The order in which we approach conceptual design involves first identifying the sources of users' misunderstandings about the systems they use. In this chapter, therefore, we highlight the key role of the user's *mental model* of the system. We see that users' mental models can take a number of very different forms; we also see how the successive stages in the user's cycle of interaction are potentially affected, in different ways, by the user's mental model. This discussion will set the stage for the next chapter's coverage of a set of methods for conceptual design.

13.2   Understanding software systems

Software systems are never easy for people to understand. Partly because software is so inaccessible, hidden away inside the memories of computers, and partly because it can be so complex, people constantly have difficulty in getting it to do what they want, and are constantly surprised by the results. We shall start, therefore, by looking at the nature of the misunderstandings of software users. As we shall see, many of them are better described as *misconceptions*, that is, as false or inaccurate concepts about the software's structure and functionality.

13.2.1   Programmers' misunderstandings

It is important to realize, right from the start, that misconceptions about software are not limited to non-programmers. The people who design and build programs often have their own difficulties in understanding the other software modules on which their program depends. As a result, they cannot always make their own programs work as they should.

For example, the designers of an emergency dispatch system tried to make it run faster by using a 'screen pre-load' feature to store all of the frequently used screen displays on the system's disk; in this way the images wouldn't have to be generated afresh each time they were needed. The effect was to make the system run slower, however. It turned out that the images occupied so much disk space that the system kept running out of space for process swapping (London Ambulance Service, 1993). The system's designers were labouring under a misconception, namely that 'screen pre-loads always improve speed of response'. A more accurate statement would be that pre-loads can improve response, and so can efficient swapping, but both of them contend for the same disk-memory resource.

Before we look at users' misconceptions, therefore, we need to accept that designers themselves have only an incomplete understanding of how the system works. They too have a model of the system, in this case a model of the hardware and software which we call the **system model** – a concept introduced in Chapter 6. The system model may bear some similarity to the user's mental model, since both are views of the same system. But there are always differences, and we need to be fully aware of them.

13.2.2   Users' problems with conceptual mismatch

When non-programmers are confronted by software they face a different set of problems from the programmer's. We should remember that these people do not, as a rule, perform activities purely for the sake of interacting with a computer. Instead they are concerned with goals such as dispatching ambulances to scenes of accidents, cashing cheques, telephoning friends or borrowing books from a library. The concepts involved in these activities are not necessarily easy to translate into the terms demanded by the software system.

Users therefore encounter difficulties of many kinds. Routine use of office software, for example, may involve problems such as these:

- The sizes of documents are measured in bytes, not pages or words.

- Finding a document involves remembering a file name such as *jhb-8-29-94.txt*, not a location in a file-cabinet drawer.

- Entering simple data, such as a date, may involve translation into an obscure format, for example, 29th August 1994 may become 940829.

- Recognizing a person's name may mean allowing for missing letters, for example, the name 'E. Pedersen' may become EPEDERSE.

- Interpreting error messages may involve dealing with codes such as 'C5' and knowing that this means that the printer is out of paper.

In every one of these cases, the user is being confronted with concepts drawn from the designer's system model. In each case there has been a failure to match the concepts of the user interface to the concepts of the user's activity. First and foremost, the role of conceptual design is to overcome these kinds of mismatch.

13.2.3   The problem of learning on the job

Another vital role for conceptual design lies in reducing the user's problems in learning to use the system. If the user interface can be made more obvious and self-explanatory, the user will be less reliant on formal training, and more capable of dealing with unfamiliar tasks when they arise.

This is an important design issue, because the trend these days is always towards reducing training. There is a consequent danger that users will never learn to use systems properly, and will instead learn slow or unreliable ways of performing tasks. They may never learn more than a fraction of the system's functionality, as was shown in a study by Rosson; she found that average users of a word processor made use of only one-sixth of the available functions (Rosson, 1983). Another study, by Kraut *et al.* (1983), showed that even expert users of UNIX make use of only a small fraction of the command repertoire.

Conceptual design methods can come to the rescue by making systems easier to learn by exploration. If users can gain an adequate understanding of the system just from using it, their reliance on training becomes much less. We therefore try increasingly to support exploratory learning by users. We employ design strategies that make the system's functionality and behaviour more obvious, and we test our designs with methods such as the Cognitive Walkthroughs of Chapter 8.

13.3 The user's mental model

Conceptual design is concerned with helping people to accumulate knowledge about the systems they use. As they gain experience of a particular system, they acquire knowledge about the system's behaviour, and on this basis they are able to develop theories about its inner workings (Olson, 1992). They gradually form a working 'model' of the system around which they organize their knowledge and theories. This is their *mental model* of the system.

Mental models can in fact be formed through many kinds of user experience – through use of the system, through observation of other users at work, through training, through reading documentation. Some of the common processes by which mental models arise are shown in Figure 13.1.

We deliberately use some of the same symbols here as earlier in the book, for some of the components are the same as before. Note, however, that these are processes performed by the *user*, not by a designer. To avoid confusing the two, different arrow symbols are used. Where systems or activities occur as models they are shown in fainter or broken lines.

13.3.1 Runnable mental models

In Chapter 3 we encountered the distinction between static and dynamic models. Dynamic models have the property that they can be 'run' over a sequence of actions; either over observed actions in order to explain them or, as shown in Figure 13.2, over possible future actions in order to predict what may happen.

When we study people's mental models we see evidence of both kinds of model. We find cases where users have static models of how information is stored in the system (Figure 13.3(a)). We also observe users with dynamic models of 'what will happen if I do this', runnable models that help the user to look ahead in the dialogue (Figure 13.3(b)).

A runnable mental model is a model of **causality**, that is, of relations between cause and effect (Moray, 1992). It is a model of the causal links by which actions on one object cause actions on others. The simple model of Figure 13.3(b) reminds the user of the causal link between deleting a folder and deleting all of its contents. A more complex causal model is learned by users of the UNIX mv command for renaming files, described earlier in

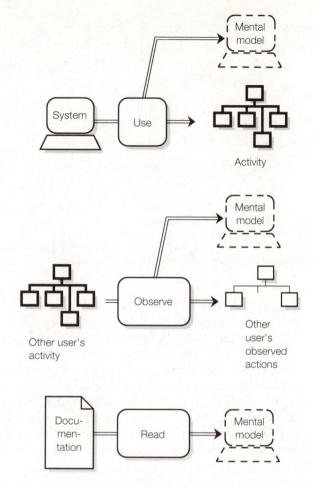

Figure 13.1   Some of the processes by which users form mental models: by use, by observation of other users, from documentation. Thinner or broken lines are used here to denote models of real activities or systems, rather than the activities or systems themselves.

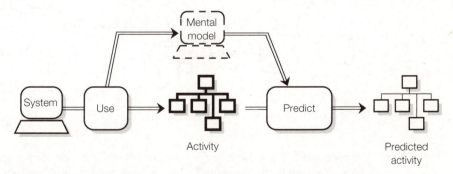

Figure 13.2   How the user may rely on a mental model to make predictions about the outcome of using the system.

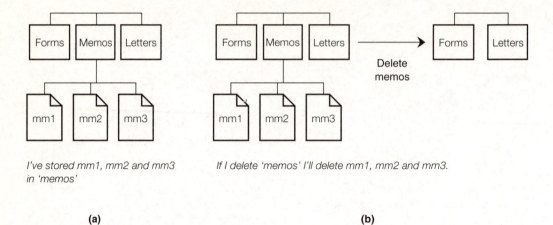

I've stored mm1, mm2 and mm3 in 'memos'

If I delete 'memos' I'll delete mm1, mm2 and mm3.

(a)   **(b)**

Figure 13.3   (a) A static mental model of how information is stored; (b) a dynamic, 'runnable' mental model of what will happen if a folder is deleted.

Figure 12.3; they learn that the command mv abc xyz not only renames the file *abc* to be called *xyz*, but also deletes any existing file *xyz*.

There are parallels between the runnable mental models on which users rely and the dynamic models we use in design, such as the Keystroke-Level Model or the model of exploratory learning. For example, when users are faced with two alternative methods for performing a task, they may try to predict which method will be faster (Figure 13.4), in a manner that resembles a designer using keystroke-level analysis to choose between two user interfaces (Young and MacLean, 1988). However, we should avoid making the assumption that users and designers have the

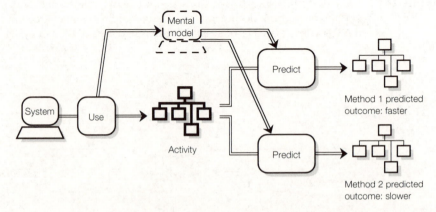

Figure 13.4   The user makes predictions of the outcome of two methods of operation, in order to decide which method to adopt. On this basis, method 1 is chosen as likely to be faster.

same dynamic models of systems. Indeed for the most part we cannot be sure what mental models our users have, because we cannot look inside their heads. This makes conceptual design a challenging task.

13.3.2   Running a mental model: A simple example

The notion of a 'runnable' mental model has been raised, and we will explore it further with the aid of an example.

When we make a telephone call we have a mental model of the stages that the call will go through between first picking up the phone and finally

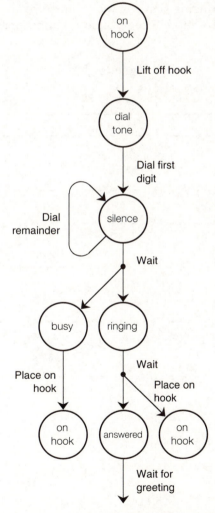

Figure 13.5   A user's mental model of the stages in placing a phone call, and the actions to be performed.

hearing an answering voice. As we mentally run this model, it predicts that there will be a short silence after we finish dialling and before the call is connected, and then usually a ringing signal, which will break off when someone answers the call or when we hang up (Figure 13.5).

Suppose we make a call to a foreign country for the first time. We will probably hear some unexpected sounds, and we can try to explain these by running the model. Thus we can account fairly easily for a longer silence than usual after dialling, for our model tells us that the call is being connected, and this country is located at an unusually distant part of the phone network. If the silence is then broken by an unfamiliar signal such as a sequence of very rapid 'pips', our model cannot immediately provide a clear-cut explanation, but may offer suggestions – the line is busy or this is the ringing signal in the country we are calling. If the pips shortly give way to a more recognizable ringing signal, our model is back in action,

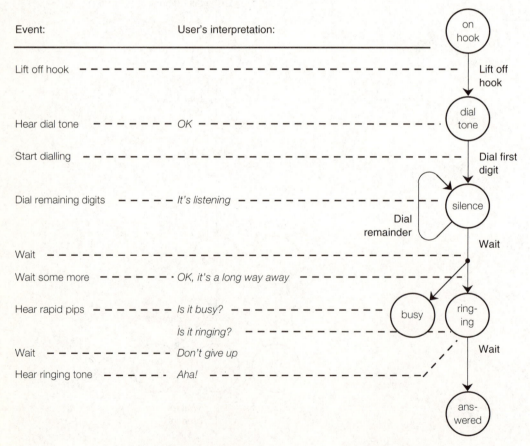

Figure 13.6   How the user's mental model serves in support of an unfamiliar task – placing a call to a foreign country.

'locking on' to this familiar sound and telling us that someone should answer soon (Figure 13.6).

This example illustrates an important point: when we design a system, we must try to help the user form a runnable mental model that will assist him or her in using the system. Thus if we were to set up a new telephone network in a foreign country, we might adopt one of the following two strategies:

(1) We might try to adopt a switching system that worked in accordance with people's mental models of the existing phone system. Of course this might be difficult to achieve if (due to the existing system's peculiarities) local subscribers had acquired highly unusual mental models.

(2) We might try to find a solution capable of steering local users towards a more 'international' model.

Almost certainly we would try to avoid a system that conflicted with all existing conventions, both local and international. Whatever our final decision, just by considering these alternatives we would be engaging in an exercise in conceptual design.

13.3.3   How the system image helps form mental models

We saw earlier how the user forms a mental model from using the system and observing its behaviour or, in some cases, observing its use by someone else. Thus their mental model is not based on knowledge of the internal structure of the system, but on observation of its external behaviour. It is based on the generated image of the system, visible or audible, which Don Norman has called the **system image** (Norman, 1986). To a large extent the system image is presented via the user interface.

The system image helps the user to understand the state of the system. Sometimes this assistance is largely unplanned by the designer; for example, dishwashers gratuitously emit various clicks and swishing noises that inform us about the progress of the wash cycle. But in complex interactive systems it is normal design practice to take advantage of the visual and auditory channels to help the user understand what the system is doing. In this sense the system image is an important factor in conceptual design, a point to which we will return in Section 14.4.

13.4   The form of the mental model

Any mental model that can be 'run' will have some form or structure, linking together the various items of knowledge and causal relationships learned by the user. Among users of the same system, the form of the model probably won't be the same, because people's mental models are influenced by their personal experiences with the system. However, we can often see

Electricity Was Leaking All Over The House

Figure 13.7   James Thurber's grandmother adhered to the 'flowing waters' model of electricity to an extreme degree. From Thurber (1961). Copyright © 1933, 1961 James Thurber. From *My Life and Hard Times*, published by HarperCollins.

recurring forms of model; for example, Gentner and Gentner studied people's models of electricity and found two dominant models, analogous to 'flowing waters' or 'teeming crowds' (Gentner and Gentner, 1983). The humorist James Thurber wrote about his grandmother's mental models of technology; her model of electricity 'leaking out of empty sockets' can be viewed as a rather bizarre form of the 'flowing waters' model (Figure 13.7).

Some systems tend to suggest one particular form of model more than any other. Thus an electronic piano will suggest, just through its appearance, a mental model of a conventional keyboard musical instrument. This mental model will be reinforced by the experience of playing it. Any other model that might have been suggested at the outset, perhaps of a sideboard in the shape of a piano, will quickly be dispelled.

During system design it helps to know that a particular form of model is likely to arise. We can design the user interface around this model, reinforcing it in ways that we think will help the user. We can make various assumptions about the concepts that the user is likely to transfer from previous experience; for example, we can assume that a set of buttons, laid out in three rows and labelled Q, W, E, R, T, Y, and so on, will be treated as keys for text entry. The existence of a single dominant mental model makes conceptual design easier.

13.4.1   Recurring forms of mental model

What are the forms of mental model that arise most frequently with users of interactive systems? In this section we will look briefly at four common forms of model:

- State transition models
- Object-action models
- Mapping models
- Analogies.

We will see that some of these are associated with user interfaces of a particular style; for example, a direct-manipulation interface is very likely to suggest an object-action model. A more comprehensive discussion of forms of mental model can be found in Young (1983).

13.4.2   State transition models

In some cases, systems tend to encourage users to form mental models around observed changes in the system's overall state. We have already encountered an example of such a system in the telephone switching network: the basic transitions that the user expects during a successful phone call were shown in Figure 13.5.

A state transition model is likely to arise if the system is seen to switch between different modes of behaviour, e.g., if it changes its overall appearance or if it responds differently to the user's actions (Williams *et al.*, 1983). The phone network's state transitions are designed to be audible to the person placing the call, but they can equally well be displayed visually, and indeed many fax machines do this. Many users of telephones are aware not only that the network changes state during a call, but also that it alters its response to user actions as it changes state. For example, the network doesn't usually react at all to keystroke actions while the phone is in its cradle, nor while the number is ringing.

13.4.3   Object-action models

Users' mental models of interactive systems almost invariably include concepts about **objects** accessible via the user interface (Williams *et al.*, 1983). They are aware of the existence of these objects, of their respective states and attributes, and of causal relationships between them. They are also often aware of **actions** they can perform on these objects; hence they acquire an **object-action** mental model.

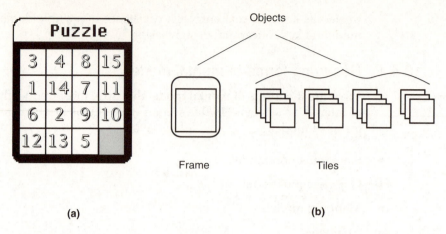

(a)   **(b)**

Figure 13.8   A 'squares' puzzle, (a) as it appears on the screen, (b) as represented as a set of conceptual objects in the user's mental model.

The user of a 'squares' puzzle game, for example, is aware of the existence of 15 numbered tile-like objects and a frame within which these can be slid around (Figure 13.8(a)). Thus the user depends on a model in which two different kinds of object are represented: a frame, and a set of tiles (Figure 13.8(b)).

When systems offer the user an object-based mental model, they usually offer a set of actions applicable to specific objects. The squares puzzle offers only a single *slide* action applicable to tiles. A richer example is found in graphical desktops, which present a number of different objects, including icons representing documents, folders and applications (Figure 13.9(a)). Actions that users know they can generally apply to icons include moving, selecting, opening and deleting. The user's mental model of a set of icons might therefore take the form shown in Figure 13.9(b). It shows that icons can be in different states, for example, selected or unselected, opened or closed; it also shows that each icon has a label, in effect a sub-object owned by the icon, which the user can change. The model is shown here as a *lattice* of concepts about objects, actions and attributes; lattices are discussed further in Section 13.5 below.

Object-action models provide a basis for organizing knowledge about the system's functionality. Thus the user of a graphics editor will be aware of the various displayed lines, boxes, circles, and text items in the drawing, and also of the actions that can be performed on each one, for example, deleting an object, moving it, duplicating it and rotating it. Some actions will be known to apply to certain objects but not to others; for example, boxes and circles can be filled with a selected pattern, while text items can be set to a different typeface, but not *vice versa*. When the system's functionality is explicitly organized according to object types, the user tends to operate it with the aid of an object-action model.

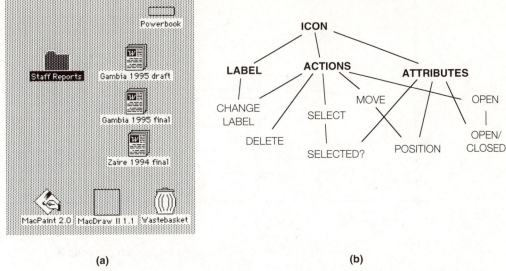

(a)   (b)

Figure 13.9   Macintosh desktop icons: (a) as they appear on the screen, and (b) a possible object-action mental model of an icon. Icon designs: courtesy Claris Corporation; Microsoft Inc.

13.4.4   Mapping models

Just as users always have some knowledge of the objects within the system, they also know how to 'map' their intentions into sequences of actions. An airline check-in clerk forms the intention of querying the system about passenger Mik Lamming, and maps this into the command line LLAMMING/M. On a four-function calculator, the intention of adding 2517 to 781 and subtracting 688 would be mapped into pressing the following keys:

$$2\ 5\ 1\ 7 + 7\ 8\ 1 - 6\ 8\ 8 =$$

Mapping models are especially likely to arise in systems that involve repetitive sequences of actions. Here, even if the system basically behaves according to a state transition or object-action model, the mapping model can 'take over'. In other words, the mapping model is the one that the user retrieves from memory and runs. An experienced user of a word processor, for example, will tend to learn mappings for the more common commands (for example, 'double-click, control-I to set a word to italic') and to rely on these rather than the basic object-action model.

In some cases the user must rely primarily on mappings because the system does not suggest any other form of mental model. This is the case with the four-function calculator. It does have a set of internal objects in the form of memory registers, and the push-buttons perform actions on these objects, but the internal model is far too complex to be understood

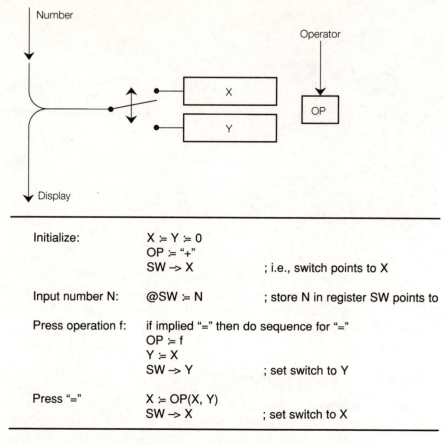

Initialize:	X ≔ Y ≔ 0	
	OP ≔ "+"	
	SW –> X	; i.e., switch points to X
Input number N:	@SW ≔ N	; store N in register SW points to
Press operation f:	if implied "=" then do sequence for "="	
	OP ≔ f	
	Y ≔ X	
	SW –> Y	; set switch to Y
Press "="	X ≔ OP(X, Y)	
	SW –> X	; set switch to X

Figure 13.10   Register model for the four-function calculator. From Young (1983).

or run by the average user (Figure 13.10). Studies by Young have suggested that the user instead learns a number of 'core mappings' for simple tasks such as the one above, and extends or repeats these mappings to perform more complex calculations (Young, 1983).

13.4.5   Analogical models

An analogical model is likely to arise when the user encounters a new system that closely resembles a system they are familiar with. What we see then is the user's adoption of a model for the new system that is similar or identical to the model held for the old one. The adopted model may be of any form, including the forms we have already discussed, that is, state transition, object-action or mapping. Gentner and Gentner have discussed the nature of analogical models at some length in their study of people's models of electricity (Gentner and Gentner, 1983).

Figure 13.11   A flight simulator of the type on which airline pilots gain much of their training; it depends on achieving an exact analogy. Courtesy Thomson Training and Simulation.

Interactive systems often draw analogies from the real world; a well-known example is the 'desktop' user interface with its objects analogous to paper documents, folders, files, wastebaskets, and so on. However, these analogies serve mainly to introduce the user to the concepts of the user interface; they are offered as *metaphors* rather than as strict analogies. Much more exact analogies are found in simulation programs, especially those that attempt to simulate systems in real time. Flight simulators, for example, are designed to be exactly analogous with cockpits of real aircraft, to the extent of providing realistic background noise and a 'cockpit' that tilts and vibrates just as a real aircraft would in flight (Figure 13.11).

13.5 Mental models of complex systems

Users may be able to form state transition or object-action models of simple systems, but how do they deal with highly complex, constantly changing systems such as nuclear power stations or spacecraft? How do their models change over time? And how do we apply our knowledge about mental models to system design?

13.5.1 Lattices of causal relationships

We will start with the question of how users deal with complex systems. Studies by Moray suggest that their mental models rely on the same kinds of causal links as in, say, a mental model of the telephone network.

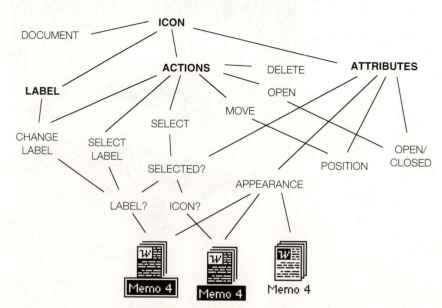

Figure 13.12   A comprehensive mental model of Macintosh icons. Icons here and in Figure 13.13 courtesy of Microsoft Inc.

However, there are many levels of understanding, each forming a *lattice* of relationships, different parts of which are called into use depending on the task (Moray, 1992).

The object-action model of Figure 13.9(b) is a simple example of a lattice. It shows only the causal relationships that might exist between objects and actions, however. A more complete lattice model might be as shown in Figure 13.12. In comparison with Figure 13.9(b), it shows some of the causal relationships that the user might form between, say, the CHANGE LABEL action and the LABEL-SELECTED attribute – if the label is not selected, the icon is not ready for it to be changed. The expert user relies on this kind of understanding to operate the user interface efficiently.

The beginner's lattice will be less complete, as shown in Figure 13.13. Actions may be missing, such as DELETE and CHANGE LABEL in this example. There may be erroneous connections in the lattice; here the user believes that icons have only one 'selected' state and just one appearance when selected. This mental model will hamper the user, who won't know how to delete icons, nor how to change their labels.

How do flaws in the conceptual lattice affect people's ability to operate more complex systems? Moray quotes an example of a pasteurization plant which is operated with the aid of the status display shown in Figure 13.14(a), and with means of controlling feedstock pump rates, steam pump rates and heater settings. As they become more experienced, operators build up an increasingly powerful set of lattices of causal

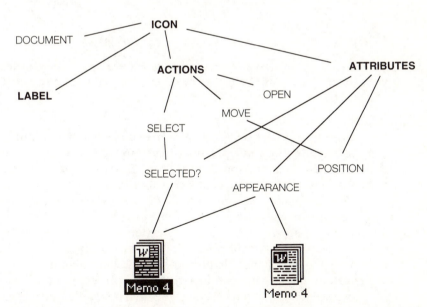

Figure 13.13   An incomplete mental model, belonging to a user who has not learned about the DELETE action or about the separate ways of selecting the icon and its label.

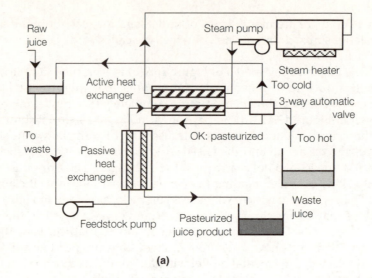

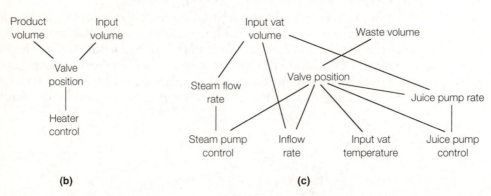

Figure 13.14   (a) An orange-juice pasteurizing plant, and two causal-lattice mental models of it formed by operators: (b) of a novice operator, and (c) of an expert. From Moray (1992).

relationships. A novice operator may believe only that product volume is affected by the valve position, which in turn is affected by input volume and heater control position (Figure 13.14(b)). An experienced operator may know about a great many causal links, as shown in Figure 13.14(c). These are not the only levels of understanding that operators may acquire: they also learn how supply rates affect displays, for example, and they develop models of state transitions and mappings (Moray, 1992).

Moray was able to explain differences in users' performance of tasks with the aid of these lattice models. He built a simulator of the pasteurization plant, and conducted tests with users of different levels of experience. Figure 13.15 shows how two operators tackled the same task of dealing with a fault in the juice pump. Each diagram shows how the operator's focus of attention shifted from one part of the plant to another, and

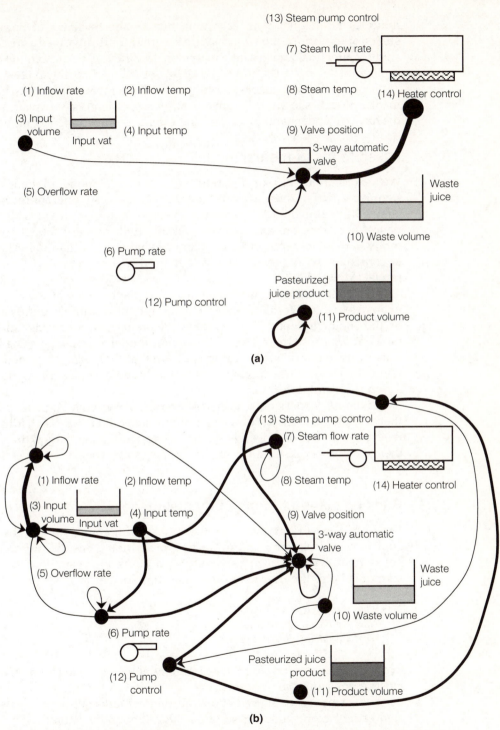

Figure 13.15   Sequences of focus of attention while dealing with a juice pump failure in the pasteurizing plant of Figure 13.14(a), by (a) a novice operator, (b) an expert operator. From Lee J. D. (1992).

indicates the frequency of each transition by the thickness of lines. The skilled operator's sequence (shown in Figure 13.15(b)) involved a number of shifts of attention but very little repetition, leading to quick resolution of the problem. The novice (Figure 13.15(a)) focused almost entirely on two areas of the plant, and was unable to rectify the fault after many attempts. The two mental models shown in Figures 13.14(b) and 13.14(c) help explain why – the novice's understanding of the plant extended only to a few components.

13.5.2   Mixed forms of mental model

We looked briefly at four different forms of mental model in the last section. We saw that there is evidence that each of these different forms can arise while users operate interactive systems. However, there is also evidence that users can maintain several different forms of model concurrently in order to represent the system's behaviour (Williams, 1983). This is consistent with Moray's view that users maintain several levels of model (Moray, 1992).

Someone placing a phone call, for example, is aware of the existence of an object in the form of a telephone at the called number, and is aware of the moment when this invisible telephone starts ringing and the moment when it stops. This object-action model supplements the basic state transition model. The caller is aware that by hanging up their own phone they can cause ringing to cease at the other end – this is another action they can perform indirectly.

Likewise, experienced users of interactive systems learn mappings that complement their knowledge about states and objects. Ultimately they may come to rely heavily on these mappings, and resort to the use of their deeper understanding of the system only when it behaves in an unusual way.

13.5.3   Running different forms of mental model

The form of mental model of course makes a difference to how the user applies it to explaining and to making predictions. But the difference is not as great as we might expect. For the purposes of explanation, the mental model helps the user to answer questions such as,

> What am I now seeing?
> What did the system just do?
> What did I do to make it do that?

In other words, by running the mental model the user can reconstruct the most recent sequence of events.

For the purposes of prediction, the mental model supports the user in answering a corresponding set of questions about the future:

What can I do next?
What if I do this?
What will the system do then?
What will I see as a result?

Here the user runs the mental model in order to anticipate the next sequence of events.

The common property of all of these examples is the underlying *cycle of interaction*, the same cycle that we first encountered in Chapter 3. In running the mental model over past events the user is stepping through recent stages in the interaction cycle, and in running the model predictively he or she is playing out the next few stages. Section 13.6 takes up this point and shows how the interaction cycle provides a basis for engaging in conceptual design.

13.6 The interaction cycle and the user's understanding

The *cycle of interaction*, with its seven stages of user action, was introduced in Chapter 3. It is shown again diagramatically in Figure 13.16.

Each of the seven stages depends on the user's level of understanding. The stages most strongly affected by the mental model are shown highlighted in Figure 13.16.

The stages draw on knowledge of different kinds. The 'execution stages' on the left are particularly dependent on the user's understanding of the system's *functions*. They depend on understanding what functions are available and how to put together a sequence of actions that will have the desired

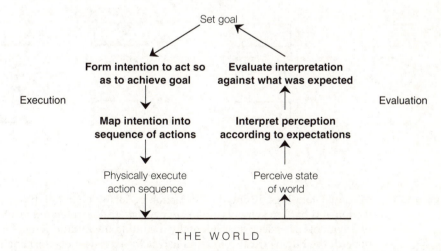

Figure 13.16   The user's interaction cycle. Based on Norman (1986).

effect. In contrast, the 'evaluation stages' on the right rely on the user's understanding of the system's *state*. Only by correctly recognizing the current state can the user tell whether the desired effect has been achieved.

Accordingly, if we want to avoid misconceptions, we must attend to these stages in the cycle. We must understand the way mental models support each stage, and help the user build adequate models of the system's function and state. We must understand how conceptual breakdowns can occur, and try to prevent them.

How conceptual breakdowns occur: An example

An example helps illustrate the kinds of breakdowns that can arise during the interaction cycle. It shows a number of ways in which faulty mental models can lead the user to take inappropriate action.

Figure 13.17(a) shows a simple line drawing prepared on a computer, consisting of three symbols. The user wishes to change the top and bottom symbols to point to the right instead of the left, as shown in Figure 13.17(b). She therefore selects the symbols, and the system responds by showing 'selection marks' as in Figure 13.17(c). So far, so good. However, when she applies the function to reverse the symbol, the result is quite unexpected: the selected symbols remain unaltered, and the middle symbol changes out of all recognition (Figure 13.17(d)). At this point the user gives up, and decides to redraw the entire figure.

Several misunderstandings, occurring at different points in the interaction cycle, have combined to cause this unwanted outcome:

(1)   *Failure to appreciate the system's state* (**Interpret perception** stage). The user had selected the symbols by drawing diagonally across them. She had

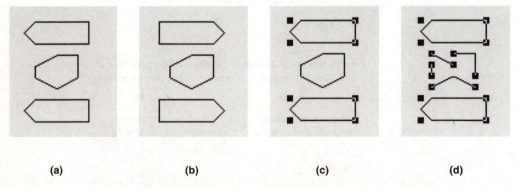

(a)   (b)   (c)   (d)

Figure 13.17   Misunderstandings during the interaction cycle: (a) the initial drawing, in which the top and bottom symbols are to be reversed; (b) the intended result; (c) the two symbols are selected, accidentally including the middle symbol in the selection; (d) the **Flip Vertical** command leaves the two symbols unchanged and the middle symbol in a mess.

therefore selected the six-sided symbol in the middle, but the selection marks on this symbol were invisible because the pairs of marks coinciding at each vertex cancelled each other out (see Figure 13.17(c)). The first mark was generated by turning all white pixels to black, and black to white; the second mark was created in the same way, returning all pixels to their original state.

(2) *Failure to select the appropriate action* (**Map intention** stage). The user applied the **Flip Vertical** command, thinking this meant 'flip about a vertical axis'. She should have used **Flip Horizontal** instead. Then, at least, the top and bottom symbols would have reversed direction.

(3) *Inadequate evaluation of the resulting state of the system* (**Evaluate interpretation** stage). The user could not relate the result of Figure 13.17(d) to the action she had just taken. The system appeared to have 'gone beserk'; in fact it had merely flipped each component of the drawing vertically about its midpoint.

(4) *Lack of intention to take recovery action* (**Form intention** stage). Due either to panic or lack of training, the user didn't take the opportunity to apply the **Undo** command to return the symbols to their previous state.

This example illustrates the user's shifting dependence on models of function and state during the execution and evaluation halves of the cycle. Failures 2 and 4 occur on the execution side, and are failures in taking action. Failures 1 and 3 occur on the evaluation side, because of misunderstanding the system's state.

13.6.1 In conclusion: How we tackle conceptual design problems

Problems of misunderstanding by users provide us with a basis for improving designs. When we see users repeating the same mistakes, we see evidence of inadequate mental models, and we can learn from these examples how to achieve better conceptual designs.

The next chapter discusses a number of conceptual design methods; but we can already see, in the preceding example, the basis on which analysis of conceptual designs can be performed. The cycle of interaction offers us a framework for conducting walkthroughs of tasks that may give users trouble. At each stage in the cycle we can look at the kinds of problems we have observed, and relate them to possible flaws in their mental models. Then we can modify the system's design so as to help users acquire the mental models they need.

In the case of Figure 13.17, for example, we can rectify one of the user's problems by making clear exactly which objects are selected. Selection marks should not cancel each other out completely; we need to devise a means of making overlapping marks visible. A second problem, confusion over the meaning of **Flip vertical**, can be rectified by a change of name, for example, to **Vertical-axis flip**.

We will explore this technique, and several others, in Chapter 14. In this continued discussion, we will build extensively on this chapter's presentation of different forms of mental model.

Exercises

(1)   Explain the terms *mental model, system model, system image*.

(2)   Describe three ways in which mental models may be formed by users.

(3)   Give three examples of users' models of causality of actions.

(4)   List four major kinds of mental model, and give an example of each.

(5)   Describe the form of mental model that a telephone caller might have concerning (a) the receiver's phone, and (b) the receiver's answerphone.

(6)   Describe the mappings used by car drivers when moving off from a stationary position, (a) using a stick shift, (b) using an automatic transmission.

(7)   Observe a checkout clerk, and try to establish what mappings he or she uses.

(8)   Draw a lattice describing a user's mental model of (a) a check box, (b) a scroll bar. Which parts of the lattice might users not include in their models?

(9)   Describe a possible user's model of the system in Figure 12.11.

(10)   Make a list of all of the mappings you know for a four-function calculator.

Further reading

Norman D. A. (1986). Cognitive engineering. In *User Centered System Design* (Norman D. A. and Draper S. W., eds.), pp. 31–65. Hillsdale NJ: Lawrence Erlbaum Associates

A valuable presentation by Norman of his Cycle of Interaction and of aspects of conceptual design and direct manipulation.

Norman, D.A. (1988). *The Psychology of Everyday Things*. New York: Basic Books

An entertaining book on mental models and conceptual design, with many examples.

Young R. M. (1983). Surrogates and mappings: Two kinds of conceptual models of interactive devices. In *Mental Models* (Gentner D. and Stevens A. L., eds.), pp. 35–52. Hillsdale NJ: Lawrence Erlbaum Associates

A useful summary of types of mental model, coupled with an analysis of mental models of several devices including calculators.

CHAPTER 14

Conceptual design: Methods

Chapter objectives:

We need methods to to help us identify the kind of mental model our users should acquire, and to design the user interface so that the user will indeed acquire this model. Several such methods are presented here, including:

- Defining the intended mental model
- Hiding the technology of the system
- Designing a suitable system image
- Analysing by Cognitive Walkthrough
- Applying appropriate design guidelines.

14.1 Introduction

In Chapter 13 we discussed mental models, the different forms they take and their support for interaction – material that provides a basis for methods of conceptual design. This chapter picks up the story, and presents a number of conceptual design techniques for improving users' chances of understanding how to operate systems, effectively and efficiently. In other words, it explains how to promote system usability through conceptual design.

The methods presented here, like those in this book as a whole, are a combination of synthesis and analysis. They help us to synthesize designs in terms of appropriate forms of mental model, and they provide ways of analysing designs in terms of their support for the stages in the interaction cycle. The methods include:

- Identifying the form of mental model we wish the user to acquire

- Hiding the system model

- Encouraging the acquisition of this mental model by designing a suitable system image

- Analysing the design by means of detailed Cognitive Walkthroughs

- Application of appropriate design heuristics and guidelines.

We will study each of these techniques with the aid of a number of simple design cases and examples.

14.2 The intended mental model

The first and most obvious approach to conceptual design is to choose the mental model we would like the user to adopt. This is the **intended mental model**. Once we have chosen it, we then design the user interface to present and reinforce this model, and we analyse the model's ability to support the user during the interaction cycle.

It is important to realize that this is only an *intended* mental model, and the real mental model adopted by the user may be quite different. As Norman points out, the individual user's own mental model is personal and idiosyncratic, while the designer's intended model is generalized to suit the 'typical user' (Norman, 1986). Consider the user of a word processor, for example, who typically knows only a fraction of the command repertoire (Rosson, 1983); the designer's intended model probably extends much further. One of the aims of iterative conceptual design is to try to bring the intended and actual mental models into closer alignment.

14.2.1 How the choice of mental model influences design

We can view the definition of the intended mental model as a precursor to design. We start out with a 'design' for the intended mental model, and transform this into a design for the system itself (Figure 14.1).

For example, we might approach the design of a document retrieval system by choosing the sets of objects and actions available to the user, including objects such as documents and folders, and actions such as opening, viewing, scrolling and closing. On this basis we could define the object-action mental model we would like the user to adopt. We could then design a user interface, and underlying software, to present and reinforce this model. We would probably adopt a direct-manipulation style in this instance; in Section 14.4.1 we will see examples of such a user interface.

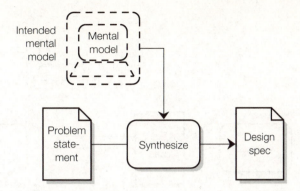

Figure 14.1   Designing the system on the basis of an initial 'design' for an intended mental model.

14.2.2   Retrofitting the mental model

Ideally we should define the intended mental model at the outset, before we get too deeply into user interface design. However, there are situations where this is difficult, for example, where we must retain compatibility with an existing system or must interface to an existing machine.

For these and other reasons it is quite common to 'retrofit' an intended mental model after the initial stage of system design, as shown in Figure 14.2. This initial stage usually involves choosing an appropriate style of interaction and a set of functions, and the intended mental model is fitted around these, influencing further enhancements of the design.

An alternative document retrieval system, for example, might be built onto an existing menu-based office system. It would need to use a menu-based interaction style, allowing the user to search through a hierarchy of document directories. This in turn would suggest a state transition mental model. We might sketch out the set of states that we intended the user to be aware of, and develop the design further in terms of this state transition model.

14.2.3   The intended mental model and the style of interaction

The intended mental model may take any of the general forms discussed in Chapter 13, for example, it may be a state transition model, an object-action model or a mapping model. Our choice of interaction style will usually be strongly linked to this choice of form of mental model, whichever is chosen first. Thus:

- **An object-action mental model** is likely to encourage the adoption of a direct-manipulation style of user interface, in which each of the conceptual objects is represented as a manipulable screen object.

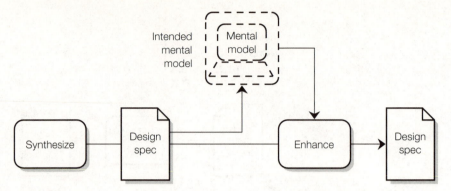

Figure 14.2   Fitting the intended mental model around the initial system design.

- **A state transition mental model** is likely to make sense as an intended model if a menu-based or voice-based style of interaction has been chosen, as in the example above.

- **A mapping model** may arise as a result of choosing a command-line or function-key style.

- **An analogical mental model**, such as a desktop metaphor, might be chosen as a basis for a system with a direct-manipulation style of interaction, or to assist in introducing new objects to an existing such system.

14.2.4   In summary

Conceptual design involves identifying the structure of the mental model we intend the user to acquire. If we can, we identify it prior to user interface design; if not, we determine the mental model from the user interface. Either way, we will find links between the mental model and the style of interaction that the user interface presents.

14.3   Hiding the system model

User interfaces are often designed to allow computer-based control of machinery and to access existing systems. We can see countless examples of this, in telephone answering machines, VCRs, automated tellers, automobile test equipment, flight automation systems, digital heating controls, home security systems, digital phone switchboards, and so on. In these situations, conceptual design faces the problem of hiding those aspects of the machine or system that might interfere with the user's performance of his or her activities (Gentner and Grudin, 1990). In effect, we need to *hide the system model* wherever its visibility may cause problems.

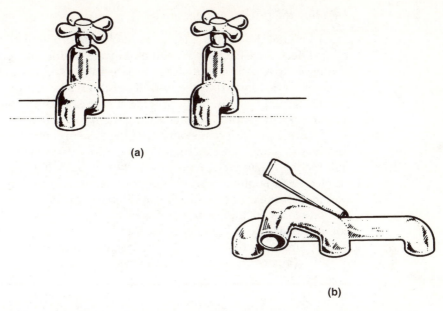

(a)

(b)

Figure 14.3   Water supply (a) revealing the two-temperature system model, (b) hiding it. Based on Norman (1988).

Some examples

A simple example of revealing the system model, quoted by Norman, is the provision of separate hot and cold water taps, as shown in Figure 14.3(a) (Norman, 1988). Why is this done? What task, other than connection to a washing machine, could conceivably demand separation of hot and cold supplies? All we need is a single outlet of water at a controlled temperature, as shown in Figure 14.3(b). But of course, the supply system provides water at two temperatures – the system model says you can have either hot water or cold. This is the system model that two taps fail to hide.

As in the case of water taps, hiding the system model is usually a matter of finding a simpler model. In the case of automobile control, digital systems have been applied towards making the task of starting a car extremely simple: all that the driver does is insert a key and turn it. In the days of vintage cars the task was much more complex and failure-prone; it involved advancing and then retarding the ignition, adjusting the fuel mixture, repositioning the fuel jets, and possibly pumping atomized fuel into the induction manifold; it also involved knowing whether the car was fitted with coil or magneto ignition (Wheatley and Morgan, 1964). Over time, ways have been found to hide these features of the internal mechanism, one by one. This example still serves to remind us that one of the difficulties in hiding system models is to recognize *all* of the elements of the model that can be hidden without loss of usability.

Defining the virtual system model

In conceptual design we attempt to avoid the problem of system models by, in effect, replacing the machine or system with a different *virtual system model* to which a more appropriate user interface can be designed. This involves converting the outputs of the real system to a different set for the virtual system, and applying a corresponding conversion to the virtual system's inputs before feeding them to the real inputs.

Figure 14.4 shows an example of the system-model interface problem and its solution. A user interface to an audio-video switch, based on a system model, is shown in Figure 14.4(a): it requires the user, wishing to be connected to another user, to type four separate commands defining the parameters of each of four audio or video connections. It suffers from various problems, including a high risk of typing error, lack of help regarding command syntax or available names, and an unavoidable step-by-step connection process which causes the connection to be revealed piece by piece.

```
> connect newman v1-out lamming v1-in
```
note: now lamming sees newman but newman's screen remains blank
```
> connect lamming v1-out newman v1-in
```
now both parties can see each other but there is no audio
```
> connect newman a1-out lamming a1-in
```
lamming can now hear newman but cannot be heard
```
> connect lamming a1-out newman a1-in
```
finally, the connection is complete.

(a)

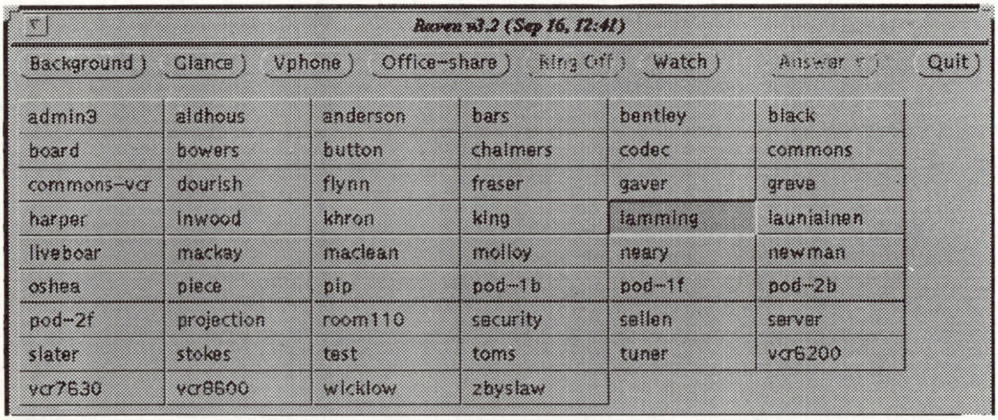

(b)

Figure 14.4 Setting up an audio-video link using (a) a device-based interface, (b) a user interface that hides the system model, based on the Portholes system (Dourish and Bly, 1992).

In Figure 14.4(b) a much simpler menu-based interface has been designed in which connections are made simply by selecting a name. In effect, this has been done by defining a 'virtual audio-video switch' that differs in two important respects from the real switch: it provides a list of names of all accessible users, and it allows a complete connection to be set up as a single 'atomic' operation. It provides a virtual system model we can design to.

14.3.1 In summary

One way of thinking about conceptual design is, therefore, as *redefining the system model* – as a task of surrounding the existing machine or system with a new one, to which an appropriate user interface can easily be fitted. This is sometimes called 'bottom-up' design, because it starts with the technology and works outwards towards the user interface. However, as we saw at the start of this section, sometimes we have no means of influencing the choice of technology; we must simply focus on making it comprehensible.

14.4 Designing the system image

The system image, as we saw in Chapter 13, is the means by which the functionality and state of the system are presented to the user. In introducing the notion of a system image, Don Norman also drew attention to its value as a basis for conceptual design (Norman, 1986). In his words,

> ... in many ways, the primary task of the designer is to construct an appropriate System Image, realizing that everything the user interacts with helps to form that image: the physical knobs, dials, keyboards, and displays, and the documentation, including instruction manuals, help facilities, text input and output, and error messages.

He went on to discuss the implications for the system designer:

> If one hopes for the user to understand the system, to use it properly, and to enjoy using it, then it is up to the designer to make the System Image explicit, intelligible, consistent. And this goes for everything associated with the system. Remember too that people do not always read documentation, and so the major (perhaps entire) burden is placed on the image that the system projects.

Let us look at some of these implications in more detail.

14.4.1 The user interface as the presenter of the system image

Display-based user interfaces are capable of presenting the user with a comprehensive picture of the system. They can show, for example, the entire 'desktop' on which the user's working set of documents are arranged (Figure 14.5(a)); they can show a menu of all of the main categories of function available via sub-menus (Figure 14.5(b)); they can show diagrammatically all of the main stages in the steam process of a nuclear power station (Figure 14.5(c)).

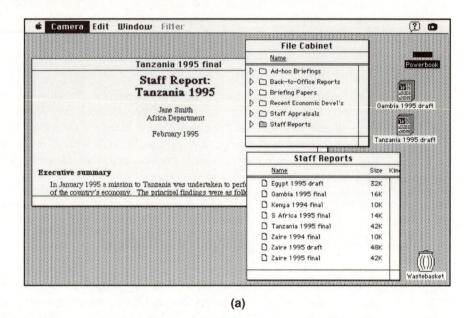

(a)

```
CAMBRIDGE UNIVERSITY LIBRARY ON-LINE CATALOGUE SYSTEM:

1. University Library Main Building - catalogue of post-1977
   imprints

2. University Library Main Building - title index of pre-1978
   borrowable books

3. Union Catalogue of Departmental & College Libraries

4. Cambridge Union List of Serials

5. Cambridge Libraries Directory (including abbreviations)

To finish searching type END at any numbered menu prompt.
Type option (1,2,...)  and press RETURN: 1
```

(b)

Figure 14.5   Examples of displays showing comprehensive views of systems: (a) a graphical desktop (Apple, 1987); (b) a top-level menu of categories of function; (c) a process flow display (Rasmussen and Goodstein, 1988). Courtesy Apple Computer; Microsoft Inc.; Cambridge University Library.

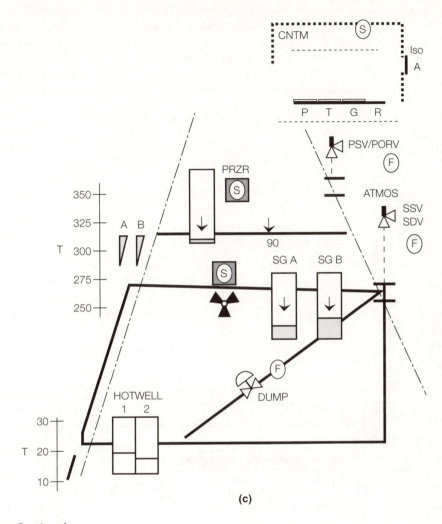

(c)

Figure 14.5   *Continued*

These overall views are powerful mechanisms for presenting a system image. They allow us to transform the intended mental model into pictorial or texual form, and display it on the screen. This is a very direct way of getting across an intended mental model. However, when we use this technique for presenting the system image, we must take care to maintain the two properties of *currency* and *consistency*.

14.4.2   Maintaining the currency of the system image

The display should show the state of the system as it is now, not as it was some time ago. Otherwise it will convey the wrong mental model to the user.

A simple failure to maintain display currency contributed to the 1979 accident at Metropolitan Edison's Three Mile Island power station. The light indicating the status of a pilot-operated relief valve misled the control-room staff, who thought it showed that the valve was closed. In fact it showed only that the relay to close it had been actuated; the valve itself was stuck open. As the President's Commission reported:

> Had the valve closed as it was designed to do, or if the control room operators had realized that the valve was stuck open, or if they had simply left on the plant's high pressure injection pumps, the accident at Three Mile Island would have remained little more than a minor inconvenience for Met. Ed.

The cost of this failure was estimated at upwards of $1 billion in 1979 dollars (President's Commission, 1979).

14.4.3   Maintaining system-image consistency

Likewise, each successive display that the user receives should reinforce the system image rather than conflict with it. In Figure 14.6 we see an example of inconsistent displays of a desktop folder's contents. The panel on the left could confuse the user into believing the folder has documents missing.

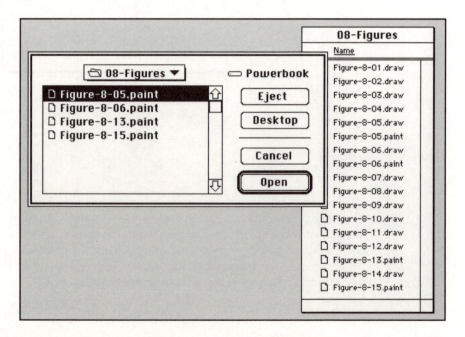

Figure 14.6   Two displays of a folder's contents. On its own, the display on the left could suggest that items are missing. Courtesy Apple Computer.

14.4.4   Progressive reinforcement of the system image

Reinforcement of the system image can also have a powerful cumulative effect. Sometimes this is the only way to get the intended mental model across – the available communication channel is too restrictive, or the model too complex, for a comprehensive display.

Voice-based interaction relies extensively on progressive reinforcement to build up and maintain an adequate mental model. In designing a voice message system, for example, we need to present the user not only with a state-transition model of the available functions, but an object-action model of the stored messages. We may find it particularly vital to reinforce the stored-message model, because the user relies heavily on this part of their mental model in order to perform the task. Thus it probably wouldn't be adequate to prompt the user with the initial message:

> *Press 2 to hear your first new message*

because this would give no indication of the number of stored messages. A more helpful message would be:

> *You have three new messages. Press 2 to hear your first new message.*

The user is already able to build up a simple model of the stored messages and of the likely effect of pressing the '2' key (Figure 14.7).

14.4.5   In summary

The system image offers an invaluable means for presenting and re-inforcing the mental model of our choice. It can be presented via a variety of channels, including display, audio feedback, training and documentation. It is important to maintain currency and consistency in the system image, and to consider ways of reinforcing it as the interaction proceeds.

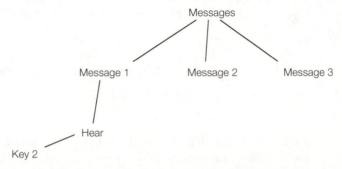

Figure 14.7   The mental model that starts to build in response to the prompt, *You have three new messages. Press 2 to hear your first new message.* The user learns about message-objects, and a 'hear' action that can be invoked by the mapping 'press 2'.

14.5 Walkthrough analysis

Synthesis techniques, such as designing the intended mental model or creating a system image, are useful only if we are also able to analyse the results for usability. This is one of the more difficult areas of conceptual design, for there is no tangible mental model that we can analyse. We can analyse the mental model we intend for the user, but of course there is no guarantee that the user will adopt it. Alternatively we can try to determine what mental model our user has adopted, but this is a slow and error-prone task, and by the time we find out it may be too late to rectify mistakes in the design.

In this section we will look at a way of extending Cognitive Walkthrough methods so that they help us analyse our conceptual designs.

14.5.1 Cognitive Walkthroughs: The technique in outline

The Cognitive Walkthrough method has already been described in Chapter 8, and its underlying theory of exploratory learning was presented in Chapter 3. For the reader's convenience the method itself is summarized in Figure 14.8.

The primary purpose of the technique is to analyse user interfaces in terms of problems users may encounter due to lack of understanding of the user interface. It is often used to analyse walk-up-and-use interfaces.

14.5.2 Extending the walkthrough technique

If we want to use the walkthrough technique to analyse designs in terms of users' mental models, we can modify the three iterated questions, and add a fourth, to read as follows:

Q1: Will the correct action be sufficiently evident to the user *via their existing mental model or via the system image*?

Q2: Will the user connect the correct action with what he or she is trying to do, *either via his or her own mental model* or via its description?

Q3: Will the user interpret the system's response to the chosen action correctly, that is, will the user know from this response, *and from his or her own mental model*, if he or she has made a right or a wrong choice?

Q4: *Will the user's mental model be affected? Will new concepts be added, or existing concepts lost?*

As with the basic walkthrough technique, we iterate until the task is complete or until we encounter a design problem that justifies halting.

With the addition of the questions in italics the technique becomes more challenging. It involves identifying the user's probable mental

Analysis by Cognitive Walkthrough involves simulating the way users explore and gain familiarity with interactive systems, with the aid of a simple step-by-step model:

0   The user starts with a rough plan of what he or she wants to achieve – a task to be performed;
1   The user explores the system, via the user interface, looking for actions that might contribute to performing the task;
2   The user selects the action whose description or appearance most closely matches what he or she is trying to do;
3   The user then interprets the system's response and assesses whether progress has been made towards completing the task.

The analysis involves simulating steps 1, 2 and 3 at each stage of interaction, by asking questions of the form:

Q1:   Will the correct action be made sufficiently evident to the user?
Q2:   Will the user connect the correct action's description with what they are trying to do?
Q3:   Will the user interpret the system's response to the chosen action correctly, that is, will the user know if he or she has made a right or a wrong choice?

The process is repeated until the task sequence is completed or until the analysis succeeds in identifying sufficient problems to make further analysis unnecessary.

Figure 14.8   The basic Cognitive Walkthrough technique, from Chapter 8 (Lewis *et al.*, 1992).

model at the outset, and keeping it updated by answering question Q4 at each step. Question Q4 involves assessing the user's capacity to remember the new concepts that are presented, and this is difficult. Nevertheless, the technique can be very useful in helping to identify conceptual design problems. Three short examples follow, illustrating this use of the technique.

Example 1: Changing an icon's label

To introduce this use of the Cognitive Walkthrough method we will analyse a simple example: the novice Macintosh user attempting to change the name of an icon. As we saw in the last chapter, a novice user may not appreciate that icons can be selected in two ways, and that the label itself must be selected in order to change it, as shown in Figure 14.9(a).

The correct initial action, then, is to click on the label, as shown in Figure 14.9(a). Instead the user clicks on the icon itself, as shown in Figure 14.9(b). Here is the first stage in the analysis of this sequence:

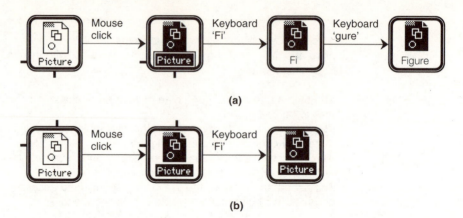

(a)

(b)

Figure 14.9   Changing the label on a Macintosh icon by selecting and retyping: (a) the correct method; (b) an incorrect method – the user selects the body of the icon. Icons courtesy Claris Corporation.

Q1:   Will the correct action be sufficiently evident to the user via his or her existing mental model or via the system image?

Answer: No. As we can see in Figure 14.10, the user's mental model lacks the distinction between selecting the icon and selecting the label. The icon's appearance does not immediately suggest that there are two objects here.

Q2:   Will the user connect the correct action with what he or she is trying to do, either via his or her own mental model or via its description?

Answer: Possibly. But this user hasn't made the connection.

Q3:   Will the user interpret the system's response to the chosen action correctly, that is, will the user know from this response, and from his or her own mental model, if he or she has made a right or a wrong choice?

Answer: No. The system responds by highlighting the entire icon, including the label. This doesn't tell the user that the icon itself, not the label, has been selected.

Q4:   Will the user's mental model be affected? Will new concepts be added, or existing concepts lost?

Answer: No. If anything, the system's response has reinforced the user's view of the icon as a single object.

Thus the system has encouraged the user to view the icon as a single entity. Now we'll analyse the second step. The correct action would be to select the label, but the user types the new contents instead. The analysis of this step runs as follows:

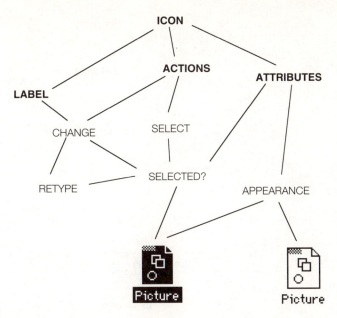

Figure 14.10   The novice user's mental model of the icon, showing just those concepts relating to changing the label. Icons courtesy Claris Corporation.

Q1:   Will the correct action be sufficiently evident to the user via his or her existing mental model or via the system image?

Answer: Probably not. The icon looks as if it is selected. There is nothing to suggest that the user should point at the label.

Q2:   Will the user connect the correct action with what he or she is trying to do, either via his or her own mental model or via its description?

Answer: As before, possibly, but the user's mental model is getting in the way.

Q3:   Will the user interpret the system's response to the chosen action correctly, that is, will the user know from this response, and from his or her own mental model, if he or she has made a right or a wrong choice?

Answer: Yes. The system doesn't respond at all to the characters that the user types, so it is obvious that this is the wrong choice of action.

Q4:   Will the user's mental model be affected? Will new concepts be added, or existing concepts lost?

Answer: Probably. The user may now wonder if selecting and retyping is the correct method. His or her mental model may be weakened, as shown in Figure 14.11.

    If the user were now to select the label itself, he or she might then complete the task successfully and learn about the two parts of the icon as

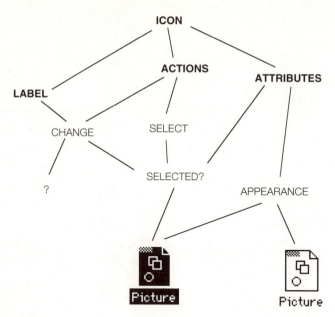

Figure 14.11   How the novice user's mental model of the icon may be affected by failure to change the label. Icons courtesy Claris Corporation.

a by-product. The detailed analysis of this sequence is left as an exercise for the reader.

We may wonder whether this problem might be avoided by changing the user interface of the icon. One possibility might be to invert only the body of the icon when it is selected, but this could be confused with an icon whose label is being retyped. There is no obvious solution to this design problem.

Example 2: An audio-video link

In this second example we will analyse a simple conceptual design of a two-way audio-video link of the kind introduced in Figure 14.4. We will apply the Cognitive Walkthrough method to the situation where one of the cameras has been turned off, unknown to the person at the other end of the link (Figure 14.12).

User A and User B have established an audio-video link between their two offices – a form of video-mediated 'office sharing'. With experience, this kind of link tends to build the mental model, 'If I can see them, they can see me', that is, a model of reciprocal visibility (Adler and Henderson, 1994). We will explore how this model affects the course of events.

During his lunch break, User A rearranges the cables in his office, and forgets to turn his camera back on. However, User B's camera is still on, and so the connection appears perfectly OK to User A. When User B

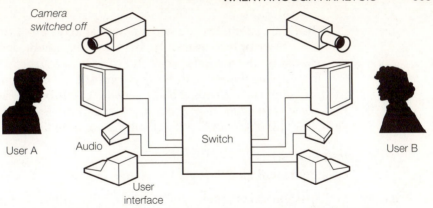

Figure 14.12   An audio/video link, in which User A's camera has been switched off.

returns from lunch, she sees a blank screen, and assumes that the connection has been closed intentionally by User A. She needs to have a private phone conversation anyway, so she takes no further action.

Let's analyse the situations for both users. We will consider User A first, at the point when he has finished rearranging the cables; at this point, his correct action should be to *switch the camera on*:

Q1:   Will the correct action be sufficiently evident to the user via his or her existing mental model or via the system image?

Answer: No. The mental model User A has acquired is, 'If I can see her, she can see me'. He can see User B's office, so he assumes he is visible on her video monitor. As for the 'system image', it consists of a tiny red light which is no longer on, and this goes unnoticed. The user interface shows the connection still in effect.

Q2:   Will the user connect the correct action with what he or she is trying to do, either via his or her own mental model or via its description?

Answer: No. At this time, User A is not trying to achieve any goal that depends on being visible to User B; if he were, however, the correct action would be obvious.

Q3:   Will the user interpret the system's response to the chosen action correctly, that is, will the user know from this response, and from his or her own mental model, if he or she has made a right or a wrong choice?

Answer: No. User A's 'chosen action' – to leave the camera switched off – generates no response from the system.

Q4:   Will the user's mental model be affected? Will new concepts be added, or existing concepts lost?

Answer: No. User A is unaware that anything is wrong.

Thus the system has allowed a potential invasion of privacy to occur, through its lack of response to the switched-off camera, and through User A's reliance on the mental model, 'If I can see her, she can see me'.

To complete the analysis, we will look at User B's situation on returning from lunch, and seeing a blank screen. At this point, the correct action for User B is to *notify User A* that there is a problem with the connection, since it is still open but is not delivering a picture to her.

Q1:   Will the correct action be sufficiently evident to the user via his or her existing mental model or via the system image?

Answer: Perhaps. She too maintains the mental model, 'If I can see him, he can see me', and on this basis will form an assumption that the connection has been closed. The user interface shows the connection still open, but User B may not notice this – the control panel may no longer be visible to her.

Q2:   Will the user connect the correct action with what he or she is trying to do, either via his or her own mental model or via its description?

Answer: No. User B's mental model now tells her that the connection is closed; she is not aware of any problem.

Q3:   Will the user interpret the system's response to the chosen action correctly, that is, will the user know from this response, and from his or her own mental model, if he or she has made a right or a wrong choice?

Answer: No. She takes no action, and receives no response.

Q4:   Will the user's mental model be affected? Will new concepts be added, or existing concepts lost?

Answer: User B has simply formed a temporary model of a closed audio-video link.

How does this potentially damaging situation get resolved? At worst, User B begins her private phone call, User A overhears it via the audio link, wonders why she is being so indiscreet, puts two and two together, and checks his camera to see if it is on. In a more likely scenario, User B returns to her office and soon picks up the sounds of User A in his office via the audio link. She realizes that the connection is open after all, and takes suitable action: 'Hey, I can hear you but I can't see you. Is your camera out of action?'

How might we redesign this system to prevent such a potentially embarrassing situation from arising again? One solution might be to build an integrated audio-video station, incorporating camera, monitor and audio, with a single on-off switch. Had this been installed, User A would have lost his picture when he powered the station down, and would have been reminded by this to power it up. Other solutions might be to provide an extra feedback monitor showing each user the pictures on their own cameras, or to have the system sense the absence of a video signal and take appropriate action, for example, close the connection.

Example 3: Setting editor preferences

Often we will need to walk through a series of actions, as in the following simple example of direct-manipulation data entry. Here we are concerned with a user who has recently begun to use a document database. She wishes to use the same editor as she had been using before, `emacs`, for preparing documents.

The database system allows a variety of preferences to be modified. The first step is to select **Preferences** from a system menu; this brings up the panel shown in Figure 14.13(a). The user can click on any or each of the preference buttons to bring up individual panels (Figure 14.13(b)), change the settings (Figure 14.13(c)), and then click on **Save** to store the settings.

We will assume that this user has had experience of other similar systems, also offering a choice of editors, and has experience too of the window environment in question. She will have transferred these concepts to her mental model of the new system.

Our Cognitive Walkthrough analysis starts with just the main system window visible, and runs as follows:

Q1: Will the correct action be sufficiently evident to the user via his or her existing mental model or via the system image?

Answer: Yes. The correct action is to select **Preferences** in the system menu. The system image makes it sufficiently evident.

Q2: Will the user connect the correct action with what he or she is trying to do, either via his or her own mental model or via its description?

Answer: Yes. From her existing mental model she knows that this term covers functionality such as choice of editor.

Q3: Will the user interpret the system's response to the chosen action correctly, that is, will the user know from this response, and from his or her own mental model, if he or she has made a right or a wrong choice?

Answer: Yes. The panel displayed in response includes an **Editor** button.

Q4: Will the user's mental model be affected? Will new concepts be added, or existing concepts lost?

Answer: No. But the user will have confirmed her expectation that editor-selection is one of the preference-setting functions available.

The first cycle of our analysis has exposed no problems in the conceptual design. We move on to the next cycle, in which the user displays the editor panel by clicking on the button:

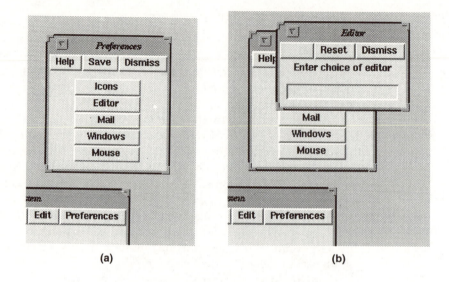

(a)   (b)

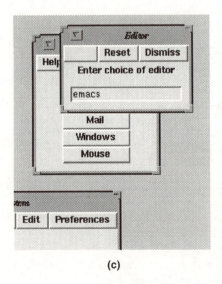

(c)

Figure 14.13   Setting editor preferences: (a) opening the PREFERENCES panel; (b) opening the EDITOR subpanel; (c) entering the choice of editor.

Q1: Will the correct action be sufficiently evident to the user via his or her existing mental model or via the system image?

Answer: Yes. The **Editor** button is clearly visible.

Q2: Will the user connect the correct action with what he or she is trying to do, either via his or her own mental model or via its description?

Answer: Yes. The meaning of the **Editor** description is clear.

Q3: Will the user interpret the system's response to the chosen action correctly, that is, will the user know from this response, and from his or her own mental model, if he or she has made a right or a wrong choice?

Answer: Yes. The display of a new panel, with a box for entering the editor name, confirms that the action was correct.

Q4: Will the user's mental model be affected? Will new concepts be added, or existing concepts lost?

Answer: No. The panel's appearance suggests nothing unusual.

Thus the second cycle is completed successfully. The third cycle involves typing in the editor name, emacs (Figure 14.13(c)), and this again raises no problems for the user, so we will omit this step in the analysis. We will proceed directly to the fourth and final step, clicking on the **Save** button:

Q1: Will the correct action be sufficiently evident to the user via his or her existing mental model or via the system image?

Answer: No. The user's preference – select the emacs editor – is stated in the panel she has just modified. According to her mental model of direct-manipulation interfaces, any action on this preference statement should be made by means of one of the buttons on the panel; but none of them offers the action she wants to take. The correct action, **Save**, involves a button on another panel. Furthermore, this **Save** button may be obscured by the current panel.

Q2: Will the user connect the correct action with what he or she is trying to do, either via his or her own mental model or via its description?

Answer: No. The **Save** button will be connected with the panel displaying the set of functions. The user's existing mental model would probably suggest not using this button, because she doesn't know what information will be saved.

Instead, therefore, the user simply closes the two panels, hoping that this has altered the editor preference. Again, experience with other systems that allow this kind of preference changing (for example, Apple Macintosh) might have suggested that no further action is needed.

Q3:   Will the user interpret the system's response to the chosen action correctly, that is, will the user know from this response, and from his or her own mental model, if he or she has made a right or a wrong choice?

Answer: No. The system provides no confirming response. Until she tries to edit some text, she won't know whether the preference has taken effect.

Q4:   Will the user's mental model be affected? Will new concepts be added, or existing concepts lost?

Answer: Yes. She will now be uncertain of the object-action model underlying the preference choosing user interface.

We see here an example of a common mistake, attaching an action to the wrong object. A **Save** button on the second panel would solve the problem.

14.5.3   In summary

When we design an interactive system, we need to rework our intended mental model progressively, in parallel with the user interface. We can manage this reworking process by walkthrough analysis of the conceptual design. Each analysis generates findings that influence both the intended mental model and the system design, as shown in Figure 14.14. One or more analyses may be undertaken at each stage, based on a representative set of *benchmark tasks*. We have worked through three such tasks:

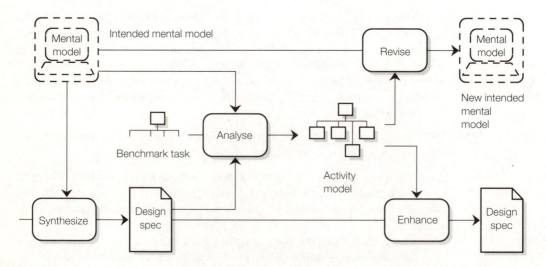

Figure 14.14   Processes involved in analysis of conceptual designs. The intended mental model and the design are developed in parallel, by means of a series of analyses in terms of benchmark tasks.

changing an icon's label, re-cabling a camera, and altering the text-editor preference. Other examples of conceptual design analyses can be found in Payne (1984) and Norman (1988).

We need to allow time for this kind of analysis during the design process. If possible, we should conduct walkthroughs in which we simulate the problems of users with different levels of understanding; we should try to track their acquisition of new concepts. This is not something that can be done quickly. However, walkthrough analysis generates invaluable design feedback. Although analysis poses many questions that we may find difficult to answer, the exercise of answering them will usually improve our overall understanding of the design problem.

14.6 Conceptual design heuristics

When we design a user interface, many of the decisions we take are based on experience and advice. Already, this chapter has passed on several basic pieces of advice, which might be summarized as follows:

- Choose the mental model you intend the user to adopt, preferably before attempting to design the user interface.

- Link your choice of mental model to your choice of style of interaction.

- Hide all those aspects of the system model that conflict with the user's performance of his or her activity.

- Exploit the system image to convey the intended mental model.

- Take steps to ensure currency and consistency in the system image.

These are examples of **design heuristics**, strategies that help us to improve the outcome of design. Design heuristics often enable decisions to be made quickly, without the need for extensive analysis. Not only are they useful in guiding design decisions, but they can also be applied to evaluation, as we saw in Chapter 8: we write down the set of heuristics we think the design should comply with, and then inspect the design, looking for lack of compliance and other problems.

The list of conceptual design heuristics doesn't stop with the five given above. In this final section a few additional heuristics are offered, to indicate the kind of assistance they can provide to the process of conceptual design. They are drawn from a number of sources, including Rubinstein and Hersh (1984), Apple (1987), Carroll and Olson (1988), and Mayhew (1992), which are recommended to readers in search of more such heuristics.

14.6.1   A sample of conceptual design heuristics

First of all, heuristics can help us remember how varied our user population is. Not only do users come to a new system with a wide range of prior experience, but they continue to maintain different sets of concepts about the system.

- Take into account the mental models that users will bring with them to the new system.

This heuristic, from Mayhew (1992), protects us from assuming we can invent any intended mental model we like. Carroll and Olson (1988) have put it another way, *investigate whether people have and use mental models of various kinds*. There is an implication that we should make the effort to understand what concepts our users already possess. We need to allow time for this.

- Promote the development of both novice and expert mental models.

We cannot guarantee that all our users will be fully trained when they first use the system in earnest. This heuristic, also from Mayhew (1992), tells us to keep a range of possible mental models in mind. It tells us to design the system image so that the extra information the novice needs is available. When we conduct analyses, we should take the extra effort to analyse in terms of both novices and experts.

The next two heuristics relate to the use of *metaphors*. As we saw in Chapter 13, metaphors provide ways of introducing concepts to users with the aid of analogies with familiar real-world objects. In effect, they *transfer* mental models from the real world so that the user has a basis for understanding the new system.

- Use concrete metaphors and make them plain, so that users have a set of expectations to apply to computer environments.

This heuristic, from Apple (1987), makes clear the basic strategy for the use of metaphors. *Make them plain* reminds us that a metaphor does no good if the user fails to recognize it. A well-known example is the American mailbox symbol shown in Figure 14.15; it has no meaning to a European user.

- Adhere to familiar metaphors as much as possible without sacrificing power.

The unconstrained use of metaphors can lead to inefficient interfaces. Every action involves dragging an object to some other object, and commands that could be stated quickly via the keyboard involve the user in a succession of pointing and clicking steps. This heuristic, based on Mayhew

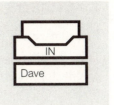

Figure 14.15 The use of a metaphor to convey an electronic mail function. The icon on the left is unrecognizable to many Europeans; the icon on the right is more universally recognizable.

(1992), tells us to analyse our metaphor-based interfaces for speed of operation, perhaps with the aid of the Keystroke-Level Model of Chapter 8.

- When there's a choice, have the least surprising thing happen to the user.

Our final heuristic is based on Dan Swinehart's 'Law of least astonishment' (Thimbleby, 1990). Choosing the least surprising design is consistent with maintaining an existing mental model. Choosing something surprising risks undermining the concepts the user already has. This principle has become increasingly important as more and more systems are designed for use within standard window environments with their own conventions. Here, the law of least astonishment tell us to abide by the conventions of the environment unless there are very good reasons for doing something different.

14.6.2   In summary

Heuristics provide us with sets of rules to keep in mind as we synthesize and analyse the design. Through their judicious use, we can sometimes make rapid design progress. However, heuristics aren't a substitute for the other tools we have covered for design synthesis and analysis. They have specific domains of applicability, and they sometimes come into conflict with each other (Barnard and Grudin, 1988). They don't offer explicit solutions to design problems, nor do they tell us how to measure the usability of our designs. Their main value lies in the knowledge and experience they encapsulate.

In this final section we have started to enter into a method of design that applies much more widely to interactive system design – the use of **guidelines**. We need to understand how heuristics arise, what knowledge they encapsulate, and how to make good use of them. These and other issues are explored in the final chapter.

Exercises

(1)   Summarize the five ways of approaching conceptual design.

(2)   How does choice of style influence the user's mental model? To what extent does our choice of intended mental model influence our choice of style?

(3)   Give examples of (a) parts of the automobile's system model that have been successfully hidden; (b) new user concepts that have been added to the automobile.

(4)   How would you hide the system model of (a) a mountain bike's 27 gears? (b) telephone numbers? (c) file names, in the specific situation where files A and B have got their names transposed? Describe the virtual system models you would introduce in their place.

(5)   Devise more helpful system images for (a) a pay phone, (b) a dishwasher, (c) a telephone answering machine.

(6)   How would you rectify the problem exposed in Figure 14.6?

(7)   Conduct an extended Cognitive Walkthrough on two of the following: (a) the example of Figure 13.17; (b) dragging a floppy disk to the Apple Macintosh wastebasket; (c) the UNIX *cat* command; (d) the direct-manipulation interface shown in Figure 12.11; (e) the voice-based interface shown in Figure 12.10.

(8)   What are design heuristics? How would the heuristic, 'Promote the development of both novice and expert mental models', affect your answers to question 5(c)?

(9)   How would you overcome the problems listed in Section 13.2.2?

(10)   Why is it important that fax machines should have displays that show when the number is being dialled and so on? What sorts of problems are likely to arise when they don't?

Further reading

Smith D., Irby C., Kimball R.M., Verplank W. and Harslem E. (1982). Designing the Star User Interface. *Byte*, **7** (4), April

An example of a carefully worked out conceptual design, highly innovative in its day.

CHAPTER 15

Designing to guidelines

Chapter objectives:

Guidelines offer advice regarding design problems, and suggest solutions. They help with aspects of design that lie outside the scope of analytical tools or empirical evaluation. This chapter explains how guidelines are used in interactive system design, by addressing the following issues:

- The roles played by guidelines in design
- Limitations of guidelines
- Guidelines as general principles
- The use of guidelines in specific contexts, for example, screen design, use of colour, designing within a specific style, design of user interface components.

15.1 Introduction

This is the final chapter on user interface design, and the last chapter in the book. Any reader who started at the beginning and has had the stamina to reach these last few pages will have realized that there are many limitations to the methods presented so far. Virtually any design problem, however small, is going to pose questions that these methods cannot answer in full. There will be many questions of detail, for example, concerning screen design or the use of colour. There will be questions about the use of specific windowing systems and user interface 'house styles.'

373

We can sometimes answer these kinds of questions by drawing on *guidelines*. Guidelines have already appeared in this book under various disguises, in particular during the discussion of heuristics at the end of the last chapter. A great many more guidelines are available to designers of interactive systems, for example, in the works of Shneiderman (1992) and Mayhew (1992). They cover a vast range of issues in user interface design. Although they solve some design problems, they can create problems of their own. In particular, it can be difficult to find or select the right guideline for the problem at hand.

This chapter is about the effective use of guidelines in user interface design. It makes no attempt to offer a compendium of guidelines, because these already exist in books such as those just cited. Instead it explains the roles of guidelines in design, points out some of their limitations, and identifies some of the different design contexts in which they are useful. It then discusses the use of guidelines in each of these contexts, illustrating how they address a specific design problem, the Economic Update system of Chapters 6 and 7.

15.2 Guidelines: What are they, and why do we need them?

We will start with an explanation of what guidelines are. **Guidelines** provide us with advice on the solution of design problems, and suggest possible solution strategies. Each guideline has a context or domain within which it applies, that is, a range of design problems to which it is applicable. When we apply a guideline to such a problem, we treat it as a *heuristic*, that is, we draw on assumptions derived from past experience with this kind of problem. In many cases, the experience we draw on includes empirical research.

Some examples

Figure 15.1 shows a representative set of guidelines, drawn from a variety of sources. These examples illustrate a number of the points just made. Thus we can see that guidelines vary considerably in the *context* to which they apply, all the way from the general consistency principle (A) to specific advice on adjusting the fields of view of video-link cameras (D). Some of them are phrased as gentle hints (C) while others are mandatory or even statements of fact (E, F). Some may read as obvious common sense derived from design experience (A); others may surprise us, and lead us to wonder how they were arrived at (B, D).

15.2.1 Why do we need guidelines?

The role of guidelines is particularly prominent in interactive system design, to the extent that books of guidelines have been written to help

A   Strive for consistency.

B   In menu-based interaction, where users make frequent selection and the set of options does not change over time, use letter identifiers paired to each option.

C   Consider voice synthesis as an output device when the user's eyes are busy, when mobility is required, or when the user has no access to a workstation or screen.

D   When using a video link to support collaboration of individuals, adjust camera fields of view wide enough to show other people at the connected locations, not just the heads and shoulders of the principal users.

E   When closing a document, the user must be able to choose whether to save any changes made to the document since the last time it was opened.

F   A standard window has a **close box**. When the user clicks the close box, the window goes away .

Figure 15.1   Examples of guidelines, concerning (A) consistency (Shneiderman, 1992); (B) menu selection (Perlman, 1984); (C) voice-based interaction (Mayhew, 1992); (D) use of video communication (Dourish *et al.*, 1994); (E and F) closing documents and windows (Apple, 1987).

designers in this field (Rubinstein and Hersh, 1984; Brown, 1988). Why is there so much dependence here on guidelines?

The answer lies in the frequency with which unfamiliar design problems arise. As interactive system designers we constantly find ourselves in new problem domains, designing systems to support activities we have never studied before. Even when we work in familar domains we often adopt new forms of solution, either by necessity or by preference. Thus we may be obliged to use a windowing environment we have never experienced before, for example, or we may see an opportunity to improve usability by incorporating a new user interface technique. For whatever reason, we find ourselves in unfamiliar design territory. And this happens constantly; it may happen, to some extent, with every new design problem we tackle.

In the course of designing interactive systems, therefore, we often need help in dealing with unfamiliar design problems. Guidelines can provide a source of help by encapsulating the results of other people's experience and research. In a sense they offer the kind of 'packaged experience' that we need when we are working in unfamiliar design territory.

15.3   How we use guidelines

Before looking at further examples of guidelines we need to understand how to make good use of them. Guidelines have a number of different *roles* in design – they can serve different purposes. They also have *limitations*, which mean that we must apply them with care. Also, as we have seen, every guideline has a *context* within which it applies, and applying it outside this context may be risky. We look briefly at each of these topics.

15.3.1   The roles of guidelines

Guidelines can be used for many purposes, but they are more effective in some roles than in others. For example, it is not easy to learn how to design user interfaces by simply reading a book of guidelines, although compilers of guidelines have been known to recommend this. But there are things that guidelines do well, and this is where their true roles lie.

Guideline use in the design enhancement process
The roles we shall be discussing shortly are illustrated in the process diagram of Figure 15.2. In terms of the design representations of Chapter 4 we can regard each guideline as a miniature 'investigation report'. It may report on actual research, or it may draw from accumulated experience.

We select the guideline on the basis of its match with the problem we are solving, or with a particular question that has arisen about the design. We apply it to the solution in its current form, typically with a view to enhancing it. Alternatively we simply document any problems that the guideline may have helped identify; this list of problems is shown in Figure 15.2 as an evaluation report.

The process diagram highlights four major roles played by guidelines in design: *raising awareness, assisting in choices, offering strategies* and *supporting evaluation*. These have been documented in reports on actual studies of guideline use, principally by Tetzlaff and Schwartz (1991) and by Nielsen and Molich (1990).

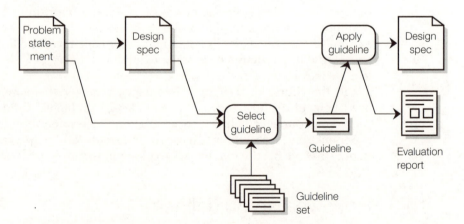

Figure 15.2   The process by which guidelines are applied. We can regard each guideline as a miniature investigation report.

Raising awareness of concepts

A guideline may introduce a concept that we have not encountered before, for example, the following from Microsoft (1992) illustrated in Figure 15.3(a):

- A cascading or hierarchical menu is a submenu (also known as a child menu) attached to the right side of a menu item ... Cascading menus can be added to drop-down menus, contextual menus, or even other cascading menus.

We might encounter this guideline while searching for information of another kind. If we have never experienced tear-off menus before, this will be a new concept that we can retain for possible use at a later date (Figure 15.3(b)).

Assisting in design choices

When we need help with a difficult decision, we may find the answer in a guideline. Suppose we are designing a command-line style of user interface, and need to allocate the command line itself to a place on the screen. Should it be at the top or the bottom? The following, based on research by Granda *et al.* (1982), is quoted by Mayhew (1992):

- Locate the command line near the bottom of the screen unless it is clear that the user's gaze will be elsewhere.

In other words, we should adopt the layout of Figure 15.4(b) rather than follow Figure 15.4(a).

Offering strategies for solving design problems

Solving a design problem involves finding an overall strategy, and we can sometimes find the strategies we need in sets of guidelines. We may be led to a strategy while investigating a specific question.

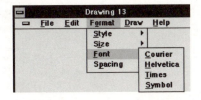
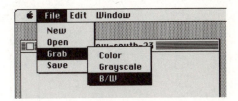

(a)   (b)

Figure 15.3   Cascading menus: (a) an example (in Microsoft Windows) that raises awareness of the concept; (b) the concept put to later use, in a different windowing environment (Apple Macintosh). Courtesy Microsoft Inc.; Apple Computer.

```
┌─────────────────────────────────┐        ┌─────────────────────────────────┐
│ Enter number, press RETURN:     │        │     BETTERTOOLS ON-LINE CATALOGUE │
│                                 │        │                                 │
│     BETTERTOOLS ON-LINE CATALOGUE │      │ Jones Stillson wrenches:        │
│                                 │        │                                 │
│ Jones Stillson wrenches:        │        │ 1.   9 in, 3/4 in. jaw    $15.99 │
│                                 │        │ 2.  12 in, 1 in. jaw      $18.99 │
│ 1.   9 in, 3/4 in. jaw   $15.99 │        │ 3.  15 in, 1 1/2 in. jaw  $19.99 │
│ 2.  12 in, 1 in. jaw     $18.99 │        │ 4.  20 in, 2 in. jaw      $34.49 │
│ 3.  15 in, 1 1/2 in. jaw $19.99 │        │ 5.  30 in, 3 in. jaw      $79.99 │
│ 4.  20 in, 2 in. jaw     $34.49 │        │                                 │
│ 5.  30 in, 3 in. jaw     $79.99 │        │ Type the number for the product you want, │
│                                 │        │ and press the RETURN key.       │
│ Type the number for the product you want, │ Enter 0 to return to the previous menu. │
│ and press the RETURN key.       │        │ Enter 9 to return to the initial menu. │
│ Enter 0 to return to the previous menu. │                                   │
│ Enter 9 to return to the initial menu. │ Enter number, press RETURN:      │
└─────────────────────────────────┘        └─────────────────────────────────┘
```

(a)   (b)

Figure 15.4   The command line (a) placed at the top (not recommended), and (b) at the bottom (recommended).

Thus we might encounter a problem in enabling users to navigate quickly through large files of customers' invoices stored online. We might investigate solutions based on scrolling techniques, and come across the following guideline in Sun (1991):

- When your application organizes data logically into pages, provide page-oriented scroll bars.

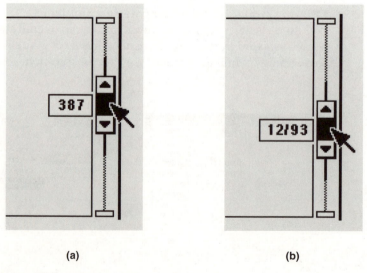

(a)   (b)

Figure 15.5   An OPEN LOOK page-oriented scroll bar adapted for use in scrolling through date-ordered invoices. Based on Sun (1991). Copyright owned by Sun Microsystems, Inc. Used herein by permission. All other rights reserved.

The page-oriented scroll bar guideline, illustrated as shown in Figure 15.5(a), might inspire the provision of a date-oriented scroll bar as shown in Figure 15.5(b).

The provision of overall design strategies is a common role of the 'desktop' style guides written in support of proprietary software systems. They illustrate how guidelines can assist in the process of enhancing the design, in a fashion that Thimbleby has called *generative* (Thimbleby, 1984).

Supporting evaluation

We have already encountered the use of heuristic guidelines to support evaluation in Chapter 8. On a more informal basis, we can use guidelines as usability checklists. Thus we might be conducting a review of the menu design shown in Figure 15.6(a); we might decide to check it against the guidelines for menu-based interaction offered by Mayhew (1992), which include the following:

- Facilitate backwards navigation.

As a result, we might change the design by adding the option shown in Figure 15.6(b) for returning to the previous menu.

15.3.2   Limitations of guidelines

Guidelines have their limitations, and we need to bear these in mind. Most of the limitations apply to the way we select guidelines and apply them, not to the content of the guidelines themselves.

Problems in selecting guidelines

We need to be sure we select guidelines that apply to the problem in question; but there may be a lot of these, scattered throughout the guideline set. We must guard against the tendency to apply the first relevant guideline we find, a tendency noted by Tetzlaff and Schwartz (1991). It is

```
1.  PCN on Russian debt, 12-17-93

2.  PCN on Belarus application, 12-1-94

3.  PCN on Russo-Latvia accord, 15-1-94

4.  PCN on Ukrainian exports, 22-2-94

5.  PCN on Estonian loan, 24-6-94

6.  PCN on FSU policies 95-96, 8-8-94

Type number, RETURN, to display document
```

```
1.  PCN on Russian debt, 12-17-93

2.  PCN on Belarus application, 12-1-94

3.  PCN on Russo-Latvia accord, 15-1-94

4.  PCN on Ukrainian exports, 22-2-94

5.  PCN on Estonian loan, 24-6-94

6.  PCN on FSU policies 95-96, 8-8-94

Type number, RETURN, to display document
Type 0, RETURN, for previous menu
```

(a)   (b)

Figure 15.6   Evaluation in terms of a guideline: (a) before, (b) after applying the guideline concerning facilitation of backwards navigation.

sometimes hard to select the most important guidelines to apply from among many, and tempting to apply only those that make the enhancement task easy.

Problems in applying guidelines

In applying a guideline, we rely on explanations and illustrations to supplement the wording of the guideline itself. Guidelines themselves are usually stated in the minimum number of words. By itself, this wording may convey rather little, and we may miss the guideline's significance entirely. Consider the following guideline for text layout offered by Tullis (1988):

- Reduce search times by minimizing the number of groups of items while designing each group to subtend a visual angle as close as possible to 5 degrees.

This guideline is attempting, among other things, to help us avoid screen layouts in which text or graphic items merge together when they should be distinct. It is illustrated in Figure 15.8 (intentionally *not* placed on this page), where it is applied to improving the hardware catalogue design of Figure 11.11. Without the help of this example we might not appreciate the usefulness of the guideline. Examples and explanations are key to the successful use of guidelines. But we must be careful not to focus our attention on the example and ignore the actual advice offered by the guideline, another tendency noted by Tetzlaff and Schwartz (1991).

The other problem we face in applying a guideline is knowing whether it has the desired effect. How can we be sure that the enhanced design in Figure 15.6 is more usable than the unenhanced design? The guideline itself will not help us to measure usability. We must apply some other means of testing usability, for example, an appropriate analytical tool or an empirical evaluation. Sometimes this is inconvenient or impossible. We must then simply rely on the guideline to do its job.

Problems with multiple guidelines

We often find that several guidelines apply to the problem we are trying to solve. The order in which we then apply the guidelines may affect the outcome. Thus applying guideline 1 and then guideline 2, as shown in Figure 15.7(a), may lead us in a different direction than applying them in the reverse order.

This kind of problem may be avoided if we apply guidelines in conjunction, as in Figure 15.7(b). But we may then find that the guidelines conflict, and this may make the design problem more difficult. Consider the following two OPEN LOOK guidelines, from Sun (1991), concerning the order of menu items:

- Use a logical order (if one exists) to help guide users through the process.
- Put most important or most frequently used functions at the top of the menu.

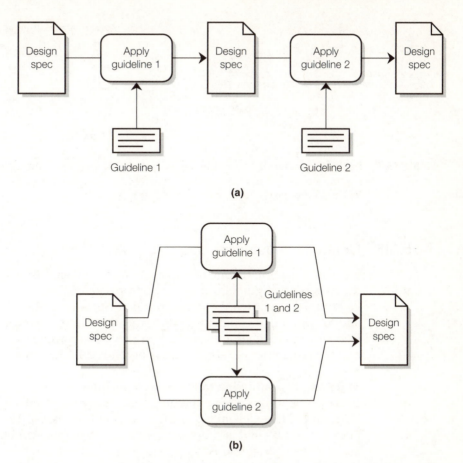

(a)

(b)

Figure 15.7   Applying guidelines in order to enhance the design, (a) one at a time, (b) two or more at a time.

It is quite likely that a logical ordering (for example, **Open** before **Close** and **Save**) will not result in placing the most frequently used function at the top of the menu. Barnard and Grudin (1988) have written about this problem, and have given further examples of guideline conflict.

Such conflicts arise partly because guidelines are based on different theories and experiences concerning the improvement of usability factors, and because there are many such factors. Thus we may find ourselves trying to apply one guideline that improves efficiency and another that reduces errors. There is no particular reason why they should be easy to apply together.

Conflicts also arise because guidelines have limited scope of application. Some apply to menu-based interfaces, for example, while others apply to direct manipulation. Guidelines for one windowing system may not apply to another. For this reason we need to be very careful about the *context* in which we use guidelines.

Available in five sizes, click to order:		
(order)	Model WS09 9 in, 3/4 in. jaw	$15.99
(order)	Model WS12, 12 in, 1 in. jaw	$18.99
(order)	Model WS15, 15 in, 1 1/2 in. jaw	$19.99
(order)	Model WS20, 20 in, 2 in. jaw	$34.49
(order)	Model WS30, 30 in, 3 in. jaw	$79.99

Available in five sizes, click to order:				
	model	length, in	jaw, in	price
(order)	WS09	9	3/4	$15.99
(order)	WS12	12	1	$18.99
(order)	WS15	15	1 1/2	$19.99
(order)	WS20	20	2	$34.49
(order)	WS30	30	3	$79.99

(a)   (b)

Figure 15.8   Evaluation in terms of a guideline: (a) before, (b) after applying guideline concerning visual groups (see subsection 'Problems in applying guidelines' above). Based on the design of Figure 12.11.

15.3.3 Contexts of guideline use

We come therefore to one of the most important aspects of guideline use, the matching of guidelines to the appropriate design context. This is the key to tracking down the guidelines that can solve the problem at hand, and to applying them in a way that suits this context. For this reason, collections of guidelines are generally organized according to context of use, and the remainder of this chapter is organized in the same way.

Matching the guideline to the design problem
Every guideline is suited to helping solve design problems of a particular kind, and is less well suited to other kinds of problems. Thus the guidelines we discuss in this chapter are suited to designing problems in interactive system design; this is the *overall context* to which they apply. They apply less well to problems in industrial design, and not at all to the design of bridges and earth-filled dams. Most guidelines are even more selective than this: they apply to particular interaction styles, for example, or to user interface components. According to the kinds of problems they suit, there is a range of problems for which they are less well suited.

For example, the well-known guideline, 'Minimize depth in favour of breadth', applies to menu-based interaction, but not necessarily to the design of overlapping windows or of database searches. The guideline, 'Use an output rate of approximately 180 words per minute', applies to voice-based interaction but not to the display of text.

We need to select guidelines whose context of use overlaps with the problem we are trying to solve. We can do this by checking each of the components of the problem statement, as defined in Chapter 2:

(1)   Is the guideline appropriate to the **activity** that the design is to support?

(2)   Is it applicable to the type of **user** who will perform the activity?

1

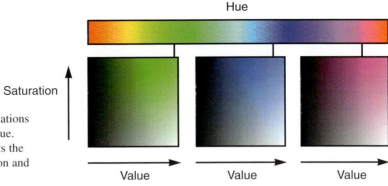

Hue

Saturation

Value Value Value

Plate 1 Effects of variations in hue, saturation and value. Each of the squares shows the effect of varying saturation and value while keeping hue constant.

2(a) 2(b)

3498	Brown, Peter
3467	Carroll, Henry P.
2233	Ericsson, Sol
3412	Goldberg, Tony
7077	Heitmeyer, Herman
7076	Ishida, Hiro
3497	Kawasaki, Toru
3499	Lebrun, Pierre
2017	Ng, Desmond
7071	Reisen, Pik
3866	Saraswat, K.K.
4444	Szczur, Amy
1974	Tutu, Jonas
1133	Wang, Chu
3423	Barberris, Santiago
1433	Xu, Lixia

Plate 2 Use of colours to differentiate between items: (a) too many colours; (b) five colours, the recommended maximum.

3(a) 3(b)

3498	Brown, Peter
3467	Carroll, Henry P.
2233	Ericsson, Sol
3412	Goldberg, Tony
7077	Heitmeyer, Herman
7076	Ishida, Hiro
3497	Kawasaki, Toru
3499	Lebrun, Pierre
2017	Ng, Desmond
7071	Reisen, Pik
3866	Saraswat, K.K.
4444	Szczur, Amy
1974	Tutu, Jonas
1133	Wang, Chu
3423	Barberris, Santiago
1433	Xu, Lixia

Plate 3 The use of colours to indicate staff levels: (a) arbitrary colours assigned to levels; (b) staff levels indicated by position in the spectral order.

Plate 4   The use of different cursor colours: (a) yellow, hard to follow; (b) red, easier to follow.

Plate 5   The effect of high-saturation colours: (a) distracting effect of placing high-saturation colours adjacent to each other; (b) avoidance of this effect by placing them on a neutral background.

The battery level indicators at the bottom of this page show that blue is better than red for items that will be viewed on the periphery; the effect can be seen best when focusing on this caption.

4(a)

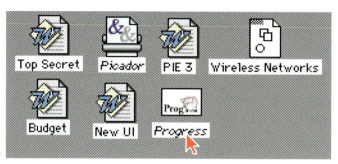

4(b)

5(a)

🟩	3498	Brown, Peter
🟦	3467	Carroll, Henry P.
🟥	2233	Ericsson, Sol
🟧	3412	Goldberg, Tony
🟨	7077	Heitmeyer, Herman
🟦	7076	Ishida, Hiro
🟩	3497	Kawasaki, Toru
🟩	3499	Lebrun, Pierre
🟥	2017	Ng, Desmond
🟥	7071	Reisen, Pik
🟥	3866	Saraswat, K.K.
🟧	4444	Szczur, Amy
🟩	1974	Tutu, Jonas
🟥	1133	Wang, Chu
🟩	3423	Barberris, Santiago
🟨	1433	Xu, Lixia

5(b)

🟩	3498	Brown, Peter
🟦	3467	Carroll, Henry P.
🟥	2233	Ericsson, Sol
🟧	3412	Goldberg, Tony
🟨	7077	Heitmeyer, Herman
🟦	7076	Ishida, Hiro
🟥	3497	Kawasaki, Toru
🟩	3499	Lebrun, Pierre
🟥	2017	Ng, Desmond
🟥	7071	Reisen, Pik
🟥	3866	Saraswat, K.K.
🟧	4444	Szczur, Amy
🟩	1974	Tutu, Jonas
🟥	1133	Wang, Chu
🟥	3423	Barberris, Santiago
🟨	1433	Xu, Lixia

1 hr 30 min

1 hr 30 min

Plate 6 Colour coding of function keys: (a) unfamiliar colours; (b) familiar colours.

Plate 7 Catering for users with colour deficient vision: (a) two buttons that will be difficult for these users to tell apart; (b) the buttons made more distinguishable by adding markings.

Plate 8 The difference between the gamuts of a typical printer and a typical colour display. Significant regions of the display lie outside the printer's gamut; colours in these regions can be displayed but cannot be printed. A small range of colours can be printed but cannot be displayed. *Source:* Maureen C. Stone *et al*.

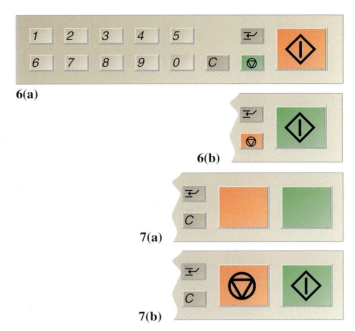

6(a)

6(b)

7(a)

7(b)

8

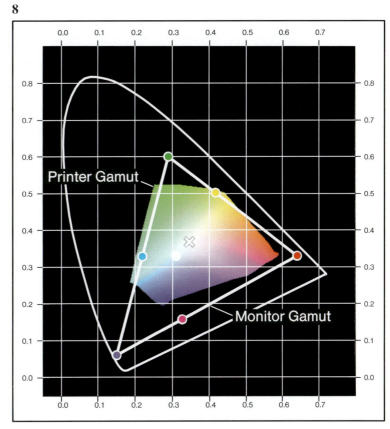

Plate 9   How the same specifications of colour may be rendered on different displays. *Source*: Lamming and Rhodes (1991)

(3)   Does it address the particular **levels of support** or **usability factors** that determine the success of the design?

(4)   Is it appropriate to the **form of solution** chosen?

By asking these kinds of questions, we can select those guidelines appropriate to the problem at hand. As we focus in on narrower problems, such as the design of components, we can narrow the range of guidelines that we apply.

Guideline categories

By looking at guidelines in this way, we can identify a number of different categories. There are far more such categories than a single chapter can cover. However, the following five contexts cover the spectrum of different types of guideline:

- **General principles** that apply to any user interface, more or less independently of the supported activity, the user, and the form of solution (see Section 15.4 below);

- Guidelines that apply to forms of solution for **interactive display layouts**, including those that use **colour** (Sections 15.6 and 15.7);

- Guidelines for use with specific **interaction styles** (Section 15.8);

- Sets of guidelines offered in **style guides** associated with proprietary systems and standards (Section 15.9);

- Guidelines for the design of individual **user interface components** supporting particular user tasks, for example, menus and icons (Section 15.9).

The rest of this chapter looks briefly at each of these levels of guideline use. Each section treats a particular category of guideline, and suggests ways to use them effectively in design.

15.4 General design principles

The fact that all interactive systems support human activity means that they all share certain properties, and achieve success by adhering to certain common rules. This is the source of a number of *general design principles*, applicable to virtually any problem in interactive system design. In terms of the context-checking questions above, these principles apply to the support of virtually any human activity, performed by anybody; they address the full range of usability factors and apply to virtually any form of solution.

15.4.1   General principles

A fundamental principle of interactive system design is the need to support the user's activity. Our concerns with aspects of the user interface are all part of our underlying concern to ensure that the user's task or process is performed quickly and well. We therefore need to design with an eye for *task compatibility*, as Mayhew puts it (Mayhew, 1992); with an understanding of the fundamental principles behind human action and performance (Norman, 1986). The need to design with a view to supporting human activity is so basic that it often gets left out of people's general principles or 'golden rules'. So it needs to be stated here at the outset:

- Design with a view to supporting the user's task or process.

A second principle relates to the need to address the concerns of the user. If we know who this user is, and have some familiarity with his or her special needs, we can orient our design strategy accordingly. But we often lack this understanding. A fundamental guideline to follow is Hansen's 'user engineering principle' (1971):

- Know the user.

By a combination of studying the users' activities and learning about their skills, knowledge, roles and responsibilities, we can design according to these two principles.

What other general principles should we apply during design? A number of writers have offered lists of design principles (Mayhew, 1992; Shneiderman, 1992; Hix and Hartson, 1993). The list of 'golden rules of dialogue design' proposed by Shneiderman is shown in Table 15.1.

Shneiderman's list includes some design principles with obvious links to usability factors. Thus the provision of short cuts improves speed of operation, feedback reduces errors and eases learning, and so on. These usability principles complement the principles of supporting the task and knowing the user. They cover the third component of problems in interactive system design: ensuring adequate levels of support to the user's activity.

But there are also some principles here whose links to usability are less obvious. The recommendation to *design dialogues to yield closure* relates to Norman's seven-stage cycle of interaction; in effect, it suggests building in closure points that signal the successful conclusion of a group of actions. Here the link to usability is made via a more fundamental model of human information processing. The same is true of the suggestion to *reduce short-term memory load*. The recommendation to *support internal locus of control* refers to the need to give users the sense that they are in charge – the *initiators* of actions rather than the *responders* (Gaines, 1981). These principles are less concerned with reminding us of usability factors, and more aimed at suggesting useful basic design strategies.

Table 15.1 General design principles: Shneiderman's golden rules of dialogue design (1992) and the evaluation heuristics suggested by Nielsen and Molich (1989).

Shneiderman	*Nielsen and Molich*
Strive for consistency.	Be consistent.
Enable frequent users to use short cuts.	Provide short cuts.
Offer informative feedback.	Provide feedback.
Design dialogues to yield closure.	
Offer simple error handling.	Good error messages.
Permit easy reversal of actions.	Provide clearly marked exits.
Support internal locus of control.	
Reduce short-term memory load.	Minimize user memory load.
	Simple and natural dialogue.
	Speak the user's language.
	Prevent errors.

We saw earlier that guidelines can be used in support of evaluation. In Table 15.1 we see a second set of principles drawn up for this very purpose – the evaluation heuristics of Nielsen and Molich, first introduced in Chapter 8. Almost all of these have direct links with usability, as we might expect from a set of principles chosen for this particular purpose. However, there is some overlap with the principles of the first column; in both cases the guidance is in the same general direction.

Choosing a set of general principles

Is one set of general principles better than another? In the main, yes, we are better off with a set of principles that relate directly to the support of the user's actions, that focus on the user, that remind us of key usability requirements, and that are derived directly from our knowledge about human resources and limitations. In this respect, lists like those in Table 15.1 are sound sources of guidance.

It is also the case that each and every designer has a preferred set of strategies and heuristics that 'work' for him or her personally. Thus one designer will find it particularly helpful to try to 'speak the user's language', while another will have found the principle 'permit easy reversal of actions' helpful.

In conclusion, therefore, the following four 'general principles of general principles' can be followed in drawing up a personal set of golden rules:

- Follow design principles that you can relate to supporting the user's task or process.

- Follow principles that you can easily relate to meeting the user's special needs.

- Follow principles that help you in meeting usability factors and that assist you in linking to knowledge about human resources and limitations.

- Adopt a set of principles that suits your personal approach to design.

15.5 An example: The design of the Economic Update system

At this point we will switch our attention to an example, the design of an Economic Update retrieval system. This problem was introduced in Chapter 6, and provided a basis for Chapter 7's dicussion of requirements definition. We return to it in order to experience the use of general design principles and of other categories of guideline to be discussed in the following sections.

15.5.1 The Economic Update problem

Let us recapitulate the Economic Update design problem. We saw the design team, working with economists from the Commission, come up with a one-sentence problem statement:

> Design a means of providing Commission economists with immediate access to economic updates, based on stored data, that reflect the recency of the data and the need for interpretation.

The purpose of the system is to support economists in the preparation of pre-contact notes and other documents. Each Economic Update is a short document covering recent economic trends and data concerning a particular country. Special display techniques, for example, highlighting and emphasis, are to be used to indicate recency and reliability of data in the updates. The design has now reached the form shown in Figure 15.9: it provides a menu of countries (Figure 15.9(a)), from which the user can make a selection in order to view the country's update (Figure 15.9(b)).

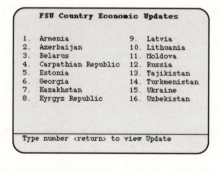

(a)

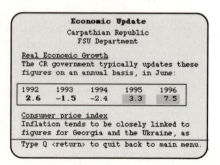

(b)

Figure 15.9   The design of the Economic Update system, as developed in Chapter 6: (a) the main menu of countries; (b) an example of an update.

15.5.2   Applying general principles

The solution already reflects some of the design principles discussed in Section 15.4. The nature of the economists' work processes has been factored into the design through study and analysis, and the inclusion of economists in the design team has helped the designers to get to know their users better.

Let us look at how some of the other general principles can be applied, e.g., Shneiderman's golden rule, 'Strive for consistency'. To pursue this point, we need to investigate what happens as the user reads through an update. Since updates may extend beyond one screenful, the user will need to scroll downwards through the text. Figure 15.10(a) shows how the update might appear while the user is halfway through reading it; we see that the title of the update, visible in Figure 15.9(b), has disappeared. The display is now inconsistent with both Figures 15.9(a) and 15.9(b) in this respect. To enable the user to see at all times what is being displayed, we can include a label field at the top of the screen as shown in Figure 15.10(b).

A second general principle we should apply is, 'Reduce short-term memory load'. The scroll-like display of Economic Updates places an extra load on the reader, because tables are separated by text and often cannot be viewed simultaneously. Thus the reader would have difficulty viewing economic growth figures together with inflation rates, and would have to rely on memory to compare figures from two tables. To solve this problem, we could provide an 'outline view' mode in which only section headings and tables would appear (Figure 15.11).

A more compact format even than this might be needed in order to minimize the system's load on short-term memory.

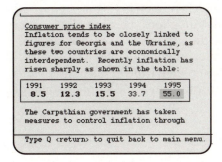
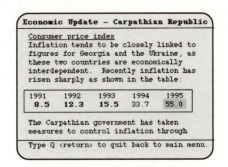

(a)   (b)

Figure 15.10   The Economic Update system's screen layout, (a) without a title, (b) with title added.

```
┌─────────────────────────────────────────────────┐
│ Economic Update - Carpathian Republic           │
│ Real Economic Growth                             │
│ ┌───────────────────────────────────────────┐   │
│ │ 1992    1993    1994    1995    1996       │   │
│ │ 2.6    -1.5    -2.4     3.3     7.5        │   │
│ └───────────────────────────────────────────┘   │
│ Consumer price index                             │
│ ┌───────────────────────────────────────────┐   │
│ │ 1991    1992    1993    1994    1995       │   │
│ │ 8.5    12.3    15.5    33.7    55.0        │   │
│ └───────────────────────────────────────────┘   │
│ Money supply                                     │
│ ┌───────────────────────────────────────────┐   │
│ │ 1991    1992    1993    1994    1995       │   │
│ └───────────────────────────────────────────┘   │
│ Type Q <return> to quit back to main menu.       │
│ Type F <return> to return to full text.          │
└─────────────────────────────────────────────────┘
```

Figure 15.11   Reducing the user's short-term memory load by allowing several tables to be displayed at once for comparison.

15.5.3   Applying other categories of guideline

A design project such as the Economic Update system will involve focusing on a large number of individual problems, varying in breadth and depth. By considering the nature of each problem, and asking ourselves the questions listed in Section 15.3.3, we can identify the types of guideline most likely to help us. This approach to guideline selection is illustrated in the next sections.

15.6   Guidelines for the design of effective displays

We have already seen an illustration, in Figure 15.8, of guidelines' ability to help in the design of screen layouts. This is one area where we can usually expect to benefit from guidelines, because almost every interactive application presents us with a problem in screen design. It is an area where aesthetics and graphic design principles have a particularly important role to play. This section reviews the kinds of guidelines available to help us with screen design problems, and applies some of them to the Economic Update system's design.

15.6.1   Screen design guidelines

Screen design guidelines include a number of helpful suggestions on how to design screen-based systems that are faster or less error prone in operation. These guidelines achieve their impact – that is, help improve usability – by suggesting ways to design screens that can be read more quickly or that are less likely to be misread. We will see some examples of how they do this. For a full discussion of such guidelines, see Tullis (1988), Marcus (1992) and Mayhew (1992), from whose writings most of these examples are taken.

15.6.2   Graphic design guidelines

Guidelines for graphic design of screen layouts have been presented by Marcus (1992) and by Tufte (1983, 1990). These guidelines have a different flavour from those just described, for they draw on experience and aesthetics rather than on psychological research. They attempt to teach through advice and suggestions what is normally learned in schools of design.

Some of Marcus' most valuable suggestions cover the design of layered displays, such as systems of overlapping panels and windows. Here the screen designer has the challenging task of finding an effective way of distinguishing overlapping objects. He suggests a number of depth cues, such as drop shadows, gradually changing texture, perspective, and so on (Marcus, 1992).

15.6.3   Applying screen design guidelines to the Economic Update application

The Economic Update design presents us with a number of individual problems in screen design, all of which are likely to take the form:

Design the layout of the screen to support rapid, error-free reading of ... [type of information] by economist users.

The problem statement reflects our constant concern to speed up task performance and reduce errors by effective screen design. The guidelines we use address these concerns; some offer advice on screen design in general, some apply to specific types of displayed data, such as graphics or tables of numbers.

Some general guidelines on display layout have been proposed by Tullis (1988), on the basis of extensive research into display designs for improved readability. He makes the overall point that users' task performance generally improves with reduction in the *density* of displayed information, that is, with the proportion of the screen that the information covers. An obvious way to tap into this source of usability is to avoid presenting unneeded information that would increase density. Hence the following general principle:

● Present only what is necessary for the activity's performance.

A more specific principle emerging from Tullis' research concerns the need to design in terms of visual grouping. If two items are too close together they will fuse into one visual group, and if the members of a group are too far apart they will form separate groups. These factors affect how fast information can be scanned, and lead to the following guideline:

- Assist associations between items by placing them within 5 degrees' visual angle of each other

This guideline can be used in conjunction with the guideline illustrated in Figure 15.8. Some examples of its use in the Economic Update application are illustrated in Figure 15.12. Figure 15.12(a) complies with both guidelines; Figure 15.12(b) involves large groups in which the

Lending country	Total debt, US$	Schedule	Rate
Azerbaijan	12,673,119	96 to 99	4.30
Belarus	35,122,703	99 to 02	3.35
Georgia	4,716,000	95 to 97	5.00
Kyrgyz Republic	801,339	98 to 99	4.40
Latvia	18,773,101	97 to 01	6.04
Ukraine	104,336,000	99 to 02	2.55

(a)

```
Azerbaijan    12,673,119    96 to 99    4.30
Belarus    35,122,703    99 to 02    3.35
Georgia    4,716,000    95 to 97    5.00
Kyrgyz Republic    801,339    98 to 99    4.40
Latvia    18,773,101    97 to 01    6.04
Ukraine    104,336,000    99 to 02    2.55
```

(b)

Azerbaijan	12,673,119	96	to	99	4.30
Belarus	35,122,703	99	to	02	3.35
Georgia	4,716,000	95	to	97	5.00
Kyrgyz Republic	801,339	98	to	99	4.40
Latvia	18,773,101	97	to	01	6.04
Ukraine	104,336,000	99	to	02	2.55

(c)

Figure 15.12   Spacing of groups: (a) reducing the number of visual groups to the minimum (four) for minimum search time; (b) lack of vertical alignment leads to formation of one large visual group; (c) large spacing leads to additional visual groups.

```
Cabinet minisiters: V. A. Vanov
   (Prime Minister), T. Y.
   Karaskinov (Foreign Minister),
   I. P. Rumanov (Minister of
   Finance), G. I. Karalyn (Home
   Affairs), A. B. Grevitska
   (Minister of Culture), ...
```

```
Cabinet minisiters:
   V. A. Vanov          Prime Minister
   T. Y. Karaskinov     Foreign Minister
   I. P. Rumanov        Minister of Finance
   G. I. Karalyn        Home Affairs
   A. B. Grevitska      Minister of Culture
```

(a)   (b)

Figure 15.13   Text presented (a) as running horizontal text, (b) more readable in vertical columns.

individual items are hard to locate; and Figure 15.12(c) involves unduly widely spaced group members, which tend to be seen as separate components. These guidelines apply equally to text and graphic items.

Other guidelines have been developed by Tullis more specifically for text displays, e.g.:

- Present lists in vertical columns rather than running horizontal text.

This guideline draws attention to the common mistake of running together lists of text items that are scanned much more easily if laid out in a vertical list. Figure 15.13 illustrates the guideline's use.

We might also find a use for graphic design guidelines in the Economic Update application if, for example, we were to use a more elaborate user interface allowing one table to overlay another. Figure 15.14 shows the kind of problem that arises in differentiating tabular data, and illustrates the use of drop shadows to alleviate the problem.

17.34	6.68	8.50
19.34	1.45	0.53
17.20	3.75	4.43
99.52	24.75	5.92
104.02	19.87	2.37

17.34	6.68	8.50
19.34	1.45	0.53
17.20	3.75	4.43
99.52	24.75	5.92
104.02	19.87	2.37

(a)   (b)

Figure 15.14   Overlaid tables (a) without, (b) with drop shadows.

15.7 Guidelines for the use of colour

Guidelines for the use of colour are of increasing importance as colour displays become increasingly widespread. Problems in effective screen design frequently turn out to involve making effective use of colour. We have a particular need here for guidance, because questions of colour are rarely a matter of simply applying common sense or intuition. For example, what colour would we use for an indicator light embedded in a shift-lock key on a keyboard, indicating that it is pressed down? Would red or green be better than yellow or blue? Rather than guess at the answers to these kinds of questions, as manufacturers have sometimes done in the past, we should study colour guidelines and see what they can tell us.

We will start with a brief summary of colour terminology, and then review a number of colour guidelines. Several of these guidelines turn out to be useful in dealing with problems in the design of a colour-display version of the Economic Update system. The examples are illustrated in Plates 1 to 9; some are also shown in the text in monochrome.

15.7.1 Colour terminology

Many modern computer displays are capable of displaying millions of different colours. We can specify any one of these colours in terms of three properties, shown in Plate 1:

- **Hue**, that is, the place of the colour in the spectrum, from red to violet. Hue is measured in terms of spectral wavelength.

- **Saturation** or **chroma**, which measures the purity of the colour. As saturation approaches zero, colours turn to shades of grey.

- **Value** or **intensity**, that is, the darkness of the colour. As value approaches zero, displayed colours turn to black.

The human eye perceives images with the aid of *rod* and *cone* photo-receptors in the retina. Only cones are sensitive to colour, and most of them are in the central region of the eye, or *fovea*.

15.7.2 Choice of colours

Two colour guidelines, from Marcus (1992), help us in choosing appropriate colours for differentiating and ordering items:

- For item differentiation, use a maximum of five colours (plus or minus two) to match the user's short-term memory capacity.

- For item ordering, follow the spectral order: red, orange, yellow, green, blue, indigo, violet.

In Plate 2(a) we see a list of names of staff members of the Commission, where the Economic Update system is used; a different colour has been used for each nationality represented, far too many to remember. Plate 2(b) uses five colours to represent European, Asian, African and North and South American nationals. In Plate 3 we see colour assigned to staff levels; in Plate 3(a) there is no attempt to correlate colours with levels, whereas Plate 3(b) shows seniority by position in the spectral order.

15.7.3   Colour vision limitations

Other guidelines can assist us in designing within the limitations of normal colour vision. Since the majority of cone photoreceptors are in the central region of the eye we must take care how we use colour for large areas of the screen such as backgrounds. Red and green cones are especially scarce in the peripheral region, while blue cones are scarce in the centre, and the following guideline reflects these limitations:

- Use red and green within the eye's central focusing area, and avoid relying on them on the periphery.

This guideline is illustrated in Plate 4. In Plate 4(a) we see a yellow cursor, less easy to follow than the red cursor of Plate 4(b). At the top of the same page we see alternative designs for a battery-level indicator, in which red is incorrectly chosen, on the left, to alert the user to the need to recharge or switch off. A better choice is blue (or yellow), as shown on the right.

Some further useful guidelines exist for the use of of high-saturation colours:

- Avoid use of extreme changes of hue in adjacent high-saturation colours.
- Use familiar colour codings, for example, red for stop or danger, green for go.

These are illustrated in Plates 5 and 6. Plate 5(a) illustrates the distracting effect of adjacent, high-saturation colours, which is avoided in Plate 5(b). In Plate 6 we see how the transposition of familiar colours on a photocopier's control panel increase the risk that the controls will be confused.

15.7.4   Colour vision impairment

The following guideline on colour screen design is an important one, because about eight per cent of male users have some impairment in colour vision:

- Use additional coding methods, for example, shape, size or texture, to cater for users with colour-deficient vision.

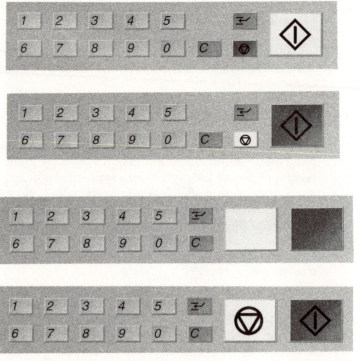

Figure 15.15   Dealing with vision impairments: labelling copier button colours to avoid reliance on colour. The upper pair of designs, from Plate 6, are indistinguishable by a seriously impaired user. The lower pair of designs, from Plate 7, illustrate how labelling can assist the impaired user.

We cannot rely exclusively on colour to distinguish between items on the screen, because these people will have difficulty in telling them apart. Therefore we may need to introduce redundancy, adding texture or labelling as shown in Plate 7 and in Figure 15.15, to help the user distinguish between different items.

15.7.5   Accuracy in colour rendering

All of the colour guidelines offered so far have focused on the question, 'Which colour or colours will achieve the desired effect?' Unfortunately the problem of colour selection is not as simple as this, because we cannot rely on the hardware of the interactive system to deliver the chosen colour to the user. We cannot be sure, for example, that the light green colour we have chosen for an on-screen printer control panel will always have the hue, saturation and value that we chose. The button may appear muddy green on some displays, yellow on others, grey on others still. If we print a picture of the control panel, the button may come out brown.

The guideline we must follow to limit the risk of these occurrences is as follows:

- Use colour in such a way that you can be sure that the effects will be achieved despite normal differences in colour rendering by displays and printers.

The term *rendering* is used here to apply to the mechanism by which coded information is transformed into a visible image. As Plate 8 shows, the *gamut* of colours that a printer can produce is typically much more limited than that of a colour monitor. Colours that lie outside the printer's gamut but within the monitor's are colours that can be displayed but not hard-copied. At the same time, there are some small regions of the printer gamut that the monitor cannot reproduce.

The implication of this guideline is that we should understand the likely degree of variation among the different display devices that will be used when our system is in operation. We should not rely on precise colour values, or expect users to be able to distinguish between similar colours, if rendered colours are likely to vary widely. Some of the problems that may arise are illustrated in Plate 9. For further discussion of this issue, see Lamming and Rhodes (1990).

15.8 Guidelines in support of interaction styles

As we saw in Chapter 12, adoption of a particular interaction style means that we can take advantage of know-how relating to the style we have selected. By committing to a particular style we define the design problem more narrowly: a problem statement of the form 'Design an interactive system...' is transformed into 'Design a form fill-in system...' or 'Design a direct-manipulation system...'. We narrow the context of design to a point where we can take advantage of guidelines that apply to the particular style we have chosen.

15.8.1 The contribution of research

Not only are there a lot of style-specific guidelines, but many of them are backed up by empirical research. This is especially true of interaction styles that have a strong influence on the user's sequence of actions, for example, voice-based interaction or forms fill-in. Here the researcher is able more easily to hold constant those variables that might interfere with experiments, and take samples that show significant results. The results lead in turn to the discovery and publishing of guidelines (Newman, 1995).

The overall effect of this style-specific research has been to build up quite substantial bodies of knowledge in certain design contexts. Research into forms fill-in, for example, has given us guidelines not just about form-filling in general, but about designing fields and captions on forms, and about choosing data entry formats (Mayhew, 1992).

Guidelines for menu-based systems

Another context where we find a relatively good supply of guidelines is the design of menu-based systems, that is, of systems like our Economic Update retrieval system. Guidelines on menu-based interaction draw not only on the more obvious common-sense fruits of experience, as in the 'Facilitate backwards navigation' guideline quoted earlier; they also present some less obvious research findings. Miller's well-known discovery concerning menu hierarchy is a good example of a design guideline that we might never discover through our own experience:

- Prefer broad and shallow to narrow and deep.

The wording here is Shneiderman's (1992), based on the original research conducted by Miller (1981). Miller tested a range of menu hierarchies on users, each one containing 64 possible choices but varying in depth (1–6 levels) and breadth (64 down to 2 choices per level). He found that selection times and error rates were least for two levels with eight choices per level. His findings might be useful if we were building a worldwide Economic Update system, covering a hundred or more national economies rather than under a dozen. We would be inclined to use a two-level menu hierarchy, as shown in Figure 15.16(c), rather than the over-shallow and over-deep hierarchies of Figures 15.16(a) and 15.16(b) respectively.

Guidelines for graphical direct manipulation

By way of contrast, guidelines to help us design graphical direct-manipulation interfaces are in short supply. Controlled experiments are harder to conduct here, because direct-manipulation systems place relatively few constraints on users' task sequences. It is relatively hard to design an experiment in which the task is externally valid *and* in which nuisance variables are kept under control.

One aspect of direct manipulation that has been reasonably thoroughly researched, however, is the design of icons. Indeed some of the very earliest research into the design of graphical desktops was oriented towards the choice of icon designs (Verplank, 1988). A more recent example of icon research is the document-retrieval study by Byrne (1993) indicating that simple pictorial icon designs are preferable to blank icons or complex icons. If we were to adopt a direct-manipulation interface for the Economic Update system, we might find Byrne's results useful (Figure 15.17).

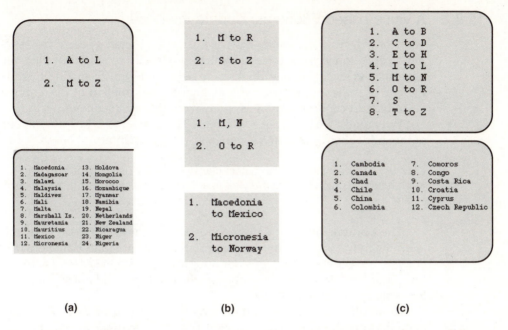

(a)   (b)   (c)

Figure 15.16   Menu hierarchies: (a) excessively wide and shallow hierarchy; (b) too tall and narrow; (c) two-level hierarchy, eight menus of roughly twelve items each.

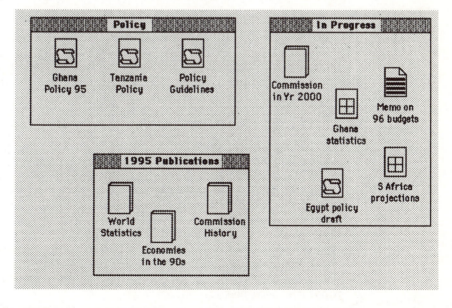

Figure 15.17   An icon-based Economic Update system, using simple icons as recommended by Byrne (1993).

15.8.2   A voice-based Economic Update interface

Voice-based systems, using recorded or synthesized speech and tele-phone-style touch pads, have become popular only recently, but there are nevertheless some useful guidelines to help us design them. To illustrate the use of these guidelines, we will explore the problem of designing a voice-based Economic Update system accessible by telephone.

Why might we build such a system? The answer is to be found in one of the guidelines quoted at the very start of this chapter:

● Consider voice synthesis as an output device when the user's eyes are busy, when mobility is required, or when the user has no access to a workstation or screen.

The Commission staff's mission responsibilities keep them frequent-ly on the move and unable to connect to the Commission's data network. For this reason we might consider supporting voice-based access to the Economic Update system, even though the need for it did not surface dur-ing systems analysis and design.

A simple voice-based solution would offer the user the same infor-mation as presented in Figures 15.9(a) and 15.11. In other words, the user dialling into the system would first be presented with a list of countries, and on selecting a country would hear the headings and data. Mayhew (1992) offers two guidelines for designing the wording of the messages:

● In a prompting message, present the goal first and the action afterwards.

● In a message of predictable form whose purpose is to provide variable informa-tion, place this information at or near the start of the message.

The wording of the initial list and update information might be as shown in the example of Figure 15.18. We can see that the first of these

---

On dialling the system:
Welcome to the Commission's Economic Update system.
For the Azerbaijan update, press one; for Byelorus, press two; for Carpathia, press three; for Estonia, press four; for Georgia, press five; for Kazakhstan, press six; for Latvia, press seven; for more countries, press eight; to repeat this message, press nine.
User presses '3'.
To exit from this message, press zero. Carpathia economic growth, 1992 to 1996, [confident voice] two point six, minus one point five, [normal voice] minus two point four, [uncertain voice] three point three, seven point five. Consumer price index, ...

Figure 15.18   Voice-based interface to the Economic Update system.

guidelines has a strong influence on the choice of words. The second guideline, which applies to wordings such as 'Three new voice messages in your mailbox', is less relevant here.

The weakness of this design lies in the lengthy second message, which might keep the user waiting for a minute or more for a particular item of information. Accordingly, the second message might be divided up into shorter messages accessed via a second-level menu, as shown in Figure 15.19.

Two further guidelines, from Mayhew (1992), would enable the user to proceed more quickly through the data, and to deal with poor-quality telephone lines:

- Provide a means of skipping the remainder of partially heard messages.

- Provide a means of repeating messages.

Message-skipping can be supported merely by allowing commands to be entered as soon as the announcement begins. To provide the 'repeat' function an extra key, for example, '#', would need to be dedicated to it, and the user would need to be told about it. Figure 15.20 shows the use of skipping and repeating.

Finally, we would find this guideline useful in estimating the speed of retrieval of information:

- Use an output rate of approximately 180 words per minute.

At 180 words per minute, the second message in Figure 15.19 (*'Carpathia economic growth...'*) would take about fifteen seconds to recite. If we know how long messages take to play we can estimate task performance times and optimize the design of messages.

User presses '3' after initial message.
To exit from this message, press zero. For Carpathia economic growth, press one; for consumer price index, press two; for money supply, press three; for sector data, press four.
User presses '1'.
Carpathia economic growth, 1992 to 1996, [confident voice] two point six, minus one point five, [normal voice] minus two point four, [uncertain voice] three point three, seven point five. For more data, press one; to return to the country list, press two.
User presses '1'.
For consumer price index, press two; for money supply, press three; for...

Figure 15.19   Adding a second level of hierarchy to the voice-based interface to reduce the length of messages.

On dialling the system:
Welcome to the ...
User presses '3' to skip rest of message.
To exit from ...
User presses '1'.
Carpathia economic growth, 1992 to 1996, [confident voice] two point six, minus one point five, [normal voice] minus two point four, [uncertain voice] three point three, seven point five. For more data, press ...
User presses '#' to repeat message.
Carpathia economic growth, 1992 to 1996, [confident voice] two point six, minus one point five, [normal voice] minus two point four, [uncertain voice] three point three, seven point five. For more data, press ...
User hangs up.

Figure 15.20   The voice-based interface in the hands of an expert user, making use of 'skip' amd 'repeat' capabilities.

15.9 The use of style guides

This chapter has looked at a succession of design contexts and at the types of guidelines available in each context. Each context has had the effect of limiting the range of guidelines we need to consider. This final section discusses a type of design context in which we are especially likely to find ourselves – the context of designing according to a 'house style', to a standard or to a software developer's style guide. The design problems we face here are likely to be stated as follows:

Design an application for the Apple Macintosh ...
Design a system to run in the Microsoft Windows environment ...
Design a system using the OSF/Motif windowing system ...
Design a database to be accessed via the World Wide Web ...

The problem statement may even call for a style-independent solution:

Design a system to run under any of the major windowing environments ...

Problems in style-independent design represent an especially severe test of user interface design skill, and lie beyond the scope of this chapter. It is worthwhile, however, to look briefly at the kinds of information provided in style guides and at the kinds of assistance they provide to design. This section looks first at a fairly simple example, the NCSA Style Guide for designing documents to be accessed via the World Wide Web (Berners-Lee *et al.*, 1994), and then at guides on graphical 'desktop' windowing styles.

15.9.1 Style guidelines for the World Wide Web

We have had a brief introduction to the World Wide Web in Section 12.4.3. The 'Web' is a worldwide hypertext system, connecting users to hypertext documents via the Internet. It is an exciting recent development in interactive computing, important partly because of its very rapid growth in user population (usage has tended to double every four months) and partly because of its reliance on a consistent style of user interface, supported by standard languages and communication protocols.

Rapid growth in Web usage has been matched by the growth in information added to the Web. This in turn has created an important role for style guidelines on preparation of hypertext documents in general, and Web documents in particular. Good examples of each can be found in Shneiderman (1992) and Berners-Lee *et al.* (1994).

Example: Putting Economic Updates on the Web

To illustrate the application of Web style guidelines, let us explore what it would mean to put Economic Updates onto the Web. This is perhaps an unusual way to make available the kinds of confidential information included in Updates. There are mechanisms for ensuring security, however, and Web technology is indeed attracting attention as a basis for sharing private information. An advantage of using the Web is its support for a wide range of data types, including text, graphics, images, audio and video.

Authoring a hypertext document is different from normal authoring in some fundamental ways, as Shneiderman points out. A major challenge is to create a structure of linked documents that the reader can navigate successfully, without getting lost. As Shneiderman puts it, we must *ensure that meaningful structure comes first*. In the words of Berners-Lee *et al.*:

- It helps readers to have a tree structure as a basis for the book: it gives them a feeling of knowing where they are.

In the Economic Update system, therefore, we would probably retain a structure similar to the two- or three-level menu structure used in the earlier designs. We would need to organize the material into suitably-sized linked documents. Shneiderman reminds us to *respect chunking* and suggests 'chunks' that deal with one topic, theme or idea, less than 10 000 words in length. Berners-Lee *et al.* propose the following guides for document size on the Web:

- For on-line help, and for menus giving access to other things: small enough to fit onto 24 lines.

- For textual documents, of the order of half a letter-sized (A4) page up to five pages.

A set of pages from the Web-based Economic Update system, based on these guidelines, is shown in Figure 15.21.

15.9.2   Style guides for windowing environments

Windowing environments provide software developers with pre-coded interactive components, and with means for interconnecting these components in order to build *integrated* applications supporting a range of functions. Without these environments, the development of integrated applications would involve so much effort that they might never get built. But each windowing environment, while assisting design, imposes its own design conventions, and designers must learn what these conventions are and how to follow them. This, as Hix and Hartson have pointed out, is the essential role of style guides (Hix and Hartson, 1993).

Styles guides need to provide information of three main kinds:

(1)   **General principles** of user interface design, similar to those discussed in Section 15.4;

(2)   **Global rules**, usually fairly few in number, applying to the entire user interface;

(3)   **Design guidelines for components**, usually very numerous and making up the bulk of the style guide.

How do we make use of this information? The *general principles* are always well worth reading at the outset, even if some of them may seem familiar. What makes them special is the amount of real-world experience they encapsulate – the developers of windowing systems work directly with the designers of packaged software and come to know a great deal about the factors that underlie successful design. The 'Philosophy' section introducing the Apple Human Interface Guidelines is a good example (Apple, 1987).

Global rules need to be understood thoroughly before we tackle the detailed design of an interactive system. They cover such matters as the conventions for use of mouse buttons, assignments of text editing keys, general methods of selecting objects on the screen, pointer shapes, and so on. We may have gained familiarity with much of this material just through prior use of the windowing system, but there will always be details that we have missed. We need to gain complete familiarity with the environment's global design rules, because the system we design must be fully compatible with them.

The material on *components* and their design usually begins with an overview of the range of components available: windows, menus, icons, control panels and dialogue boxes, alerts, and so on. In this overview, guidelines are offered for choosing the appropriate component for the job. Here, for example, are some quotes from OPEN LOOK's style guide (Sun, 1991):

```
┌─────────────────────────────────────────────────────────────────────┐
│ ▽                        NCSA Mosaic: Document View                   │
├─────────────────────────────────────────────────────────────────────┤
│  File   Options   Navigate   Annotate                        Help    │
├─────────────────────────────────────────────────────────────────────┤
```

Document Title: FSU Economic Updates List

Document URL: file://localhost/tmp_mnt/home/newman/html/test/commission1.html

FSU Country Economic Updates

Updates are available for the following countries:

- Armenia
- Azerbaijan
- Belarus
- Carpathian Republic
- Estonia
- Georgia
- Kazakhstan
- Kyrgyz Republic
- Latvia
- Lithuania
- Moldova
- Russia
- Tajikistan
- Turkmenistan
- Ukraine
- Uzbekistan

Also, full back index available for FSU Economic Updates.

```
[Back] [Forward] [Home] [Reload] [Open...] [Save As...] [Clone] [New Window] [Close Window]
```

Figure 15.21   An Economic Update system in the style of the World Wide Web. NCSA Mosaic™ is copyrighted by and is property of the Board of Trustees of the University of Illinois.

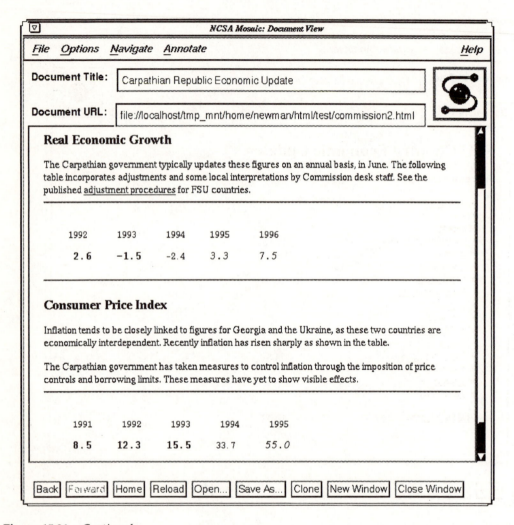

Figure 15.21   *Continued.*

Abbreviated buttons provide the same functionality as buttons but take up less space. Abbreviated buttons are small square buttons with no text label inside them.

Gauges are used to give a visual indication of how full or empty an object is or to show what percentage of a job is complete.

The *base window* is the primary window in which you present your application.

Each base window must have its own *icon*.

A *notice* is a special type of pop-up window used by the application to inform users of important conditions or to inform them that a serious error has occurred.

Following the overview are the detailed descriptions that specify the exact behaviour of each component and provide guidelines on configuring them for the application.

15.9.3   Designing the components of windowed applications

The components of windowed applications are sometimes known as *widgets*. They have also been called *design algorithms*, in the sense that they are design rules encapsulated in runnable software (Smith, 1986).

Style guides include large amounts of advice and guidance on designing widgets. In many cases these can be viewed as results of usability analysis rather than experience or research; the well-defined sequences of operation of widgets make analysis relatively easy. For example, we find the following guidelines in the style guide for Microsoft Windows (Microsoft, 1992):

- Dragging to a submenu item requires extra coordination to negotiate the change in direction.

- Accessing the submenu item by means of mouse clicks requires an extra click and a change in mouse direction.

Our task, in designing an interactive application, is not so much to design these components as to customize them or configure them to suit our requirements. To do so, we need to understand two aspects of the component's design.

First, we need to gain a thorough understanding of the component's built-in user interface. This is almost always more complex than apparent on the surface. We saw an example of how complex even the simplest widget can be in Chapter 11's description of the user interface of Macintosh check boxes. Other widgets, such as pull-down and drop-down menus, involve much lengthier descriptions; for example, the description of Windows drop-down menus in Figure 15.22 covers only the way simple menus are made to appear with the mouse; it does not

5.3.1.1.1 Displaying Drop-Down Menus. To display a drop-down menu, the user uses the mouse to point to the menu title and presses the mouse button. This procedure highlights the title and opens the menu. If the user releases the button while the pointer is still on the menu title, the menu remains open so that the pointer can be moved to the desired menu item. Alternatively, the pointer can be moved to the item while the button is still held down. If the user moves the pointer to a second menu title before releasing the button, the first menu closes and the second menu opens. This lets users switch easily from one menu to another or see an overview of all menus by dragging the mouse across the menu bar. If the user drags the pointer out of a menu frame to any other location than a menu title, the menu remains open. However, if the user then releases the mouse button outside the menu frame, the menu closes without initiating any commands.

Figure 15.22   Detailed description of basic mouse-operated menu display in Microsoft Windows (Microsoft, 1992). Details of cascading menu display, keyboard operation and response to menu choice are not included here.

cover cascading menus (see Figure 15.3), nor does it describe what happens when a menu choice is made. It also omits details of how menu selection is made via the keyboard, an important capability of Windows (Microsoft, 1992). Yet we need to understand these details in full because, again, this is the user interface that we will be customizing.

The second step in understanding how to work with these components is to become familiar with the relevant design rules and guidelines. Most style guides are extremely thorough in documenting this material, and we may not want to learn it by heart. The next section illustrates how we can apply rules and guidelines in the course of setting up the drop-down menus for a Windows-based version of the Economic Update system.

15.9.4   Designing drop-down menus for a windowed Economic Updates system

When we follow rules and guidelines for designing with widgets, we are working in a particularly narrow design context. Our problem statement will typically take the form, 'Design a set of menus for a Windows-based design for ...'. In these narrow confines, we tend to use guidelines primarily to answer questions and to evaluate the design.

Why would we want to redesign the Economic Update system to make use of a windowing environment? The most likely reason is that the initial system has been a success, and there is now a demand to make it more widely available throughout the Commission. The new, extended user community will include people who are already using Windows for other purposes.

Responding to requests for new features

A second reason why we might choose to reimplement the Economic Update system for a windowing environment is in response to requests for additional features. These may be difficult to add to a simple menu-based system. Let us suppose the following suggestions have been made by users:

- It should be possible to keep two or more updates open on the screen at one time.

- It would be useful if just the text of the update could be displayed, without the tables, much like the existing display for tables and no text (see Figure 15.11).

- A Help facility would be useful.

- Sometimes it is important to know the identity of the author of text, or source of data.

- If parts of updates could be printed, instead of the whole document, there would be saving of time and paper.

Responding to this list of requests will involve a major design exercise. We will look just at the task of designing a set of menus for the new system. We will base our design around Microsoft Windows' drop-down menus, and make use of the Windows style guide (Microsoft, 1992).

The list of menu commands

Our first task is to make a list of all of the commands we will need to accommodate in the set of menus:

Open documents, even when there is a document currently displayed.

Print document.

Print selected part of document.

Show tables only as in the existing system, 'toggling' between the 'show tables' and 'hide tables' state.

Show text only as requested, also a toggling command.

Help.

We must also find a means of showing authors' names and data sources. One possible solution is the use of pop-up menus, which appear close to a selected item. However, we encounter the following advice in the style guide:

- Pop-up menus are designed primarily for mouse users

In other words, there is no means of operating pop-up menus from the keyboard. It is unwise to demand that users should operate the system with a mouse, just for the sake of two commands. So we decide to add two more toggling commands to our drop-down menus:

Show authors.

Show sources.

The menu structure

Now we are ready to assign commands to menus. The first step is to see whether any commands should be incorporated in standard menus. Some of the commands clearly belong in a **File** menu, following the style guide's recommendation:

- Applications that use data files should include a **File** menu, which provides all the commands the user needs to open, create, and save files.

The style guide's illustrative example also includes the **Print** command, and so we assign the following commands to the **File** menu:

Open document.

Print document.

Print selected part of document.

Exit from the Economic Update program.

The **Exit** command is added as an afterthought, to maintain consistency with other Windows applications. Another relevant standard menu is the **Help** menu, to which we assign the 'Help' command.

We are left with four toggling commands, **Show tables**, **Show text**, **Show authors** and **Show sources**. These are all of a similar nature, and so we include them in the same menu, which we give the title **Show**. This complies with two guidelines relating to titles:

- Titles for drop-down and cascading menus should represent the entire menu and should reveal as clearly as possible the purpose of all items on the menu.

- Each menu title should contain an underlined mnemonic access character that gives direct access through the keyboard. The access character should be (in suggested order of preference) the first letter of the menu title ... .

The four items in the **Show** menu fall into two groups of two, the first controlling the hiding or revealing of text and data, the second controlling the addition of author and source information. Therefore we divide the menu accordingly, as suggested in the following guideline:

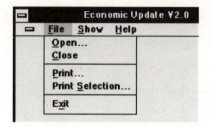
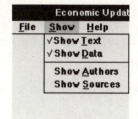
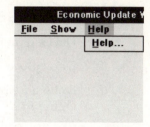

Figure 15.23   The design of menus for the Windows-based Economic Update system. Courtesy Microsoft Inc.

- Whenever a menu item contains items that fall into logical groups, the groups should be separated by a line.

We apply the same guideline to the choice of groups for the **File** menu. The final design for the set of menus is shown in Figure 15.23.

15.10   Conclusion

This chapter has explored a wide range of user interface design guidelines, and has illustrated their use on a number of design problems. It has shown how guidelines can help at various stages in the design. In so doing, it has provided a glimpse of how some of the **detailed design** of user interfaces is carried out. This is where much of the effort goes during the design of interactive systems.

The use of guidelines is not limited to detailed design, of course. Indeed guidelines have many uses, and can be used in a variety of ways, all the way from identifying design strategies to conducting heuristic evaluations. Sets of guidelines can also play a useful role in bringing together the fruits of research and the results of practical design experience – two bodies of knowledge that intersect less than they should.

As we have seen from the earlier chapters in this book, guidelines take their place alongside other design methods. These other methods include both analytical techniques and methods for synthesizing solutions. Some of them apply, like guidelines, to the detailed stages; others are more useful in the early stages, style-selection methods being an example. But there are serious gaps in the range of methods for analysis and synthesis. Guidelines help fill some of these gaps, and thus enable us to achieve success in the design of interactive systems.

Exercises

(1)   Devise a more compact outline format than Figure 15.11.

(2)   Draw process diagrams to illustrate the four roles of guidelines.

(3)   Draw an Object State Transition Chart to describe the user interface of Figure 15.23.

(4)   Would guideline B in Figure 15.1 apply to the original design for the Economic Update system? If so, modify the design to comply with the guideline.

Further reading

Mayhew D. J. (1992). *Principles and Guidelines in Software User Interface Design*. Englewood Cliffs, NJ: Prentice Hall

> A particularly thorough style-oriented text on user interface design, with several hundred guidelines presented under the headings of the appropriate styles. Research overviews provide useful background to the guideline material.

Apple Computer (1987). *Apple Human Interface Guidelines*. Addison-Wesley

> Includes a useful, concise set of general principles, plus advice and descriptive material on Macintosh 'widgets'.

Microsoft Corporation (1992). *The Windows Interface: An Application Design Guide*. Redmond WA: Microsoft Press

> The corresponding guideline book for Microsoft Windows, with detailed descriptions and discussions of interactive objects.

Byrne M. D. (1993). Using icons to find documents: Simplicity is critical. In *Proc. InterCHI '93 Human Factors in Computing Systems*, April 24–29, Amsterdam, Netherlands, pp. 446–53. New York: ACM/SIGCHI.

> Describes an investigation of the use of different styles of icon and their effect on ease of retrieval.

Designing a
human memory aid

Chapter objectives:

This purpose of this chapter is to illustrate the use of interactive design methods in an innovative project, the problem here being the design of a portable memory aid. The case study covers:

- The definition of the problem
- Preliminary studies of people's memory problems
- Early feasibility studies
- Establishment of some basic requirements
- The design of a prototype system, Forget-Me-Not.

B.1   Introduction

This case study describes the design of an innovative interactive system: a portable memory aid. The story here is rather different from the first case study, which described an attempt to make incremental improvements to a well-established solution. Here we are concerned with the solution of a hitherto unsolved design problem – overcoming people's difficulties in recalling events and retrieving 'lost' information. We follow the invention of a solution, the conduct of a number of early investigations, and the design and construction of a prototype. The activities described here were conducted by members of staff of the Rank Xerox Research Centre in Cambridge, UK, with the assistance of researchers from the Medical Research Council's Applied Psychology Unit in Cambridge. Some of the work was carried out in the Computer Science Laboratory of Xerox Corporation's Palo Alto Research Center in California.

The case of the portable memory aid illustrates virtually all of the methods described in this book. We shall see that studies and evaluations played a key role in helping to define the functional requirements of the eventual prototype. So too did methods of user interface design, especially when it came to choosing an appropriate mental model to present to the system's user. The story illustrates the degree to which innovative projects can stretch available methods to their limits.

The project also involved solving a number of problems in the design of system software, and it depended on the development of a small portable terminal. These two projects lie outside the scope of this book, and are therefore mentioned only in passing here.

What follows is of necessity a simplified account. Like any leading-edge research project, this one encountered dead ends, had lucky breaks, solved one problem when trying to solve another, did things in the wrong order, and had alternating periods of furious activity and relative calm. To tell the full story would take many more pages, and would involve explaining things that, in the end, had little influence on the eventual design. Instead this case study covers the principal stages of the project. Their chronological order, and the order in which they are discussed here, are shown in Figure B.1.

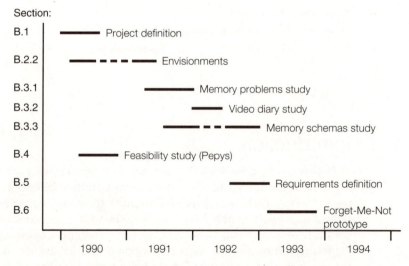

Figure B.1   The chronology of the project. Section numbers in this case study are shown along the vertical axis.

B.2 The design problem and its origins

The origins of this particular problem lie in a situation of very broad concern. The modern world places great demands on human memory, and to a large extent computer systems add to the demand rather than relieve it. They ask users to recall command sequences for a variety of different interactive systems, for example, and to remember the names under which they have filed away documents, perhaps many months or even years ago. As people come to rely on more and more systems, and store more and more information electronically, the burden on their memories must increase. There is a need to find ways to reverse this trend.

B.2.1 Defining the problem: Finding a form of solution

This is an example of a very broadly defined problem area. The basic design problem is fairly obvious: 'Design a system to help people remember things'. But there is no means of telling whether this is at all soluble. The problem needs to be narrowed down. One way to do this is to define the problem in terms of a more explicit form of solution.

Early in 1990 the project team hit upon a form of solution, involving the use of stored **context** to assist the user in retrieving information and recalling events. This idea came partly from studying the literature on human memory, and human *autobiographical memory* in particular (Rubin, 1986). According to psychological studies, people reconstruct the context of past events in order to recall the events themselves or to retrieve information concerning the event. For example, to remember where we put our reading glasses we may replay the sequence of events when we last used them; to remember who was at a farewell dinner party we may try to reconstruct the events at the restaurant (Reiser *et al.*, 1985).

Technological developments also contributed to the idea. The proposed form of solution lay in using computer technology to help build the essential context for recall and retrieval. This could be done by building a personal information system that could not only store the information to which the user might need access – documents, phone numbers, online help – but could also record the context in which access was made, for example, the phone number dialled after a document was retrieved.

In this way the system might be able to assist in answering questions of the form, 'Where's that document I discussed with Jenny on the phone last Tuesday?' Given the context, *before a phone call to Jenny*, it could present a list of the user's actions matching this description, including the retrieval of the document in question. A number of forms of contextual data could potentially be stored in the memory aid: the user's workstation activities and use of electronic mail, details of phone calls made and times when calls were received, use of card keys, and so on.

(a)

(b)

Figure B.2   Envisionments of the memory aid: (a) a simple cardboard mockup, (b) a sketch of a scenario suggesting how the memory aid might be used.
Courtesy Rank Xerox.

B.2.2   Envisioning the solution

It was not at all obvious what physical form such a memory aid would take. To assist in defining the problem, a variety of envisionments and scenarios were constructed. Some were built out of cardboard (Figure B.2(a)) while others took the form of cartoons illustrating how the memory aid might work (Figure B.2(b)). All of these helped to explain the idea and engage others in discussions of how the problem might be formulated and addressed.

The envisionments were particularly helpful in underlining the need to design a *portable* memory aid. It became obvious that problems in recall and retrieval could arise anywhere and at any time. If the system were available only in the user's office, it would be limited in its ability to help. Somehow, the system must be incorporated into a device small and light enough to carry around all the time.

In the course of these early envisionments the project team began also to understand better the kinds of memory problems such a system might help solve. By using stored context to help people find things and recall events, the system would reduce the user's reliance on explicit *indexing* of information, that is, attaching labels or filing in specific places. It would not be obligatory to give everything a carefully chosen name, for example, *memo-3-Jun-93-from-Bob-re-93-budget*. The system would be able to help find things that had simply been stored away anonymously. In other words, it could help in *unanticipated retrievals* of information, where the need for future retrieval had not been foreseen at the time the information was first stored.

B.2.3   The problem statement

The idea for the context-based approach, and the understanding gained from the early envisionments, assisted the project team in defining the design problem. After the fact, and using the notation of Chapter 2, we can state it as follows:

> Design a portable context-based system to enable people to recall events and retrieve information more easily, including events and information that they may not have realized they might need to access again.

This represents the project team's understanding of the problem towards the end of 1990. By this time several studies and prototyping activities were under way.

B.3   Preliminary studies of everyday memory

The activity that this interactive system was to support – recall and retrieval – is one of the most common human activities. People access their memories many thousand times a day. It should have been quite easy to study such a common activity, and there should have been plenty of prior studies to draw upon. However, the project team became aware at an early stage that the workings of human memory are hard to study because they are hard to observe. Furthermore, although psychologists have conducted a wide range of memory studies (see Baddeley, 1990), most of these have involved artificial activities in the laboratory, such as retrieving words from a memorized list, rather than situations in the real world.

There was a need to learn more about memory's support for 'everyday activities', and particularly for the routine activities of the workplace. Therefore several studies were undertaken, focusing on questions such as:

- What memory problems arise most often in the workplace, and which of them do people find most troublesome?

- What characterizes an 'event' that someone will remember?

- Of the events that occur during the working day, what kinds are people most likely to forget? What kinds of events are they most likely to retain, and use later as context for recall and retrieval?

Three separate studies were conducted. The first was a study of *memory problems at work* conducted with the aid of a questionnaire. The second involved recording the events of people's days on video. The third was based on a set of interviews, and led to two separate analyses, a classification of *basic work activities* and an analysis of people's use of *daily schemas* in recalling the events of the day.

B.3.1   The study of memory problems at work

The objective of the study of memory problems at work was to determine which problems people considered to be most frequent and most severe. It was conducted partly to help decide where to focus the project team's efforts, and partly to understand how frequently people might use a memory aid. A full report on the study can be found in Eldridge, Sellen and Bekerian (1992).

The study was conducted by issuing a simple questionnaire, listing about 20 types of memory problem, and asking subjects to rate them for frequency and severity. Each question had to be answered with a frequency rating for the problem's occurrence, ranging from 'never' to 'daily or more'. In addition, people were asked to indicate the three problems they considered to be the most severe.

The questionnaire was issued to about 400 people in an engineering organization, using the organization's e-mail system. Replies were received from 118 respondents. The results are summarized in Table B.1 and the questions are shown in Figure B.3 on pages 420–21. The questions are arranged in order of decreasing frequency, and scores are shown both

Table B.1   Results of memory lapse study, from Eldridge, Sellen and Bekerian (1992).

Question Number	Question	Mean Frequency Rating[a]	Severity[b]
5b	How often do you forget someone's name whom you have only met once or twice?	2.38	37
12	How often do you forget one or more items from a set of items you are holding in mind (e.g. a mental list of things to do or say)?	2.27	41
6a	How often do you forget where you put a paper document or book?	2.01	40
3	How often do you forget to take things with you, or leave things behind and have to go back for them?	2.00	27
7	How often do you have trouble remembering a particular word (i.e. when on the tip of your tongue)?	1.92	17
1	How often do you plan to do something or say you'll do something, and then completely forget about it until later?	1.87	37
2	How often do you start doing something, get interrupted, and then forget your previous activity?	1.79	19
6b	How often do you forget where you put some other physical object? [*i.e., not a document*]	1.70	14
10c	How often do you remember some fact or facts, but forget something important about who said it, where you read it, or where it came from?	1.62	7
6c	How often do you forget where you stored an electronic document or application on your computer?	1.61	22
11a	How often do you forget details of how to do something, even though you have done it once or twice before? [*i.e., on a computer*]	1.51	19
5a	How often do you forget someone's name whom you know well?	1.30	15
4	How often do you go somewhere to do something, then forget why you're there when you get there?	1.21	4
10a	How often do you forget something important about what was said in a conversation or meeting, but remember details about who was there, where it was, or when it took place?	1.17	14

Table B.1 *Continued.*

Question Number	Question	Mean Frequency Rating[a]	Severity[b]
11c	How often do you forget details of how to do something, even though you have done it once or twice before? [*i.e., not on a computer*]	1.01	3
10b	How often do you have trouble recalling important details of a conversation or meeting, such as who was there, or where or when it took place?	.97	6
9a	How often do you forget whether you have done something or not for some event that took place very recently?	.91	7
8	How often do you remember some information, and then find out later that it is incorrect?	.86	4
9b	How often do you forget whether you took part or took some action in a distant past event?	.74	1
11b	How often do you forget details of how to do something, even though you have done it many times before? [*i.e., on a computer*]	.59	1
11d	How often do you forget details of how to do something, even though you have done it many times before? [*i.e., not on a computer*]	.37	0

[a] Based on the following scale: 0 = never, 1 = rarely, 2 = monthly, 3 = weekly, 4 = daily.
[b] Numbers are the number of respondents (out of 118) indicating that problem as severe.

for frequency and for severity of the problem. Frequency scores are based on the use of a numeric scale to code responses (0 = never, 1 = less than monthly, 2 = monthly or more, 3 = weekly or more, 4 = daily or more). Severity scores indicate the number of people who marked the problem as severe for them.

The study indicated that the most frequent problems were a mixture of prospective memory lapses (that is, forgetting about future events) and retrospective memory lapses (forgetting about past events). The proposed system, which was aimed at helping with retrospective memory lapses, had the potential to help with five out of the ten most frequent problems, and six out of the ten most severe. The reported frequencies of problems were not high, but there was a lot of variation in the average frequency ratings of individuals, some of whom indicated they had problems at least once a week, while others indicated they rarely had memory problems of any kind.

B.3.2   The video-diary study

The second study took a very different approach, attempting to simulate the effect of technology in jogging people's memory. It focused on the potential of video recording. Three subjects volunteered to be videotaped continuously for an extended period; they were later interviewed to discover how well they could reconstruct the events of the period in question.

This study showed, not unexpectedly, that there was a marked drop-off in ability to reconstruct events over a period of four weeks. It also showed that playing back the video record was surprisingly effective in reminding subjects of what they were doing. The sight of a shopping bag, for example, acted as a reminder that the subject had been to the shoe repairer earlier in the day. So powerful was the video record as a memory aid that subjects were able to remember as much after four weeks *with* the video record as they could after one week *without* it (Eldridge, Lamming and Flynn, 1992).

B.3.3   The memory schemas study

The purpose of the third study was to understand how the system should describe events in people's working days, and how it should select events in order to present a recognizable sequence from some previous day. A complete report on the study can be found in Eldridge, Barnard and Bekerian (1994).

The project team needed to know how to display a sequence of past events to the user of the memory aid. During early feasibility studies, the team had experimented with descriptions such as the following:

10:00	Meeting with Department Director [16 mins]
10:16	Working on monthly report [25 mins]
10:41	Phoned Peter [3 mins]
10:44	Working on monthly report [8 mins]
10:52	Reading electronic mail [35 mins]
11:27	Visited Kitchen [2 mins]
11:29	Talking to Frances in her office [21 mins]
11:50	Returned to office, phoned home [3 mins]
11:53	Thunderstorm, workstation crashed [30 secs]

But how realistic were these descriptions? What types of events did people actually use to describe their own working days? If these questions could be answered, it would be easier to construct descriptions of past events that users would recognize.

It was already clear from the video-diary study that some events would be more helpful than others in jogging the user's memory. But there were unanswered questions here too. Should the system try to distinguish between routine and non-routine events, for example, and

Memory Lapse Questionnaire
(by Abi Sellen and Marge Eldridge)

At Rank Xerox we are designing a system which we hope will help people deal with the kinds of lapses or memory problems that everyone experiences from time to time. In order to do this effectively, we need to have some idea of what kinds of memory problems are the most frequent, and which are the most problematic. It would help us a great deal if you would fill out the following questionnaire. THIS SHOULD TAKE ABOUT 10–15 MINUTES. In return, we will be happy to summarise the results for those who are interested.

Be assured that your data will be kept confidential. We are interested in overall results rather than individual answers. If you wish to respond by e-mail, please forward this note by the 15th of May to the return address supplied. If you have any concerns about confidentiality, feel free to print a hard copy of this note and return it anonymously in the enclosed envelope.

INSTRUCTIONS

MALE OR FEMALE (Optional):   AGE (Optional):

Part 1: Rating the Frequency of Memory Problems at Work
To indicate your frequency judgements, please use your best estimate of how often these things happen to you AT WORK, using the LAST SIX MONTHS as a basis for making these judgements. Please estimate frequency by choosing ONE of the following options for each question:

Never   never in the last six months
Rarely   less than monthly
Monthly   at least monthly but not weekly
Weekly   at least weekly but not daily
Daily   daily or more

If you are responding by e-mail, indicate your answers by deleting the options that do not apply. If you are responding on hard copy, circle the answer that applies. Please give only one answer per question.

Part 2: Rating the Severity of Memory Problems at Work
After you have rated the frequency of each problem, would you please put an asterisk (*) next to the number (or letter) of the THREE problems which tend to be the most problematic for you when they occur. In other words, indicate those 3 problems which require the most time and effort to deal with when they happen, regardless of how often they occur.

MEMORY LAPSE QUESTIONNAIRE
Note: The responses appeared as follows after each question:
    Never in the last 6 months   Rarely
    Monthly   Weekly
    Daily.

Figure B.3   Memory lapse questionnaire, from Eldridge, Sellen and Bekerian (1992). Note that the format of the questionnaire as sent out by e-mail varied slightly from this due to the limited formatting options available in the electronic mail system.

1. How often do you plan to do something or say you'll do something, and then completely forget about it until later?
2. How often do you start doing something, get interrupted, and then forget your previous activity?
3. How often do you forget to take things with you, or leave things behind and have to go back for them?
4. How often do you go somewhere to do something, then forget why you're there when you get there?
5a. How often do you forget someone's name whom you know well?
5b. How often do you forget someone's name whom you have only met once or twice?
6a. How often do you forget where you put a paper document or book?
6b. How often do you forget where you put some other physical object?
6c. How often do you forget where you stored an electronic document or application on your computer?
7. How often do you have trouble remembering a particular word (i.e., when it's on the tip of your tongue)?
8. How often do you remember some information, and then find out later that it is incorrect?
9a. How often do you forget whether you have done something or not for some event that took place very recently?
9b. How often do you forget whether you took part or took some action in a distant past event?
10a. How often do you forget something important about what was said in a conversation or meeting, but remember details about who was there, where it was, or when it took place?
10b. How often do you have trouble recalling important details of a conversation or meeting, such as who was there, or where or when it took place?
10c. How often do you remember some fact or facts, but forget something important about who said it, where you read it, or where it came from?

Please answer 11a and 11b for COMPUTER ACTIVITIES ONLY

11a. How often do you forget details of how to do something, even though you have done it once or twice before?
11b. How often do you forget details of how to do something, even though you have done it many times before?

Please answer 11c and 11d for NON-COMPUTER ACTIVITIES ONLY

11c. How often do you forget details of how to do something, even though you have done it once or twice before?
11d. How often do you forget details of how to do something, even though you have done it many times before?
12. How often do you forget one or more items from a set of items you are holding in mind (e.g., a mental list of things to do or say)?

***** Don't forget to add the asterisks (see instructions for Part 2.) *****

THANK YOU FOR TAKING THE TIME TO RESPOND TO THIS
QUESTIONNAIRE!

Figure B.3   *Continued.*

display only the non-routine? The following kind of display, omitting routine events, seemed more likely to provide a useful context:

10:00   Meeting with Department Director [16 mins]
10:16   .. other events ...
11:53   Thunderstorm, workstation crashed [30 secs]

The study was designed to elicit descriptions of subjects' 'typical days', and then to compare these typical-day descriptions with descriptions of actual days – the previous day, and the day one week previous. The use of a typical-day description was influenced by earlier research suggesting that people use generalized structures, or *schemas*, to assist in remembering past events (Alba and Hasher, 1983). Twelve subjects, from the same engineering organization as before, were interviewed and audio-taped.

Analysis of basic activities
In the first stage of analysis the individual activities of the subject's actual days were identified. This was done by looking for changes in the subject's location, in the objects involved in the activity, or in the people present. Evidence of these changes made it possible to identify the *basic activities* of the working day. These were then divided into categories, giving the following distribution between categories:

	Number	Per cent
Meetings, conversations, etc.	118	24
Changing location in building	59	12
Telephone calls	55	11
Desk activities	54	11
Electronic mail work	52	11
Other workstation activities	50	10
Other	104	21
Total	492	100

By investigating these data in more detail, it became clear that a large proportion of basic work activities could be incorporated into the user's stored context. A system capable of capturing details of meetings, location changes, telephone calls and workstation tasks would be able to store nearly 85 per cent of the average user's basic work activities. If the system were capable of keeping track of desk activities, the total would be closer to 95 per cent.

Analysis of recall
The follow-on analysis focused on the differences between the descriptions of the previous day and of the day one week before. What kinds of activities did people forget during the intervening week? How did they relate to the typical-day schema? The unexpected result of this analysis was that people were more likely to forget the atypical activities than the

typical during the course of the week; indeed their ability to recall typical activities was hardly diminished, as the following table of mean values shows:

	Number of activities recalled		
	Typical	Atypical	Total
Recalled from yesterday	5.36	12.00	17.36
Recalled from a week ago	5.88	4.88	10.75

These results suggested that a model of the user's typical day might be a useful basis for retrieval. At the same time, they highlighted the user's relative difficulty in recalling atypical activities, and suggested that the system might be especially helpful in recalling these activities. Besides offering these insights, the study also raised doubts about the practice of using short, semi-structured interviews as a basis for systems analysis and design, a point that has been mentioned in Chapter 5.

B.4   An initial feasibility study

While these studies were in the planning stages, a preliminary feasibility study was conducted, in which a prototype memory aid was built and tested. At this stage, almost none of the necessary technology was available to support the collection of the user's contextual data. Nor did any portable terminal exist suitable for accessing stored records. Nevertheless there was a need to answer some preliminary questions about the feasibility of the whole project, questions that could not be answered purely by user studies or analyses.

In particular, it was important to understand the feasibility of generating recognizable and useful descriptions of past events by means of software. The basic usage scenario developed by the project team involved four steps, illustrated in Figure B.4:

(1)   The user describes the context in which the event in question was thought to have occurred;

(2)   The system searches for matching sequences of events;

(3)   The system presents one or more candidate sequences for selection;

(4)   The user recognizes the sequence and explores it in more detail to find the event in question.

How successfully could the system handle Steps 2 and 3, the generation of recognizable descriptions of past events? An opportunity to answer this question arose through the availability of active-badge technology for collecting data about the user's location. The technology had been developed by Olivetti Research and had been successfully tested by Want *et al.* (1992). Active badges, worn by individuals, could be tracked

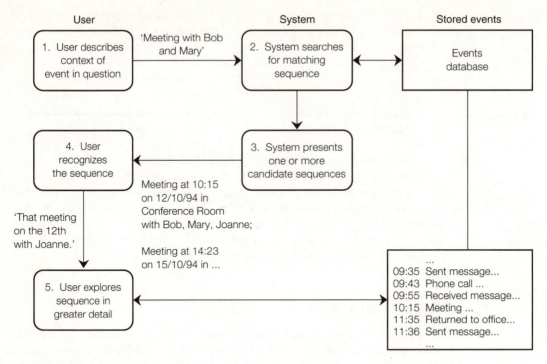

Figure B.4   Steps in the scenario of using the memory aid.

by wall-mounted sensors and the data used, for example, to direct telephone calls to people's current location. An active badge system, installed at the Rank Xerox laboratory, was used as the basis of an experiment in generating descriptions of location-based events.

B.4.1   The Pepys system

The software system for interpreting location data was known as *Pepys*, after the seventeenth-century diarist, because it generated diaries describing people's days. These were delivered to each of the subjects in the experiment at the start of the next working day, via e-mail. A typical diary is shown in Figure B.5.

The Pepys system was eventually kept in service for two years, because some of the subjects in the experiment found the diaries useful, for example, in filling out timesheets or writing six-monthly reports. The badges themselves were not universally liked, however, because they represented a threat to people's privacy. The badge system involved the use of centralized data collection, rather than a personal data-collection device, and this tended to remind people of 'Big Brother'. Furthermore, the badges were found less useful by Rank Xerox research staff than they had been by the badges' original developers, for reasons that have been

Diary for Tuesday, October 30, 1990

14:14   In office [50 mins]
15:04   In and out of event in Nathan's office; with W. Nathan, R. Hatton
        [45 mins]
15:50   In office [10 mins]
16:00   In Conference Room [4 mins]
16:05   Attended part of event in Commons; with B. Andrews, M. Morton,
        R. Hatton [7 mins]
16:13   Mostly in office [44 mins]
16:57   Attended event in Wright's office; with P. Wright [7 mins]
17:04   Looked in on event in Morton's office; with I. David, M. Morton
        [1 min]
17:05   Mostly in office [2h 3m]
        17:05   In office [5 mins]
        17:11   In event in office; with P. Wright, I. David [1h 2m]
        18:13   In office [36 mins]
        18:50   Meeting in office; with W. Nathan [13 mins]
        19:03   In office [5 mins]
19:09   In 2nd floor rear area [2 mins]
19:11   Last seen

Figure B.5   An example of a Pepys diary; from Newman *et al.* (1991).

explained by Harper *et al.* (1992). In 1993 the badge system was taken out of service, having served its purpose.

Three useful results emerged from studies of the use of Pepys. First, a study of the accuracy of the event descriptions showed that between 80 and 90 per cent of them matched people's own descriptions of the events in question. This was an encouraging result from a first attempt at constructing recognizable descriptions. Second, the video diary study (described in Section B.3.2) indicated in passing that access to a Pepys diary enabled people to recall roughly twice as many events as they could in free, unassisted recall (Eldridge, Lamming and Flynn, 1992). This was one of the first indications that a useful memory aid might be achievable, that is, that a solution to the originally defined problem might be found. Third, the project brought to the surface the need to preserve the user's privacy. This became one of the fundamental requirements to be met by the memory aid. All of the subsequent designs for user interfaces and supporting software reflected this requirement.

B.5   Requirements definition

Following these initial investigations, the project went through a phase of analysing different technical options, and trying to define specific requirements. In a less innovative project, this phase could have been expected to arrive at a more precise definition of the solution and its performance targets. This project still presented many questions, however, most of them so difficult to answer that a clear picture of the solution could not be gained.

Instead, therefore, the project team decided to take stock of all the knowledge that they had gained from the earlier work. They were able to identify a small number of general requirements scoping the functionality of the system and its underlying software. They were also able to identify some basic performance requirements. A prototyping exercise was then undertaken, not so much to refine these requirements in the manner described in Chapter 7, as to add some understanding of the technical and user interface issues. This prototyping project is described in the next section. Here we look at the general requirements that were emerging from the research so far.

B.5.1 Functional requirements

The functional requirements for the memory aid amounted to guidelines on how to apply technology towards supporting the system's interactive functions. In other words, they defined an overall technical strategy rather than a set of interactive functions. The five components of this strategy were:

- **Sensing the user's environment.** The system would be more effective in supporting retrieval and recall if it could build a rich description of the user's context. This might involve sensing a wide range of aspects of the user's environment: the user's location, his or her use of telephones and other equipment, other people present, current weather conditions, and so on.

- **Automatic data capture.** The system should not rely on the user for the entry of contextual data, nor should the user be expected to interpret or categorize these data. Instead these operations should be carried out automatically by the system. Only in this way would the system be able to help in situations where the need to access events had not been anticipated at the time the events took place.

- **Manual data capture.** Although the vast majority of contextual data would be captured automatically, the user would need the capability to annotate events and take notes for future reference. In particular, it would be valuable if the memory aid could support the recording of future events so as to provide reminders later.

- **Focus on relevant information for retrieval.** An important aspect of the system's functionality would be its support for searching and browsing through biographical data. It should provide simple ways to constrain the search to relevant parts of the event archive.

- **Integrated with other applications.** The memory aid should be available for use in conjunction with other information systems, e.g., in retrieving documents and recalling methods of operation. It should also record computer-usage events as part of the user's context.

Performance requirements
The remaining four requirements proposed some general yardsticks against which the system's performance should be assessed:

- **Available where needed.** Memory problems strike at all times and in all places. The system should be small enough and light enough to carry everywhere, and should continue to maintain its automatic data sensing and capture, regardless of the user's location.

- **Easy to use.** As a tool for assisting in remembering things, the memory aid would compete with the user's own memory, in the sense discussed in Chapter 2. In other words, the user would have a choice of method for recall or retrieval, and would tend to choose the method he or she found most effective. If the memory aid was too difficult or time-consuming to operate, the user would probably give up using it. Therefore the system should not place a greater cognitive load on the user than would be imposed by having to remember the event in question unaided.

- **Reliable and fail-safe.** Another important attribute of the memory aid, if it was to compete successfully with the user's own memory, was its reliability. The autobiographical record should be complete and accurate, otherwise the user would come to mistrust it. If the system should fail, the user should be informed, and a record of its failure should be included in the archive.

- **Respectful of privacy.** The memory aid would record a great deal of personal information about the user, much more invisibly than would be recorded in a pocket calendar, for example, or an itemized phone bill or a list of personal expenditures. The system should offer the user clear guidelines on what was being recorded and what was not. It should also work to strict rules on what could be disclosed to other people, for example, about presence at meetings. All of these aspects should be tailorable, and all data should be secure against unauthorized access by others.

These functional and performance requirements are documented more extensively in Lamming *et al.* (1994).

B.6 The Forget-Me-Not prototype

The development of a working prototype became feasible with the availability of a small, portable, networked terminal, the PARCTab, or 'Tab' for

Figure B.6   The ParcTab. Courtesy Rank Xerox.

short (Figure B.6). At the same time, the results of earlier studies, tests and requirements exercises were beginning to build an adequate basis for the design of the prototype. This section will briefly describe the design and implementation of the Forget-Me-Not prototype. We shall see that it involved two tightly interwoven activities: the choice and refinement of a *conceptual design*, and the choice of a *style of user interface* suitable for the Tab's very small screen. More details of the user interface are to be found in Lamming and Flynn (1994).

The Tab provided a stylus-sensitive LCD bitmap display measuring 50 by 35 mm, divided into 128×64 pixels. It had three function buttons mounted along one edge. It was light enough and small enough to be carried around, clipped to a belt or carried in a pocket. The Tab has been described in Schilit *et al.* (1993) and in Weiser (1993).

B.6.1   Conceptual design: The Threads model

The conceptual design of Forget-Me-Not centred around the choice of a suitable set of objects and actions to form the intended user's mental model. As we shall see, an important component of the design was the concept of a Thread connecting events with a common property. This concept played a prominent role in early designs, but retreated into the background as the design took shape, continuing nevertheless to play an important guiding role. In this section we will look at how the Threads model arose.

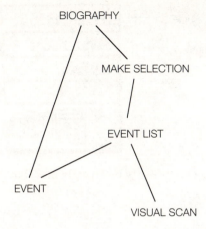

Figure B.7   The basic conceptual model, shown as a lattice of events, event lists and searching back and forward.

From the very outset of the project, the solution to the design problem
was seen to involve presenting the user with autobiographical data – with
lists of past events. The conceptual design took shape around this central
idea. The basic objects of the user interface were *events*, and these formed
event lists through which the user could scan visually for recognizable
sequences. The form of this conceptual model is shown in Figure B.7.
Around this simple set of concepts, further objects and actions were
added.

By the time work began on Forget-Me-Not, the project team had a
clear notion of the properties of events, thanks to the earlier memory-
schema studies. The criteria for distinguishing between basic activities –
change of location, change in people present, change of focus – were used
to define event properties:

- **location** of the event

- **people present** during the event

- **focus** of the event: meeting, document, phone call, and so on.

In addition, the **time** at which the event occurred, and the person or
subject experiencing it, should both be included in the definition. Thus
each event had five basic properties; this idea was retained throughout
the course of the design.

An early model of Forget-Me-Not consisted simply of a display showing one event, including its five basic properties. This is shown in Figure
B.8. To see the previous or next event, the user clicked on the upper or
lower button of the Tab.

Figure B.8   A single-event display on an early model of Forget-Me-Not. Courtesy Rank Xerox.

This design was never viewed as a complete solution, for it could not have met the ease-of-use requirement, that is, the requirement to minimize the effort involved in locating events. The user's biography would probably involve thousands of events like the one shown in Figure B.8, and the user would take a very long time to search for an event matching a particular description.

A second idea dating from the earliest stages of the project was the inclusion of a means of specifying patterns of events in order to narrow down the search. In early discussions, this idea had taken the form of search requests such as 'Find the document I retrieved before making a phone call to Jenny'. This was a potentially very powerful means of specifying events of interest. It allowed the user to specify complex temporal relationships between events, and thus to locate particular events in relatively few steps.

At the same time, the conceptual design would be made a lot more complicated by the introduction of such a powerful pattern-matching capability. In the course of building and evaluating mock-ups it became clear that this design, like the simple design of Figure B.8, failed the ease-of-use requirement, but failed it for the opposite reason: finding an event involved very few steps, but the steps would involve deep knowledge of the user interface and careful specification of patterns.

B.6.2   The use of filters

To achieve a middle ground, the project team chose a simple *filtering* model. Events were specified simply by listing their essential properties. The user would not specify temporal sequences, but would search for these sequences visually after filtering out non-matching events. The user would specify a filter, the system would respond with a list of matching events, and the user would select one of these events and display the full list of events before and after it.

How should the user specify a filter? A number of methods were considered, and the discussion led not only to the adoption of a particular method but to the 'discovery' of the Threads model. The first idea came from observing that each event had a displayable set of properties; by specifying some or all of these properties a set of similar events could be retrieved. A filter for use in finding these events could be constructed by editing the properties of a currently displayed event. The user could then ask to see the next event matching this filter, and then the next after that, and so on. Figure B.9 shows an early sketch for this user interface.

The idea of 'skipping' between events matching a set of properties could be applied to single properties; for example, it would allow the user to follow the sequence of all events at one location, or all events involving one particular other person, one particular document, and so on. This introduced the concept of Threads, and the accompanying idea of treating the properties of events as *objects* in their own right. Each location, person, document, and so on, could be viewed by the user as a separate object. Each such object could be viewed as possessing a Thread linking all of the events in the user's autobiography in which the object took part. Figure B.10(a) shows one of the first sketches in which the Threads idea was discussed, and Figure B.10(b) describes the Threads model more completely.

The Threads model allowed users to locate events by 'travelling in time' backwards and forwards along the Thread of a particular object. Thus user Greg, in the example of Figure B.10(b), could follow his own thread back to his brief presence at the meeting in the Conference Room; he could then switch to the Conference Room's thread and follow it forward to his next meeting there. The Threads model offered users a different way of thinking about filters: by specifying a filter containing two or more properties, the user would be searching for points in time where two or more objects' Threads came together.

Figure B.9   A display layout supporting the specification of events by properties, and the provision of functions for viewing the next or previous matching event. Courtesy Rank Xerox.

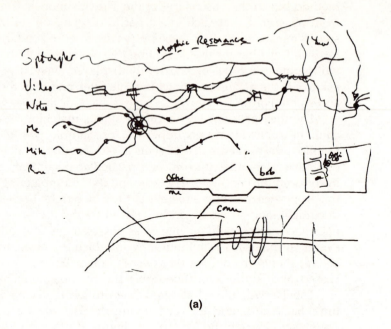

(a)

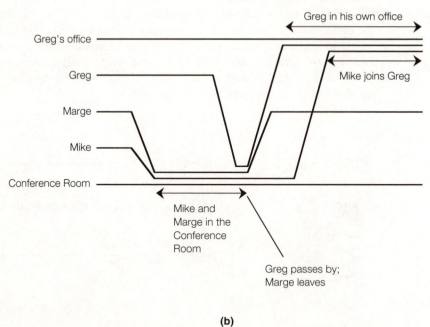

(b)

Figure B.10   The Threads model: (a) an initial sketch; (b) the form of the model. Courtesy Rank Xerox.

B.6.3   Testing the initial conceptual design

Until now, prototypes of the user interface had shown one event at a time, because it did not seem feasible to show more than this on the Tab's tiny screen. This user interface was subjected to various kinds of analysis. In particular, walkthrough techniques were used to test each of the principal functions.

These analyses exposed problems with the one-event display. The user relied on short-term memory to recognize a sequence of events, and this was inefficient and error-prone. As a result of this analysis, the display layout was changed to show more events simultaneously. Different layouts were tried; for example, at one time the single-line format shown in Figure B.11 was adopted. This list was still scrolled up and down in the same way as before, using the Tab's buttons.

B.6.4   Designing for the small screen: An icon-based design

Much design effort was needed to find a satisfactory way of dealing with the Tab's small screen. A solution to this problem was found in earlier work by Balabanovic, who had used *icons* to represent objects in a Tab-based portable control device (1993). This idea was well suited to the Threads-based design for the memory aid, in which event properties were treated as objects.

This led to the adoption of an iconic design for Forget-Me-Not. Each object – location, person, document, and so on – would have its own icon. Events would be displayed as a combination of icons and text describing their properties. A Thread would be specified by selecting a particular icon. Filters would be constructed by selecting a set of icons. Figure B.12 shows the final layout chosen for the Forget-Me-Not display.

To allow the construction of filters from icons in a natural way, a graphical direct-manipulation interface was designed. The user could

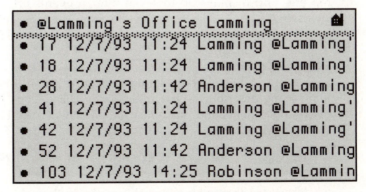

Figure B.11   An early multi-event display design. Courtesy Rank Xerox.

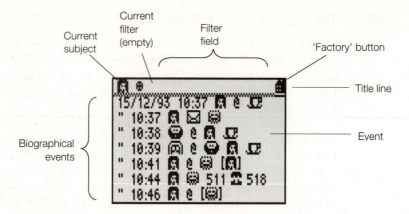

Figure B.12 The screen layout of the Forget-Me-Not display. The system is currently showing the biography of Mike, and since the filter field is empty the system is showing all events in his biography. The 'factory' button gives access to a full set of icons. Courtesy Rank Xerox.

build a filter by pointing at icons and dragging them up to the top row of the display in order to add them to the filter displayed there. Icons could be removed from the filter by dragging them out of the top line. To switch to a different thread, the user dragged the appropriate icon up to the top left corner of the screen. This 'drag and drop' interface was combined with the function-key interface for scrolling through events. The two styles of interaction, function-key and direct-manipulation, provided an effective way of using the very small amount of screen space available.

B.6.5 The full user interface

The full Forget-Me-Not user interface is shown in Figures B.12 to B.16. The primary display, shown in Figure B.12, shows the current filter on the top line, and displays up to seven filtered events on the lines below, in chronological order. These are events from the biography of the current *subject*, whose icon appears in the top left corner of the display.

Event descriptions
Each event includes a time-stamp indicating when it began, and one or more icons describing what took place. These icons represent people, places, documents and, in some cases, actions taken. Here, for example, are five people-icons:

Places are shown by pictorial icons or, in the case of people's offices, by the person's icon in brackets:

⌨ The Kitchen   ⯗ Area 2B   [🎨] Mike's office   ⎣ Conference Room

Documents are shown by the ✉ symbol, indicating electronic mail. The pair of icons ✉ 🎨 indicates an electronic message from Marge. Action icons include the following:

ê   Encountered or went to, e.g., 🎨 ê 👾 means 'Marge encountered Peter.'

✐   Edited by, e.g., ✉ ✐ 👾 means 'Message edited by Greg.'

↦   Sent to, e.g., ✉ ↦ 👾 indicates 'Message sent to Greg.'

☎   Called, e.g., 511 ☎ 518 means 'Called extension 518 from extension 511.'

Event descriptions start with the time-stamp, and then indicate the subject, the action performed and the place, in that order. Examples include:

15/12/93 10:37 🎨 ê ⌨   Mike went to the Kitchen

15/12/93 10:39 🎨 ê 👾 🎨 ⌨   Marge encountered Peter and Mike in the Kitchen

15/12/93 10:41 🎨 ✉ ↦ 👾   Marge sent a message to Greg

15/12/93 10:46 🎨 ê [👾]   Mike went to Greg's office (which was unoccupied).

Scrolling through the biography
To navigate through the biography the user clicks on the top or bottom button of the Tab. The top button reveals the preceding seven events, the bottom button reveals the next seven. This is shown in Figure B.13.

Editing the title line
Changes are made to the title line by dragging icons into it and out of it. Four such 'drag and drop' functions are supported:

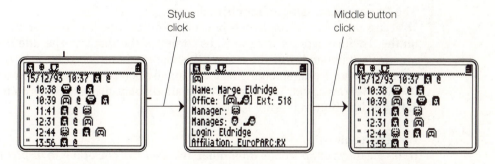

Figure B.13   Scrolling down and up through events by means of the Tab's buttons.

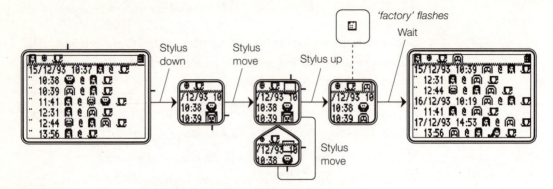

Figure B.14   A 'drag and drop' operation, in which an icon is added to the filter and the biography display is reconstructed.

- **Adding an object to the current filter.** The user points to an icon somewhere among the displayed events, presses down with the stylus, drags it to the filter region of the title line and releases the stylus (Figure B.14). The 'factory' icon on to the right of the filter will flash until the system has reconstructed and displayed events according to the new filter.

- **Removing an object from the filter.** The user drags the icon from the title line to anywhere in the region below the title line. The biography display is reconstructed in accordance, and the 'factory' icon flashes while this is in progress.

- **Clearing the filter.** The user drags the separator symbol, to the right of the subject icon in the title line, to anywhere below the title line. The biography display is revised, and the 'factory' icon flashes to show this is in progress.

- **Changing the subject.** The user drags the appropriate icon to the top left corner of the screen. Again, the 'factory' icon flashes while the biography display is reconstructed.

The Factory: Accessing other objects
To access an object whose icon is not shown on the display, the user clicks on the 'Factory' icon in the top right corner of the display. The title line remains unchanged, but the rest of the display is replaced by a 'warehouse' of icons from which the user can make a selection in order to modify the filter or subject. To return to the main display, the user clicks on the Tab's middle button (Figure B.15).

Inspecting an icon
If the meaning of an icon is unfamiliar, the user can click on it to *inspect* it. The main display is replaced with seven lines of information about the

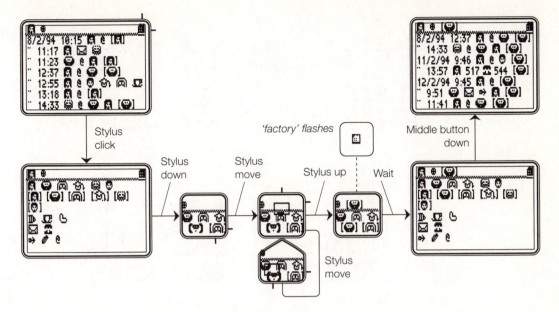

Figure B.15   Accessing the 'Factory' to select an icon not visible in the main display.

object represented by the icon. The middle button of the Tab is pressed in order to return to the main display (Figure B.16).

B.6.6   An example: Locating an item of electronic mail

We will conclude with a simple example of how Forget-Me-Not can be used to help with memory problems. In this instance, Greg (🔳) is reading an electronic-mail message reporting on a meeting with two other people, Peter (😃) and Prof (😼). He wants to look at the message he sent after the previous such meeting, but he cannot remember where he filed it.

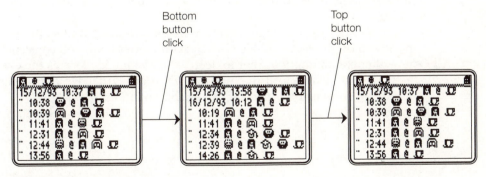

Figure B.16   Inspecting an icon.

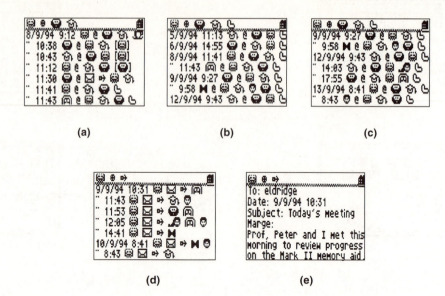

(a)   **(b)**   **(c)**

(d)   **(e)**

Figure B.17   An example of the use of Forget-Me-Not. Greg (🈂) needs to find a message relating to a previous meeting with Peter and Prof (🈂 🈂): (a) he constructs an initial filter but there are too many matching events; (b) he recalls that the meeting was in the Common Room (🈂) and thus narrows down the search; (c) he identifies the meeting, at 9:30 on 9/9/94, and scrolls this event to the top of the screen; (d) he constructs a new filter to locate messages he has sent, and identifies the message at 10:31; (e) he clicks on the message icon to display it.

His first step is to set up a filter, 🈂 🈂, to select events involving Peter and Prof. The resulting display still includes a very large number of events, since he has met many times with Peter and Prof (Figure B.17(a). Greg recalls that the meeting took place in the Common Room (🈂). He therefore extends the filter to include the Conference Room as a component (🈂 🈂 🈂). Now the number of events is manageable, and Greg can see the meeting in question, at 9:27 on the 9th of September (Figure B.17(b)).

To identify the message, Greg scrolls the meeting event to the top of the screen (Figure B.17(c)). He now clears the filter field, and constructs a new filter containing the 'Sent to' icon (🈂). He quickly locates the event, at 10:31, in which he sent the message (Figure B.17(d)). He clicks on the message icon to inspect its contents, as shown in Figure B.17(e).

B.7 Conclusion

This final case study of interactive system design has described a programme of research and development with an emphasis on innovation. A deliberately challenging problem was identified and was tackled through a combination of studies, envisionments, requirements analysis and design. One of the major outcomes was a prototype 'human memory prosthesis', Forget-Me-Not, working on a small hand-held terminal.

The story of Forget-Me-Not is very different from the previous case study, in which the enhancement of a telephone operator's workstation was discussed. There is much less emphasis here on meeting quantified performance requirements, and much more emphasis on research into surrounding issues. The aim of the design work here is not so much to improve on a previous design as to find an initial form of solution to a hitherto unsolved problem.

What we see here is an instance of the kind of design work that sets in motion the process of innovation. This process can lead to a succession of design enhancements, and to a gradually enlarging body of knowledge about the solution. It can give rise to guidelines that help the designers of future versions of the system, and to analytical models that enable them to evaluate the designs they produce. If the innovation process follows its full course, the original idea is transformed into a well-established, mature piece of technology – such as a telephone operator's workstation – capable of serving an important function in society. The role of the design methods described in this book is to assist in the development of interactive systems that can serve such functions.

Further reading

Lamming M.G., Brown P., Carter K., Eldridge M., Flynn M., Louie G., Robinson P. and Sellen A. (1994). The design of a human memory prosthesis. *Computer Journal*, **37**, 153–63

> A general paper on the idea of designing a human memory aid, discussing some of the requirements such a system should meet.

Eldridge M. A, Lamming M. G. and Flynn M. (1992). Does a video diary help recall? In *People and Computers VII* (Monk A. *et al.*, eds.) , pp. 257–69. Cambridge: Cambridge University Press

> An account of a study of the use of recorded video to help people recall past events.

DESIGN PROBLEMS

These problems offer opportunities for larger-scale exercises in the use of interactive system design methods. Each one is stated as a situation of concern, and provides a starting point for one or more stages of design, for example:

- Problem definition
- User studies and analysis
- Requirements definition
- User interface design and usability analysis
- Prototyping and evaluation

The problems are given in roughly ascending order of difficulty.

1   A telephone answering machine

Telephone answering machines present a number of problems to their users. For example, sharing a single machine among several people may lead to the loss of messages, and may not provide enough privacy. Another cause for concern is the high level of functionality on modern machines, which discourages first-time users.

Discuss with members of your design team the problems they consider most serious. Undertake studies if necessary, and take the problem through the stages of requirements definition and user interface design.

2   A group online calendar

A group of about 50 professionals need a system to help them schedule meetings. They hold a lot of meetings among themselves and with clients. The group's administrators spend a great deal of time trying to set up meetings and schedule meeting rooms. Many meetings have to be rescheduled several times, sometimes because other meetings have overrun. In the present situation, scheduling is done by hand on a wall calendar, but this calendar is inaccessible to staff who are out of town, and valuable time is spent telephoning them to notify them of changes. Also, entries are sometimes erased by accident. A lot of time is being lost due to scheduling problems.

3   A translation aid

The staff of a European press agency receive newspapers and other publications in a dozen different languages. Each member of staff is responsible for reading publications in two or three languages, and identifying passages to be photocopied and supplied to the agency's clients.

Although familiar with the languages, staff often come across words they cannot immediately translate. They need a rapid means of looking up the meanings of these words – ordinary dictionaries are too slow. Likewise, typing in each word to an online translation package is unlikely to save time because of typing errors and difficulties in entering accents. A means is needed of quickly scanning the word on the printed page, and presenting one or more possible translations back to the user.

4   A tool for managing audio recordings

Students with impaired vision need to keep audio notes of lectures. Later they need to listen to the recordings and index the material. This involves selecting passages and adding voice annotations. The process can be performed on a double cassette recorder, but is slow and cumbersome. A more efficient device is needed, capable of simplifying and speeding up the management of audio material.

5   A visitor reception system

Visitor reception is often a cause for concern, especially in security-conscious organizations. The work of checking in visitors tends to bunch around the hours and the half-hours, causing long check-in delays and late arrivals at meetings.

You may find that your own organization has plenty of problems with visitor reception, and can be used as the focus of the design exercise. Or you can visit some other organization and talk to the receptionists to find out what problems they have.

As a further alternative, consider the following case. A nuclear research centre is obliged to issue its visitors with radiation measurement tags ('dosimeters') and to retain long-term records of measured radiation for each visitor. While on-site, visitors must be escorted at all times to make sure they do not stray into hazardous areas. The visitor reception procedures involve gaining prior signed approval for each visitor from the hosting department of the centre, before the day of the visit. On arrival, each visitor is issued with a badge and a numbered dosimeter. The visitor's passport or ID is retained as security, and is returned when the visitor hands in the dosimeter and leaves the centre. These procedures cause long delays in visitor reception at peak hours. When visitors have not been approved ahead of time the delays are even worse. Yet the centre cannot afford to hire more receptionists. Could an interactive system help resolve this situation?

6   A traffic control system

The city nearest you is experiencing such severe traffic congestion that it has decided to introduce a traffic control system based on the principles of air traffic control. Every driver must, except under emergency circumstances, file a journey plan before setting out on any journey of more than a minimum length. The traffic control system will issue the driver with a time slot, and thus will even out the flow of traffic during the day.

To define and solve this problem, you will need to consider the nature of journeys made on the urban road system, and the kind of interactive technology drivers might use in order to file their journey plans. One possible form of solution might be a telephone-based system with synthesized voice feedback. Another might be a telephone with a small screen. You will need to consider how many plans drivers may make in advance, and how complex their journeys are.

To keep the problem simple, you may wish to focus only on the problem of supporting drivers filing journey plans. A second part of the problem is to control the flow, handling any departures from plan by drivers and any requests for changes to plan while on the road. This will require some means of communication with drivers. To solve this part of the problem, you will probably want to learn more about how air traffic control is done, for example, from Hopkin (1988) or Harper *et al.* (1995).

BIBLIOGRAPHY

Ackroyd S., Harper R., Hughes J. A., Shapiro D. and Soothill K. (1992). *New Technology and Practical Police Work*. Buckingham, UK: Open University Press

Adler A. and Henderson D. A. (1994). A room of our own: Experiences in a direct office share. In *Proc. CHI '94 Human Factors in Computing Systems*, Boston MA, April 24–28, pp. 138–44. New York: ACM/SIGCHI

Alba J. W. and Hasher L. (1983). Is memory schematic? *Psychological Bulletin*, **93**, pp. 203–31

Alexander C. (1967). *Notes on the Synthesis of Form*. Cambridge MA: Harvard University Press

Annett J. and Duncan K. D. (1967). Task analysis and training design. *Occupational Psychology*, **41**, 211–21

Apple Computer (1987). *Apple Human Interface Guidelines*. Reading MA: Addison-Wesley

Atwood M. E., Gray W. D. and John B. E. (in press). *Project Ernestine: analytic and empirical methods applied to a real-world CHI problem*. San Mateo CA: Morgan-Kaufman

Baddeley A. (1990). *Human Memory*. Cambridge: Cambridge University Press.

Balabanovic M. (1993). Private communication.

Ballas J. A., Heitmeyer C. L. and Pérez M. A. (1992). Evaluating two aspects of direct manipulation in advanced cockpits. In *Proc. CHI '92 Human Factors in Computing Systems*, Monterey CA, May 3–7, pp. 127–34. New York: ACM/SIGCHI

Barnard P. (1991). Bridging between basic theories and the artifacts of human–computer interaction. In *Designing Interaction: Psychology at the Human–Computer Interface* (Carroll J.M., ed.). Cambridge: Cambridge University Press

Barnard P. and Grudin J. (1988). Command names. In *Handbook of Human–Computer Interaction* (Helander M., ed.), pp. 237–56. Amsterdam: North-Holland

Benson, D. (1993). Police and information technology. In *Technology in Working Order: Studies of Work, Interaction and Technology* (Button, G., ed.), pp. 81–97. London: Routledge

Berners-Lee T. *Style Guide for Online Hypertext*. URL http://www0.cern.ch/hypertext/WWW/Provider/Style/Overview.html

Berners-Lee T., Cailliau R., Luotonen A., Nielsen H. F. and Secret A. (1994). The World-Wide Web. *Comm. ACM*, **37**(8), 76–82 (August)

Bingham J. and Davies G. (1992). *Systems Analysis*. Basingstoke: Macmillan.

Bly S. and Minneman S. (1990). Commune: A shared drawing surface. In *Proc. COIS '90, Conference on Office Information Systems*, Cambridge MA, April 25–27, pp. 184–92

Boehm B. W. (1981). *Software Engineering Economics*. Englewood Cliffs NJ: Prentice-Hall

Boehm B. W. (1988). The spiral model of software development and enhancement. *IEEE Computer*, **21**(5), 61–72

Brown C. M. (1988). *Human–Computer Interface Design Guidelines*. Norwood NJ: Ablex

Button G., ed. (1993). *Technology in Working Order: Studies of Work, Interaction and Technology*. London: Routledge

Byrne, M.D. (1993). Using icons to find documents: simplicity is critical. In *Proc. InterCHI '93 Human Factors in Computing Systems*, Amsterdam, Netherlands, April 24–29, pp. 446–53. New York: ACM/SIGCHI

Callahan D., Hopkins M., Weiser M. D. and Shneiderman B. (1988). An empirical comparison of pie versus linear menus. In *Proc. CHI '88 Human Factors in Computing Systems*, Washington DC, May 15–19, pp. 95–100. New York: ACM/SIGCHI

Card S. K., Moran T. P. and Newell A. (1983). *The Psychology of Human Computer Interaction*. Hillsdale NJ: Lawrence Erlbaum Associates

Carey M. S., Stammers R. B. and Astley J. A. (1989). Human–computer interaction design: the potential and pitfalls of hierarchical task analysis. In *Task Analysis for Human–Computer Interaction* (Diaper D., ed.). Chichester: Ellis Horwood

Carmody S., Gross W., Nelson T. H., Rice D. and Van Dam A. (1969). A hypertext system for the /360. In *Pertinent Concepts in Computer Graphics* (Faiman M. and Nievergelt J., eds.), pp. 291–330. Urbana IL: University of Illinois Press

Carroll J. M. and Mack R. (1984). Learning to use a word processor: by doing, by thinking and by knowing. In *Human Factors in Computer Systems* (Thomas J. and Schneider M., eds.), pp 13–52. Norwood: Ablex

Carroll J.M. and Olson J. R. (1988). Mental models in human–computer interaction. In *Handbook of Human–Computer Interaction* (Helander M., ed.), pp. 45–65. Amsterdam: North-Holland

Checkland P. and Scholes J. (1990). *Soft Systems Methodology in Action*. Chichester: John Wiley

Constant E. W., II (1980). *The Origins of the Turbojet Revolution*. Baltimore MD: Johns Hopkins University Press

Coulouris G. F. and Thimbleby H. (1993). *HyperProgramming: Building Interactive Programs with HyperCard*. Reading MA: Addison-Wesley

CREST Project Team (1994). *CREST: Principles and Requirements (revised)*. London: Bank of England

Dalton M. (1959). *Men who Manage*. New York: John Wiley

Davis A. M. (1990). *Software Requirements Analysis and Specification.* Englewood Cliffs NJ: Prentice-Hall

DeMarco T. (1979). *Structured Analysis and System Specification.* Englewood Cliffs NJ: Prentice-Hall

Desurvire H. W., Kondziela J. M. and Atwood M. E. (1992). What is gained and lost when using evaluation methods other than empirical testing. In *People and Computers VII* (Monk *et al.*, eds.). Cambridge: Cambridge University Press.

Diaper D., ed. (1989a). *Task Analysis for Human–Computer Interaction.* Chichester: Ellis Horwood

Diaper D. (1989b). Task observation for human–computer interaction. In *Task Analysis for Human–Computer Interaction* (Diaper D., ed.). Chichester: Ellis Horwood

Dourish J. P. and Bly S. (1992). Portholes: supporting awareness in a distributed work group. In *Proc. CHI '92 Human Factors in Computing Systems*, Monterey CA, May 3–7, pp. 541–7. New York: ACM/SIGCHI

Dourish J. P., Adler A., Bellotti V. M. E. and Henderson D. A. (1994). Your Place or Mine? Learning from Long-term Use of Video Communication. *Technical Report EPC-94-105*, Rank Xerox Research Centre, 61 Regent Street, Cambridge CB2 1AB, UK

Eldridge M. A., Lamming M. G. and Flynn M. (1992). Does a video diary help recall? In *People and Computers VII* (Monk A. *et al.*, eds.), pp. 257–69. Cambridge: Cambridge University Press

Eldridge M. A., Sellen A. and Bekerian D. E. (1992). Memory Problems at Work: Their Range, Frequency and Severity. *Rank Xerox EuroPARC Technical Report EPC-92-129*, 61 Regent Street, Cambridge, UK

Eldridge M. A., Barnard P. and Bekerian D. E. (1994). Autobiographical memory and daily schemas at work. *Memory*, **2**(1), 51–74

Emery F. E. and Trist E. L. (1960). Socio-technical systems. In *Management Science Models and Techniques*, Vol 2. London: Pergamon

Engelbart D. C. and English W. K. (1968). A research center for augmenting human intellect. *AFIPS Conf. Proc.*, **33**, pp. 395–410, Fall 1968 Joint Computer Conf. Washington: Thompson Books

Ferguson E. S. (1992). *Engineering and the Mind's Eye.* Cambridge MA: MIT Press.

Fitts P. (1954). The information capacity of the human motor system in controlling amplitude of movement. *J. Exp. Psych.* **47**, 381–91

Frohlich D. M. (1988). On the organization of form-filling behaviour. *Information Design J.*, **5**, 43–59

Gaines B.R. (1981). The technology of interaction: dialogue programming rules. *Intnl. J. of Man–Machine Studies*, **14**, 133–50

Gaver W. W. (1989). The SonicFinder: an interface that uses auditory icons. *Human Computer Interaction*, **4**, 67–94

Gaver W. W., Moran T. P., MacLean A. *et al.* (1992). Realizing a video environment: EuroPARC's Rave System. In *Proc. CHI '92 Human Factors in Computing Systems*, Monterey CA, May 3–7, pp. 27–35. New York: ACM/SIGCHI

Gentner D. and Gentner D.R. (1983). Flowing waters or teeming crowds: mental models of electricity. In *Mental Models* (Gentner D. and Stevens A. L., eds.), pp. 99–129. Hillsdale NJ: Lawrence Erlbaum Associates

Gentner D. R. and Grudin J. (1990). Why good engineers (sometimes) create bad interfaces. In *Proc. CHI '90 Human Factors in Computing Systems*, Seattle WA, April 1–5, pp. 277–82. New York: ACM/SIGCHI

Gentner D. and Stevens A.L., eds. (1983). *Mental Models*. Hillsdale NJ: Lawrence Erlbaum Associates

Goodwin C. (1981). *Conversational Organization: Interaction between Speakers and Hearers*. New York: Academic Press

Goodwin C. and Goodwin M. H. (in press). Seeing as situated activity: formulating planes. In *Cognition and Communication at Work* (Middleton D. and Engestrom Y., eds.). New York: Cambridge University Press

Goodwin M. H. (1991). Assembling a response: setting and collaboratively constructed work talk. Presented at the Invited Session on Communicative Acts as Socially Distributed Phenomena, American Anthropological Association Annual Meetings, Chicago, 24 November 1991

Gordon M. J. C. (1988). *Programming Language Theory and its Implementation*. Chichester: John Wiley

Gould J. D. (1988). How to design usable systems. In *Handbook of Human–Computer Interaction* (Helander M., ed.), pp. 757–89. Amsterdam: North-Holland

Granda R. E., Teitelbaum R. C. and Dunlap G. L. (1982). The effect of VDT command line location on data entry behaviour. *Proc. Human Factors Soc. 26th Annual Meeting*, pp. 621–4

Gray W. D., John B. E. and Atwood M. E. (1992). The précis of Project Ernestine or, an overview of a validation of GOMS. In *Proc. CHI '92 Human Factors in Computing Systems*, Monterey CA, May 3–7, pp. 307–12. New York: ACM/SIGCHI

Gray W. D., John B. E. and Atwood M. E. (1993). Project Ernestine: validating a GOMS analysis for predicting and explaining real-world task performance. *Human Computer Interaction, 8*, 237–309

Greatbatch D., Luff P., Heath C. and Campion P. (1993). Interpersonal communication and human–computer interaction: an examination of the use of computers in medical consultations. *Intnl. J. of Interacting with Computers, 5*, 193–216

Green T. R. G. and Payne S. J. (1984). Organization and learnability in computer languages. *Intnl. J. of Man–Machine Studies, 21*, 7–18

Greenbaum J. and Kyng M., eds. (1991). *Design at Work: Cooperative Design of Computer Systems*. Hillsdale NJ: Lawrence Erlbaum Associates

Grudin J. (1989). The case against user interface consistency. *Commun. ACM* **32**(10) pp. 1164–73

Grudin J. (1992). Obstacles to participatory design in large product development organizations. In *Participatory Design* (Schuler D. and Namioka A, eds.). Hillsdale NJ: Lawrence Erlbaum Associates

Hansen W. J. (1971). User engineering principles for interactive systems. *Proc. Fall Joint Computer Conf. 39*, Montvale NJ: AFIPS Press, pp. 523–32.

Harper R. H. R. (1991). The computer game: detectives, suspects and technology. *British J. of Criminology*, **31**(3), pp. 292–307

Harper R. H. R., Newman W. M. and Lamming M. G. (1992). Locating systems at work: implications for the development of active badge applications. *Interacting with Computers*, **4**(3), 343–63.

Harper R. H. R., Hughes J. A., Randall D., Shapiro D. Z. and Sharrock W. W. (1995, in press). *Order in the Skies: Sociology, Collaborative Work and Technology*. London: Routledge

Hartson H. R. and Smith E. C. (1991). Rapid prototyping in human–computer interface development. *Interacting with Computers*, **3**(1), 51–91

Hartson H. R., Siochi A. C. and Hix D. (1990). The UAN: a user-oriented representation for direct manipulation interface designs. *ACM Trans. on Information Systems*, **8**(3), pp. 181–203

Heath C., Jirotka M., Luff P. and Hindmarsh J. (1993). Unpacking collaboration: the interactional organisation of trading in a city dealing room. *Proc. Third European Conf. on Computer-Supported Cooperative Work – ECSCW '93*, pp. 155–70. Dordrecht: Kluwer

Hick W. E. (1952). On the rate of gain of information. *Quarterly J. of Experimental Psychology.* **4**, 11–26

Hix D. and Hartson H. R. (1993). *Developing User Interfaces: Ensuring Usability through Product and Process*. New York: John Wiley

Hopkin V. D. (1988). Air traffic control. In *Human Factors in Aviation* (Wiener E. L. and Nagel D. C., eds.), pp. 639–63. San Diego CA: Academic Press

Hopkins D. (1991). The design and implementation of pie menus. *Dr Dobbs Journal*, Dec. 1991, 16–26

Howell D. C. (1989). *Fundamental Statistics for the Behavioral Sciences.* Boston MA: PWS–Kent

Howes N. R. (1988). On using the user's manual as the requirements specification. *IEEE Tutorial on Software Engineering Project Management* (Thayer R. H., ed.) pp. 172–7. Washington DC: IEEE Computer Society Press

John B. E. (1990). Extension of GOMS analyses to expert performance requiring perception of dynamic auditory and visual information. In *Proc. CHI '90 Human Factors in Computing Systems*, Seattle WA, April 1–5, pp. 107–15. New York: ACM/SIGCHI

John B. E. and Gray W. D. (1994). *GOMS Analyses for Parallel Activities*. CHI '94 Tutorial notes. New York: ACM

Johnson P. (1992). *Human–Computer Interaction: Psychology, Task Analysis and Software Engineering*. Maidenhead: McGraw-Hill

Kendall K. E. and Kendall J. E. (1992). *Systems Analysis and Design.* Englewood Cliffs NJ: Prentice-Hall

Keppel G. (1973). *Design and Analysis: A Researcher's Handbook.* 2nd edn. Englewood Cliffs NJ: Prentice-Hall

Keppel G. and Saufley W. H., Jr. (1980). *Introduction to Design and Analysis: A Student's Handbook*. San Francisco CA: Freeman

Klugh H. E. (1986). *Statistics: The Essentials for Research*. New York: John Wiley

Koved L. and Shneiderman B. (1986). Embedded menus: menu selection in context. *Comm. ACM*, **29**, 312–18

Kraut R. E., Hanson S. J. and Farber J. M. (1983). Command use and interface design. In *Proc. CHI '83 Human Factors in Computing Systems*, Boston MA, December 12–15, pp. 120–4. New York: ACM/SIGCHI

Kuhn, T. S. (1962). *The Structure of Scientific Revolutions*. Chicago IL: University of Chicago Press

Lammers S. M. (1986). *Programmers at Work*. Redmond WA: Microsoft Press

Lamming M. G. and Flynn M. (1994). Forget-me-not: intimate computing in support of human memory. *Technical Report TR-94-103*, Rank Xerox Research Centre, 61 Regent Street, Cambridge CB2 1AB, UK

Lamming M. G. and Newman W. M. (1992). Activity-based information retrieval: technology in support of personal memory. *Personal Computers and Intelligent Systems: Information Processing 92*, pp. 68–81. Amsterdam: North–Holland

Lamming M.G. and Rhodes W. R. (1990). A simple method for improved color printing of monitor images. *ACM Trans. on Graphics*, **9**(2), 346–75

Lamming M.G., Brown P., Carter K. *et al.* (1994). The design of a human memory prosthesis. *Computer Journal*, **37**, 153–63

Landauer T. K. (1988). Research methods in human–computer interaction. In *Handbook of Human–Computer Interaction* (Helander M., ed.), pp. 905–28. Amsterdam: North-Holland

Landauer T. K. and Nachbar D. W. (1985). Selection from alphabetic and numeric menu trees using a touch-screen: breadth, depth and width. In *Proc. CHI '85 Human Factors in Computing Systems*, San Francisco CA, April 14–18, pp. 183–8. New York: ACM/SIGCHI

Lee J. D. (1992). *Trust, Self Confidence and Operators' Adaptation to Automation*, Ph.D. Thesis, Univ. of Illinois

Lee L. (1992). *The Day the Phones Stopped*. New York: Donald I. Fine Inc.

Lewis C. H. and Polson P. G. (1990). Testing a walkthrough methodology for theory-based design of walk-up-and-use interfaces. In *Proc. CHI '90 Human Factors in Computing Systems*, Seattle WA: April 1–5, pp. 235–42. New York: ACM/SIGCHI

Lewis C. H., Polson P. G., Rieman J., Wharton C. and Wilde N. (1992). *Cognitive Walkthroughs: A Method for Theory-Based Evaluation of User Interfaces*. CHI '92 Tutorial Notes, Monterey CA, 4 May 1992. New York: ACM

London Ambulance Service (1993). *Report on the Inquiry into the London Ambulance Service*. Available from: Communications Directorate, South West Thames Regional Health Authority, 40 Eastbourne Terrace, London W2 3QR, UK

Marcus A. (1992). *Graphic Design for Electronic Documents and User Interfaces*. New York: ACM Press

Martin J. (1973). *Design of Man–Computer Dialogues*. Englewood Cliffs NJ: Prentice Hall

Martin, J. (1987). *Recommended Diagramming Standards for Analysts and Programmers*. Englewood Cliffs NJ: Prentice-Hall

Mattson H. F., Jr. (1993). *Discrete Mathematics with Applications*. New York: John Wiley

Mayhew D. J. (1992). *Principles and Guidelines in Software User Interface Design*. Englewood Cliffs NJ: Prentice-Hall

MacKenzie I. S. (1992). Fitts' law as a research and design tool in human–computer interaction. *Human Computer Interaction*, **7**, 91–139

McShane W. R. and Roess R. P. (1990). *Traffic Engineering*. Englewood Cliffs NJ: Prentice-Hall

Microsoft Corporation (1992). *The Windows Interface: An Application Design Guide*. Redmond WA: Microsoft Press

Miller, D.P. (1981). The depth/breadth tradeoff in hierarchical computer menus. In *Proc. of the Human Factors Soc. 25th Annual Meeting*, pp. 296–300

Moray N. (1992). Mental models of complex dynamic systems. *Mental Models and Everyday Activities*, Proceedings of 2nd Interdisciplinary Workshop on Mental Models (Booth P. A. and Sasse A., eds.), Robinson College, Cambridge, UK, March 1992, pp. 103–31

Morgan C., Williams G. and Lemmons P. (1983). An interview with Wayne Rosing, Bruce Daniels and Larry Tesler. *BYTE* **8**(2) 90–114

Mumford E. (1983). *Designing Human Systems for New Technology: The Ethics Method*. Manchester: Manchester Business School Press

Myers B.A. and Rosson M.B. (1992). Survey on user interface programming. In *Proc. CHI '92 Human Factors in Computing Systems*, Monterey CA, May 3–7, pp. 195–202. New York: ACM/SIGCHI

Neumann P. G., ed. (1989). Risks to the Public. *ACM Software Engineering Notes* **14**(5) 3–23

Newell A. and Simon H. A. (1972). *Human Problem Solving*. Englewood Cliffs NJ: Prentice-Hall

Newman W. M. (1968). A system for interactive graphical programming. In *AFIPS Conf. Proc.*, 1968 Spring Joint Computer Conf. Washington, DC: Thompson Books, pp. 47–55

Newman W. M. (1988). The representation of user interface style. In *People and Computers IV* (Jones D. M. and Winder R., eds.), pp. 123–43. Cambridge: Cambridge University Press

Newman W. M. (1994). A preliminary analysis of the products of HCI research, based on pro forma abstracts. In *Proc. CHI '94 Human Factors in Computing Systems*, Boston MA, April 24–28, pp. 278–84. New York: ACM/SIGCHI

Newman W. M. (1995). Analysis and evaluation of multimedia systems. In *Multimedia Systems and Applications* (Earnshaw R.A., ed.). London: Academic Press

Newman W. M., Eldridge M. A. and Lamming M. G. (1991). Pepys: generating autobiographies by automatic tracking. In *Proc. Second European Conf. on Computer-Supported Cooperative Work – ECSCW '91*, pp. 175–88. Dordrecht: Kluwer

Newman W. M. and Wellner P. (1992). A desk supporting computer-based interaction with paper documents. In *Proc. CHI '92 Human Factors in Computing Systems*, Monterey CA, May 3–7, pp. 587–92. New York: ACM/SIGCHI

Nielsen J. (1992). Finding usability problems through heuristic evaluation. In *Proc. CHI '92 Human Factors in Computing Systems*, Monterey CA, May 3–7, pp. 373–80. New York: ACM/SIGCHI

Nielsen J. (1993). *Usability Engineering*. San Diego CA: Academic Press

Nielsen J. and Molich R. (1989). Teaching user interface design based on usability engineering. *ACM SIGCHI Bulletin*, **21**(1), 45–8

Nielsen J. and Molich R. (1990). Heuristic evaluation of user interfaces. In *Proc. CHI '90 Human Factors in Computing Systems*, Seattle WA, April 1–5, pp. 249–56. New York: ACM/SIGCHI

Norman D. A. (1986). Cognitive engineering. In *User Centered System Design* (Norman D. A. and Draper S. W., eds.), pp. 31–65. Hillsdale NJ: Lawrence Erlbaum Associates

Norman D. A. (1988). *The Psychology of Everyday Things*. New York: Basic Books

Norman D. A. and Draper S. W., eds. (1986). *User Centered System Design*. Hillsdale NJ: Lawrence Erlbaum Associates

North West Regional Health Authority (1990). *First Edition Operational Requirement for a Nursing System for Resource Management*. NW Regional Health Authority, Manchester, UK

Ogden W. C. (1988). Using natural language interfaces. In *Handbook of Human–Computer Interaction* (Helander M., ed.), pp. 281–99. Amsterdam: North-Holland

Olson J. S. (1992). The what and why of mental models in human computer interaction. *Mental Models and Everyday Activities*, Proceedings of 2nd Interdisciplinary Workshop on Mental Models, Robinson College, Cambridge, UK, March 1992

Orr J. (1990). Talking about machines: an ethnography of a modern job. PhD Thesis, Cornell University. *Technical Report SSL-91-07 [P91-00132]*, Xerox Palo Alto Research Center, 3333 Coyote Hill Road, Palo Alto CA

Payne S. J. (1984). Task action grammars. In *Human Computer Interaction – Interact '84* (Shackel B., ed.), pp. 139–44. Amsterdam: North Holland

Pedersen E. R., McCall K., Moran T. P. and Halasz F. G. (1993). Tivoli: an electronic whiteboard for informal workgroup meetings. In *Proc. InterCHI '93 Human Factors in Computing Systems*, Amsterdam, Netherlands, April 24–29, pp. 391–8. New York: ACM/SIGCHI

Perlman G. (1984). Making the right choices with menus. In *Human Computer Interaction – Interact '84* (Shackel B., ed.), pp. 291–5. Amsterdam: North-Holland

Polson P. G. and Lewis C. H. (1990). Theory-based design for easily learned interfaces. *Human Computer Interaction*, **5**, 191–220

Preece J., Rogers Y., Sharp H., Benyon D., Holland S. and Carey T. (1994). *Human–Computer Interaction*. Wokingham: Addison-Wesley

President's Commission (1979). *Report of the President's Commission on the Accident at Three Mile Island*. New York: Pergamon Press

Rasmussen J. and Goodstein L. P. (1988). Information technology and work. In *Handbook of Human–Computer Interaction* (Helander M., ed.), pp. 175–201. Amsterdam: North-Holland

Reiser B. J., Black B. J. and Abelson R. P. (1985). Knowledge structures in the organization and retrieval of autobiographical memory. *Cognitive Psychology*, **17**, 00. 89–137.

Rogers G. F. C. (1983). *The Nature of Engineering: A Philosophy of Technology*. London: Macmillan

Rosson M. B. (1983). Patterns of experience in text editing. In *Proc. CHI '83 Human Factors in Computing Systems*, Boston MA, December 12–15, pp. 171–5. New York: ACM/SIGCHI

Rouse W. B. (1991). *Design for Success*. New York: John Wiley

Rubin D. C. (1986). *Autobiographical Memory*. New York: Cambridge University Press

Rubinstein R. and Hersh H. (1984). *The Human Factor: Designing Computer Systems for People*. Bedford MA: Digital Press

Schegloff E. A. (1979). Identification and recognition in telephone conversation openings. In *Everyday Language* (Psathas G., ed.), pp. 23–78. New York: Academic Press

Schilit B. N., Adams N., Gold R., Tso M. and Want R. (1993). The ParcTab Mobile Computing System. In *Proc. 4th Workshop on Workstation Operating Systems (WWOS-IV)*, Napa CA: IEEE

Schroeder M.D., Birrell A.D. and Needham R.M. (1984). Experience with Grapevine: the growth of a distributed system. *ACM Trans. on Comp. Sys.* **2**(1), 3–23

Sellen A.J. (1992). Speech patterns in video-mediated conversations. In *Proc. CHI '92 Human Factors in Computing Systems*, Monterey CA, May 3–7, pp. 49–59. New York: ACM/SIGCHI

Shneiderman B. (1983). Direct manipulation: a step beyond programming languages. *IEEE Computer*, **16**(8), 55–78

Shneiderman B. (1992). *Designing the User Interface: Strategies for Effective Human–Computer Interaction*, 2nd edn. Reading MA: Addison-Wesley

Simon H. A. (1981). *The Sciences of the Artificial*. Cambridge MA: MIT Press

Siochi A. C. and Hartson H. R. (1989). The UAN: a task-oriented notation for user interfaces. In *Proc. CHI '89 Human Factors in Computing Systems*, Austin TX, April 30–May 4, pp. 183–8. New York: ACM/SIGCHI

Smith D. C., Irby C., Kimball R. M., Verplank W. and Harslem E. (1982). Designing the Star user interface. *BYTE*, 7(4)

Smith S.L. (1986). Standards versus guidelines for designing user interface software. *BIT* **5**, 47–61

Smith S. L. and Mosier J. N. (1986). Guidelines for Designing User Interface Software. *Report ESD-TR-86-278*, Electronic Systems Division, The Mitre Corporation, Bedford MA. Available from the National Technical Information Service, Springfield VA

Sommerville I. (1994). *Software Engineering* 4th edn. Wokingham: Addison-Wesley

Stifelman L. J., Arons B., Schmandt C. and Hulteen E. A. (1993). VoiceNotes: a speech interface for a hand-held voice notetaker. In *Proc. InterCHI '93 Human Factors in Computing Systems*, Amsterdam, Netherlands, April 24–29, pp. 179–86. New York: ACM/SIGCHI

Stone M. C., Cowan W. M. and Beatty J. C. (1988). Color gamut mapping and the printing of digital color images. *ACM Trans. on Graphics*, **7**(4) 249–92

Strauss A. L. (1987). *Qualititative Analysis for Social Scientists*. Cambridge: Cambridge University Press

Suchman L. (1987). *Plans and Situated Actions*. Cambridge: Cambridge University Press

Suchman L. and Wynn E. H. (1984). Procedures and problems in the office. *Office: Technology and People*. **1**, 133

Sun Microsystems (1991). *OPEN LOOK Graphical User Interface Application Style Guidelines*. Reading MA: Addison-Wesley

Tetzlaff L. and Schwartz D.R. (1991). The use of guidelines in interface design. In *Proc. CHI '91 Human Factors in Computing Systems*, New Orleans LA, April 28–May 2, pp. 329–33. New York: ACM/SIGCHI

Thimbleby H. (1984). Generative user-engineering principles for user interface design. In *Human Computer Interaction – Interact '84* (Shackel B., ed.), pp. 661–6. Amsterdam: North-Holland

Thimbleby H. (1990). *User Interface Design*. Reading MA: Addison-Wesley

Thornton G. and Harper R. H. R. (1991). Detectives or Clerks? An Examination of the Work of Detectives. *Rank Xerox EuroPARC Technical Report EPC-91-109*, 61 Regent Street, Cambridge, UK

Thurber J. (1961). *My Life and Hard Times*. New York: HarperCollins

Trist E. L. and Bamforth K. W. (1951). Some social and psychological consequences of the long-wall method of coal-getting. *Human Relations*, **4**, 3–38

Tufte E. R. (1983). *The Visual Display of Quantitative Information*. Cheshire CT: The Graphics Press

Tufte E. R. (1990). *Envisioning Information*. Cheshire CT: The Graphics Press

Tullis T. S. (1988). Screen design. In *Handbook of Human–Computer Interaction* (Helander M., ed.), pp. 377–411. Amsterdam: North-Holland

US Department of Labor Statistics (1993). *Occupation Outlook Handbook.* Washington DC: US Dept. of Labor

US Government Accounting Office (1979). Contracting for Computer Software Development—Serious Problems Require Management Attention to Avoid Wasting Additional Millions. *GAO Report FGMSD 80-4*, Nov. 1979

Verplank W. L. (1988). Graphic challenges in designing object-oriented interfaces. In *Handbook of Human–Computer Interaction* (Helander M., ed.), pp. 365–76. Amsterdam: North-Holland

Vincenti W. G. (1991). *What Engineers Know and How They Know It.* Baltimore MD: Johns Hopkins University Press

Want R., Hopper A., Falcao V. and Gibbons J. (1992). The active badge system. *ACM Trans. on Office Information Systems*, **10**(1), 91–102

Weinberg G. M. (1988). *Rethinking Systems Analysis and Design.* New York: Dorset House

Weiser M. D. (1991). The computer for the 21st century. *Scientific American*, September, pp. 66–75

Wellner P. (1991). The DigitalDesk calculator: tangible manipulation on a desk top display. In *Proc. ACM UIST '91 Conf.* Nov, Hilton Head NC

Wheatley R. C. and Morgan B. (1964). *The Maintenance and Driving of Vintage Cars.* London: Batsford

Whiteside J., Bennett J. and Holtzblatt K. (1988). Usability engineering: our experience and evolution. In *Handbook of Human–Computer Interaction* (Helander M., ed.), pp. 791–817. Amsterdam: North-Holland

Williams M. D., Hollan J. D., and Stevens A. L. (1983). Human reasoning about a simple physical system. In *Mental Models* (Gentner D. and Stevens A. L., eds.). Erlbaum

Wilson, J., and Rosenberg, D. (1988). Rapid prototyping for user interface design. In *Handbook of Human–Computer Interaction* (Helander M., ed.). Amsterdam: North-Holland

Woodmansee G. H. (1984). The Visi On experience – from concept to marketplace. In *Human Computer Interaction – INTERACT '84* (Shackel B., ed.), pp. 871–5. Amsterdam: North-Holland

Young R. M. (1983). Surrogates and mappings: two kinds of conceptual models of interactive devices. In *Mental Models* (Gentner D., and Stevens, A. L., eds.), pp. 35–52. Hillsdale NJ: Lawrence Erlbaum Associates

Young R. M. and MacLean A. (1988). Choosing between methods: analysing the user's decision space in terms of schemas and linear models. In *Proc. CHI '88 Human Factors in Computing Systems*, Washington DC, May 15–19, pp. 139–43. New York: ACM/SIGCHI

Zuboff S. (1988). *In the Age of the Smart Machine: The Future of Work and Power.* New York: Basic Books

INDEX

Key: **bold** numbers indicate definitions or main entries; *italic* numbers refer to illustrations.

A

abstraction 47
acceptance and rejection of systems 66–7
Ackroyd S. 62
action research 103
active badge 423–5
activity, human 16
   level of support for 16, *17*
     see also usability
   need to support xii, 6, 12
   purpose 55
Adler A. 362
Aegis weapons system 9
air traffic control 63–6, 73, 76–7
   requirements for *144*
airline check-in 277, *278*
   mental model of 335
airport control 53–4, 73–4, 279–81
Alba J. W. 422
analogy
   and interaction style 350
   mental models based on 336–8
analysis
   dependence on models 83–4, 167
   in design 11, 83–4, 272–3
   in requirements validation 156–7
   two stages of 167–9, *168*
   of usability 81, 163–82
Annett J. 117
answering machine 55–6
   design problem 441
anthropological theories of human behaviour 53–7
appearance of user interface
   describing 278–9, *279*
Apple Computer
   field testing at 207
   Human Interface guidelines 370, 402, 410
   Macintosh 33, 200, 283
     see also Macintosh
applications
   air traffic control 63–6, 73, 76–7
   airline check-in 277, *278*
   answering machine 55–6
   audio-video communication 57, 352–3, 362–5
   automated teller machine 61, 187

clock, digital 273, 277
cockpit display 243–5
computer-aided design (CAD) 217
crime detection 62–3
crime reporting 63
critical 9, **193**
   evaluation of 193–4
door security system 295–6
Economic Update (EU) system 135–7
flight simulator 338, *337*
hardware-store catalogue 184–6, 299–318
human memory aid 287–9, 411–39, *5*, *287*, *288*
mail order 23–6, 28, 199
meeting support tool 210–12
order entry 219–20
patient registration 78–80, *80*, *84*
Pre-Contact Note (PCN) system 133–5
shared drawing tool 207–8
TAO workstation 17–18, 36, 116, 158, 249–68
ticket machine 16–21, 120–3, 178–82
voice mail 357
voice note-taker 34–6, *35*, 205
Applied Psychology Unit 412
arc, in state transition diagram **276**
ATM, *see* automated teller machine
Atwood M. E. 187, 250, 252, 268
audio recording, design problem 442
audio-video communication
   and gaze direction 57
   mental model of 352–3
   walkthrough analysis of 362–5
autobiographical memory 413, 429
automated teller machine 61, 187
automation
   coalmine 53
   deficit 243–5
   of tasks 27
autopilot
   automation deficit 243–5

B

Baddeley A. 416
Balabanovic M. 433
Ballas J. A. 243–4
Bamforth K. W. 53

Barnard P.   49, 371, 381, 419
basic activities
  distribution   422
  of the working day   422
Bekerian D. E.   416–17, 419, 420
benchmarks   **168**
  in conceptual design   368–9
  in TAO workstation evaluation   263
  in usability measurement   168
Bennett J.   214
Benson D.   62
Benyon D.   108
Berners-Lee T.   303, 400–1
between-group experiment   247
Bingham J.   95
Bly S.   207, 214, 352
Boehm B. W.   126, 157
Brown C. M.   375
Brown P. J.   439
business process   23
  see also process, human
Button G.   67
Byrne M. D.   396, *397*, 410

C
CAD *see* computer-aided design
calendar, on-line, design problem   441
Callahan D.   217
callee   250
Campion P.   68
Card S. K., *see* Card S. K., Moran T. P and
      Newell A.
Card S. K., Moran T. P and Newell A.   45–7,
      50, 68, 139, 167, 172–4, 187, 195, 259,
      263
Carey M. S.   24
Carey T.   108
Carroll J. M.   369–70
Carter K.   439
case studies
  air traffic control   63–5
  cockpit display evaluation   243–5
  crime detection   62–3
  crime reporting   63
  meeting support tool evaluation
  210–12
  telephone operator workstation
  249–68
      see also TAO, Project Ernestine
  ticket machine   16–21, 120–3, 178–82,
  200–3, 240–3
      see also ticket machine, design of
CASE tools   125
categorical data   239
causal link   17
  human activity as   19–20
check box   283–4
Checkland P.   6, 16, 39
chi square analysis   239–40
choice, between tools and systems, *see* com-
      petition

chroma   392
Cinematrix Inc   *4*
Civil Aviation Authority   64
client
  for interactive system design   17, 38,
  145–7
  stakeholder   144–5
clock, digital
  user interface   *273*
  state transition chart   *277*
coalmine automation   53
cockpit display
  evaluation case study   243–5
cognitive subsystem   48–51, *49*, 257
cognitive walkthrough   83, *84*, 176–82
  in conceptual design   358–69
  in requirements validation   156
collaborative systems
  audio-video link   *352*
    mental model of   352–3
  evaluation of   194
  shared drawing tool   207–8
  Tivoli meeting support tool   210–12
collect call
  handling   250
  interaction sequence   253
  parallelism in   257
collection, of unpaid bills   97–8
colour, use of   392–5, Plates 1–9
  choice of colour   392–3
  rendering, accuracy of   394–5
  vision impairment   393–4
  vision limitations   393
command-line interaction   **315**, 315–16
  properties   316
Commission, the   128–30
  analysis of study   128–9
  data models   *128, 129, 129*
  Economic Update (EU) system   135–7
  identifying functions   129–30
  participative design   133–7
  Pre-Contact Note (PCN) system   133–5
  scenario   *134*
  requirements definition   148–56, *155*
communication, in design   272, 274
competition
  between tools   23, 65–7
  between tools and systems   66
components
  widgets   405
  windowed applications   405–9
computer-aided design (CAD)   217
  menu design example   217–18
conceptual design   xv, 81, 323–71
  design process   348–50, 368–9
  of human memory aid   428–33
  and learning, users'   325–9
  methods   347–71
    choice of intended mental model
    348–50
    design of system image   353–7

use of heuristics   369–71
  hiding the system model   350–3
  walkthrough analysis   358–69
misconceptions, users'   324–5
telephone call example   329–31
cone, retinal   392
  distribution of cones   393
confidence interval   **236**
  derivation   236–38
  example   238
confidence level, experimental   219–20
  methods of establishing   224–30
confounding, in experiments   223
Constant E. W.   36
context
  of guideline use   382–3
  stored, and human memory   413
  of system development   79–80, 145–7
Coulouris G. F.   290
CPM-GOMS   257–67
  and basic GOMS   258–9
  modelling method   259–62, *261*
  schedule chart   **260**
    examples   *262, 264*
    templates   260–1
credit-card call
  CPM-GOMS model   *264*
  interaction sequences   253, 262–3
  parallelism in   257
  redefined procedures   266–7
crime reporting   63
critical applications   9, **193**
  evaluation of   193–4
critical path   257, **261**
  plotting, in CPM-GOMS modelling   261–2
cycle of interaction   **59–60**, 81, 324, 343–5, 348

D

Dalton M.   103
data collection methods   93–107
  interviews   94–9
  observation   99–103
  questionnaires   103–6
data flow diagram   *26*, 125–9, *127, 128, 129*
data modelling   125
Davies G. W. P.   95
Davis A. M.   125, 161
dealer rooms   99, *100*
degrees of freedom, in experiments   **232**
DeMarco T.   143
dependencies, in human activity   24–5
  multiple   25–6
  reduction of   27–8
dependent variable   **222**
design
  activities involved in   70, 272
  engineering   10
  heuristics   183
  sketching in   272–3

design principles, general   383–7
  and Economic Update problem   387
  general principles of   385
  and human information processing   384
  in style guides   402
  and usability factors   384
design processes   69–87
  analysing the design   83–4
  developing the specification   78–82
  empirical evaluation   85–6
  modelling the user's activity   75–8
  studying the user   72–5
  symbols used   72
desktop   296, *297*, 338, *354, 356*
Desurvire H. W.   187
detailed design of user interface   373, 405–9
detective, police   26–7, 62–3, *102*
DFD, *see* data flow diagram
Diaper D.   20, 93, 108, 119, 167
DigitalDesk   *5*
direct manipulation   296–7
  forms fill-in   296, 313–15
  graphical   **296**, 311–13
  guidelines for   396
  and object-action mental models   349
  properties of   296–7, 312–13
directed graph   276, 303
display design
  guidelines for   388–91
  reduction in density   389
  visual grouping   389–91
distribution   **225**
  normal   **225**, *225*, 225–7
doctor and patient, interaction between   43–4, *43*
domain knowledge   98
door security system   295–6
Dourish J. P.   210, 352, 375
drag-and-drop operations
  in human memory aid   434
Draper S. W.   91, 346
drop shadow   *391*
Duncan K. D.   117
dynamic model   44–6
  of human behaviour   55
  mental model   326

E

Economic Update (EU) system   135–7
  applying guidelines   386–409
  icon-based interface   396, *397*
  problem statement   135, 386
  requirements   *137*, 148–56, *155*
  specification   136
  user identification   149–50
  voice-based interface   398–400
  see also the Commission
Eldridge M. A.   96, 416–17, 419–20, 425, 439

emacs   365
Emery F. E.   58, 131
empirical law, of human behaviour   44
Engelbart D. C.   276
engineering design   10
    creativity in   10
    see also design
English W. K.   276
enhancement, of solutions
    guideline use in   376
    in solving problems   36
entity-relation diagram   126
envisionment   **132**
    examples   133–4, *136*
    of human memory aid   415, *414*
    see also prototyping
errors, user   7, 8, 31, 220
    statistical analysis of   238
ethnography   **101**
    ethnographic field study   101–2
evaluation   xv, 182–6, 189–212
    basic stages in   194
    controlled   215–24
    in controlled conditions   194
    in cycle of interaction   60
    documentation   196–8
    empirical   85–6, 189–212
    field tests, iterative   207–10
    formative   **190**, 190–1
    heuristic   182–6
        see also heuristic evaluation
    learning by prototyping   203–4
    and performance requirements   191
    with predictable usage   216–18
    prototypes, informal tests of   204–8
    studies in support of   92
    summative   191–2
execution, in cycle of interaction   60
experiment, controlled   193, 215–24
    between-group   246
    confounding the result   223
    when needed   194
    stages   223–4
    multi-factor   246
    of user-interface components   217
    within-group   247
experimental design   217–18
    and analysis   195–6
    of telephone operator workstation field
        trial   255–6
    two-sample   220–4
    variables, choice of   222
expert system, for police detection   62–3, 66
explanatory theory, of human behaviour
        42–4
exploration
    of interactive system   61
    in design   272–3
exploratory learning, theory of   **61–2**, 76,
        123, 176–7
    direct manipulation and   312

externally valid task   **199**, 223
    choice of, in experiments   221

F
feature, of human process   26
field test   193, 207–12
    case study   210–12
    iterative   207–10
    participative nature   207
    stages in   209–10
Ferguson E. S.   70, 272
Fitts P.   52
    Fitts' Law   44, **51–2**, 67, 76, 172, *173*
flight information display   279–80
flight progress strip   64–5
flight simulator   338, *337*
Flynn M.   *4*, 419, 425, 428, 439
Forget-Me-Not   427–39, *5*
    see also human memory aid
form of solution   16, *17*, 32–7
forms fill-in interface   313–15
    properties of   315
fovea   392
function-key interface   307–9
    example   *308*
    interactive devices   307
        activation of   309
    principles   307–9

G
Gaines B. R.   384
gamut, colour   395
Gaver W. W.   198, 210
gaze direction, models of   56–7
Gentner D.   332, 336, 346
Gentner D. R.   332, 336, 346, 350
global rules, for windowing systems   404
goal   20–1, 58, 66, 117
    in cycle of interaction   59–61
    in Goms analysis   170
    subgoal   117
    in walkthrough analysis   168
golden rule
    see design principles, general
Goms analysis   **170**, 169–76
    CPM-Goms extension   257
        see also CPM-Goms
    see also keystroke-level model
Goodwin C.   56–7, 280
Goodwin M. H.   53, 280
Gordon M. J. C.   42
Gould J. D.   205
Granda R. E.   377
Gray W. D.   36, 54, 116, 158, 225, 250, 252,
        254, 259, 261–5, 267–8
Greatbatch D.   43, 68
Greenbaum J.   131
Grudin J.   137, 183, 350, 371, 381
GUI, *see* user interface, graphical

guidelines   81, 373–409, **374**
    categories of   383
    for conceptual design   369–71
    contexts of use   382–3
        colour   392–5
        display layout   388–91
        general principles   383–7
        interaction styles   395–9
        style guides   400–5
        user interface components   404–9
    generative role   379
    heuristics as   183, 374
    as investigation reports   376
    limitations, problems with   379–81, *382*
    multiple guidelines, use of   380
        conflicts between   381
    the need for   374–5
    roles in design   376–9
    style-specific   320
    use of   375–83

H
Hansen W. J.   384
hardware-store catalogue example   184–6,
        299–318
    activities involved   299–300, *300*
    heuristic evaluation   184–6
    problem statements   301, 305, 307, 309,
        311, 313, 315, 317
    situation of concern   299
Harper R. H. R.   26–7, 63–5, 102, 210, 425,
        444
Harslem E.   372
Hartson H. R.   285, 290, *see also* Hix D. and
        Hartson H. R.
Hasher L.   422
Hawthorne effect   103
HCI, *see* human-computer interaction
Heath C.   68, 99–100
help, on-line   401
Henderson D. A.   362
Hersh H.   369, 375
heuristic   **183**
    use in conceptual design   369–71
    as general design principle   385
    style-specific   320
    see also guidelines
heuristic evaluation   182–6
    example   184–6
    method   183–4
    style-specific   320
Hick W. E.   44
    Hick's Law   44, *45*
hierarchic task description   **21–2**
Hix D.   285, *see also* Hix D. and Hartson
        H. R.
Hix D. and Hartson H. R. 167, 190, 192, 200,
        204, 214, 224, 285, 290, 384, 402
Holland S.   108
Holzblatt K.   214
Hopkin V. D.   130, 444

Hopkins D.   217
Howell D. C.   216, 248
Howes N. R.   161
HTML, *see* World Wide Web
HTTP, *see* World Wide Web
hue   392
human activity *see* activity, human
human-computer interaction (HCI)   vii,
        xiii, 108
human memory aid   287–9, 411–39, *5*, *288*,
        289
    conceptual design   428–33
    design of   411–39
    envisionments   414–15
    event filters   430–8
    feasibility studies   423–5
    Forget-Me-Not prototype   427–39
    icons   433–5
    portability of   415
    preliminary studies   415–23
    privacy issues   424, 427
    problem statement   415
    requirements for   425–7
    use, example of   437–8
    user interface   434–8
human virtual machine   xii, 42, **47**, 46–67
    and telephone operator activities   257
HyperCard   157, 200–3
    example of use   287–9
    HyperTalk language   202–3, *203*
    overview   200–2
HyperTalk, *see* HyperCard
hypertext   **303**, 301–3
hypothesis, in statistical analysis   229–30
    experimental   **230**
    null   **230**

I
icon
    design guidelines   396
    in human memory aid   433–5
    label changing
        cognitive walkthrough   359–62
        user interface   274, *285*, 286
    user's mental model
independent variable   **222**
indexing of information   415
innovation   10, **36**, 36–7
    innovative solutions   36
    need for   37
    requirements and   158–9
input device
    activation of   309
    in function-key interfaces   307
input syntax   **276**
    notations for   276–8
    see also notation
inspection, usability   167, 182–6
intended mental model
    choice of   348–50
    retro-fitting   349

intensity, colour   392
interaction style   **294**, 293–321
    categories of   294–9
        direct manipulation   296–7, 311–15
        key-modal   295–6, 300–11
        linguistic   297–9, 315–19
    choice of   319–21
        hardware constraints on   319
        and usability requirements   319–20
    combining styles   320–1
    guidelines in support of   395–9
    for human memory aid   428, 433–4
    style-specific design knowledge   320
        see also guidelines
    and user's mental model   349–50
interactive objects   279–82, *281*
    notations for describing   281–4
    in an airport control room   279–81
interactive system   xi, **6**
    why we design them   6–7, 18–19
    design
        creativity in   10
        maintaining success   9–10
        measuring success   7–8
        methods used   10–12
        results of failure   8–9
interview   73, 94–9
    bad   *95*
    effective   96–8, *97–8*
    method   94–6
    recording   99–100
    structure   94
investigation
    in design   85–6
    plan   85
    pro formas   197–8
        examples   197, *198*, 206, 211, 212
    report   86
Irby C.   372
iteration in design   11–12

J
John B. E.   250, 259, 261–2, 268

K
Kendall J. E. and Kendall K. E.   *75*, 99, 103,
        108, 139
Keppel G.   216, 248
key-modal interaction styles   295–6
    function key   307–9
    menu-based interaction   300–4
    question and answer   305–7
    voice-based   309–11
keystroke-level model   45–6, 76, 171–6,
        286, 371
    analysis   *84*
    descriptive   115
    examples   173–6
    normative   115
    in requirements validation   157
    of telephone operator task   258–9

Kimball R. M.   372
Klugh H. E.   216
Kondziela J. M.   187
Koved L.   303
Kraut R. E.   325
Kuhn T. S.   36
Kyng M.   131

L
Lammers S.   87, 113, 146
Lamming M. G.   *4*, 287, 395, 419, 425,
        427–8, 439
lattice
    as mental model   338–42, *429*
    incomplete   339, *339, 340*
learning, ease of   7, 31
    and conceptual design   325–9
    requirements for   152–3
Lee J. D.   341
Lee L.   9, 13
level of performance
    analysis of   83–4
    of tasks and processes   30–2
level of support for user   16, *17*
        see also usability
Lewis C. H.   61
linguistic interaction styles   **297**, 297–9,
        315–19
    command-line interaction   **297**, 315–16
    text-based natural language   **297**,
        317–19
London Ambulance Service   9, 13, 324
long-term memory   49
Lotus 1-2-3   113
Louie G.   439
Luff P.   68

M
Macintosh, Apple   33, 200, 283, 359, 367,
        400
    check box   283–4
    desktop   296, *297*
    folder icon   *285*, 286
    interactive objects   *281*
mail order   23–6, 28, 199
    data model   126
    task model   117–19
mapping mental model   335–6
Marcus A.   389, 392
Martin J.   278
Mattson H. F.   42
Mayhew D. J.   31, 322, 369–70, 374–5, 377,
        379, 384, 389, 396, 398, 399, **410**
MacKenzie I. S.   52
MacLean A.   328
McShane W. R.   198
mean   **196**, 219
    population   218
    sample   219
medical practice interaction   43–4, 47–8,
        115

Medical Research Council   412
meeting support tool, case study   210–12
memory
    aid, *see* human memory aid
    autobiographical   413
    lapses   418
    long-term   49
    problems at work, study of   416–18
    schema   422
        influence on memory-aid design
        429
        study of   422–3
    working   49
mental model, user's   323–45, **326**
    of complex systems   338–43
    examples
        of audio-video link   352–3, 362–5
        of dishwasher cycle   331
        of document retrieval system   348–9
        of editor preferences selection
        365–9
        of electricity   332
        of four-function calculator   335–6,
        336
        of graphics editor   334
        of human memory aid   428–31
        of icon   *335*, 338–9, 359–62
        of pasteurization plant   339–42
        of 'squares' puzzle   334
        of starting a car   351
        of telephone call   329–31, 333, 342
        of Unix *mv* command   326–8
        of voice mail   357
        of water taps   351
    form of   331–8
    intended by designer   348
    lattice representation   334, *335*, 338–42,
    429
    mixed forms   342
        example   357
    recurring forms of   333–8
        analogy   336–8
        mapping   335–6
        object-action   333–4
        state-transition   333
    retro-fitting   349
    runnable   326–9
    running the model   342–3
mental preparation
    in keystroke-level modelling   45
    in task performance   172–3, *174*
menu
    breadth *vs.* depth guideline   396
    CAD design example   217–18, *218*
    drop-down   405–9
    pie   217
    pop-up   407–8
    pull-down   217
    variants   301
menu-based interaction   300–4
    design principles   301

examples   *302, 304*
    guidelines for   396
    menu variants   301
    properties   303
metaphor   338, 370
methodology   10
Microsoft Windows   400
    NT   33
    style guide   405–10
Miller D. P.   223, 396
Minneman S.   207, 214
misconceptions about software systems
    by programmers   324
    by users   325
        how they occur   344–5
modal user interfaces, *see* mode
mode, user interface   295
model
    descriptive   114–16
    mental *see* mental model
    normative   114–16
    of human activity   11, 29, 72, 75–8,
    114–31
        approaches   114–16
        process-based   114
        in requirements definition   149
        task-based   114, 117–23
model human processor   47, 48–9, 58
    and guidelines   384
modelling the user's activity, *see* model
Molich R.   183–4, 376, 385
Moran T. P. *see* Card S. K., Moran T. P and
        Newell A.
Moray N.   24, 326, 338–42
Morgan B.   28, 351
Morgan C.   207
morphic resonance   *432*
Motif, OSF   400
Mumford E.   114, 131
mv command   298, 326–8
Myers B. A.   199–200

N
natural language interaction   299
    text-based   317–19
NCSA   400
Nelson T. H.   303
Neumann P. G.   9
New England Telephone   116, 253
Newell A.   58, *see also* Card S. K.,
        Moran T. P. and Newell A.
Newman W. M.   197, 276, 322, 395, 424
Nielsen J.   183–4, 376, 385
node, in state transition diagram   276
normal distribution   **225**, 225–7, *225*
normal technology   36
Norman D. A.   8, 59–61, 91, 331, 343, 346,
        348, 351, 353, 369, 384
notation, user interface   81, 271–89
    for input syntax   276–8
    state-transition chart   276–7

text-based interaction   277, *278*
nuisance variable   223
null hypothesis   229–30, **230**
NYNEX   253–6

O
object, interactive   279–84
    in direct manipulation interfaces   296–7
    in graphical interfaces   281–4
    in hardware store example   *313*
    notations for describing   281–4
    user's mental model of   333–4
object-action mental model   333–4
    and direct manipulation style   349
object-oriented design   124
    see also Object State Transition Chart
Object State Transition Chart   274, **282**,
    282–4
    defining methods of operation   284–6,
    286
    examples   *284, 286, 434–8*
obligation, user's   66–7
observation   99–103
    action research   103
    concurrent verbal accounts   100
    ethnographic   101–2
    passive   100
    video recording and   99–100
Ogden W. C.   317
Olivetti Research Ltd.   423
Olson J. S.   326, 369–70
OPEN LOOK   378, 380
    style guidelines   404–5
operating system   33
order entry, evaluation example   219–20
    see also mail order
organization of human activity
    analysis of   83
    theories of   57–67
Orr J.   101
OSTC *see* Object State Transition Chart

P
Page J.   146, 161
PARC, *see* Xerox
PARCTab   427–8, *428*
participative (participatory) design   131–7,
    131
    example   133–7
    method in outline   131–3
    pros and cons   136–7
patient registration   78–80, *80, 84*
Payne S. J.   369
Pedersen E. R.   198, 210
Pepys diary system   424–5
perception
    auditory   49
    visual   49
performance levels, *see* levels of perfor-
    mance
Perlman G.   375

phone call
    mental model of   329–31, 333
    opening sequences   55–6, *56*
pointing at a target, speed of   51–52
police   26–7, 62–3, *102*
Polson P. G.   61
population   **218**, 218–20
    mean   219
prediction
    dependenence of design on   41–2
    of activity performance   84
Preece J.   103–4, 108, 186
privacy   424–5, 427
pro formas   197–8
    examples   197, *198*, 206, 211, 212, 242,
    243, 245
probability   220
    of sample belonging to population
    226–7
problem, design   17
problem definition   xiii, 15–38, **17**
problem solving   58
problem statement   **16–17**
    and contexts of guideline use   382–3
    examples
        Economic Update system   135, 386
        hardware store   301, 305, 307, 309,
        311, 313, 315, 317
        human memory aid   415
        patient registration   78, 80
        telephone operator workstation   37,
        254
        ticket machine   *17*, 120
        tollbooth   37
    and form of solution   32–3
    as the initial specification   78
process, human   **23**, 23–9
    representing activities as   76–7, *77*
processes, of interactive system design
    69–87
    of conceptual design   348–50, 368–9
    of evaluation   190–6
    of forming and using mental models
    326, *327*
    of guideline use   376, 380–1
    of requirements definition   147–56
    of systems analysis and design   110–13
    of usability analysis   167–9
Project Ernestine   249–68
    benchmark task identification   263
    cost benefit analysis   254
    CPM-GOMS model building   263–5
    explaining workstation performance
    265–7
    field trial   255–6
        unexpected result of   256
    sources of error in predictions   256–7
protocol, verbal   73, 99–101
prototypes and prototyping   xv, 67,
    198–210
    in controlled experiments   223–4

in describing the user interface   287–9
documenting in requirements specifications   157–8
in engineering   198–9
informal testing   204–8
   examples   205–7, *207*
learning from   193, 203–4, *204*
in requirements definition   157–8
in systems analysis and design   111–13
tools for   200–3
psychological models of human information processing   48–52

Q

question and answer interaction   305–7
   properties of   306–7
questionnaire   73, 103–6
   design issues   103–5
   by electronic mail   105–6, *106*, 416
   example   *104*, 420–1

R

radical solutions   36–7
Rank Xerox Research Centre   xvi, 412, 424
Rasmussen J.   354
RD3 air traffic control system   63–5
readership of this book, intended   xii–xiii
reasoning, users'   65–7
recording
   audio   99, 100
   interviews   98–9
   video   99–100
Reiser B. J.   413
rendering of colours   395
representations   272–89
   design   70–87, **71–2**, *72*
   strategies for use   274–6
   strategies for user interface description   276–89
   transformation between   274
   user interface   81, *82*
requirements   38, 79–80, 141–60, **142**
   contexts of use   145–7, *146*
      development under contract   145
   definition   144–60
      for human memory aid   425–7
   document   79
      outline   80
   evaluation and   191
   examples   122, 130, 137, *144, 146*, 426–7
   and experimental design   220
   functional   149, 151
   and innovation   158–9
   for interactive systems   147–54
   non-functional   151
   performance   151–4
   serving design   142–4
   as targets   143
   and technology layers   154–6

usability   152–4
validation   79, 143
research
   in engineering design   10
   vs. evaluation   247
   in guideline development   395–6
Rhodes W. R.   395
Robinson P.   439
rod, retinal   392
Roess R. P.   198
Rogers G. F. C.   10, 13, 70, 199
Rogers Y.   108
Rosson M. B.   199–200, 325, 348
Rouse W. B.   144
routine design tasks
   in innovative projects   159
   and requirements definition   143–4
routine events, recall of   422–3
Rubin D. C.   413
Rubinstein   369, 375
runnable model   44–5, 76
   mental models   **326**, 326–9
      different forms of   342–3
      example   329–31
   see also dynamic model

S

Sachs J.   113
Saufley W. H.   216, 248
Schegloff E.   55–7
schema   275–6
Schilit W.   428
Scholes J.   6, 16, 39
Schroeder M. D.   210
Schwartz D. R.   376, 379–80
score   219
script   202
   see also HyperTalk language
scroll bar
   page- and date-oriented   378–9
selection of method by user   170–1, 328
Sellen A. J.   248, 416–17, 419–20, 439
sensitivity, of task performance to design changes   221, 223
Sharp H.   108
Shneiderman B.   206, 303, 317, 319–22, 374–5, 384–5, 387, 396, 401
significance, statistical   196, **220**
   targets   220
   methods of testing for   224–30
Simon H. A.   xii, 58
simulator, flight   *337, 338*
Siochi A. C.   285
situated action   21
situation of concern   xiii, 6, 16–17, **18**
   examples   18, 34, 299
Smith D. C.   372
Smith S. L.   405
social setting   54
sociological theories of human behaviour
   fine-grained   53–7

group organization   62–7
software engineering   xi, xiii, xv
    tools   199–200
software requirements analysis, *see* soft-
    ware systems analysis
software systems analysis   125–31
    see also systems analysis
solution, form of   16, *17*, 32–7
Sommerville I.   126, 139, 162, 166
specification, development of   78–82
speech recognition   34–6
speed of operation   7, 31, 84
    analysis of   169–76
        keystroke-level   45–6, 170
    pointing at target   51–2
    statistical analysis of   241–2
spiral development process   157
stakeholder *see* client
standard, usability   194
standard deviation   **228**, 227–9
    calculation of   231–3
state, of user interface   276
    user's mental model of   333
state transition chart   276–7
    example   277
state-transition mental model   333
    and interaction style   350
statistical analysis methods   230–40
    basic calculations   231–3
    t test   233–6
    deriving confidence intervals   236–8
    chi square   239–40
Stifelman L. J.   34, 206
Strauss A. L.   93
studies, user   72–5, 91–107
    ensuring quality in   93
    when to conduct   92
style of interaction, *see* interaction style
style guide   400–5
    for windowing environments   402–9
        components   404–9
        general principles in   402
        global rules   404
    for World Wide Web   400–2
subdivision of the design   80, *81*
subgoal   117, 170
    in telephone operator activities   250–1
subjects, in controlled experiments   224
substitute command   *74*
subsystem, cognitive   48–9
    cycle times   50
subtask   117, 170
Suchman L.   21, 24, 47, 97
sum of squares of differences from the
        mean   **231**
    calculation of   231
    worked example   232
Swinehart D. C.   371
synthesis in design   11
system
    computer-based   27

    misconceptions about   324–5
system image   **331**
    designing   353–7
    maintaining currency and consistency
        355–6
    progressive reinforcement   357
system model   **129**, 129–31, 324–5
    hiding   350–3
    virtual   352–3
systems analysis   **124**, 124–31
    and design   xiv, 109–38, **110**
        processes   110–13
        prototyping and evaluation in
            111–13
    using data flow diagrams   126–31
    software systems analysis   125–31
    viewpoints on   124–5

T
t test   233–5
    deriving confidence intervals   236–8
    examples   235–6, 238
    table of values   234
Tab, *see* PARCTab
TAO (toll and assistance operator)   17–18,
        36, 116, 158, **250**
    call categories   251, 256, 263
    greeting   251
    parallelism in tasks   257
    task structure of work   250–7
    workstation, evaluation and analysis of
        249–68
        benchmark tasks   263
        CALL RELEASE key   251
            repositioning   254–5, 265–6
        CPM-GOMS analysis of design
            262–5
        display   251, *252*, 255, 266
        keyboard sequences   255
        user interface   251
        see also Project Ernestine
task   **20**, 20–3
    externally valid   **199**, 221
    focus   25
    hierarchic description of   **21–2**, *76*, 116,
        118, *119*
    object   24
    performance, models of   59
        analysis of   119
    resources   24–5
    subtask   117
task analysis and design   117–23
    example   120–3
    Hierarchic Task Analysis   117, *119*
Tcl/Tk   200
teaching, from this book   xiii–xv
telephone call
    mental model of   329–31, 333
    opening sequences   55–6
telephone operator, *see* TAO
telephone tag   24

Tesler L. G.   207
Tetzlaff L.   376, 379–80
text-based interaction, notations for
    describing   277, *278*
theories
    of the human user   41–68
    of social behaviour   55–7
    used in design   42–6
Thimbleby H.   290, 371, 379
Thornton G.   26–27, 102
thread-based mental model   428–33
Three Mile Island   356
Thurber J.   332, *332*
ticket machine design   16–21, 120–3,
    178–82
    analysis by cognitive walkthrough
        178–82
    HyperCard prototype   200–3
    problem statement   *17*, 120
    requirements   122–3
    statistical analysis   240–3
    task analysis and design   120–3
Tivoli meeting support tool   210–12, *211*
toll and assistance operator, *see* TAO
tool   22–3
traffic control system, design problem   443
transcripts, symbols used in   *43*
translation aid, design problem   442
Trist E. L.   53, 58, 131
Tufte E. R.   389
Tullis T. S.   380, 389, 391

U
UAN, *see* User Action Notation
UNIX™   175, 298
    command repertoire, users' knowledge
        of   325
    mv command   298, 326–8
    xwd, *xpr* commands   175
US Naval Research Laboratory   243–5
usability   16, **30**, 30–2, 75
    analysis of   11, 81–4, 167–86
    approaches to measuring   166–7
    factors   7, 30–1
        as dependent variables in experi-
            ments   222
        and guidelines   381, 384
        use of models in predicting   75–6
        table of   8, 30–1, *76*
    inspection   167, 182–6
    predicting   75–6
    questions about   165–6
    target   31
        ease of learning   152–3
        speed of operation   153–4
usable functional form   **147**, 153
user   16, *17*, **29–30**, 72
    identifying the   149–50
    needs   29
    studies, *see* studies, user
    tests, informal   193

User Action Notation (UAN)   285–7,
    289–91
user-centred design   xii, 91
user interface   **6**, 33
    architecture   **294**, 319
    design of   xiii, xv, 80–2
        conceptual   347–71
        detailed   373, 405–9
        documentation   271–89
        guidelines in   373–409
        importance   272
    graphical (GUI)   vii, 281
    notations   81, 272
        see also notations
    as presenter of system image   353–4
        see also system image
user participative design, *see* participative
    design
USS Vincennes   9

V
validation   79, **143**
    requirements   156–8
variable, experimental   222–3
    dependent   222
    independent   222
    nuisance   223
variance   **228**, 227–9
    calculation of   231–3
verification   **143**, 159
Verplank W. L.   372, 396
video diary study   419
Vincennes, USS   9
Vincenti W. G.   199
virtual machine   47
    human   ix, 42, **47**, 46–67, 257
Visi On   39
visitor reception system, design problem
    442
Visual Basic   157, 200
voice-based interaction   309–11
    examples   *310*, *398*–400
    guidelines   *398*–9
    user's mental model of   357
voice mail, example   357
voice note-taker   34–6, *35*, 205–6
    evaluation of   205–6

W
walk-up-and-use system   30, 152
    interaction styles   295
walkthrough   46, 83
    in activity sequence modelling   168
    analysis, cognitive   83, *84*, 176–82,
        358–69
    human memory aid analysis   433
    program   47
Want R.   423
Weinberg G. M.   109, 114, 139
Weiser M. D.   428
Wellner P.   *4*

Wheatley R. C.   28, 351
Whiteside J.   30, 214
widget   **405**, 410
    see also components
Williams M. D.   333, 342
windowing environments   **402**
    style guides for   402–9
Windows, Microsoft   400
    NT   33
    style guide   405–10
within-group experiment   246
Woodmansee G. H.   39
word processor   28
working memory   49
World Wide Web   301–3, 400
    Economic Update system   401–2, *403–4*
    Hypertext Transfer Protocol (HTTP)
    303

Hypertext Markup Language (HTML)
303
    support for menu–based interaction
    301–3
    style guide   400–2
Wynn E.   96, 97

X
X Windows   33
Xerox Palo Alto Research Center (Xerox
    PARC)   412

Y
Young R. M.   328, 333, 336, 346

Z
zigzag line, speed of drawing   50
Zuboff S.   8